Programming Domino 4.6 with Java™

Programming Domino 4.6 with Java™

Bob Balaban

An Imprint of IDG Books Worldwide, Inc.
An International Data Group Company
Foster City, CA ✦ Chicago, IL ✦ Indianapolis, IN ✦ Southlake, TX

Programming Domino 4.6 with Java™

Published by
M&T Books, an imprint of IDG Books Worldwide, Inc.
An International Data Group Company
919 E. Hillsdale Blvd., Suite 400
Foster City, CA 94404
www.idgbooks.com (IDG Books Worldwide Web site)

Copyright © 1998 Looseleaf Software, Inc. All rights reserved. No part of this book, including interior design, cover design, and icons, may be reproduced or transmitted in any form, by any means (electronic, photocopying, recording, or otherwise) without the prior written permission of the publisher.

Library of Congress Catalog Card No.: 97-77230

ISBN: 1-55851-583-6

Printed in the United States of America

10 9 8 7 6 5 4 3 2 1

1DD/QR/QR/ZY/NY

Distributed in the United States by IDG Books Worldwide, Inc.

Distributed by Macmillan Canada for Canada; by Transworld Publishers Limited in the United Kingdom; by IDG Norge Books for Norway; by IDG Sweden Books for Sweden; by Woodslane Pty. Ltd. for Australia; by Woodslane Enterprises Ltd. for New Zealand; by Longman Singapore Publishers Ltd. for Singapore, Malaysia, Thailand, and Indonesia; by Simron Pty. Ltd. for South Africa; by Toppan Company Ltd. for Japan; by Distribuidora Cuspide for Argentina; by Livraria Cultura for Brazil; by Ediciencia S.A. for Ecuador; by Addison-Wesley Publishing Company for Korea; by Ediciones ZETA S.C.R. Ltda. for Peru; by WS Computer Publishing Corporation, Inc., for the Philippines; by Unalis Corporation for Taiwan; by Contemporanea de Ediciones for Venezuela; by Computer Book & Magazine Store for Puerto Rico; by Express Computer Distributors for the Caribbean and West Indies. Authorized Sales Agent: Anthony Rudkin Associates for the Middle East and North Africa.

For general information on IDG Books Worldwide's books in the U.S., please call our Consumer Customer Service department at 800-762-2974. For reseller information, including discounts and premium sales, please call our Reseller Customer Service department at 800-434-3422.

For information on where to purchase IDG Books Worldwide's books outside the U.S., please contact our International Sales department at 415-655-3200 or fax 415-655-3295.

For information on foreign language translations, please contact our Foreign & Subsidiary Rights department at 415-655-3021 or fax 415-655-3281.

For sales inquiries and special prices for bulk quantities, please contact our Sales department at 415-655-3200 or write to the address above.

For information on using IDG Books Worldwide's books in the classroom or for ordering examination copies, please contact our Educational Sales department at 800-434-2086 or fax 817-251-8174.

For press review copies, author interviews, or other publicity information, please contact our Public Relations department at 415-655-3000 or fax 415-655-3299.

For authorization to photocopy items for corporate, personal, or educational use, please contact Copyright Clearance Center, 222 Rosewood Drive, Danvers, MA 01923, or fax 508-750-4470.

> LIMIT OF LIABILITY/DISCLAIMER OF WARRANTY: AUTHOR AND PUBLISHER HAVE USED THEIR BEST EFFORTS IN PREPARING THIS BOOK. IDG BOOKS WORLDWIDE, INC., AND AUTHOR MAKE NO REPRESENTATIONS OR WARRANTIES WITH RESPECT TO THE ACCURACY OR COMPLETENESS OF THE CONTENTS OF THIS BOOK AND SPECIFICALLY DISCLAIM ANY IMPLIED WARRANTIES OF MERCHANTABILITY OR FITNESS FOR A PARTICULAR PURPOSE. THERE ARE NO WARRANTIES WHICH EXTEND BEYOND THE DESCRIPTIONS CONTAINED IN THIS PARAGRAPH. NO WARRANTY MAY BE CREATED OR EXTENDED BY SALES REPRESENTATIVES OR WRITTEN SALES MATERIALS. THE ACCURACY AND COMPLETENESS OF THE INFORMATION PROVIDED HEREIN AND THE OPINIONS STATED HEREIN ARE NOT GUARANTEED OR WARRANTED TO PRODUCE ANY PARTICULAR RESULTS, AND THE ADVICE AND STRATEGIES CONTAINED HEREIN MAY NOT BE SUITABLE FOR EVERY INDIVIDUAL. NEITHER IDG BOOKS WORLDWIDE, INC., NOR AUTHOR SHALL BE LIABLE FOR ANY LOSS OF PROFIT OR ANY OTHER COMMERCIAL DAMAGES, INCLUDING BUT NOT LIMITED TO SPECIAL, INCIDENTAL, CONSEQUENTIAL, OR OTHER DAMAGES.

Trademarks: All brand names and product names used in this book are trade names, service marks, trademarks, or registered trademarks of their respective owners. IDG Books Worldwide is not associated with any product or vendor mentioned in this book.

Copyright 1997 Sun Microsystems, Inc., 901 San Antonio Road, Palo Alto, CA 94303-4900 USA, All rights reserved. Java, Java Servlet Development Kit and other Java related marks are trademarks or registered trademarks of Sun Microsystems, Inc. in the U.S. and other countries.

© 1998 Lotus Development Corporation. Used with permission of Lotus Development Corporation. LSX Toolkit is a trademark of Lotus Development Corporation.

An Imprint of IDG Books Worldwide, Inc.
An International Data Group Company

ABOUT IDG BOOKS WORLDWIDE

Welcome to the world of IDG Books Worldwide.

IDG Books Worldwide, Inc., is a subsidiary of International Data Group, the world's largest publisher of computer-related information and the leading global provider of information services on information technology. IDG was founded more than 25 years ago and now employs more than 8,500 people worldwide. IDG publishes more than 275 computer publications in over 75 countries (see listing below). More than 60 million people read one or more IDG publications each month.

Launched in 1990, IDG Books Worldwide is today the #1 publisher of best-selling computer books in the United States. We are proud to have received eight awards from the Computer Press Association in recognition of editorial excellence and three from *Computer Currents'* First Annual Readers' Choice Awards. Our best-selling *...For Dummies*® series has more than 30 million copies in print with translations in 30 languages. IDG Books Worldwide, through a joint venture with IDG's Hi-Tech Beijing, became the first U.S. publisher to publish a computer book in the People's Republic of China. In record time, IDG Books Worldwide has become the first choice for millions of readers around the world who want to learn how to better manage their businesses.

Our mission is simple: Every one of our books is designed to bring extra value and skill-building instructions to the reader. Our books are written by experts who understand and care about our readers. The knowledge base of our editorial staff comes from years of experience in publishing, education, and journalism — experience we use to produce books for the '90s. In short, we care about books, so we attract the best people. We devote special attention to details such as audience, interior design, use of icons, and illustrations. And because we use an efficient process of authoring, editing, and desktop publishing our books electronically, we can spend more time ensuring superior content and spend less time on the technicalities of making books.

You can count on our commitment to deliver high-quality books at competitive prices on topics you want to read about. At IDG Books Worldwide, we continue in the IDG tradition of delivering quality for more than 25 years. You'll find no better book on a subject than one from IDG Books Worldwide.

John Kilcullen
CEO
IDG Books Worldwide, Inc.

Steven Berkowitz
President and Publisher
IDG Books Worldwide, Inc.

Eighth Annual Computer Press Awards ≥1992

Ninth Annual Computer Press Awards ≥1993

Tenth Annual Computer Press Awards ≥1994

Eleventh Annual Computer Press Awards ≥1995

IDG Books Worldwide, Inc., is a subsidiary of International Data Group, the world's largest publisher of computer-related information and the leading global provider of information services on information technology. International Data Group publishes over 275 computer publications in over 75 countries. Sixty million people read one or more International Data Group's publications each month. International Data Group's publications include: **ARGENTINA:** Buyer's Guide, Computerworld Argentina, PC World Argentina; **AUSTRALIA:** Australian Macworld, Australian PC World, Australian Reseller News, Computerworld, IT Casebook, Network World, Publish, Webmaster; **AUSTRIA:** Computerwelt Osterreich, Networks Austria, PC Tip Austria; **BANGLADESH:** PC World Bangladesh; **BELARUS:** PC World Belarus; **BELGIUM:** Data News; **BRAZIL:** Annuário de Informática, Computerworld, Connections, Macworld, PC Player, PC World, Publish, Reseller News, Supergamepower; **BULGARIA:** Computerworld Bulgaria, Network World Bulgaria, PC & MacWorld Bulgaria; **CANADA:** CIO Canada, Client/Server World, ComputerWorld Canada, InfoWorld Canada, NetworkWorld Canada, WebWorld; **CHILE:** Computerworld Chile, PC World Chile; **COLOMBIA:** Computerworld Colombia, PC World Colombia; **COSTA RICA:** PC World Centro America; **THE CZECH AND SLOVAK REPUBLICS:** Computerworld Czechoslovakia, Macworld Czech Republic, PC World Czechoslovakia; **DENMARK:** Communications World Danmark, Computerworld Danmark, Macworld Danmark, PC World Danmark, Techworld Denmark; **DOMINICAN REPUBLIC:** PC World Republica Dominicana; **ECUADOR:** PC World Ecuador; **EGYPT:** Computerworld Middle East, PC World Middle East; **EL SALVADOR:** PC World Centro America; **FINLAND:** MikroPC, Tietoverkko, Tietoviikko; **FRANCE:** Distributique, Hebdo, Info PC, Le Monde Informatique, Macworld, Reseaux & Telecoms, WebMaster France; **GERMANY:** Computer Partner, Computerwoche, Computerwoche Extra, Computerwoche FOCUS, Global Online, Macwelt, PC Welt; **GREECE:** Amiga Computing, GamePro Greece, Multimedia World; **GUATEMALA:** PC World Centro America; **HONDURAS:** PC World Centro America; **HONG KONG:** Computerworld Hong Kong, PC World Hong Kong, Publish in Asia; **HUNGARY:** ABCD CD-ROM, Computerworld Szamitastechnika, Internetto online Magazine, PC World Hungary, PC-X Magazin Hungary; **ICELAND:** Tolvuheimur PC World Island; **INDIA:** Information Communications World, Information Systems Computerworld, PC World India, Publish in Asia; **INDONESIA:** InfoKomputer PC World, Komputek Computerworld, Publish in Asia; **IRELAND:** ComputerScope, PC Live!; **ISRAEL:** Macworld Israel, People & Computers/Computerworld; **ITALY:** Computerworld Italia, Macworld Italia, Networking Italia, PC World Italia; **JAPAN:** DTP World, Macworld Japan, Nikkei Personal Computing, OS/2 World Japan, SunWorld Japan, Windows NT World, Windows World Japan; **KENYA:** PC World East African; **KOREA:** Hi-Tech Information, Macworld Korea, PC World Korea; **MACEDONIA:** PC World Macedonia; **MALAYSIA:** Computerworld Malaysia, PC World Malaysia, Publish in Asia; **MALTA:** PC World Malta; **MEXICO:** Computerworld Mexico, PC World Mexico; **MYANMAR:** PC World Myanmar; **NETHERLANDS:** Computer! Totaal, LAN Internetworking Magazine, LAN World Buyers Guide, Macworld Netherlands, Net, WebWereld; **NEW ZEALAND:** Absolute Beginners Guide and Plain & Simple Series, Computer Buyer, Computer Industry Directory, Computerworld New Zealand, MTB, Network World, PC World New Zealand; **NICARAGUA:** PC World Centro America; **NORWAY:** Computerworld Norge, CW Rapport, Datamagasinet, Financial Rapport, Kursguide Norge, Macworld Norge, Multimediaworld Norge, PC World Ekspress Norge, PC World Nettverk, PC World Norge, PC World ProduktGuide Norge; **PAKISTAN:** Computerworld Pakistan; **PANAMA:** PC World Panama; **PEOPLE'S REPUBLIC OF CHINA:** China Computer Users, China Computerworld, China InfoWorld, China Telecom World Weekly, Computer & Communication, Electronic Design China, Electronics Today, Electronics Weekly, Game Software, PC World China, Popular Computer Week, Software Weekly, Software World, Telecom World; **PERU:** Computerworld Peru, PC World Profesional Peru, PC World SoHo Peru; **PHILIPPINES:** Click!, Computerworld Philippines, PC World Philippines, Publish in Asia; **POLAND:** Computerworld Poland, Computerworld Special Report Poland, Cyber, Macworld Poland, Networld Poland, PC World Komputer; **PORTUGAL:** Cerebro/PC World, Computerworld/Correio Informático, Dealer World Portugal, Mac*In/PC*In Portugal, Multimedia World; **PUERTO RICO:** PC World Puerto Rico; **ROMANIA:** Computerworld Romania, PC World Romania, Telecom Romania; **RUSSIA:** Computerworld Russia, Mir PK, Publish, Seti; **SINGAPORE:** Computerworld Singapore, PC World Singapore, Publish in Asia; **SLOVENIA:** Monitor; **SOUTH AFRICA:** Computing SA, Network World SA, Software World SA; **SPAIN:** Communicaciones World España, Computerworld España, Dealer World España, Macworld España, PC World España; **SRI LANKA:** Infolink PC World; **SWEDEN:** CAP&Design, Computer Sweden, Corporate Computing Sweden, Internetworld Sweden, it.branschen, Macworld Sweden, MaxiData Sweden, MikroDatorn, Nätverk & Kommunikation, PC World Sweden, PCaktiv, Windows World Sweden; **SWITZERLAND:** Computerworld Schweiz, Macworld Schweiz, PCtip; **TAIWAN:** Computerworld Taiwan, Macworld Taiwan, NEW ViSiON/Publish, PC World Taiwan, Windows World Taiwan; **THAILAND:** Publish in Asia, Thai Computerworld; **TURKEY:** Computerworld Turkiye, Macworld Turkiye, Network World Turkiye, PC World Turkiye; **UKRAINE:** Computerworld Kiev, Multimedia World Ukraine, PC World Ukraine; **UNITED KINGDOM:** Acorn User UK, Amiga Action UK, Amiga Computing UK, Apple Talk UK, Computing, Macworld, Parents and Computers UK, PC Advisor, PC Home, PSX Pro, The WEB; **UNITED STATES:** Cable in the Classroom, CIO Magazine, Computerworld, DOS World, Federal Computer Week, GamePro Magazine, InfoWorld, I-Way, Macworld, Network World, PC Games, PC World, Publish, Video Event, THE WEB Magazine, and WebMaster; online webzines: JavaWorld, NetscapeWorld, and SunWorld Online; **URUGUAY:** InfoWorld Uruguay; **VENEZUELA:** Computerworld Venezuela, PC World Venezuela; and **VIETNAM:** PC World Vietnam.

3/24/97

CREDITS

Associate Publisher
Paul Farrell

Editor
Debra Williams Cauley

Managing Editor
Shari Chappell

Technical Editor
Jeff Eisen

Copy Editor Manager
Karen Tongish

Copy Editor
Suzanne Ingrao

Production Editor
Kitty May

This book is lovingly dedicated to Samantha, David, and Irene. Thanks for everything, you're the best.

FOREWORD

There is an old saying in the computer business that goes something like this. It's easy to tell the hardware engineers from the software engineers. When confronted with a computer problem, a hardware engineerwill propose a whole new computer architecture, whereas a software engineer propose a whole new programming language. The corollary to this is that most of the time, the new computer architecture or the new programming language may be completed eventually, but the engineers never seem to find time to solve the original problem.

True to our upbringing as software engineers, when the four of us who invented Notes first started working on it in January 1985, we had lots of discussions about whether we should develop a new programming language as part of the Notes application development environment.

Fortunately (or unfortunately, depending on your point of view), we decided to scrap the idea of inventing a new language. We were afraid our project would follow the usual path and result only in a new language, and the original groupware system would have been lost in the dust.

Instead of developing a new language for Notes Release 1.0, we decided to adopt the *formula* language that was developed for the Lotus 1-2-3 spreadsheet. The Lotus 1-2-3 formula language was originally a nonprocedural language, and novices found it very easy to use. It also turned out that the formula language was extremely efficient to compile and execute. And best of all, it worked quite well as a query selection language for building views from documents in a Notes database.

As time and Notes releases marched on, we gradually adapted the formula language so it would be somewhat more useful for programming user interface macros and Agents. Some people thought we pushed the Notes formula language a bit too hard, but we were able to keep things together until the next big thing came along.

In late 1993, while we were busily working on Notes Release 4, a team at Lotus was busily working on a new procedural language that was eventually called LotusScript. It is a descendant of the ancient BASIC language, but LotusScript also has some great object-oriented extensions. Like BASIC, LotusScript turned out to be easy for novices to use to build simple applications but sophisticated enough for professionals to build complex applications.

In 1993 and 1994, a team of engineers, including Bob Balaban, added LotusScript and the so-called "Notes back-end classes" to Notes Release 4.0. The original idea was to just support Agents. We quickly expanded that idea to include all kinds of scripting for both the Notes Client and Server. We also built an object library for the product, called the Notes Object Interface (NOI). We breathed a sigh of relief thinking that Notes finally had a great language

The addition of LotusScript and the NOI increased the sophistication and elegance of the groupware applications that people built with Notes. When we re-architected the server for release 4.5 by adding the Web and other Internet protocols to Notes (and renamed it Domino), LotusScript and NOI became even more useful for building sophisticated Internet applications.

However, around the time that Release 4.0 shipped but unknown to us, a team of engineers at Sun Microsystems was again proving the old saying to be true by inventing a new language as part of an effort to build a consumer electronics system. And, as the corollary says, when the dust finally settled the only thing left was the new language: Java. But this time, the new language, first released in 1995, turned out to be a result any group of engineers would be proud of.

The only problem was that we had just shipped Notes Release 4.0, and it already had LotusScript. Luckily Bob Balaban started tinkering with Java, and he realized that he could create a Java interface to NOI to sit beside the LotusScript classes. The LotusScript Extension (LSX) architecture that Bob had developed made adding new interfaces pretty easy. So, through a little programming sleight-of-hand and lots of late nights, Bob got essentially the same classes to work with Java.

Finally, in September 1997, Bob and the rest of the team shipped Notes/Domino Release 4.6 with Java.

Now that Bob is working on his own, it appears he's finally had a chance to catch his breath and explain to all of us the cool Java things he has been working on for the last year or so. I think you'll find no better guide to the world of Notes, Domino, and Java than the person who designed and built it.

Len Kawell, Vice President, Iris Associates
November 1997

PREFACE

WHY JAVA? WHY DOMINO? WHY THIS BOOK?

Are all authors (especially first-time authors) so defensive that they feel they have to explain why they're writing a book? Perhaps not. Still, I can't assume that the gazillion people out there who work at developing killer collaborative/groupware/client-server/Internet/intranet applications understand why they should care about Lotus Domino, or Java, or both.

After ten and a quarter years (ten years, three months and six days, to be precise) of writing software for Lotus Development Corp. and its subsidiary Iris Associates, I left to work on other projects, this book included. While I was at Lotus/Iris, I spent about four and a half years working on Notes, which was later renamed Domino. I watched the product get reinvented a couple of times on its way to becoming what it is now—a terrific tool for building collaborative and group aware applications—although the journey is not yet finished.

Lots of people now know how good Domino is. Lots of people (not always the same ones) also now know how good the Internet is at facilitating communication among computers. Lots of people have also figured out that Java is a great tool for building all kinds of Internet-aware applications. I figured that it was time more people became aware that Domino and Java are an amazingly powerful combination.

The point of this book is to show you how to use the Java programming language to manipulate Domino objects. I'll leave it to you to decide how best to use those Domino objects to create your next killer Internet app. I'll stick to showing you how to use the features of Java and Domino to best advantage.

Is Domino 4.6 (the first release of the product that includes a Java API) perfect? By no means. As with most software products, it evolves and improves over time. In some respects, the Java features in Domino 4.6 represent baby steps, to be improved upon in future releases. You decide.

Much of this book is about something called the Notes Object Interface, or NOI. No matter how great a development platform Domino/Notes is, it won't *really* support robust, production-quality applications unless it's programmable. Intuitive user interfaces, wizards, and all that are great to have, but there are times when you need to really get down and tell the product *how* to do something. That's why Notes has always had a formula language, why LotusScript was added in release 4.0, and why a Java interface was added in release 4.6.

Both the LotusScript and Java interfaces to Notes expose a set of *objects* particular to the Domino/Notes product. Each object type is a *class*, and each class exposes certain attributes (*properties*) and behaviors (*methods*). The classes are things like Database, Document, View, Agent, and so on—all the objects with which you may have already become familiar by using the product. Together, these classes make up the Notes Object Interface.

Most of what you do when you use Java to program Domino is write code that manipulates NOI objects in some way. This book shows you how to do that. It goes beyond the excellent on-line documentation provided with the product to give you more in depth discussion and analysis of how the classes work together and why they are the way they are. I've put together lots of examples, all of which are discussed in some detail. All of the source code for the examples, and all the Notes databases that go with them, are available on the CD-ROM you'll find at the back of the book.

Who should read this book? I think two groups of people would benefit most:

1. Notes/Domino application developers who already know LotusScript and want to learn Java to see how it can help them create better Inter/intranet apps.
2. Java programmers who want to learn how to use the Notes Object Interface.

This book is not meant to teach you the Java programming language if you don't already know it. It is meant to teach you how to use Java to the fullest advantage when programming NOI. What we're striving for here is to give you a richness and depth of understanding that you won't get from the Domino on-line documentation, with lots of examples plus maybe a few surprises. I'll point out a few places where the Domino 4.6 documentation is incorrect (there aren't very many).

CHAPTER OVERVIEW

Chapter 1, "Domino/Notes Programmability Overview," is a survey of the commonly used Internet programming languages and how they are, or might be, used in the context of a Domino server and/or a Notes Client. It attempts to set the stage for the following chapters by giving you an overview of the Notes Object Interface (NOI) and scripting (both client side and server side).

Chapters 2–6 provide an in-depth look at the individual classes that make up the NOI. Each class's Java binding is discussed in some detail, and examples are given. All code examples (and any of the Notes databases used in the examples) are provided on the CD-ROM found at the back of this book, as well as on my Web site (http://www.looseleaf.net).

Chapter 7 is all about writing standalone applications using Java and NOI. It goes into some detail on how to write both single and multi-threaded programs.

Chapter 8 tells you how to code Java Agents for Domino, both single and multithreaded. Chapter 9 shows you how to use third-party Java development tools to debug Java Agents.

Chapter 10 goes into more detail on multithreaded Java programs using NOI, and discusses how (and how not) to share Notes objects across threads.

Chapter 11 tells you about servlets and how to write them (in case you are using an HTTP server other than Domino, such as Lotus Go). It also tells you how to convert your servlets into Agents, for when you upgrade to Domino. Again, all the code and databases used in the examples are on the CD.

Chapter 12 discusses Java Beans and their relationship to NOI.

Chapter 13 shows you how to conveniently (and profitably) use JDBC in combination with NOI to write Java programs that mix and match Notes and relational DBMS access.

Finally, Chapter 14 gives you a sneak preview of some upcoming Domino technologies, and my personal theories on where some of this stuff is headed in future releases of Domino/Notes.

I'd love to hear what you think of this book, and invite you to visit my Web site at http://www.looseleaf.net. Enjoy.

Acknowledgments

Jeff Eisen provided lots of technical review and assistance with the manuscript. Whatta guy. Thanks also to Bob Congdon for help with and advice on the servlet examples. No list of thank yous could be complete without acknowledging the years of support and assistance and inspiration I received at Iris Associates from Len Kawell and Tim Halvorsen. And thanks to Lance and Willie for being their respective selves.

Contents at a Glance

Foreword ix
Preface xv
Chapter 1: Domino/Notes Programmability Overview 1
Chapter 2: NOI Part 1: Session, DbDirectory, Database, ACL, ACLEntry . . .15
Chapter 3: NOI Part 2: Document, DocumentCollection, View, ViewColumn . .69
Chapter 4: NOI Part 3: Item, RichTextItem, RichTextStyle,
    EmbeddedObject, DateTime, DateRange 131
Chapter 5: NOI Part 4: Agent, AgentContext, International, Form, Name . .167
Chapter 6: NOI Part 5: Registration, Newsletter, Log 185
Chapter 7: Writing NOI Applications 217
Chapter 8: Writing NOI Agents 243
Chapter 9: Debugging NOI Agents 277
Chapter 10: Sharing Objects Across Threads 295
Chapter 11: Upgrading Servlets to Agents 313
Chapter 12: NOI and Java Beans 339
Chapter 13: JDBC and NOI 357
Chapter 14: A Look Ahead to Domino 5.0 379
Bibliography 403
Appendix A: Useful Links and References 407
Appendix B: Notes Object Interface Class Diagram 419
Appendix C: Domino Setup for Writing Java Programs 421
Appendix D: Notes Object Interface Exceptions 429
Appendix E: Creating LSXs 443
Appendix F: What's on the CD-ROM 447
Index 451
License Agreement 467
Installation Instructions 468

CONTENTS

Foreword ix

Preface xv

Chapter 1: Domino/Notes Programmability Overview ... 1
    The Notes Object Interface (NOI) 2
    Applications 2
    Downloaded Applets 3
    Servlets 4
    Agents 5
    CGI (Common Gateway Interface) 7
    Location and Triggering 8
    Notes Object Interface 9
    Java vs. LotusScript vs. JavaScript vs. VBScript 10
        LotusScript 10
        JavaScript 12
        VBScript 13
    Summary 13

Chapter 2: NOI Part 1: Session, DbDirectory, Database, ACL, ACLEntry 15
    Overview of NOI 15
    NOI Containment Hierarchy 18
    Introduction to the Class Descriptions 19
    The lotus.notes.NotesThread Class 21
    Exceptions 22
    The lotus.notes.Session Class 23
        Session Initializers 24
        Session Properties 24
        Session Child Object Creation 29
        Session Other Methods 31
    The lotus.notes.DbDirectory Class 37
    The lotus.notes.Database Class 40

The lotus.notes.Database Class 41
    Database Properties 41
    Database Design Elements 48
    Database Searching 50
    Database Administration 57
The lotus.notes.ACL Class 60
    ACL Properties 61
    ACL Methods 62
The lotus.notes.ACLEntry Class 64
    ACLEntry Properties 64
    ACLEntry Methods 67
Summary 67

Chapter 3: NOI Part 2: Document, DocumentCollection, View, ViewColumn 69

The lotus.notes.Document Class 69
    Document Properties 71
    Document Management Methods 88
    Item and Value Accessor Methods 98
The lotus.notes.View Class 107
    View Properties 108
    View Document Searching Methods 114
    View Document Navigation Methods 119
    View Miscellaneous Methods 121
The lotus.notes.ViewColumn Class 122
    ViewColumn Properties 122
The lotus.notes.DocumentCollection Class 123
    DocumentCollection Properties 124
    DocumentCollection Navigation Methods 125
    DocumentCollection Other Methods 126
Summary 129

Chapter 4: NOI Part 3: Item, RichTextItem, RichTextStyle, EmbeddedObject, DateTime, DateRange 131

The lotus.notes.Item Class 131
    Item Value Properties 132

Item Attributes 133
　　　Item Methods 138
　The lotus.notes.RichTextItem Class 143
　　　RichTextItem Properties 143
　　　RichTextItem Methods 144
　The lotus.notes.RichTextStyle Class 148
　　　RichTextStyle Constants 149
　　　RichTextStyle Properties 151
　The lotus.notes.EmbeddedObject Class 155
　　　EmbeddedObject Properties 157
　　　EmbeddedObject Methods 158
　The lotus.notes.DateTime Class 159
　　　DateTime Properties 160
　　　DateTime Methods 162
　The lotus.notes.DateRange Class 164
　　　DateRange Properties 165
　Summary 166

Chapter 5: NOI Part 4: Agent, AgentContext, International, Form, Name 167

　The lotus.notes.Agent Class 167
　　　Agent Properties 168
　　　Agent Methods 170
　The lotus.notes.AgentContext Class 171
　　　AgentContext Properties 171
　　　AgentContext Methods 174
　The lotus.notes.International Class 175
　　　International Properties 175
　The lotus.notes.Form Class 177
　　　Form Properties 178
　　　Form Methods 180
　The lotus.notes.Name Class 180
　　　Name Properties 180
　Summary 183

Chapter 6: NOI Part 5: Registration, Newsletter, Log ..185

　The lotus.notes.Registration Class 185
　　　Discussion of Example 189

Contents

Registration Properties 191
Registration Methods 194
The lotus.notes.Newsletter Class 200
    Newsletter Properties 201
    Newsletter Methods 203
The lotus.notes.Log Class 209
    Log Properties 209
    Log Methods 211
Summary 215

Chapter 7: Writing NOI Applications 217

Single-Threaded Applications Using NOI 217
Skeleton Multithreaded Program 220
Multithreaded Applications Using NOI 226
    Discussion of Ex74Multi 228
A Multithreaded Web Crawler 233
Discussion of the WebCrawler 238
Summary: Multithreaded NOI Applications 242

Chapter 8: Writing NOI Agents 243

Agent Infrastructure: The lotus.notes.AgentBase Class 244
Agent Identity 250
Agent Security 254
    Agent Access Control 255
    Agent Administration 256
    Agent Latency, Or, Why Won't My Agent Run? 260
    Other Interesting Environment Variables 264
Multithreaded Agents 264
Summary of Agent Output Options 271
Special Functionality for Web Agents 271
Summary 276

Chapter 9: Debugging NOI Agents 277

Sample Debuggable Agent 279
    Original Agent 279
    Debug Class Extensions: DbgSession 283
    Debug Class Extensions: DbgAgentContext 286

Summary 293

Chapter 10: Sharing Objects Across Threads 295
Why Share Objects Across Threads? 295
NOI and Thread Safety 296
What Isn't Thread Safe? 301
    Multithreading Restrictions on DbDirectory 301
    Thread Unsafe Algorithms 302
    Memory Management and lotus.notes.Session 307
Summary 311

Chapter 11: Upgrading Servlets to Agents 313
What Is a Servlet? 313
Setting Up Domino To Run Servlets 314
Writing a Servlet 318
Transforming Servlets to Agents: The Servlet/Agent Adapter ...323
    Servlet-Running Agent 325
    Discussion of the RunServlet Agent 330
    Discussion of HelloNOIServlet2 334
Processing Optional Arguments 336
Summary 336

Chapter 12: NOI and Java Beans 339
Background: What About Beans? 340
Java Beans Technologies 342
    Method Naming Conventions 342
    Event Model 343
    Introspection and BeanInfo 345
    Visibility 346
    Serialization 347
NOI and Builder Tools 352
Summary: Are NOI Objects Java Beans? 355

Chapter 13: JDBC and NOI 357
What is JDBC? 357
Why Do We Care About JDBC? 359
Layer Upon Layer 360

Testing Strategies 363
Installing JDBC and ODBC 364
JDBC Example 366
    Driver and Database Selection 366
    The Code 368
    Discussion of Data Retrieval Example 376
A Word on Agent Security 377
Summary 378

Chapter 14: A Look Ahead to Domino 5.0 379

Domino 4.6 Programmability: Summary 380
Java NOI 380
Java Agents 381
Java Servlets 382
Overview of Forthcoming Enhancements 383
Java Development Environment 383
Remote Access Technologies for Domino NOI 384
    CORBA and Domino 386
    Domino Server ORB 388
    Applet Access to Domino Server ORB: NOI for
        ORB Clients 390
    Remote Method Invocation (RMI) 392
    DCOM 395
    Summary: Whither Remote Objects for Domino? 396
Other Programmable Interfaces for Domino 398
Summary 400

Bibliography 403

Appendix A: Useful Links and References 407

Agents 407
CORBA 409
Domino Publications 410
General Notes Info 410
Home Pages 411
IMAP 412
Java Beans 412

Java Development .... .413
JDBC and ODBC .... .414
LDAP .... .415
Other Tools .... .415
RMI .... .415
Servlets .... .416
Web Server .... .416

Appendix B: Notes Object Interface Class Diagram ...419

Appendix C: Domino Setup for Writing Java Programs ..421

System Requirements .... .421
Development Tool Options .... .423
Path and Classpath Setup .... .425
    JDK .... .425
    JBuilder .... .426
    Visual Cafe .... .427
    Developing Domino Agents and Servlets .... .427
Supported Java Versions .... .428

Appendix D: Notes Object Interface Exceptions 429

Exception Codes and Messages .... .430

Appendix E: Creating LSXs 443

Appendix F: What's on the CD-ROM 447

Installation Instructions .... .449

Index 451

License Agreement 467

Installation Instructions 468

1

DOMINO/NOTES PROGRAMMABILITY OVERVIEW

Believe it or not, this is a big topic all by itself. If we use a broad definition of the word *programmabilty*, we have to mention LotusScript, cover the Notes Object Interface (NOI), and at least touch on each of the ways in which LotusScript and Java programs can be formulated (agents vs. applications vs. servlets vs. applets vs. CGI), triggered (foreground, HTTP, scheduled, new mail), where each kind of program can run (client, server, both), and how each can be edited and debugged.

Were we to cover all these topics in depth, you'd be holding an encyclopedia instead of a book. Still, we can at least categorize, compare, and contrast to give you an overview of which technology you might want to use when and where.

THE NOTES OBJECT INTERFACE (NOI)

We'll be talking a lot in this book about NOI: how to use it and what you can do with it. In fact, there are five whole chapters that document every call in the Java version of the API. For now, we'll say only that NOI is a class library, that is, a group of objects that you can program using LotusScript or Java (this book focuses on the Java interface) that manipulate the Domino/Notes groupware development platform.

If you are already a Notes/Domino user, you're familiar with such product concepts as servers, databases, views, and documents. NOI provides a programming interface to those objects. As of Domino Release 4.6, those objects are available in Java. Previously, they were available only through the embedded language known as LotusScript.

The term *Notes Object Interface* is not language specific. It refers to both the Java and LotusScript APIs. The objects underneath, however, are the same. The differences in the way you use them have mostly to do with syntactical differences in the two languages.

In the discussions that follow, some familiarity with object-oriented programming concepts is assumed. If you're already a LotusScript or C++ programmer, you'll have no trouble at all.

The rest of this chapter is about the kinds of programs people write for Domino and for Internet-based applications in general. Let's start with the different kinds of programs you can write for and in Notes/Domino and define them a bit.

APPLICATIONS

For the purposes of this book, we'll use the term *application* to mean any program that you start from a system-level icon or from a command line. Applications are self-contained and reside somewhere on your computer's disk. The Domino server is an example of an application, as is a Solitaire card game. Applications almost always have some kind of user interface (UI) with which you interact. A UI can be a simple command line or a full-blown windowing environment.

Computer programs, or *applications*, can be developed in any programming language: C, COBOL, FORTRAN, Java, all kinds of assembly languages. Some programs are developed with the aid of other software tools, because developers sometimes don't know how to program in any of the traditional computer languages. For example, when you use the Notes client application to create a database and some forms that perform a business task for you (even if it's just a list of people you have to call tomorrow), that's an application. You created it using Notes, not C, but it's still an application.

DOWNLOADED APPLETS

Applets, meaning programs downloaded over a network to your local machine and (usually) executed by a *browser* program, are very different from applications. As far as I know, applets can only be written in Java. A browser is an application that knows how to find its way around a network (a LAN or the Internet) and display *pages*. The pages are "programmed" with a language called HTML (HyperText Markup Language) and may contain references to Java applets. When a page contains a reference (a network address, or Universal Resource Locator, or URL) to an embedded Java applet program, the browser fetches that program, and executes it in the context of the page it is rendering for you.

For security reasons, browsers restrict the activities that applets can perform. Applets can't, for example, load and execute programs from your local hard disk, although that is a capability of the Java language. They also can't communicate over the network with any server, except the one from which it was downloaded. If you were to write a Java applet that tried, for example, to erase the disk of the hapless user who downloaded your program, the browser would simply throw a runtime exception, and your applet would stop executing.

Applets are a lot of what makes the stuff you see on the Internet these days hop around and boogie. Most of the headache-producing jump and jive you encounter on most pages, where text flashes in different colors and icons spin around, is programmed with Java and downloaded to your machine by the browser as applets.

We won't discuss applets very much in this book, mainly because you can't use NOI from an applet. The reason is simple: the Java NOI was implemented in a very thin layer of Java code that mostly just packages some arguments and calls into the Notes DLLs (Dynamic Link Libraries) to perform the required work. One of the things that browsers prevent applets from doing is loading a DLL, so applets are incompatible with the Domino 4.6 NOI. That doesn't mean you can't develop a Web site using Domino and have applets in your pages. That works fine, because Domino simply serves up your applets along with the rest of the stuff making up your site. What doesn't work is downloading an applet to a machine that doesn't have Domino installed on it and having that applet try to use a Notes object. The code just isn't on the machine, and even if it were, the browser wouldn't let your applet load it into memory.

How does a Java program become an applet? That's easy. It just has to be a class that extends (inherits from) the standard class java.applet.Applet. Well, maybe it's not quite that easy. It also has to implement a UI of some kind, or it will be invisible in the HTML page.

SERVLETS

If an applet is a Java program that gets downloaded to a browser running on a client and is hooked into the HTML page with a special tag, then

I guess you'd expect a Java program that runs on the server when it is referenced by an HTML tag to be called a *servlet*. A servlet acts as a sort of plug-in to the server. It's a module that is invoked before an HTML page is served up to a browser and typically inserts HTML into the page on the fly. Servlets can also be explicitly invoked by name in a URL.

What would you do with a servlet? Typically, servlets are used to examine the URL that triggered the retrieval of the current page, do some application-specific processing (a relational database lookup, for example), and insert stuff into the page that goes back to the client. As a customization tool for Web pages, servlets allow application designers to have more of the processing occur on the server, offloading the slower client machine. System administrators also like them because servlets allow them to centralize access to system resources, such as back-end databases, and to simplify deployment issues.

JavaSoft (the subsidiary of Sun Microsystems that owns Java) has developed a standard servlet API, which you can download from their Web site. In Chapter 11, we'll see how you can use JavaSoft's classes to write a servlet, and then you'll see how to convert any servlet into a Domino Agent. I'll also describe in detail how to set up your Domino 4.6 HTTP server to work with servlets.

AGENTS

As with applets and servlets, a Java class becomes an Agent by extending a specified base class, in this case lotus.notes.AgentBase. Although there was an Agent-like facility in Notes Release 3.0 called *macros*, real Agents first appeared in Notes Release 4.0. You could program them using a Notes @function formula (as in Release 3), with a pick list of *simple actions*, or with LotusScript. Notes/Domino 4.6 adds the ability to write agents using Java. In Chapter 8, we'll go into great and gory detail about how to create Java Agents for Domino. For now, though, I'll just mention some of the advantages that Domino Agents give you over servlets and applications:

- Transportability. Agents live in Notes databases and are design elements, just as forms and views are. That means they travel with the database contents when the database is moved, copied, or replicated. Once created, you don't have to keep track of the Java code separately from your application.
- Security. Agents are digitally signed when they are created or modified. This lets you know who touched an Agent last. Also, the Agent, when it runs on a server, will have no greater access to any databases than the signer of the Agent does. Furthermore, users must have designer access to a database to modify Agents. Agents can be *personal* (available for editing and execution only to the person who created it) or *shared* (available for execution to anyone with access to the database, and for editing to anyone with designer access to the database).
- Tracking. Whenever an Agent is run on a server machine, the server logs the start and end execution times, custom output messages, and any errors in the server log.

Like servlets, Agents can be triggered from a URL, a form of network address that tells you where something (an HTML page, an applet, a picture, a video) lives out there in the universe. Unlike servlets, Agents can also be triggered on Domino servers in a number of other ways, as we'll see shortly. Agents run in the foreground can have a user interface, but Agents run on servers cannot.

CGI (COMMON GATEWAY INTERFACE)

CGI programs are sometimes called *scripts*. They are programs written in any programming language supported on the server (Perl and C seem to be the most commonly used languages, although you can use BASIC and even UNIX shell scripts as well), and are triggered either with a URL or an HTML tag. Like background Agents, they exhibit no UI.

We won't be exploring CGI programming in any detail, as there are already numerous books available on that topic. In addition, my personal opinion is that CGI scripting will gradually be replaced by other forms of server programmability, primarily for performance reasons. When a request comes in to an HTTP server to run a CGI script, the server must first locate the file referenced in the URL (or HTML tag) in the file system. Then it must start a new process to execute the CGI program (regardless of whether it's a C executable, a BASIC program or a Perl or shell script). Arguments to the program are passed on the command line. When the program is finished, its process is shut down. The next time a request for that same CGI program comes in, the server again starts a new process for it. There is no way to cache CGI programs or to run them in the server process.

More up-to-date servers support higher throughput (and therefore more scalable) technologies such as servlets and Agents, which usually avoid costly process overhead. In addition, using Java as your programming language is an advantage, because once a Java class has been loaded into the Java Virtual Machine (VM), the Java byte code interpreter and execution environment, it can stay there for awhile, so that successive invocations of the same Agent or servlet do not cause the class file to be reloaded from disk.

LOCATION AND TRIGGERING

Tables 1.1 and 1.2 summarize what's been said about where each kind of program runs and how each is triggered.

Table 1.1 Program Location

Program	Client Browser	Notes Client	Domino Server	Other HTTP Server
Applet	yes	yes	no	no
Agent	no	yes	yes	no
Application	no	yes	yes	yes
Servlet	no	no	yes	yes
CGI	no	no	yes	yes

Table 1.2 Program Triggering

Program	Manual	Scheduled	URL	HTML Tag	Other Event
Applet	no	no	yes	yes	no
Agent	yes	yes	yes	no	yes
Application	yes	no	no	no	no
Servlet	no	no	yes	yes	no
CGI	yes	no	yes	yes	no

Manual triggering refers to the ability to cause a program to run synchronously when you want, either from a command-line interface or by clicking on an icon or other command button. In the Notes client, for example, you can cause an Agent to run by selecting its name from the Actions menu or by selecting it in the Agent View and clicking on **Actions/Run** in the menubar. For example, applications and CGI programs can be run from a DOS command prompt.

The Other Event column in Table 1.2 refers to the fact that Domino Agents can be triggered by events such as new mail arriving in a database or by the modification of an existing document.

Both URL and HTML triggering are available anytime you have an HTTP server. Typically, to trigger an Agent or servlet or CGI program from a URL, you simply tack the program name onto the end of the URL (following the server's name, plus any subdirectory). To pass arguments or program-specific commands, you normally use the HTTP query syntax convention, of a question mark followed by more words. The HTTP server sees the program name and will run it if it can be found.

NOTES OBJECT INTERFACE

The Notes Object Interface (NOI) is a set of classes used to manipulate the functionality of Notes workstations and Domino servers. As of Domino Release 4.6, NOI is available through LotusScript and Java bindings, as well as through OLE Automation (from Visual Basic, for example). NOI implements classes such as Session, Database and Document, and by using the methods and properties of these classes, you can build extraordinarily sophisticated collaborative and workflow applications.

We'll cover the details of the NOI classes in Chapters 2, 3, 4, 5, and 6, but it's worth summarizing here what kinds of programs can make use of the NOI classes. NOI is available only on machines where Notes/Domino is installed.

Table 1.3 NOI Availability

Program	Java Client	LotusScript Client	Java Server	LotusScript Server
Applet	no	no	no	no
Agent	yes	yes	yes	yes
Application	yes	no	yes	no
Servlet	no	no	yes	no

JAVA VS. LOTUSSCRIPT VS. JAVASCRIPT VS. VBSCRIPT

Having dissected the world of Domino programmability into the various kinds of programs you can write, you might wonder why this book focuses so heavily on Java, to the virtual exclusion of all the other Internet programming languages. Well, since you asked, I'll briefly describe the major differences among Java, JavaScript, LotusScript and VBScript, and then I'll tell you why I'm ignoring almost everything except Java.

LotusScript

LotusScript is a language based on Microsoft's Visual Basic (VB). Most of its components actually come from the original BASIC language, now in the public domain. Some VB constructs are supported for compatibility. The three major benefits of LotusScript, however, beyond being familiar to VB programmers, are the object-oriented extensions to the language that provide for classes, methods, and properties; the fact that LotusScript is embedded in all Lotus software products (desktop as well as Domino/Notes); and the LotusScript eXtension (LSX) architecture.

Unlike VB, LotusScript is a fully object-oriented language. You can write your own classes with full (single) inheritance, encapsulation, and data hiding abilities (there is no polymorphism, at least not yet).

Furthermore, each of the LotusScript host products has its own set of built-in classes that allow you to manipulate the product's objects from LotusScript. Thus, 1-2-3 provides a whole set of Range, Sheet and Workbook object manipulation abilities, and Notes has a set of classes like Session, Database, View, and DateTime.

The LSX architecture is simply a way of implementing LotusScript classes as dynamically loadable libraries (*DLL* in Windows parlance, *shared library* in UNIX, and so on), so that any LotusScript hosting product can use it. Thus, 1-2-3 can load the Notes LSX (provided that Notes is installed on the machine), and the Notes classes appear in the 1-2-3 class browser as if they were native to the spreadsheet world.

In Notes/Domino, LotusScript can be used for both back-end and front-end scripting. The distinction is simply that front-end scripts manipulate the Notes Client user interface, and can only run in the context of the Client UI. Back-end scripts, by contrast, can be run in the background on a server as well as in the Client UI. Back-end classes (the ones we're interested in here) can be used anywhere, while front-end classes (NotesUIWorkspace, NotesUIDatabase, NotesUIView, NotesUIDocument) can be used only in front-end scripts (on a form button or attached to a form event, for example). Agents meant to be triggered in the context of a UI operation, such as from the Actions menu or from a form button, may use front-end classes. However, if you write an Agent using any front-end classes and then try to run that agent in the background (on a scheduled basis, for example) where there is no UI context, the agent will fail to run (the referenced UI classes will not be found). It's the back-end classes that contain all the data manipulation functionality.

LotusScript Agents can be triggered in all the ways we've already discussed: via an URL, from the Notes Client, and in the background by various events (schedule, new mail, etc.).

The big drawback of LotusScript as a programming language is that it isn't supported by any of the popular Web browsers. That means there's no way you can write an applet in LotusScript and have it be downloaded to some random machine and execute there. Still, LotusScript remains a great Notes application programming language.

JavaScript

JavaScript and Java are two completely separate languages. They have nothing in common beyond the word *Java* in their names. Whereas Java is aimed at professional programmers and runs on any machine that has an appropriate VM installed, JavaScript is meant to be used by casual developers, and it works only in the various browser products supplied by Netscape Corp. While Java programs your computer (via the VM), JavaScript can program only your browser (or whatever browser loads the Web page containing the script). So far, only Netscape's browser product fully supports JavaScript, as there's no published standard for the language. Microsoft's Internet Explorer supports a language that is very similar to JavaScript, called JScript, but you'll find that there are subtle (and important) differences.

Make no mistake, JavaScript fills a real need. People authoring interesting Web pages need a way to "wire" the different elements of the page together and to provide a way for the browser to handle certain UI events (mouse clicks, typing, and so on) properly. JavaScript can be used, for example, to catch a mouse click and route the event to an embedded Java applet.

Is JavaScript a real programming language? Yes and no. It is interpreted, like Java and BASIC, and it has some common programming constructs like arrays and for loops. Its drawbacks have to do more with its lack of portability (it runs reliably only with Netscape's browser) and with the fact that when you write JavaScript code, you give away your source code every time your page is downloaded. The JavaScript sources are encoded directly into the HTML stream of the page and are interpreted from source (unlike Java, which is compiled down to a cross-platform interpretable byte stream) directly by the browser. This latter fact drives most professional developers to do as little as possible in JavaScript and to use it to simply connect the dots on the page.

VBScript

VBScript is Microsoft's alternative to JavaScript (though as I mentioned previously, Microsoft also supports a JavaScript-like language called JScript). JavaScript's syntax is not based on Java, but VBScript *is* based on Visual Basic. Apart from syntax differences, it is used in exactly the same way as JavaScript, and it has all the same advantages and disadvantages.

SUMMARY

To sum up, the world of Internet programmability is quite large. Not only do you have to figure out what kind of HTTP server you might want to use but what language(s) you want to program it in, and what kind of functionality you want to expose. Are you looking primarily at downloadable applets? Or are you more interested in server-side functionality, such as workflow and relational DBMS connectivity?

I've attempted to segment the overall space for you and narrow the focus of this book to the following main points: Domino is an incredibly powerful application development platform that incorporates an HTTP server, a couple of cool programming languages, and a great object hierarchy for you to work with. If you've settled on using Domino for your server (or you're thinking about it), then read on to learn more about Java and NOI and about the different ways you can use the tools provided by Lotus to develop your applications.

To this point we've covered the differences among applications, applets, servlets, and Agents. Chapter 2 is an overview of the role played by NOI in Domino programmability and the beginning of our in-depth look at the Notes classes. Later chapters go into much greater detail about how to write Java applications and Agents for Domino (both single and multithreaded). There are also a few chapters on advanced topics, such as how to run existing servlets as Domino Agents, and how to use JDBC with NOI.

2

NOI Part 1: Session, DbDirectory, Database, ACL, ACLEntry

This is where we start to dive deep into all the Notes Object Interface (NOI) classes. This chapter covers the top layer of the containment hierarchy, and subsequent chapters go into each of the 23 classes of interest to the Java programmer. Refer to Appendix A for a diagram of the NOI containment hierarchy and a list of all the classes.

Overview of NOI

The Notes object hierarchy does not make much use of class inheritance, but it does enforce a strict containment model, especially in the Java binding. There are no cases where using the *new* operator will result in a valid object instance, even for the top-level object, lotus.notes.Session. The main reason for this is that each Java object instance tightly wrappers a corresponding C++ object in the Notes LSX module (the library that actually implements all the object behaviors). The Java interface is really just a thin layer on top of a bunch of "native methods," which are implemented in C and C++. This allows Notes to use the LotusScript eXtension (LSX) architecture to present multiple language bindings to programmers, all based on exactly the same set of C++ code. When a new method or property (or even class) is added to the product, it can be exposed in all language bindings with only a very small incremental effort. Because each Java object instance is closely tied to an internal object, the objects' contexts must be strictly maintained. It makes no sense (at the Notes API layer, which was used to implement all this stuff), for example, to instantiate a free-floating Document object. Documents *must* have a database context in which to operate. The same is true for all the other NOI classes—each must exist only in the context of a container.

Another implication of strict containment is that if a container is closed (or destroyed), then all of that container's child objects are also destroyed. By "destroyed" I mean only that the in memory programmatic object is destroyed, and its resources are released. The actual object represented by the in memory object (the *real* database, document, or whatever) is not affected. Any modifications cached in the in memory object that have not been committed to disk are lost when the object is destroyed. Several of the objects have explicit save() calls on them to perform the commit operation.

If you're already familiar with the LotusScript binding of NOI (especially the back-end classes), you'll find the Java interface very familiar, except for the differences imposed by the differing syntaxes of the two languages. Of course, two different programming languages do impose some constraints on the mapping of identical functionality from one to the other, and not just syntactically (check out the September/October 1997 issue of the bimonthly publication on Notes technologies called *The View*—published by Wellesley Information

Services—Vol. 3, number 5. I had a detailed article on this called "An Introduction to the New Notes Object Interface (NOI) for Java"). The following table summarizes the differences.

Table 2.1 Java/LotusScript Differences

	Java	LotusScript
Derived from	C++	BASIC
Function calls	Methods only	Methods and properties
Typing	Strong	Not strong
Threading	Multithreaded	Single threaded
UI Programmability	Fully featured	Minimal
Network programmability	High-level socket, URL, and TCP classes	Notes RPC only
Naming	package lotus.notes	NotesXXX

In general, in the Notes/Domino environment, you can do anything with Java applications and Agents that you can do with LotusScript Agents (there's no way to write LotusScript applications, as LotusScript is an embedded language), and Java even provides functionality lacking (so far) in LotusScript, such as multithreaded programming and high-level network object libraries. Some beloved features of LotusScript are, however, lacking in the Java NOI. Two examples are as follows:

❐ **Variants**. The Variant data type in LotusScript is a wonderful, and frequently used, feature of NOI. Variants can contain any data type, including object instances and arrays. Thus, they are often used in NOI when a method or property returns a data value, which might be of any type, or an array of object instances. Variants have no place in a strongly typed language such as Java, however. Instead we used method overloading (to handle input arguments of many kinds) and the Object type (for single-instance return values and object instances) in the Java

NOI. In cases where we needed to return an array of values or objects, we used the java.util.Vector class, all of whose elements are of type Object (or some derivative).

- **Expanded class syntax.** The LotusScript Document class (named NotesDocument) was created as an "expanded" class. This means that when you write your LotusScript program you can specify any arbitrary property name on either the left- or right-hand side of an assignment operator. The property name you use, if not an actual registered property of the Document class, is interpreted to mean "an item of the given name belonging to the referenced Document instance." Thus, if you code something like *doc.Subject = "hello"*, it means that you want to assign the string "hello" to the item named Subject in the document, since Subject is not a registered property for that class. Likewise, if you were to use *doc.Subject* on the right-hand side of the assignment, it would mean that you wanted to get the value of the item named Subject. Java doesn't allow either of these constructs. Instead we just added more accessor and value setting methods to the Document class.

If you're not already a LotusScript programmer and you care only about Java, none of this is relevant to you, really. All you need to know is that the Java binding of NOI exposes all the functionality of the LotusScript binding (one way or another), and that you're not shortchanging yourself by using Java. In fact, as we'll see, Java offers some functionality you can't get with LotusScript.

NOI CONTAINMENT HIERARCHY

When you write a class library, you have to be concerned with inheritance hierarchies. They serve mainly to make the developer's job easier, because they allow you to reuse methods conveniently. But when you go to write a real-life application using someone's class library as a tool kit, you could (I claim) mostly care less about inheritance. What really matters is how you navigate from object to object in a *containment* hierarchy, especially when the classes are strictly contained, as they are with NOI.

In developing the Java binding for NOI for Domino Release 4.6, we had to make a trade-off between, on the one hand, "Java-ness" and on the other, "Notes-ness." Chapter 12 goes into more detail on how the Java NOI relates to Java Beans, and we'll explain in all its goryness why this particular trade-off had to be made, how it was done, and how it might be made better in the future. In any event, the containment hierarchy for NOI is both strict, and worth understanding, if you ever intend to use it. The diagram in Appendix B (and on the CD) serves as a road map to the detailed class by class descriptions that ensue.

INTRODUCTION TO THE CLASS DESCRIPTIONS

What follows in this and the next few chapters is a blow by blow, class by class description of NOI. Each class is shown with its *properties* (attributes of objects) and *methods* (behaviors), and most class descriptions include an example or two of how to use them. All descriptions are of the Java binding of NOI; no LotusScript examples are given, except to illustrate an important difference between the LotusScript and Java bindings. All examples are reproduced on the enclosed CD, together with any sample Notes databases that are necessary to run the samples. All the samples were created using the shipping build of Domino 4.6. You can find a complete description formatted for HTML by the Javadoc utility on the companion CD, in the docs directory.

For those of you unfamiliar with LotusScript, a word about properties and methods is in order. LotusScript makes a clear distinction between the two: properties are attributes of objects, while methods are behaviors. Properties can be read/write or read only, and typically (at least in the Notes hierarchy) take no arguments. Methods are what you'd expect from Java or C++: subroutine calls that might or might not take arguments or return a value of some kind.

Java, on the other hand, doesn't really have the notion of properties. It does allow for public member variables on a class, but it is rare that you'd use these for real work. For one thing, if setting an object's attribute has side effects (it usually does in a system of interesting size), then you need some code to run in order to deal with that. For another thing, it's fairly rare that you'd want to let someone set an object's attribute without at least range checking the value. It was recognized soon after Java 1.0 was released that some sort of property get/set scheme was highly desirable, and some features were added to the Java Beans specification to address this (primarily for the benefit of Bean builder tools, but we all gain by it). The Beans spec essentially just lays out a method naming convention, from which a set of properties can be induced.

For example, in the LotusScript binding of NOI there's a property on the Item class called Text. It's a read/write property, so I can both get the value of the property, and set it, like this:

```
Dim x As String
Dim i As NotesItem
x = i.Text
i.Text = "A new value"
```

The Java naming convention (which is followed by the Java binding of NOI) says that a property retrieval call starts with *get*, and a property setting call starts with *set*. If the property retrieval call returns a boolean value, you can optionally use *is* instead of *get*. So, the Item's Text "property" would be coded in Java as the following two calls:

```
String getText();
void setText(String s);
```

You use these methods just the same as any other in Java. The point of it all is that the new visual builder tools for Java Beans can "introspect" the methods of a Java class and figure out that when there's a get/set pattern conforming to the spec, as above, then it can represent that pair as a single property (String property Text, read/write in this case).

So, with that in mind, let's dive into the first NOI class. I've separated the set of methods logically into methods and properties, and now you know what that really means.

THE LOTUS.NOTES.NOTESTHREAD CLASS

One "supporting" class needs to be talked about briefly before we start in on the actual Notes classes. NotesThread is not a real Domino object class, like the Database or Document class, but nonetheless you need to know about it to use any of the other classes. NotesThread extends (inherits from) java.lang.Thread, and must be used whenever you want to manipulate any of the Notes objects.

The reason NotesThread is required is simple: It does the necessary per-thread initialization and teardown of the Notes back end code (which, as you'll remember, is implemented in C and C++, not Java). Other than that, NotesThread is exactly like Thread, and you use it in exactly the same ways. Chapters 7 and 8 will dwell at length on how to write multithreaded Java applications and Agents using NotesThread. For now, we'll just leave it that you need to run all of the Notes objects on a thread that's been initialized for Notes. There are three ways to do that (subsequent references to Notes classes will generally omit the "lotus.notes" package prefix):

1. Write a class that extends NotesThread, invoke the start() method. Your class's runNotes() method will be called from the new thread.

2. Write a class that implements the java.lang.Runnable interface. Create an instance of NotesThread using *new*, passing your class instance to the NotesThread constructor. Call start() on the NotesThread instance, and your class's run() method will be called.

3. If you can't do either of the previous two techniques, maybe because you're working on a UI where you have some event handlers that are invoked on an AWT (Abstract Windowing Toolkit, the Java UI class library) thread over which you have no control, then use the static calls on NotesThread instead. When you're in a situation where you need to initialize Notes for the current thread, and where the current thread is not an instance of NotesThread, then you can call NotesThread.sinitThread(), a static method (meaning, you don't need an instance of NotesThread to invoke it). WARNING: you must be absolutely sure, if you employ this technique, that you also call NotesThread.stermThread() exactly one time for each sinitThread() call on the thread. Making unbalanced calls to these two methods will most likely cause your program to throw an exception (if you're lucky), to crash (if you're not), or to hang on exit. Use the try/catch/finally mechanism to be sure to initialize and terminate the correct number of times per thread.

EXCEPTIONS

Many of the packages I've seen for Java (including the libraries distributed with Java itself) use a unique exception class for each kind of runtime error that could occur. Each exception has a different name, and there are inheritance hierarchies of them. This scheme did not map well onto Domino/Notes, where the C API and the LotusScript classes both use a system of error codes and associated text.

Instead, we created a single exception class (NotesException) to handle all of the package's error conditions. NotesException extends java.lang.Exception and provides one additional method: getErrorCode(). Any Notes call that throws an exception will throw an instance of NotesException containing the message and relevant error code. All the error codes that are generated by the Notes classes are defined as *public static final int*s (the Java equivalent to C++ #defines) in the NotesException class. You can use the base class methods (on the Throwable class, from which Exception inherits) getMessage(), getLocalizedMessage(), toString(), and printStackTrace() to extract the message text and/or send a stack trace for debugging purposes to the standard output stream. A complete list of NotesException error codes and messages is provided in Appendix D.

Okay, let's get into the real stuff.

THE LOTUS.NOTES.SESSION CLASS

The Session class is the root of the NOI containment hierarchy. You can't do much of anything unless you have a Session instance handed to you, or unless you create one. If you're writing an Agent, then Domino creates a Session instance for you (see Chapter 5); otherwise, use the static method newInstance to create one. Why a static method, instead of just using the *new* operator? The main reason is that a static method can return *null* if the system hasn't been initialized for some reason, or if your process is out of memory. It's also easier for a static method to raise an exception if something is wrong. *New* must pretty much always return an object reference, which doesn't give you much flexibility in your constructor to do validity checking, and so on.

The public methods of the Session class can be divided into the following categories:

1. Initializers
2. Properties
3. Child object creation
4. All others

Session Initializers

There's only one initializer that you'd ever use: the static newInstance() method we mentioned above. There are actually two public versions of this call, one with no arguments and one with an *int* argument. The second version—the one with an *int* argument—is meant for internal use only. The argument is a "magic cookie" that the Agent subsystem uses to pass agent context to a new Session instance. For your programs, just use Session.newInstance(). It returns a Session reference, or throws a NotesException instance.

Session Properties

java.util.Vector getAddressBooks()

Read only. This property returns a Vector containing a lotus.Notes.Database instance for each of the Address Books known to the system. If you're running the program on a workstation, this will typically be just your local names.nsf. If you're running it on a Domino server, it is often a series of databases, as most servers make use of the address book chaining feature.

One important difference between this method and the getDatabase() method, discussed below, is that getAddressBooks() does not open the databases that are returned. Any Database property or method that you use on an address book instance that hasn't been opened yet will either return *null* or throw an exception. To open an address book instance explicitly, use the open() method.

The example in Listing 2.1 gets the current list of address books and prints out the file name for each.

Listing 2.1 Address Books Example (Ex21AddrBooks.java)

```java
import java.lang.*;
import java.util.*;
import lotus.notes.*;
public class Ex21AddrBooks extends NotesThread {
    public static void main(String argv[])
    {
    try {
        Ex21AddrBooks e21 = new Ex21AddrBooks();
        e21.start();
        e21.join();
        }
    catch (Exception e) {e.printStackTrace();}
    }
    public void runNotes()
    {
    try {
        Session s = Session.newInstance();
        java.util.Vector v = s.getAddressBooks();
        if (v != null)
            {
            Enumeration e = v.elements();
            while (e.hasMoreElements())
                {
                Database db = (Database)e.nextElement();
                if (db != null)
                    {
                    db.open();
                    System.out.println(db.getFileName() + " / " +
                                            db.getTitle());
                    }
```

```
            }
          }
        }   // end try
    catch (NotesException e) {e.printStackTrace();}
     }
}   // end class
```

Because this is the first full example in the book, I'll point out a couple of things that have nothing to do with the getAddressBooks() call. First, you have to include the import statement for the lotus.notes package, and the Notes/Domino executable directory (the one where all the executable files are installed) must be on the path, so that the proper libraries can be loaded. Furthermore, your CLASSPATH must include the notes.jar file.

Second, note that the first method in the class is a static one named *main*. This is required in order to run the program from the command line. You'd invoke this program with the command **java Ex21AddrBooks**, and the Java interpreter will start your program at the main() function. Because main() is static, no instance of the class has yet been created when the program starts. That's why the first thing main() does is create an instance of Ex21AddrBooks. Once that instance exists, we just call start() on it. That causes our runNotes() method to be invoked on a new thread. Main() then calls join() on the new thread, to wait for it to complete before exiting. While not strictly necessary in this simple example, waiting for all child threads to exit before terminating the mainline program is good practice, and it *is* required when you're writing an Agent, as we'll see in Chapter 8. Did we have to use another thread to run this? No, certainly not. We could easily have just put all the calls in main(). But then you wouldn't be as hip as you are now to the total coolness of Java and threads.

The runNotes() method is where we put the real logic of the program. It creates a new Session instance and gets a Vector containing a

NOI Part I: Session, DbDirectory, Database, ACL, ACL Entry

list of databases. Each Database instance in the Vector is an unopened address book. We iterate over the elements in the Vector using the Enumeration interface in a simple while loop, printing out each database's file name and title. We have to open each database explicitly before we can access the title (but not the file name).

When I run the program from the command line (in my case from a DOS window on my NT system), the first thing I see is a password prompt. That's because my Java program is accessing the Notes backend, just like an API program would do, and my user id has a password on it. When I type in my password, the program continues. Then I see the names of the address books known to my system (both local address books and the ones on my default server).

AgentContext getAgentContext()

If your program is an Agent, then this call returns the context object for the current Agent. Otherwise it returns *null*. From the AgentContext class you find out all sorts of things about how the Agent is being run (current database, current user name, and so on). See Chapter 5 for details.

String getUserName()
lotus.notes.Name getUserNameObject()
String getCommonUserName()

These three calls return different versions of the user's name, as found in the current id file. The first one, getUserName() returns the fully qualified "distinguished name," for example, "CN=Bob Balaban/O=Looseleaf." The getCommonUserName() method returns only the "common" part of the hierarchical name (e.g., "Bob Balaban"), and getUserNameObject() returns the distinguished name instantiated in a lotus.notes.Name object instance (see Chapter 5 for details on this class).

lotus.notes.International getInternational()

Returns an instance of the International class, which contains a bunch of read-only properties exposing many of the international settings on your system. These include: AM/PM Strings, decimal point character, the localized word for "today," and so on. See Chapter 5 for details. There is only one instance of the International class per machine.

String getNotesVersion()

Obtains a string representing the id of the version of Notes that you have installed. The string is localized for the country and language version of the product, and usually contains the date of the release as well.

String getPlatform()

Returns the name of the operating system on which the current version of Notes is running.

lotus.notes.Database getURLDatabase()

If you have your current location record set up to refer to a Domino Web server database, whether local or remote, this call will return an instance of that Database. You can then use that Database instance to retrieve pages off the Web and convert them to Notes documents (see the write up on the Database class, later in this chapter).

boolean isOnServer()

Returns *true* if the current Agent program is running in a Domino server process. This property will be *true* for any Agent run in the back-

NOI Part I: Session, DbDirectory, Database, ACL, ACL Entry

ground by the Agent Manager, or for any Agent invoked by the HTTP server. Any other program will return *false* for this property, even if the program is being run on a server machine, if it's being run from the workstation console or from the command line.

Session Child Object Creation

These methods are similar to the properties that return other objects belonging to NOI, but these calls are not properties, because in some cases they require input arguments, and in other cases they return objects which are not (semantically speaking) attributes of the session.

lotus.notes.DateTime createDateTime(String time)

Notes has its own internal formats for dates and times. This call creates a DateTime instance using an optional date/time string. If you want to create an "empty" DateTime instance and set the value of the object later using one of the DateTime properties, just use "" or *null* as the argument value. See Chapter 4 for details on the DateTime class.

lotus.notes.DateRange createDateRange()
lotus.notes.DateRange createDateRange(lotus.notes.DateTime start, DateTime end)

A DateRange is just a pair of DateTime instances, although the DateRange object does not embed its start and end times, it merely points to them. Thus, if you use the second form of the createDateRange() call, providing starting and ending DateTime instances, you can later change the value of one or the other DateTime instance, and the DateRange will point to the new value. Be careful if you do this, you never want the starting date to be later than the ending date, or you'll have a meaningless range.

lotus.notes.Log createLog(String name)

Returns an instance of the Log class, which can be used to log action and error information to a Notes database, to a mail message, or to disk. See Chapter 6.

lotus.notes.Name createName(String name)

Creates an instance of the Name class, initialized with the provided string, usually a full distinguished name, but it doesn't have to be. If the name you provide is not a full hierarchical name, though, this class has no way of converting a common name to a distinguished name. Full discussion of the Name class is in Chapter 5.

lotus.notes.Newsletter createNewsletter(lotus.notes.DocumentCollection list)

Newsletters are usually used to format a list of Document instances into a message, often containing doclinks to the source documents and some kind of tag or title line. The input argument is a DocumentCollection instance, which contains the Document list. Chapter 3 talks about DocumentCollections, and Chapter 6 discusses Newsletters.

lotus.notes.Registration createRegistration()

The Registration class (new to Domino 4.6) allows you to create and manage user, certifier, and server ids. See Chapter 5.

lotus.notes.RichTextStyle createRichTextStyle()

The RichTextStyle class is also new to Domino 4.6, and its purpose is to allow you to add text to a rich text item using different styles. See Chapter 4 for examples.

Session Other Methods

lotus.notes.Database getDatabase(String server, String dbname)

Returns a Database instance, given a server name and database file name. If you want to access a database on your local machine, use "" as the server name.

lotus.notes.DbDirectory getDbDirectory(String name)

DbDirectories are used primarily to iterate over the databases on a particular machine. You create an instance of DbDirectory by using this call and providing the name of the server you want to use ("" for the local machine). See below for details.

String getEnvironmentString(String name)
String getEnvironmentString(String name, boolean issystem)
Object getEnvironmentValue(String name)
Object getEnvironmentValue(String name, boolean issystem)
void setEnvironmentVar(String name, Object value)
void setEnvironmentVar(String name, Object value, boolean issystem)

"Environment variables" are named values, string, DateTime, or numeric. They are stored in your system's notes.ini file. Some environment variables are used internally by Notes; these are called *system variables*. Other environment variables you can make up yourself; these will automatically have a "$" prepended to the name you supply when you set or get their values.

To retrieve the value of an environment variable as a string, use one of the getEnvironmentString calls. If you know that the variable whose value you want is a system variable (i.e., the variable's name in notes.ini is not preceded by a "$"), then you must use the variant where you specify *true* for the second argument. If the variable is not a system variable, you can use either call (if you use the second one, specify *false* for the second argument). Any environment variable can be retrieved as a string.

If you know that the environment variable you want has either a date or a numeric value, use one of the getEnvironmentValue() calls. If the value is numeric, then an Object of subclass Number will be returned. If the value is a date, or date and time, then an instance of lotus.notes.DateTime is returned. You can use the built-in Java operator *instanceof* to determine the kind of object you've retrieved. If the environment variable does not exist, getEnvironmentValue() returns an Integer object whose value is 0. There is no way to tell the difference between a missing variable and a variable whose real value is 0, unfortunately. Again, use the variant with the boolean argument to access system variables.

The setEnvironmentVar call handles all values, String, DateTime, and numeric. You invoke it with the name of the variable you want to set, the value represented as an Object, and (optionally) a boolean indicating whether the name is a system variable or not. Using Object as the value input argument type allows you to pass any of the valid formats, as all object classes extend Object somewhere in their inheritance hierarchy. If you pass in an Object that is not one of the valid formats, an exception is thrown.

The example in Listing 2.2. sets and then gets an environment variable.

Listing 2.2 Setting an Environment Variable Example (Ex22SetEnv.java)

```
import java.lang.*;
import java.util.*;
import lotus.notes.*;
public class Ex22SetEnv {
    public static void main(String argv[])
```

```
        {
        try {
            NotesThread.sinitThread();
            Session s = Session.newInstance();
            DateTime dt = s.createDateTime("today");
            s.setEnvironmentVar("Bob'sVar", dt);
            Object o = s.getEnvironmentValue("Bob'sVar");
            if (o == null)
                System.out.println("Didn't get it back, what's up??");
            else {
                if (!(o instanceof DateTime))
                    System.out.println(
                        "Got something, but it ain't a date!!");
                else System.out.println("Got " + o);
                }
        catch (Exception e) {e.printStackTrace();}
        finally {NotesThread.stermThread();}
        }
}   // end class
```

This is a simple example, but there are a couple of points worth illuminating. First, notice that all the code is in the **main()** function. We don't really need to start up another thread here, but we do need to initialize the current thread for Notes, since we aren't creating an instance of NotesThread anywhere. We do that using the static init and term methods discussed earlier. Note that the stermThread() call is in a *finally* block to ensure that it gets executed, even if there's an exception.

Second, we create a DateTime object and initialize it with a valid Notes date expression, "today." We could have also used "yesterday," "tomorrow," or any valid date format. After setting and retrieving the environment variable's value, we use *instanceof* to make sure that we got a real DateTime object back. Note that the negating operator "!" is outside a set of parentheses. That's because *instanceof* is of lower operator precedence than !; if we didn't have the parens, then we would get a compiler error saying that "o" is not a boolean type, and therefore, "!o" is invalid.

Notice also that we can just pass our DateTime object to System.out.println(), and it will print out today's date. Why does that work? Because, like several other objects in the NOI package, DateTime overrides the implementation of the toString() method, which belongs to the Object class. We can decide that printing the value of a DateTime instance means printing the actual date value. If we didn't override toString(), we'd get some weird object reference stringification from Java, which is pretty useless to us.

java.util.Vector freeTimeSearch(lotus.notes.DateRange startend, int duration, Object namelist, boolean findfirst)

This method allows you to determine the blocks of time that are available on the calendars of the people and/or group(s) you specify. The *startend* argument is a DateRange specifying the window in which you want the search to take place. The starting and ending times can be minutes, hours, days, or years apart. *Duration* is the number of minutes you want to be available for each person. If you're trying to schedule a one-hour meeting, you will enter 60, for example. Next comes the name or names that you want the system to search for. We used Object as the input type here for maximum flexibility: You can enter a single String, or a Vector containing any number of Strings. If you use one or more group names, Notes will expand each group and search for all members of the group. The *findfirst* boolean specifies, if *true*, that you just want the first available time returned. If you specify *false*, all available times within the window are returned.

The return value is a Vector containing zero or more DateRange instances. If you specified that you only wanted the first match, the Vector will have at most one DateRange in it; otherwise, it will have as

NOI Part I: Session, DbDirectory, Database, ACL, ACL Entry　　35

many DateRanges as there are available blocks of time for all participants whose names you supplied. If no available times were found for all participants, then an empty Vector will be returned.

java.util.Vector evaluate(String expression)

java.util.Vector evaluate(String expression, lotus.notes.Document context)

In LotusScript NOI Evaluate is a language construct, really a built-in global function (not associated with any object instance). The purpose of it is to pass through to the host application a "macro" expression, usually some legacy language that the host product uses. In the case of Notes/Domino, you would use Evaluate to execute an @function formula from LotusScript. (Notes inventor Ray Ozzie once referred to the Evaluate feature as "kind of like coding inline assembler for LotusScript." Shows you where he's coming from.)

Because Java doesn't have global functions (and even if it did, it would be *so* un-objectoriented to use them), we put an Evaluate method on the Session class instead. The two flavors of the Evaluate() method each take as input a String containing the formula you want evaluated. You can optionally supply a Document instance that is taken as the context for the formula. This allows you to specify field names in the formula, and the values for those fields will be taken from the document you supply.

The return value is a Vector containing the results of the formula. A Vector is needed because some formulas return lists of values, while others return scalar values. You have to use the various methods on Vector to determine how many values there are, and what kind. Let's try a simple example.

The example in Listing 2.3 uses the Session.evaluate() call to get the value of a Notes @function formula.

Listing 2.3 Using Evaluate Example (Ex23Eval.java)

```
import java.lang.*;
import java.util.*;
import lotus.notes.*;
public class Ex23Eval {
    public static void main(String argv[])
      {
      try {
          NotesThread.sinitThread();
          Session s = Session.newInstance();
          Database db = s.getDatabase("", "names.nsf");
          View v = db.getView("People");
          Document doc = v.getFirstDocument();
          String formula = "@created";
          java.util.Vector vec = s.evaluate(formula, doc);
          String result = vec.firstElement().toString();
          System.out.println("Formula result = " + result);
          }
       catch (Exception e) {e.printStackTrace();}
       finally {NotesThread.stermThread();}
       }
 }  // end class
```

In this example, we find the first entry in the People view of the machine's address book. This Document instance serves as the "context" for the formula. Not all formulas need a context, but providing a document lets you use field names and so on that can only apply to a specific document. In this case, we know that the result of the formula will be a single value, so we can just pull the first entry out of the Vector and convert it to a String. Date values are returned by evaluate() as lotus.notes.DateTime instances, and the toString() method is implemented for that class.

String toString()

Returns the name of the ID used for the current session.

THE LOTUS.NOTES.DBDIRECTORY CLASS

DbDirectory is the class you use to navigate databases on a machine. You provide a Notes server name when you create the object (using getDbDirectory() on the Session). Then you call the getFirstDatabase() method with a constant indicating what type of file you're interested in, obtaining a Database instance as the return value. Then you call getNextDatabase() until it returns a *null*.

You can also use DbDirectory to locate a database by name or replica id, locate your default mail database, or open a database only if it has been modified since a specified date.

As with the Session.getAddressBooks() call, Database instances returned by the DbDirectory navigation calls are bound to a real database, but the database is not opened. Some information about the database is available in a cached buffer, even though the database is not open, so you have a high performance way of finding out certain things about a Database instance that doesn't involve all the overhead of opening the file. The cached properties that are available in unopened databases (see the description of the Database class below for details) are:

- Last modification date
- Replica id
- Categories
- Title
- Template name
- Design template

The DbDirectory has only one property, *String getName()*, returning the name of the server. The other methods are listed as follows.

lotus.notes.Database getFirstDatabase(int type)

The constants you can use to select the type of database to search for are all *static final int* members of the class. They are:

- DbDirectory.DATABASE. All NS? files.
- DbDirecotry.TEMPLATE. All NTF files.
- DbDirectory.REPLICA_CANDIDATE. Any database that doesn't have replication turned off.
- DbDirectory.TEMPLATE_CANDIDATE. Any database that might be a design template.

This call does a search of the server's default data directory and all its sub-directories for the type of file you specify. There's no way to have it search a directory that is not the Notes data directory. Each time you call getFirstDatabase(), the search is reset for the new file type you pass in.

Because the internal Notes API mechanism that DbDirectory uses to perform the search is not thread safe, you cannot begin a search with getFirstDatabase() on one thread and then call getNextDatabase() on the same instance on another thread. The method detects this situation, and will throw an exception. I'm told that this will be cleaned up for Domino 5.0. This is the only case in the Domino 4.6 NOI where you are restricted from using certain functions on an object across threads.

lotus.notes.Database getNextDatabase()

Returns the next database in a search. If getFirstDatabase() has not been called, you'll get an exception.

NOI Part I: Session, DbDirectory, Database, ACL, ACL Entry

lotus.notes.Database openDatabase(String dbfile)

lotus.notes.Database openDatabase(String dbfile, boolean failover)

Attempt to open the database with the specified name on the server. If the open fails, a Database instance is still returned, but the database will not be open. You can use the Database.isOpen() call to tell for sure whether the call succeeded or not. If you specify *true* for the "failover" argument, then in cases where the server cannot be reached (down, or possibly overloaded), and where the server is a member of a cluster, Notes tries to locate a replica of the same database on another server in the cluster. If it can find one, it will open that one. You can tell if this happened by using the Database.getServer() call, which returns the name of the server the database lives on. If the name returned by getServer() is different from the name of the DbDirectory, then you failed over.

lotus.notes.Database createDatabase(String dbfile)

lotus.notes.Database createDatabase(String dbfile, boolean open)

Creates a new database on the server. You must have database creation rights for the machine in question (you always do for your local workstation; for a Domino server, you have to be listed in the **can create databases** field in the server's configuration record). Otherwise, you will get an exception. If you use the flavor of createDatabase() that takes a second argument, you can specify whether the database should be opened as part of this call. The default is to open the database.

lotus.notes.Database openDatabaseIfModified(String dbfile,
    lotus.notes.DateTime date)

This call is similar to openDatabase(), but will only open the database if it has been modified (design or data) since the specified date and time.

Again, check the isOpen() call to see if the database was successfully opened.

lotus.notes.Database openDatabaseByReplicaID(String rid)

Given a replica id in string form, this call will attempt to locate a database with that id on the server (the database can have any file name or title, so long as the replica id matches). If no match is found, an exception is thrown. If a match is found, but the database cannot be opened, an exception is thrown. See openDatabase() for details.

static lotus.notes.Database openMailDatabase(lotus.notes.Session session)

This call attempts to locate the current user's default mail database. If you are running your program on a workstation, the location of your mail database comes from your current location setting. If this call is executed from an Agent, the name that's used is the name of the person who last signed (created or modified) the Agent. That name is looked up in the public name and address book, and the person's mail database location is retrieved from there. This call is static because you might not know in advance what server the database is located on.

String toString()

This routine is overridden in DbDirectory to allow you to pass a DbDirectory instance to System.out.println(). The server name is returned.

THE LOTUS.NOTES.DATABASE CLASS

Database is one of the more functional, and heavily used, classes in NOI. It has a large number of properties and methods, so I've tried to organize them into a few different categories.

Database Properties

This section lists all the properties on the Database class. As always, if there is only a get call for an attribute, then that property is read-only. If there are both a get and a set call, then the property is read-write.

lotus.notes.ACL getACL()

Returns the ACL object for the current database. See below for details on ACL and ACLEntry.

java.util.Vector getAgents()

Returns a Vector containing all the Agents in the database that are visible to the current user. Unless the current user id has Manager access to the database, private Agents belonging to other users will not be included in the list. Each element of the Vector is an instance of the Agent class.

lotus.notes.DocumentCollection getAllDocuments()

Returns a DocumentCollection instance containing all the data documents in the database. Note that DocumentCollection contents are ordered, but not in any way that would be useful to a developer.

String getCategories()

void setCategories(String categories)

The categories referred to here are not the same as the categories you find in some database views. The Database Categories String can be found in the database properties box (select **File/Database Properties** from the Notes menu, go to the **Design** tab in the properties box). If you set a new category string, it is updated to the database immediately.

lotus.notes.DateTime getCreated()

Returns the date/time the database was created on the machine.

int getCurrentAccessLevel()

Returns a constant indicating the access level with which the database is currently open. The possible values are all declared *static final int* in the Database class. The choices are:

- ACLLEVEL_NOACCESS
- ACLLEVEL_DEPOSITOR
- ACLLEVEL_READER
- ACLLEVEL_AUTHOR
- ACLLEVEL_EDITOR
- ACLLEVEL_DESIGNER
- ACLLEVEL_MANAGER

See the following Database Administration section for a description of some additional methods that manipulate access control at the database level.

String getTemplateName()
String getDesignTemplateName()

If the current database is a template (NTF), then you can get the template name (which is not the same as the database name or title) using getTemplateName(). If the current database was created from a template and if it inherits its design from that template, then you can find out the name of the template from which it inherits with the getDesignTemplateName() call.

String getFileName()

Returns the database file name (the name of the actual disk file). No path information is included.

String getFilePath()

This property returns the "path," or disk location of the current database. Somewhat counterintuitively, you get different results depending on whether the database is local (on the machine where you're running the program) or remote (on a server somewhere). For local databases, you get the full file system path name.

On my Windows NT system, for example, you might get c:\notes\data\names.nsf, or, if the database is in a subdirectory of the default data directory, c:\notes\data\subdir\setup.nsf. If the database is on a remote server, then all you get is the path relative to the default Notes data directory (names.nsf, or subdir\setup.nsf, for example). This was done for security reasons: Notes should not expose the directory structure of servers.

java.util.Vector getForms()

Returns a Vector containing all the Form instances available to the current user. As with Agents, private forms belonging to other users won't be in the list.

lotus.notes.DateTime getLastFTIndexed()

The date the database's full text index was last updated. If there is no full text index, a *null* is returned.

lotus.notes.DateTime getLastModified()

The date and time of the last modification to the database as indicated. Both data and design modifications are included in the last-modified date.

java.util.Vector getManagers()

Returns a Vector containing a list of Strings. Each String is the name of a user with Manager access to the database.

lotus.notes.Session getParent()

Returns the Database's parent Session instance.

double getPercentUsed()

Returns the percentage of the database that is "occupied." This number is the same as what you see when you bring up the database properties box and click on the **% used** button in the **Information** tab.

NOI Part I: Session, DbDirectory, Database, ACL, ACL Entry

String getReplicaID()

The replica id of the database, in string format; this is useful if you want to open another replica of the same database on another machine. See DbDirectory.openByReplicaID().

String getServer()

The name of the server that this database lives on, often a hierarchical name.

double getSize()

The current size, in bytes, of the database on disk.

int getSizeQuota()
void setSizeQuota(int quota)

The "quota" for a database is set by a server administrator and represents the maximum size the administrator wishes to allow for a database. This property is different from the user-settable size limit, or maximum size to which the database can grow. The quota is only settable by a user with Administrator privileges on the server. The size is represented in kilobytes. If you set this property, the value is stored in the database immediately.

String getTitle()
void setTitle(String title)

The title of the database, as seen in the database properties box. You must have Designer or above access to the database to set the title. If you set this property, the value is stored in the database immediately.

java.util.Vector getViews()

Returns a Vector containing all the views (and folders) in the database to which the current user has access. As with Agents and forms, private views and folders belonging to other users will not appear in the list.

boolean isDelayUpdates()
void setDelayUpdates(boolean flag)

This property only has an effect when you use it on a remote database. Normally (and when the DelayUpdates property is set to *false*) when documents are updated on a server (a document delete operation also qualifies as an update, by the way), the update is written immediately to disk and the client waits for the update to complete before continuing (a "blocking," or synchronous call from the client to the server).

If you're performing a lot of updates (or deletes) in a tight loop and want to gain some performance throughput, you can set the DelayUpdates property on the remote database to *true*. This has the effect of batching up a series of update operations for later completion by the server, and the client is not blocked for the full amount of time it takes to do the update to disk. There's a risk associated with using this feature, however: If the server crashes between the time you post the update operation and the time the update is written to disk, then the change is lost.

boolean isFTIndexed()

Returns *true* if the database has a full text index.

boolean isMultiDbSearch()

Domino/Notes allows you to create a full text index that includes more than one database. The databases can all reside on a single server, but they don't have to because your index can span multiple servers. A multi-database index lives in a special database that you create. This property returns *true* if the current database has a multi-database index; otherwise, it returns *false*.

The steps for creating a multi-database index are simple:

1. Create a new database from the Search Site template (srchsite.ntf).
2. Hit **Esc** to exit the default search form that comes up first.
3. From the Create menu, select **Search Scope Configuration**. Select the scope of the databases that will be included in the index (Database, Directory, Server or Domain), and the name of the server, directory, and so on as required. This specifies where the indexer should look for databases. The server name to look on doesn't have to be the current machine, or the machine where your new search site database will live.
4. You need to mark all databases that you want to be included in the index as available for multi-database indexing. For each database that you want included, bring up the database properties box, go to the **Design** tab, and check the **Include in multi-database indexing** box.
5. Go back to your new search site database, and bring up the properties box. Go to the **Full Text** tab, and click on **Create Index**. The multi-database index will be created in the background. This may take a long time, depending on how many databases are included and on how big they are.

Any full text searches that you perform on this database will now implicitly search all databases included in the index. This is a great way to implement a site-searching feature for use by dumb browsers over the Web. See below for further discussion of full text searching.

boolean isOpen()

True if the database is open; otherwise, *false*.

boolean isPrivateAddressBook()
boolean isPublicAddressBook()

When you use the getAddressBooks() call on the Session class, you get back a list of (unopened) Database instances; each represents an address book. If the database was retrieved from the local machine, it's considered a "private" address book. If it was retrieved from a server, then it's a "public" address book. These two calls help you tell the difference. Another way of telling is to look at the string returned by the Database.getServer() call, which works even when the database is not open.

Database Design Elements

This section lists some methods that retrieve design elements from a database.

lotus.notes.Agent getAgent(String name)

Use this call to find a specific Agent in the Database by name. If the Agent exists but is a private agent belonging to another user, or if the Agent doesn't exist, then a *null* is returned.

lotus.notes.Form getForm(String name)

Finds a Form by name; it returns *null* if not found.

NOI Part I: Session, DbDirectory, Database, ACL, ACL Entry

lotus.notes.Document getProfileDocument(String key1, String key2)

Profile documents were added to Domino/Notes in Release 4.5, mainly to solve certain performance problems. Before Release 4.5, as the use of LotusScript started to mushroom, developers were finding that it was very expensive to store per-user profile information in a database in a clean and robust way. Sure, you could create a special form for the profile information and then create a special view in the database that selected only documents created with that form. But then you also had to go to every other view in the database and modify each of the other view selection formulas to exclude documents created with the profile form. Furthermore, every time you needed to look up someone's profile, you had to go to the profile view and look up the correct document, usually by the user's name. And what if you needed more than one profile per user in a database, maybe for two different workflows or something? In that case, your profile lookup had to be by a multi-field key. All in all, something of a pain.

Profile documents are a huge performance win: They are cached in the server's memory, so multiple lookups do not cause the document to be read from disk every time. They also have a two-level hash key. One is usually a user name, though it can be any string, and the other (if supplied) can also be any string. Thus, looking up a profile document is much faster than finding and accessing a data note in a view. Furthermore, profile documents are design elements, not data notes, and therefore will never appear in any view.

The getProfileDocument() call finds the profile document in the current database that has the same one- or two-level key (the second key is optional—you can specify *null* or ""). If the document doesn't exist, one is created. Once you have a valid profile document reference, you can treat it just like any other Notes Document instance (get/set item values, update, and so on). The only way to tell a profile document from a regular data document is by looking at the Document.isProfileDocument() property. See Chapter 3 for details.

lotus.notes.View getView(String name)

Returns the specified View instance (could be a view or a folder), if it exists and is accessible by the current user. Returns *null* if not found. If the name refers to a folder of type "private on first use," an exception is thrown, because these are not accessible via NOI (mainly because the newly created private folder must live in the desktop file, and there is currently no back-end access to it).

Database Searching

These calls relate to finding documents in a database.

lotus.notes.DocumentCollection FTSearch(String query)
lotus.notes.DocumentCollection FTSearch(String query, int maxdocs)
lotus.notes.DocumentCollection FTSearch(String query, int maxdocs, int sortoptions, int otheroptions)

These three flavors of FTSearch allow you to find all documents that match a query that you supply. The query can be a simple search string, or you can embed in the query special keywords. See the Domino online documentation for a full specification of the query language—there's too much of it to go into here in any detail. The result of performing a full text search is a list of Document instances that match the query. Most of the time this result set is sorted, as we'll see. The default is to sort the contents of the list by *relevance score*, a number between 0 and 100 that more or less indicates how relevant the document is to the query.

If you specify the maxdocs parameter, then no more than that many documents will be returned. This is useful in cases where a query might result in many hundreds of matches, and you don't want to spend lots of CPU cycles processing them all. There is, in any event, an upper limit of 5000 documents in a result set.

There are two parameters relating to searching and sorting options. To specify sort options, use one of the following constants (defined, as usual, as *public static final int*):

- Database.FT_SCORES. This is the default. It tells Notes to sort the result set by relevance score.
- Database.FT_DATE_ASC. This constant sorts by document modification date, ascending (earliest date first).
- Database.FT_DATE_DES. This constant sorts by document modification date, descending (latest date first).

The sort option is ignored if the database does not contain a full text index.

The other options allow you to specify the granularity of the word matching algorithm used. You can specify one or both of the following constants. If you want both options, you must add the values together:

- Database.FT_STEMS. This constant tells Notes to look for "stem" matches instead of exact matches. For example, if your query is simply "Geek," but you want variants of the word to also match (Geeks, Geekitude, Geekness, and so on), then specify FT_STEMS.
- Database.FT_THESAURUS. This constant tells Notes that synonyms of a word, as found in the system thesaurus file, also count as matches. For example, if your query specifies Geek, then you might want Propeller Head to match as well. It will, provided your thesaurus file contains the link.

These options are ignored if the database does not contain a full text index. In cases where you invoke one of the FTSearch methods on a database that has no full text index, you will get a valid result set. However, the search will take much longer than it would if there were an index, and you don't get any relevance scores or sorting options. Multi-database searches must always have a full text index.

If the database that you perform the search on is a multi-database index, then all the same options apply, but the results are a bit more interesting. Normally the result set returned by a full text search is a simple sorted array of document ids, and possibly relevance scores. With a multi-database search, however, you need to get more information back than just a document id. You need a way to find out which specific database each document is in. Thus, the result set of a multi-database search contains not just document ids, but full doclinks, which also include a database replica id. You don't really need to know this to write a valid program, however. Just access the documents in the returned DocumentCollection as you normally would (see Chapter 3). Be aware, however, that there's a performance implication when you have a list returned from a multi-database search. Instantiating a document from one of these might be expensive, because it might live in a remote database that isn't open in your program's process space yet. If that's the case, NOI will simply generate a Database instance for that database behind the scenes, and then create an instance of the correct document from that database (remember, no NOI object can be instantiated without a valid container). If you later reference that same database, you won't have to pay the performance penalty twice, as the object will already be cached for you.

When we get to our discussion of the Newsletter class (Chapter 6), you'll see a truly cool (and high performance) application of multi-database result sets.

NOI Part I: Session, DbDirectory, Database, ACL, ACL Entry

void updateFTIndex(boolean create)

Use this call to create a new full text index for a database, or to update an existing index. In the create case (you specify *true* for the input argument), default indexing options are used. If you're updating an existing index, then the options stored in the index when it was first created are used to update it. This call works for both local and remote databases. If you specify *false* for the **create** option and there is no index in the database, then nothing happens.

The **create** option is ignored if the index already exists. If the database is on a remote server, you cannot create the index (an exception is thrown), but you can update it.

lotus.notes.DocumentCollection Search(String formula)
lotus.notes.DocumentCollection Search(String formula,
   lotus.notes.DateTime cutoff)
lotus.notes.DocumentCollection Search(String formula,
   lotus.notes.DateTime cutoff, int maxdocs)

If you like to specify search criteria using the Notes @function formula language, then these calls are for you. Like the full text variety, they return a DocumentCollection instance containing the results of the search (all the documents that match the query). Also like FTSearch, there is a parameter that specifies the maximum number of documents to retrieve (0 means no limit).

Unlike FTSearch, though, there's an input argument that specifies a date/time before which documents are ignored. This is a highly efficient way of reducing the amount of time it takes to perform the search. If you don't want a time limit, then either use *null* for this argument, or pass in a "wildcard" DateTime instance (one for which you have invoked the setAnyDate() and setAnyTime() methods. See Chapter 4).

The result set of a formula search is never ordered.

lotus.notes.Document getDocumentByID(String noteid)

lotus.notes.Document getDocumentByUNID(String unid)

If you know the note id or the universal id of a document in a database, you can retrieve that document using these calls. Both values are available as properties on the Document class (see Chapter 3). Parenthetically, the note id of a document is valid only within the scope of a single database. The universal id of a document is the same for all document instances across all replicas of the database. Thus, if you get the note id of a document in one database and try to use it to find the same document in another replica of that database, you are not guaranteed success. If you use the universal id, however, you are assured long life and prosperity (unless the document was deleted in the other database and replication has not yet occurred between the two).

lotus.notes.Document getDocumentByURL(String url, boolean reload)

lotus.notes.Document getDocumentByURL(String url, boolean reload, boolean relifmod, boolean urllist, String charset, String webuser, String webpswd, String proxyuser, String proxypswd, boolean nowait)

Since Domino Release 4.5, we've had the ability to set up Web retrieval databases. They can be private (on your workstation), or shared (on a server). Your location record tells Notes which one to use. These databases are special in that they bring HTML pages in from the World Wide Web and convert them into Notes documents. The HTML syntax is translated to Notes rich text format, and the new documents are stored in the Notes database. You can then use the Notes Client to view them, just as with any document stored in a database.

Of course you can also use the built-in browser in the Notes Client to view the HTML pages directly. The neat thing about the Web Retriever feature, though, is that it can be utilized in (at least) two situations where a normal browser is useless:

NOI Part I: Session, DbDirectory, Database, ACL, ACL Entry 55

1. You can use a background agent running on a Web Retriever enabled server to bring in pages overnight, while you are safely home in bed, or maybe out drinking somewhere.

2. You can use a server-based Web Retriever to view HTML pages when your machine doesn't have a TCP/IP connection. So long as the server is able to get out to the Web, your client machine doesn't have to speak TCP at all—it communicates with the server via any of the other supported protocols using Notes RPC.

You can use the getDocumentByURL feature to explicitly load a page into the (local or remote) Web Retriever database. The simpler version of the call takes only a URL string and a flag indicating whether you want the page forcibly reloaded. If you specify *false* for the reload flag, and if the page you requested is already available in the Web Retriever database, then you just get that document. If you specify *true*, then the page is always fetched from the Internet, even if it is available locally.

The more complicated version of the call allows you to specify more options:

❒ *boolean relifmod.* Set this parameter to *true* when you want the page to be reloaded only if it has been modified since last stored in the Web Retriever database. Note: This is one of the few cases where I've ever found an error in the Domino online documentation. The description of this call in the Java Programmer's Guide database omits this parameter.

❒ *boolean urllist.* If you set this flag to *true*, Notes will find all the links on the page that you are retrieving, and create a special item named URLLinks*n* to hold them. Since there might be more than 64 KB worth of links on a page, Notes numbers the URLLinks items in sequence. So the first links item will be called URLLinks1, the second one URLLinks2, and so on. You can use the contents of this item to "worm" the page and follow the links on it. See Chapter 4 to find out how to use text list items. The default value is *false*, as this option can cause lots of extra processing.

- *String charset.* The MIME name of the character set you want Domino to use when processing the page. Domino converts the text in the page from the specified character set to its internal character set (LMBCS). The character set name for U.S. English is "ISO-8859-1," and for Japanese it's usually "ISO-2022-JP." If you don't know or don't care what character set the page is written in, use a *null* for this parameter.

- *String webuser.* Some Web pages require that you specify a site specific user name and password before you can access them. If that's the case, pass the user name here.

- *String webpswd.* The password that goes with webuser.

- *String proxyuser.* If you're using a firewall to protect an internal LAN from acts of piracy and other evil perpetrated over the Internet, then your proxy server might require you to specify a user name and password. If so, this is where it goes.

- *String proxypswd.* The password that goes with proxyuser.

- *boolean nowait.* Note: This parameter was also omitted from the online documentation for this call. If you specify *true*, then the call returns immediately, and you don't get a Document instance for the page *(null* is returned). The default is *false*. You would use this parameter if you wanted to update lots of pages in your Web Retriever database, but didn't really want to do anything with any of them right away. You might, for example, write an Agent that refreshes a few hundred pages overnight, but that doesn't need to actually look at any of them. If you use this feature, then that Agent will run much faster.

NOI Part I: Session, DbDirectory, Database, ACL, ACL Entry

Note that these calls are only valid on a Database instance that is bound to a Web Retriever database. How do you get one of those? Easy! Just use the getURLDatabase() call on the Session class. It locates and returns an instance of the Web Retriever database specified in your location record (if any).

String getURLHeaderInfo(String url, String header, String webuser, String webpswd, String proxyuser, String proxypswd)

The HTTP specification lists a number of Web page attributes that can be accessed without downloading the page itself. To see an up-to-date list of the headers that all Web pages are supposed to support, see the World Wide Web Consortium's site at http://www.w3.org. This call retrieves the value of the specified header from the page whose URL you specify. The other arguments are as described in the getDocumentByURL() call.

Database Administration

This category includes all the rest of the Database methods, most of which have to do with creating, copying or otherwise administering databases, as well as with access control and document creation.

lotus.notes.Document createDocument()

Creates an empty document in the current database and returns an instance of the Document class.

int compact()

Compacts the current database. The database must not be in use by any other user or process (such as the indexer, Agent Manager, or any API program, including any other Java program), or this call will fail. The way compacting works is that NOI closes the current database, and then makes a compacted copy of it to a new disk file, using a temporary name (the replica id and document modification dates are all preserved, as are unread marks). If that part goes well, then the original database is deleted and the new one is renamed to the original file name.

The call returns the number of bytes saved on disk by the operation, if it is successful.

lotus.notes.Database createCopy(String server, String dbfile)

Create a copy of the current database on the specified server, using the specified database file name. The new copy is NOT a replica of the original. A Database instance representing the new database is returned.

lotus.notes.Database createFromTemplate(String server, String dbfile, boolean inherit)

Create a new database using a template (NTF) file. This call will copy all design and data notes from the template file to the new database. This operation is slightly different from a regular database copy, in that the current user id is automatically given Manager access to the new database, regardless of what access it had to the template file.

If you specify *true* for the inherit parameter, then the new database will be marked as inheriting from the template. This means that if the design of the template changes, the design of the inheriting database will be automatically updated by the server. If the new database resides on a workstation, you can force the design to get updated by using the **File/Database/Refresh Design** menu command.

lotus.notes.Database createReplica(String server, String dbfile)

Use this method to create a replica of the current database on the specified server. The new database will have the file name you provide as the

NOI Part I: Session, DbDirectory, Database, ACL, ACL Entry

dbfile parameter. As usual, you can use "" as the server name if you want the replica created on the local machine.

void grantAccess(String name, int level)
int queryAccess(String name)
void revokeAccess(String name)

Query, set, or revoke the specified user's access to the current database. The level argument is one of the previously listed ACLLEVEL_XXX constants. If you revoke a user's access, be aware that it doesn't necessarily mean they now have no access to the database. Revoke simply removes the specified user name from the access control list of the database, implicitly giving that user default access rights. If you want to exclude any user (or group) from a database, you must grant them an access level of ACLLEVEL_NOACCESS.

boolean open()

This method is useful in cases where you have a Database instance that isn't open: Either you got it from the Session.getAddressBooks() call or you navigated your way to it using DbDirectory.getFirst/NextDatabase(). In the latter case, as described above, some attributes of the database are available even when it isn't open. Others, however, are not, and you will need to explicitly open the database. This method returns *true* if the operation was a success.

void remove()

Deletes the current database from disk. The current user must have Manager access, or the call will throw an exception.

boolean replicate(String server)

Replicates the current database with all databases that have the same replica id on the specified server. Usually you'd have only one replica of any database on a given server, but there's nothing that prevents you from having more than one. The replication is two-way, so changes are both sent to the server and received from the server. There is currently no way to discover programmatically how many documents were transferred as a result of this call. The results are, however, logged in the Notes log. The call returns *true* if the operation was a success.

String toString()

As with many of the other NOI classes, Database overrides the toString() method, returning the same string as the getFilePath() call returns.

THE LOTUS.NOTES.ACL CLASS

The ACL class is used to navigate through and manage a database's access control list (thus the incredibly inventive name of the class). The list acts as a container for the individual entries, represented by the ACLEntry class (see below).

You get an instance of ACL from the Database.getACL() property. You can do this multiple times on a single database, and each ACL instance will be independent of all the others. You could, in fact (though this is definitely not recommended), make different modifications to three different instances of an access control list for a given Database instance, and then update each of the three ACLs. Of course, only the changes made in the last ACL instance to save itself back into the database will win.

Note that changes you make to the ACL properties or contents are not stored in the database until you invoke the save() method.

ACL Properties

lotus.notes.Database getParent()

Returns the ACL's parent database.

java.util.Vector getRoles()

Returns a Vector of Strings, where each String is the name of a *role* in the ACL. For those of you not familiar with roles, a role is somewhat different from a user entry. You can create a role named, for example, Reviewer, in a database, and then assign Reviewer status to any number of user or group entries in the access control list. You manage roles in the Notes Client by bringing up the Database Access Control dialog box (**File/Database/Access Control** from the menu), and selecting the **Roles** panel from the list on the left side of the dialog box.

If you have a couple of roles in the database, you can "enable" a role for a given user/group entry by selecting the entry in the list box and then clicking on the role name. A check mark will appear. You can then use the role name in place of an explicit entry name when assigning access control privileges (such as reader lists) in the database. When you specifiy a role name in some access control component, it is distinguised from a user or group name with square brackets. "[Reviewer]," for example.

boolean isUniformAccess()

void setUniformAccess(boolean flag)

The "uniform access" flag on a database, if set, means that all replicas of that database will have identical access control lists. If the flag is not set, it is possible to have each replica of a database have a different ACL setup.

One side effect of using the uniform access feature affects your access to local databases. Normally your client (or any API program, including a Java program) running on your local machine has full access to any local database, because the database's access control list is not checked. This does not apply, however, to any database with the uniform access bit set. Such databases allow only the access specified to the current id in the ACL.

ACL Methods

void addRole(String rolename)

void deleteRole(String rolename)

void renameRole(String oldname, String newname)

Use these calls to create, remove, or rename roles in your database ACL. Changes you make are not stored in the database until you invoke the save() method.

lotus.notes.ACLEntry createACLEntry(String name, int accesslevel)

Creates a new entry in the ACL, with the specified access level. An ACLEntry instance is returned, and you can use the methods and properties on that class to further refine the person or group's access rights. The input access level is one of the ACLLEVEL_XXX constants previously described.

NOI Part I: Session, DbDirectory, Database, ACL, ACL Entry

lotus.notes.ACLEntry getFirstEntry()

lotus.notes.ACLEntry getNextEntry(lotus.notes.ACLEntry entry)

lotus.notes.ACLEntry getEntry(String name)

These methods allow you to navigate through the entries in the ACL, or retrieve a specific entry by name. Entries can be people, servers, or group names. If you request an entry name that doesn't exist, the getEntry() call will return *null*.

If you want to iterate through all the entries in the list, use the getFirst/NextEntry() methods. When using getNextEntry(), you must supply the previous entry's instance as an argument. The getNextEntry() call returns *null* when there are no more entries.

void save()

When you instantiate an ACL object, NOI caches in the object instance a copy of the data in the database's access control list. As you make changes to the ACL using the methods and properties on the ACL and ACLEntry classes, your modifications are stored in the in-memory copy. In order to save these changes back to the database, you must invoke the save() method.

Note that there is no replication conflict mechanism for access control lists: Whoever saves last wins. Thus, you need to be careful, especially when writing multi-threaded Java programs, not to overwrite someone else's (or your own) changes.

The current user id must have Designer (or Manager) access to the database in order to update the ACL.

THE LOTUS.NOTES.ACLENTRY CLASS

This class allows you to modify the attributes of individual entries in the access control list.

ACLEntry Properties

int getLevel()

void setLevel(int level)

The level codes are the ACLLEVEL_XXX constants described earlier in this chapter.

String getName()

void setName(String name)

The Name property of ACLEntry allows you to query the name of the current entry, or (if you call setName() with a new name) rename the entry. If you rename an entry, the new name you provide must be unique in the current access control list, or an exception is thrown.

lotus.notes.Name getNameObject()

void setName(lotus.notes.Name name)

The NameObject property is essentially the same functionality as the Name property, except that instead of getting/setting a name as a String, you can get/set an instance of the NOI Name class. The naming of this pair of functions will probably cause conniptions in Beans-oriented builder tools, as the two function names are not symmetrical. Unfortunately, Java (like C++) does not allow you to overload a method name when two definitions of the method differ only by return type. Thus, we couldn't have two getName() functions, one of which returns a String and the other of which returns a Name instance, so we had to come up with another name for the one returning the NOI object. The corresponding setName can be overloaded, as the argument types are different, but the naming should have been parallel. Ooops.

lotus.notes.ACL getParent()

Returns the entry's parent ACL instance.

java.util.Vector getRoles()

Returns a Vector containing the names of all roles that have been enabled for the current entry. Using this method is somewhat more convenient that getting a list of all roles from the parent ACL object and then iterating over each one for an entry with the isRoleEnabled() method.

boolean isCanCreateDocuments()
void setCanCreateDocuments(boolean flag)

Specify whether the current entry is allowed to create new documents in the database.

boolean isCanCreatePersonalAgent()
void setCanCreatePersonalAgent(boolean flag)

Specify whether the current entry is allowed to create private Agents in the database. Only users with Designer access can create shared Agents.

boolean isCanCreatePersonalFolder()
void setCanCreatePersonalFolder(boolean flag)

Specify whether the current entry is allowed to create private folders in the database or not. Only users with Designer access can create shared folders.

boolean isCanDeleteDocuments()
void setCanDeleteDocuments(boolean flag)

Specify whether the current entry is allowed to delete documents in the database. You might want to allow someone to create new documents, but not to delete them afterwards. The default behavior is that anyone with author (or above) access can create documents, and anyone can delete a document that she or he created. This flag modifies that behavior.

boolean isPublicReader()
void setPublicReader(boolean flag)

If this bit is enabled for an entry, it means that the user can access (for reading) public documents in the database. The feature was created in Release 4.5 primarily to allow calendar entries in a mail database to be read by other users who normally have no access to the database. This allows me to (for example) execute a free time search (see the description above in the section on the Session class) and find out if people are available to meet with me, even when I have no access to the databases in which their calendar information is stored.

boolean isPublicWriter()
void setPublicWriter(boolean flag)

This feature was also created to support the new calendaring and scheduling functionality in Release 4.5. Just as the public reader access bit allows people to see public (usually calendar related) records in a database that they normally can't access at all, so the public writer bit allows specially designated users to modify public documents in an otherwise impenetrable database. You would allow this kind of access to someone to whom you have explicitly delegated control over your calendar (an option you can set up in the Calendar Profile in the standard mail template for 4.5 and 4.6).

ACLEntry Methods

As with the ACL class, no changes to any ACLEntry instances are stored in the database until the ACL.save() method is invoked.

void disableRole(String rolename)
void enableRole(String rolename)
boolean isRoleEnabled(String rolename)

These methods are used to manage role settings for a given entry. You can find out if a given role is enabled for the current entry, enable, or disable any role. The role name you provide as an input argument must be a valid role in the database's ACL (see the preceding discussion of the ACL class for details). If it isn't, an exception is thrown. Enabling a role name for a given entry is equivalent to checking that role name for the selected entry in the Access Control List dialog box.

void remove()

Removes the current entry from the access control list.

String toString()

Returns the entry's name.

SUMMARY

Congratulations on making it through the first detailed chapter on the NOI classes and methods. Only four more chapters and 18 more classes to go! Take a deep breath, and turn to Chapter 3, where we'll cover the Document and View classes, among others.

3

NOI Part 2: Document, DocumentCollection, View, ViewColumn

In this chapter we'll cover the methods and properties belonging to a few more NOI classes.

THE LOTUS.NOTES.DOCUMENT CLASS

The Document class is in many ways the heart of Domino, because it's where all the data lives. A lot of what developers use the higher level (in the sense of higher in the containment hierarchy) classes for is aimed at sorting, searching, and accessing documents in a database. You get the document or set of documents that you're looking for (or creating), and only then can you go to town and start manipulating actual data values.

I've divided the interface to document into several sections:

- Properties
- Document management methods
- Item and value accessor methods

Don't be cowed by the number of calls in this class, most are very straightforward.

One topic worth mentioning briefly before diving into the interface concerns *items*. Notes represents a document internally in memory as a header data structure that describes the document level attributes. The header points to a chain of value blocks, called items. Each item is self-describing, in that the item data structure tells you the type of value the item contains (number, text, text list, etc.), how big the value is in bytes, and so on. The item also contains a pointer to the actual value. Items always have a name, though sometimes the name is one with a meaning special to Notes. The special item names are usually (but not always) prefixed with a $.

My main reason for bringing up the topic of items here is that there's often some confusion about the difference between an item and a field. Understanding that before going into the details of the Document interface will avoid some confusion, so let's get that out of the way here.

An item, as I've described above, is a data element that lives in a document. It has some attributes (such as data type, length, summary and name flag settings, and so on), and a value. A field, on the other hand, lives in a form, and is a design element, not a data element. Fields describe the presentation of items in the Notes UI. When you create a field in a form, you specify the display format, font, color, help string, and various other *presentation* attributes. You don't enter any actual data in the form. The way the Notes UI works when rendering a document to the screen or printer is to find all the fields in the form, then look up each corresponding data item by name in the in memory document. Any items that don't have a correspondingly named field in the form are simply not displayed. Any fields that don't have a matching item are left blank.

It is worth remembering that the back-end classes contained in NOI know nothing about fields—they only know about items. This is true of both the Java and LotusScript bindings. A field "Q" in a form might be defined as being of type number, but if you write an Agent or application using NOI which stuffs a string into an item named Q, and your form is used to render that document, a String, not a number, will appear. This might or might not cause you problems, it depends on whether you have data validation formulas or other programs that count on that item being a number. You're on your own with this, since NOI does no checking whatsoever based on form definitions.

Document Properties

java.util.Vector getAuthors()

This property returns the contents of a document's $UpdatedBy item. This item is maintained automatically by Notes and contains the names of all modifiers of the document. The value of $UpdatedBy is a text list, though sometimes it is missing, and sometimes it has only one entry. The text list is translated into a Vector containing zero or more String objects. The names in the item come from the user's id file, so it is often a hierarchical name.

java.util.Vector getColumnValues()

This property is unique, and in many ways is one of the trickiest in all of the NOI. All other NOI calls that return a Vector actually construct homogeneous lists: All the objects in the Vector are of the same type. The getColumnValues() call returns the data that you see when you look at a view in the Notes UI, often called the "summary data." Because each column in the view can be of any type, the list of column values for a document is heterogeneous (well, it doesn't *have* to be heterogeneous, but it usually is). Thus, when you delve into the contents of a Vector returned by this property, you have to be prepared to parse the type of each object (unless you know in advance what all the column types are; but even if you do, good programming practice dictates that you should still check).

Because getColumnValues() returns a list of values as you'd see them in a view, this call returns *null* if the Document instance that you invoke it on doesn't know who its parent View object is. There is only one way a Document object can know who its parent View object is: you must instantiate the Document using the View's navigational methods (see below for discussion of the View interface). When a Document instance is created in the context of a View, the View object caches all the summary data in the Document. If you instantiate a Document object in some other way, directly from the database, for example, then the summary data is not available.

The objects returned in the Vector by getColumnValues() are in the same order as the columns in the view. You can access these values directly, without causing the entire document to be read from disk, so using the column values is a great idea when you're dealing with large documents. Of course, column values don't help you much if the data you want from a Document is not summary data (doesn't appear in the view). Rich text, for one, is never allowed to be marked as summary data, due to its size. You can, however, have computed values in a column (you supply an @function formula to the column description in the view design), and those computed values show up in the stuff returned by getColumnValues() as well.

NOI Part 2: Document, DocumentCollection, View, ViewColumn

The descriptions of the View and ViewColumn classes appear later in this chapter. Listing 3.1 is a quick example of a Java application that makes use of column values.

Listing 3.1 Column Values Example (Ex31ColValues.java)

```java
import java.lang.*;
import java.util.*;
import lotus.notes.*;

public class Ex31ColValues
{
  public static void main(String argv[])
      {
      try {
          NotesThread.sinitThread();
          Session s = Session.newInstance();
          Database db = s.getDatabase("", "mail\\bbalaban.nsf");
          View v = db.getView("($Inbox)");
          Document doc = v.getFirstDocument();
          java.util.Vector vec = doc.getColumnValues();
          System.out.println("Found " + vec.size() + " column values");
          int i;
          for (i = 0; i < vec.size(); i++)
              {
              Object o = vec.elementAt(i);
              String type = null;
              if (o == null)
                  {
                  System.out.println("Object " + i + " was null");
                  continue;
                  }
              else {
                  switch (i)
                      {
```

```
                    case 0:
                    case 3:
                        if (! (o instanceof Number))
                            {
                           System.out.println("Values 0 and 3 are " +
                               "expected to be numeric icon values");
                            continue;
                            }
                        type = new String("Number");
                        break;
                    case 1:
                    case 4:
                        if (! (o instanceof String))
                            {
                           System.out.println("Values 1 and 4 are " +
                               "expected to be Strings");
                            continue;
                            }
                        type = new String("String");
                        break;
                    case 2:
                        if (! (o instanceof lotus.notes.DateTime))
                            {
                           System.out.println("Value 2 is expected " +
                               "to be a DateTime object");
                            continue;
                            }
                        type = new String("lotus.notes.DateTime");
                        break;
                    } // end switch
                } // end else
            System.out.println("Value " + i + " is type " + type +
```

NOI Part 2: Document, DocumentCollection, View, ViewColumn

```
                        ". Value = " + o);
                } // end for
        } // end try
        catch (Exception e) { e.printStackTrace(); }
        finally { NotesThread.stermThread(); }
        } // end main
} // end class
```

This is a bit longer than most simple examples because, as I said before, column values are tricky customers. A few points to note about this program (which you can find also on the CD):

- Java, like C and C++, uses the backslash character ("\") as an escape character. That's why the path specification for the mail database in the third line of the try block uses a double backslash. The Java compiler reduces "\\" to "\" in the literal string.

- The program uses Inbox from my mail database. Note that we're using a View object for Inbox, but the actual ($Inbox) object is a folder, not a view, in the database. That's okay, because programmatically they are treated the same. More on this is covered in the next section on the View class.

- We print out the count of column values, which we get from querying the Vector's size. If a column doesn't have a value for a particular document, NOI inserts a *null* in that slot in the Vector, to keep the values lined up exactly with the columns. You might notice in some databases that there are more columns according to getColumnValues() than you can see in the UI. This can happen when Notes creates "phantom" columns to use for computational purposes. They'll mostly have no content in the Vector.

- If an element in the Vector is *null*, we just skip it. Otherwise, we want to know if it's the type of object we're expecting for that column. We just use the *instanceof* operator to check for that. There are two columns that (for some, but not all Documents) display icons, one for a mood stamp, the other to indicate that the document has attachments. In the view design property box there's a checkbox that says "display value as icon," and you write a formula to return a numeric value corresponding to one of the icons that Notes knows about. Thus, the value in this column should be an int (actually, since Vectors can contain only Objects, not scalars, it would be an Integer object, not an int). However, we wrote the check to test for *instanceof* Number, not Integer. Why is that? Because all numbers are stored as double precision values in Notes. We could have written it to check for Double, but by using Number (which is a base class for both Integer and Double), we're covering ourselves a bit more.

❐ One of the columns contains a date (the message date). The getColumnValues() call can't return Notes's internal date format here, because it's meaningless in Java. Instead, date values are returned as DateTime object instances. That's what we're testing for in column 2.

❐ At the end of the for loop we can just pass the object to println(). All of the objects we might expect to find as column values implement the toString() method, so we should get a reasonable value for all of them.

lotus.notes.DateTime getCreated()

lotus.notes.DateTime getLastAccessed()

lotus.notes.DateTime getLastModified()

Returns the date and time the document was first saved to the database (getCreated()), last read by any user (getLastAccessed()), or last changed (getLastModified()).

NOI Part 2: Document, DocumentCollection, View, ViewColumn

java.util.Vector getEmbeddedObjects()

The EmbeddedObjects class is normally used for both file attachments and OLE objects. This property, however, will only return the OLE objects (and that means OLE/2, not OLE/1) used in the document. To get all objects, including file attachments, you have to use the getEmbeddedObjects() call on the RichTextItem class.

While this might seem capricious, there really is a good reason for it. Embedded objects conceptually live in rich text items, which is where they are (usually) displayed. The rich text stream in a rich text item contains rendering information for the embedded object, as well as a link to the actual object information item, also stored in the document. At the document level, we only know about the object information items (called $OLEObjInfo); we don't know anything about which rich text fields contain which objects. Notes only stores embedded object information items for OLE/2 objects, not for OLE/1 objects. File attachment information is stored in items named $FILE.

So, if you want to find all the embedded OLE/2 objects in your document, this is an efficient property to use. The getEmbeddedObjects() call works for all operating systems, and you can examine the EmbeddedObject instances that are returned. Activation of OLE objects is restricted to Windows platforms (and Macs where OLE is installed), however.

If what you wanted was to find all the file attachments in a document, this property won't help you. You can use the RichTextItem.getEmbeddedObjects() call, which returns attachments and OLE objects, but there is one situation where even that won't get you everything. In early versions of Notes (before Release 3) file attachments were supported, but the attachment icons were not stored in rich text items. Instead the $FILE items were created in the document, and no rendering was stored at all. The same situation can occur when a file attachment is created from an API program (from C, for example, not through NOI). Unless the programmer explicitly adds an icon to a rich text item, there will be no "link" from any item to the attachment. When the Notes UI comes across a $FILE item in a document that is "unreferenced" by any rich text item, it simply adds an icon for it to the bottom of the document, so that the user knows it's there, and can detach or view it.

How do you get an embedded object instance for a pre-V3 style file attachment? Never fear, there is a way. You can get a Vector containing all the Items in a Document using the getItems() property. Then you can iterate through that list and locate the Item or Items whose name is $FILE. From there you can get the name of the attached file, and then use the Document.getAttachment() call to get an EmbeddedObject instance. See the sample code for this operation under the getAttachment() call below.

See Chapter 4 for more details on the Item, RichTextItem, and EmbeddedObject classes.

java.util.Vector getEncryptionKeys()
void setEncryptionKeys(java.util.Vector keys)

This property is used when you want to encrypt a document in-place in a database. This operation is not the same as encrypting mail that you send to someone else. In the mail case, your message is encrypted as it is sent, and each recipient's public key is used to do the encryption of the copy that is being sent to that person.

When you encrypt a document in a database, you use a special key (or keys) that you create in your id file (File/Tools/Id from the menu, then click on the **Encryption** button). Doing the encryption is a three-step process:

1. Mark the items in the document that you want to be encrypted (use the isEncrypted/setEncrypted calls on the Item class). Only the items that are so marked will actually be encrypted, the rest will remain unencrypted. File attachments can be encrypted if you want, just mark the $FILE Item.
2. Create a Vector and add to it (as String objects) the name or names of the encryption keys that you want to use. Pass that Vector to the setEncryptionKeys() call.
3. Invoke the encrypt() method on the Document instance. The in-memory copy of the document is replaced with an encrypted version. You still have to invoke the save() method for the new version of the document to be written to disk.

Encrypted documents are automatically decrypted when they are accessed. If, at document open time, the current user id does not contain at least one of the keys specified at encryption time, then the encrypted items in the document will not be viewable by that user. The user will be able to see items that are unencrypted only. There is no explicit decrypt() call.

Another option for encryption is to not supply any encryption keys, in which case the encrypt() method will use the current user's public key.

int getFTSearchScore()

This property is only valid for Document instances that have been created as the result of a full text search (see Database.FTSearch() in Chapter 2). If your database has a full text index, then each document retrieved in the search will have a "relevance score" associated with it, a number between 0 and 100. This call returns that score. If the database is not indexed, or if the Document was retrieved in some other way, the getFTSearchScore() call returns 0.

java.util.Vector getItems()

This call returns a Vector containing an Item instance for each item in the Document.

String getKey()
String getNameOfProfile()
boolean isProfile()

These properties all relate to Documents that are "profile documents" (see Chapter 2, Database.getProfileDocument() for a discussion of profile documents). When you retrieve (or create) a profile document in a database you specify one or two "key" strings for it. The keys are hashed and are used internally for fast lookup. The getKey() call returns the first key, and the getNameOfProfile() call returns the second key.

If the current Document instance is not a profile document, or if one of the keys was not supplied at create time, the getKey() and/or getNameOfProfile() calls will return *null*.

Use isProfile() to determine whether a Document instance represents a profile document.

String getNoteID()
String getUniversalID()
void setUniversalID(String id)

Document identifiers can be a confusing topic, but knowing the difference between a document's "note id" and its "universal id" is important. The note id is unique to a document only within the scope of a single database, while a universal id is unique to a document across all replicas of the database. So, for example, if you have two replicas of your mail database, one on ServerA and one on ServerB, a document that exists in both copies of the database might have different note ids, but it will

NOI Part 2: Document, DocumentCollection, View, ViewColumn

(guaranteed) have the same universal id. *Universal ids* are what the replicator uses to match up documents when it synchronizes two copies of a database.

You'll have noticed that the note id property is read-only, while the universal id property is read-write. That's because the note id is assigned when a document is first saved to the database, and is based on its physical location in the database file. The universal id (often referred to as the UNID) is not related to physical location of the document, and therefore can be settable. A word of warning, however: You really have to know what you're doing when you *set* a document's UNID, or you risk corrupting data in your database. Domino's Calendaring and Scheduling system sometimes sets a document's UNID, but this must be done safely under restricted circumstances.

- Never set a document's UNID to a value that already exists in the database.
- Never change a document's UNID once it has been saved.
- UNIDs are always 32-character hexadecimal values.

The C&S system manipulates UNIDs so that, for example, when you send an invitation to a bunch of users, the invitation document in each recipient's database will have the same UNID as the original meeting document in your database. This makes the handling of responses to invitations much easier. If you want to delve into the mysteries of how it all works, you can examine the (LotusScript) source code in any Domino 4.5 or 4.6 mail template or mail database (in the main navigator expand the *Design* twistie and select **Script Libraries**. Most of the code for processing meeting invitations and responses is in there).

lotus.notes.Database getParentDatabase()
lotus.notes.View getParentView()

Document instances always have a parent Database object, since NOI maintains a strict containment hierarchy. If you navigate to a Document instance from a View, that Document will also have a parent View; if not, it won't. The getParentView() call returns *null* if the Document was instantiated from the Database.

String getParentDocumentUNID()

Sometimes you want to find the top-level parent of a given document, which might be nested seven or eight levels deep in the response hierarchy of the current view. A document is a response to another document if it contains an item named *$REF*. The $REF item contains the UNID of the response's parent document. Listing 3.2 shows how you might code a subroutine that takes a Document instance as input and returns the top-level parent of that Document. Note that this is not a full application or Agent.

Listing 3.2 Finding A Parent Example (Ex32Parent.java)

```
public lotus.notes.Document FindTopLevel(lotus.notes.Document start-
ing)
{
    String unid;
    Document parent;
    Database db;

    if (starting == null)
        return null;

    try {
        // get the document's parent database. Is starting a response?
        db = starting.getParentDatabase();
        unid = starting.getParentDocumentUNID();
```

```
            if (unid == null)
                return null;

            do {
                parent = db.getDocumentByUNID(unid);
                if (parent != null)
                    unid = parent.getParentDocumentUNID();
            } while (unid != null);

        // we're done when the parent has no parent
        } // end try
    catch (Exception e) { e.printStackTrace(); }
    finally { return parent; }
}
```

lotus.notes.DocumentCollection getResponses()

When you navigate through a view, you have a lot of flexibility in how you move around (see the description of the View class later in this chapter for details). But if you need a high-efficiency way to collect all the first-level responses to a particular Document instance without going through the view, then you can use the Responses property.

There are two important differences between the way you navigate through responses in a view and with the Document.getResponses() call:

❒ getResponses() only returns the immediate responses to the current Document. You have to write a loop in order to get the second- and lower-level responses.

❒ When you navigate through the responses to a Document in a view, you're retrieving them in the order in which they appear in the View (which in turn depends on whether and how you specified column sorting in the view's design). When you get a collection of response Documents from the getResponses() call, the

Document instances in the collection are unordered, because the retrieval is not in the context of a View.

Listing 3.3 is an example of how to "drill down" the response hierarchy of a given document. Again, this is just a subroutine, not a full fledged class.

Listing 3.3 Finding Responses (Ex33Responses.java)

```java
public int FindLowest(lotus.notes.Document starting)
{
    DocumentCollection dc;
    int level = 0;
    Document doc = starting;
    boolean done = false;
    try {
    // just gets the first one all the time, counts the levels
    while (!done)
        {
        dc = doc.getResponses();
        if (dc == null || dc.getCount() == 0)
            done = true;
        else {
            doc = dc.getFirstDocument();
            level++;
            }
        }  // end while
    } // end try
    catch (Exception e) { e.printStackTrace(); }
    finally { return level; }
}
```

NOI Part 2: Document, DocumentCollection, View, ViewColumn

String getSigner()

String getVerifier()

Putting a digital signature on a document does two things for you: It allows a user of that document to know reliably who signed it, and it allows readers of the document to detect whether the document has changed since it was signed. When a document is signed, the following things happen:

- ❐ A *digest* of all items marked for signing is computed. Think of the digest as a very large and reliable checksum.
- ❐ The digest and the signer id's certificate information are attached to the document in an item named *$Signature*.

When you ask for the signer or verifier information, the $Signature item is read, and the signature is *verified*, meaning that the saved digest is compared against the current state of the document, and Notes tries to find at least one certificate in your current id that is also in the signature.

The *signer* is the name of the person whose id was used to create the signature. The *verifier* is the name of the certifying authority that owns the certificate which you have in common with the signer, if there is one. If there is no certificate in common, the signature cannot be verified.

These properties will return *null* if any of the following is true:

- ❐ The document is not signed.
- ❐ The document has been tampered with (modified) since the signature was created.
- ❐ Your id has no certificate in common with the signer, and the signature can't be verified.

Note that section signatures are not handled (at this time) by the Document class. Having signed sections in a document is a great feature, but it causes multiple $Signature items to be added to the document. The information necessary to figure out which signature item goes with which section is maintained in the form, not in the document itself; therefore, the back-end Document class has no way to interpret section signatures.

int getSize()

The Size property tells you approximately how many bytes are consumed by the in-memory version of the current Document. I say "approximately" because the returned value doesn't include the size of some overhead data structures. It essentially computes the sum of the sizes of the individual item's values, including the size of attached files. It doesn't count the size of the document and item data structures themselves.

boolean hasEmbedded()

Returns *true* if the current Document contains any $FILE items; otherwise, it returns *false*.

boolean isEncryptOnSend()
void setEncryptOnSend(boolean flag)

Set this property to *true* if you want the document encrypted automatically when it is mailed. When you mail a document (see the description of the send() method, below), if you've specified that you want it encrypted, Notes creates an encrypted copy of the original document for each recipient specified in the To, Cc, and Bcc lists. Each copy must be separately encrypted because the recipient's public key (obtained on the fly from the mail server's public address book) is used, so that only the recipient can decrypt the message.

NOI Part 2: Document, DocumentCollection, View, ViewColumn

boolean isNewNote()

This call returns *true* if the Document has not yet been saved to disk. NOI can tell if a Document exists on disk by whether or not the Document has a note id.

boolean isResponse()

This case returns *true* if the current Document contains an item named $REF, which indicates that it is a response to some other Document. See the description above of the getParentDocumentUNID() and getResponses() calls for more information on responses.

boolean isSaveMessageOnSend()
void setSaveMessageOnSend()

If this property is *true*, the current document will automatically be saved after you send it. Note that the send() method makes a copy of the Document and makes some modifications to the copy before actually mailing it (see the description of send() below). The Document that gets saved is the *original*, unmodified version.

boolean isSentByAgent()

Wouldn't you like to be able to write a mail Agent that filters out junk mail sent to you by Agents? Well, you can do that very easily with this property. Whenever mail is sent by NOI programs a special item named $AssistMail is automatically attached to the message. The isSentByAgent() call looks for this item, and returns *true* if it finds one. This doesn't guarantee that the message was sent by an Agent, of course, since the Document.send() method can be invoked by any LotusScript or Java program. But it does let you know that the message was generated programmatically, and not by a user directly.

The standard *Out of Office* Agent that comes in the standard mail template uses this property to ignore incoming messages generated by Agents.

boolean isSigned()

This property tells you whether the current Document contains an item named $Signature. It doesn't try to verify the signature. Of course, you could have a signed section in the Document and not have the entire Document itself be signed. This property would return a potentially misleading result of *true* in that case.

boolean isSignOnSend()
void setSignOnSend()

If this property is *true*, then NOI will automatically sign all copies of the outgoing message when you send it.

Document Management Methods

lotus.notes.Document copyToDatabase(lotus.notes.Database db)

This method makes a copy of the current Document instance and inserts it into the specified destination Database. All items and attachments belonging to the Document are copied. The copy is not automatically saved in the destination database, you need to invoke the save() method explicitly.

A Document instance for the new Document is returned. If the copy fails, an exception is thrown.

NOI Part 2: Document, DocumentCollection, View, ViewColumn

lotus.notes.Document createReplyMessage(boolean replytoall)

This method is designed for use only where the current Document is a mail message. It approximates the behavior of the **Forward** command in the Notes UI: Create a new Document instance in the current Database; render the contents of the current Document into the "body" rich text item on the new Document; get the contents of the From item on the original Document, add it to the new Document as the SendTo item; if the replytoall parameter is *true*, the contents of the original Document's CopyTo item are appended to the new Document's SendTo item.

There are two additional points worth making about this method:

1. The original Document is *rendered* into the body of the new message. This means that attachments and embedded objects are not copied or transferred to the new message. If what you want is to have a *deep copy* of the document sent to another person, where all the Items in the original are preserved in the message, then you should simply use the send() method instead (see below).

2. The *replytoall* option ignores the contents of the Bcc field in the original message, since by definition we don't know who else received a blind copy.

The new message instance is returned by the method.

void encrypt()

The encrypt() method causes all appropriately marked items in the current Document to be encrypted. See the preceding description of the EncryptionKeys property for a detailed explanation of how documents get encrypted.

After invoking this method, you must also invoke the save() method to have the encrypted version of the Document written to disk. Because a private key is required to encrypt a Document, you cannot invoke this method from a background Agent; the server does not have the private key belonging to the signer of the Agent, and it would be a real bad idea to encrypt using the server's private key.

If no encryption keys are supplied via the setEncryptionKeys() call, the current id's public key is used.

void makeResponse(lotus.notes.Document newparent)

Use this method to make the current Document a response to the Document you provide as a parameter to the call. A $REF item containing the UNID of the provided Document is simply added to the current Document. You must invoke the save() method to have the modified Document written to disk. If there was already a $REF item on the current Document, it is replaced.

void putInFolder(String foldername)
void removeFromFolder(String foldername)

A *folder* in Domino is almost the same as a view—the difference being that the contents of a view are computed automatically based on a selection formula that the database designer provides, while a folder can have an arbitrary collection of documents in it. In all other respects, folders and views are the same, so NOI doesn't have a separate Folder class.

Name lookups for folders are done in a case-insensitive way.

Folders know what documents are in them by maintaining a list of Document IDs (the note id is used). To add a Document to a folder, use the putInFolder() call. NOI adds the ID of the current Document instance to the folder's list. This means that the current Document can't be new, as Documents that have never been saved to disk don't have note

NOI Part 2: Document, DocumentCollection, View, ViewColumn

ids. You provide the name of the folder to which you want the Document added, and NOI creates the folder for you if it doesn't already exist. (There is no way currently to specify what view or folder you want the new one cloned from, you get a new folder cloned from the default view in the database.) Adding a Document to a folder that already contains that Document has no effect.

If you want to remove a Document from a folder, use the removeDocumentFromFolder() call, specifying the name of the folder. Removing a Document from a folder that did not contain that Document has no effect.

There is currently no efficient way to tell for sure whether a given Document is in a given folder. Nor is there a way to generate a list of all folders containing a given Document (the link is maintained in the folder, not in the Document). You can, of course, find out what Documents are in a folder by using the View class navigation methods (see the description of the View class below).

One further restriction: This method will generate an error if you specify a folder that has been designated as "private on first use." The reason this doesn't work is a bit complicated: The private on first use feature works from a shared folder definition. The first time a user accesses the folder (usually in the UI by dragging a document to it), a private clone of the folder is automatically created, and the document is placed in the private copy, not in the shared original. When you use NOI to add a Document to a folder, it will detect that the folder is of this special type. Unfortunately, because NOI is a "back-end" service, it can't just create the private folder for you on the fly. Private folders must live in the desktop file on your machine, and NOI doesn't have access to it. Hopefully this will be fixed in a future release.

boolean remove(boolean force)

Use this method to delete a Document from the current Database. If you specify *false* for the *force* parameter, then the delete operation will fail if the on-disk Document has been modified between the time you accessed it and the time you try to delete it (this kind of thing can happen in a client/server architecture—at least Notes gives you a way to deal with it).

If you specify *true* for force, the Document is removed regardless of anyone else's changes.

The method returns *true* if the delete was successful; otherwise, it returns *false*.

boolean renderToRTItem(lotus.notes.RichTextItem destination)

This method takes the current Document and creates a rendering of it in the specified rich text item. The destination rich text item must not be in the current Document. As with the createReplyMessage() call (which, by the way, uses this method to do its work), only a rendering of the source Document is done; attachments and so on are not carried over.

If the destination RichTextItem already contains something, this method will append the Document's rendering to that Item, not replace it.

There have been reported problems with this method not always working correctly, especially when the source Document makes heavy use of subforms and sometimes shared fields. Your mileage may vary.

NOI Part 2: Document, DocumentCollection, View, ViewColumn

boolean save()

boolean save(boolean force)

boolean save(boolean force, boolean makeresponse)

boolean save(boolean force, boolean makeresponse, boolean markread)

The save() method in its various flavors allows you to write the in-memory copy of a Document to disk. There are three options that you can specify:

1. **Force**. If you specify *true* for this option, the Document is written to disk whether or not someone else has modified it since you last accessed it from disk. In a multi-user environment, it is entirely possible that between the time you get an in-memory copy of a Document from disk and the time you save it again someone else might write a new version of that Document to the disk. Specifying *true* for the force parameter tells Notes to ignore and overwrite the other user's changes. This is not the friendliest thing to do, maybe, but it is sometimes necessary. If you specify *false* for this option, and there is a conflict, then the behavior of save() depends on your choice for the *make response* parameter. If you specify *false* and there is no conflict, the save completes normally.

2. **Make response**. When you have a conflict situation and you specified *false* for the force option, then you can have your version of the Document entered into the database as a response to the version that got there ahead of you by specifying *true* for the *makeresponse* parameter. The idea here is to treat the two conflicting versions as a replication conflict, and make one version a response to the other. Because another user got her version in there ahead of you, her's gets to be the parent Document. If you specify *false* for "force" and *false* for "makeresponse," and if there's a conflict, then the Document is not written to disk.

3. **Mark read**. If you set this option to *true*, the Document is saved and marked as read in the database's unread list. Note, however, that the Document is marked as read *for the current user id only*. Thus, if you use this option from a background Agent running on a server, then whoever signed the Agent last is the one that will see the Document as read, not you.

The function returns *true* if the Document was successfully saved, and *false* otherwise. If you choose to save a Document as a response in a conflict situation and want to know (a) whether the save() was successful, and (b) whether there was a conflict, you can find out by following this little algorithm:

1. Specify *false* for force and *true* for makeresponse in your save() call. If the current Document is already a response, save the contents of the $REF item as a String (use the Document.getItemValueString() call).

2. Test the return value. If you get a *false* back, there was some error condition and the Document was not saved. Stop. If you get *true*, you know the Document was saved and you can proceed to step 3.

3. To find out whether the Document was saved as a response or not, invoke Document.isResponse(). If the original Document that you were trying to save was already a response, then proceed to step 4.

4. Get the current value of the Document's $REF item, as in step 1. Compare the original and the current values of the UNID contained in that item. If they are the same, then your Document was saved with no conflicts. If not, then the current content of $REF is the UNID of the conflict Document.

Alternatively, you could use the getParentDocumentUNID() call to get the current value of $REF.

void send(String recipient)
void send(java.util.Vector recipients)
void send(boolean attachform, String recipient)
void send(boolean attachform, java.util.Vector recipients)

Any Document can be mailed, if you specify at least one valid recipient. There are two ways to specify who should receive the message: You can create the appropriate items in the document yourself, or you can pass one or more names in as parameters.

If you want to set up your recipient list(s) yourself, use these item names (you don't have to be case sensitive):

- **SendTo**. The To: list.
- **CopyTo**. The Cc: list.
- **BlindCopyTo**. The Bcc: list.

Each of these items should contain a string or a text list. The easiest way to create these items effectively is to use the Document.replaceItemValue() call. You don't want to use appendItemValue(), because you might then end up with multiple items of the same name, whereas replaceItemValue() ensures that an existing item of that name will be replaced.

Alternatively, you can just pass a String (for one recipient) or a Vector of Strings (for multiple recipients) in the send() call itself. If you do that, then any existing SendTo item is deleted and replaced with the name(s) you provided in the call. Note that existing CopyTo and BlindCopyTo items are NOT deleted by NOI. Therefore, if you are sending a Document that was originally a mail message, you should be real careful to delete any CopyTo and/or BlindCopyTo items that might be on the original message; otherwise you're leaving yourself open to a potentially embarrassing situation.

There is currently no way (using this method) to send only blind copies or cc's; you must have at least one name in the SendTo item. The Notes UI enforces this restriction as well. To work around it you can always just put yourself in the SendTo item, and everyone else in the BlindCopyTo item.

Here are the steps that the send() method goes through to send mail for you:

- ❐ First send() makes a new in-memory copy of your Document. This ensures that any changes it makes to the document don't have to be undone later.

- ❐ Check to make sure there is at least one entry in the SendTo item, or that one was provided as an argument. If a recipient list was passed in, replace any existing SendTo item in the copy with the new list.

- ❐ For each of the recipient lists on the document (SendTo, CopyTo and BlindCopyTo), make sure that all names in each list are in canonical format. This means that any abbreviated hierarchical names (e.g., Bob Balaban/Looseleaf) are expanded to the proper distinguished name format (CN=Bob Balaban/OU=Looseleaf).

- ❐ If you specified that you wanted the form attached to the message, send() then looks for an item named "Form" in the Document. If there is one, and if it contains a string, send() then looks in the Document's database for a form of that name. If it finds one, it copies all the relevant form items into the Document. It then deletes the Form item from the document (it turns out that if you both attach the form and have a form name

NOI Part 2: Document, DocumentCollection, View, ViewColumn

specified, Notes will use the form name only when opening the document).

- ❑ Check the **SaveOnSend**, **SignOnSend**, and **EncryptOnSend** property settings.
- ❑ Attach the $AssistMail item, indicating that the message was generated programmatically (see the above description of the isSentByAgent() call), unless one was already present.
- ❑ Last but not least, send the message and throw away the copy. If the **SaveOnSend** property was set, save the original document to disk.

Note that you don't get to specify the contents of the From item in the message you're sending. If you're calling send() from anything other than a server Agent, then From will contain the name of the current id. For background Agents, From will contain the name of the signer of the Agent (also known as the *Effective user id*), not the server name. In earlier releases of Domino/Notes, the server name was used in this case, but it caused problems for many users. Most servers do not have their own mail databases, and things like return receipts and nondelivery messages that were generated by recipients of NOI-generated mail were bouncing all over the place because they had nowhere to land. So, we changed NOI to use the effective user name instead.

void sign()

This method attaches a digital signature to the current Document instance. If you want the modified Document saved to disk, you have to invoke the save() method explicitly. See the above description of the getSigner()/getVerifier() calls for more information on how digital signatures work.

NOI uses the current Notes id file to create the signature; therefore, this method will throw an exception if you invoke it from a background server Agent, as it does with the encrypt() method.

Item and Value Accessor Methods

lotus.notes.Item appendItemvalue(String itemname)
lotus.notes.Item appendItemvalue(String itemname, double value)
lotus.notes.Item appendItemvalue(String itemname, int value)
lotus.notes.Item appendItemvalue(String itemname, Object value)

These methods give you the ability to create new Items on a Document, and to optionally put a value in the new Item. Note that no checking is done to see if an Item of the same name already exists. You are free to append as many Items of a given name as you wish, but you should be aware that the Notes UI will only display the first one it finds (recall our discussion of Items vs. Fields at the beginning of this chapter). Furthermore, the getFirstItem() call will only return the first instance of the name you provide it. It is possible to get all instances of an Item with a duplicated name via the getItems() property.

The flavor of appendItemValue() with only a single argument creates an empty Item. You can use the Item class's methods later to fill in a value, or you can leave it empty. The versions of the call that take an int and a double both store the numeric value in Notes's internal format, which is double precision.

For all other data types, pass an Object instance in for the "value" argument. Allowable data types are:

❐   Any numeric type (Integer, Double, Float, etc.). Stored as double precision.

NOI Part 2: Document, DocumentCollection, View, ViewColumn

- A String. Converted to the Notes internal character set (LMBCS) and stored as an Item of type TEXT.
- An instance of DateTime or DateRange. Stored as a date or date range.
- A Vector containing one or more Number objects. Stored as a number list.
- A Vector containing one or more String objects. Stored as a text list.
- A Vector containing one or more DateTime or DateRange instances. Stored as a date list or a date range list.
- An Item instance. The value of the provided Item is copied to the new Item.

All non-rich text Items created this way have their *Summary* flags set automatically (unless the Item is too large, greater than about 15KB), making it possible for their values to appear in a view in the UI.

The new Item instance is returned by the method.

boolean computeWithForm(boolean dodatatypes, boolean raiseerror)

When you design a form for a Notes or Domino application, you get all sorts of opportunities to add automatic processing to the form: input validation formulas, data translation formulas, default value formulas, and formulas to compute a field value on the fly, either when the document is composed or when it is displayed. Frequently, execution of these formulas causes values to come or go in other fields on the document.

Wouldn't it be nice if there were a way to get this to happen when you create a new Document, or process an existing Document using NOI? Yes, and luckily we have the computeWithForm() method. ComputeWithForm() (or as we affectionately call it, CWF) will process the current Document instance according to the form specified in the

Form item. If there is no Form item in the Document, or if the specified form can't be found, an exception is thrown. Assuming the form is accessible, CWF executes all the appropriate formulas in the form until it encounters an error, at which point it stops.

You get to specify whether you want an exception thrown when an error is encountered. If you pass *false* for the *raiseerror* argument, then you need to check the return value to see whether the operation succeeded.

You can also decide whether you want CWF to validate the contents of existing Items in the Document according to the data types specified for the corresponding fields on the form. If you select *true* for this option, then CWF checks all the data types in all the Items in the Document and compares them against the field specs in the form. If they differ, it's an error.

CWF will frequently cause new Items to come into existence in a Document, or modify existing ones. You should be sure to invoke save() on the Document to preserve these modifications.

There have been reported problems with CWF when the form uses lots of subforms. We hope these problems will be fixed in a future release.

void copyAllItems(lotus.notes.Document destination, boolean replace)

This method copies all the Items in the current Document to the destination Document you pass in as an argument. It is a very efficient call—much faster than, for example, iterating over all the Items returned from a Document.getItems() call and copying each individually. Each Item retains its original name in the destination Document.

If you want to ensure that the copied Items remain unique in the destination, set the Replace argument to *true*. This makes the method run a bit slower, as it has to do its thing in two passes instead of one (the first pass to delete all occurrences of an Item name from the source in the destination, the second pass to do the copy). If, for example, you know that the destination Document is empty (maybe you just created it), then it is safe to not use this option. Otherwise, specifying *true* for Replace is recommended.

lotus.notes.Item copyItem(lotus.notes.Item sourceitem)
lotus.notes.Item copyItem(lotus.notes.Item sourceitem, String newname)

This call copies the provided Item into the current Document. The source Item can be from another Document in the same database, or from a Document in any other database. You can optionally supply a String, which is used to rename the Item in the current Document.

An instance of the new Item in the current Document is returned.

lotus.notes.RichTextItem createRichTextItem(String name)

The various flavors of appendItemValue() create Items in a Document for numbers, text, and date values. If you want to create a new rich text item, use createRichTextItem() instead. If the name you provide is already used by an Item in the Document, an exception is thrown.

lotus.notes.EmbeddedObject getAttachment(String name)

Earlier in this chapter I wrote about EmbeddedObjects and file attachments, and how you can use calls like Document.getEmbeddedObjects() to get OLE objects, but not file attachments. I promised an example of how to use getFileAttachment() to extract a specific attachment (which might not have an icon in a rich text item in the Document) from the Document. Well, the time has come to deliver. As always, Listing 3.4 is on the CD included with the book, as is the sample database.

Listing 3.4 File Attachment Example (Ex34Attachment.java)

```java
import java.lang.*;
import java.util.*;
import lotus.notes.*;
public class Ex34Attachment
{
    public static void main(String argv[])
        {
        try {
            NotesThread.sinitThread();
            Session s = Session.newInstance();
            Database db = s.getDatabase("", "book\\Ex34.nsf");
            DocumentCollection dc = db.getAllDocuments();
            Document doc = dc.getFirstDocument();
            java.util.Vector vec = doc.getItems();
            int i, j = vec.size();
            for (i = 0; i < j; i++)
                {
                Item item = (Item)vec.elementAt(i);
                String name = item.getName();
                if (name.equals("$FILE"))
                    {
                  // get the name of the attachment from the Value property
                    String attach = item.getValueString();
                    if (attach != null)
                        {
                        EmbeddedObject eo = doc.getAttachment(attach);
                        if (eo != null && eo.getType() ==
                                EmbeddedObject.EMBED_ATTACHMENT)
                            eo.extractFile("c:\\temp");
                        else System.out.println("Couldn't get attachment "
                                + attach);
                        }
```

```
                    }  // end FILE
                }  // end for
            }  // end try
            catch (Exception e) { e.printStackTrace(); }
            finally { NotesThread.stermThread(); }
        }  // end main
    }  // end class
```

The sample database (Ex34.nsf) has the attachment in the rich text item, so we didn't have to go through all this really, but this code will work for Notes Release 2 style attachments, where the attachment icon is not contained in any rich text item.

The only slightly tricky thing about this technique is that you have to get the name of the actual file that is attached. It isn't the Item's name, because all attachment Items are named $FILE. Luckily (well, it wasn't by accident, let me tell you) for Items of type ATTACHMENT, the Value property will return the name of the attached file. You use that name in the Document.getAttachment() call, and *voila*, you get your EmbeddedObject instance, which you can use to extract the file (see Chapter 4 for a full description of the EmbeddedObject class).

Note too that, as usual when we have constants to deal with, the Item type is a *static final int* defined in the Item class. See the complete description of the Item type in Chapter 4.

lotus.notes.Item getFirstItem(String name)

Use this method to get an Item instance of a given name. Why isn't this method named findItem()? Well, it's a long story. Originally (Notes Release 4.0), we had decided to expose the "real" way Items worked in Notes. Rich text items, in particular, can be strange. They are a single "logical" item, but because of their size they can actually be made up of more than one individual item in the Document; because a single in-memory Item can't be bigger than 64KB. So, the implementation for rich text always has been to chain multiple items of the same name, and keep track of their sequencing.

As I said, the original 4.0 release of NOI exposed this fact by having two calls: getFirstItem() and getNextItem(), where getNextItem() took as an argument an Item. This would allow you to explicitly access, say, the third piece of a multi-part rich text item.

This turned out to be a really bad idea, for two reasons:

1. **Dangerous**. If you were to (accidentally or not) remove the second item of three in a rich text chain, it would give the Notes UI conniptions. Similarly, if you messed with any of the flags or other settings, the UI might get very confused.
2. **No benefit**. There isn't anything valid you can really do with the individual pieces of a rich text item anyway. You can't use it to access, say, just the third paragraph or something.

So, getNextItem() was removed from the interface. But of course, we couldn't change the name of getFirstItem(), as it was already in a released product, and changing the name would break existing LotusScript applications.

So there you have it. You should always treat RichTextItems as a single logical Item, even if you know in your heart that it isn't really implemented that way. It'll be our little secret.

java.util.Vector getItemValue(String name)
double getItemValueDouble(String name)
int getItemValueInteger(String name)
String getItemValueString(String name)

You've already seen one of these value accessors in action in the preceding file attachment example. Together these calls make it very convenient, at the Document level, to get an Item's value in whatever format suits you best. All versions of this call take only an Item name as input.

The first flavor returns *all* the values in the Item, packed up in a Vector. You use this when you have an Item that contains (or might contain) multiple values, such as a text list or a number list. In LotusScript such values are returned as arrays. In Java we use the Vector class. This makes it much easier to parse multi-valued Items, as each separate value is a separate Object instance in the Vector. It's up to you to figure out what the type of each element is, and how many there are, but that's easy: Vector.size() tells you how many, and you can use *instanceof* to test for Number, String, DateTime or DateRange values. There are other ways to find out as well, but they involve actually instantiating the Item object, and those techniques are described in Chapter 4.

The other versions of the call (getItemValueInteger/ Double/String) each return a single value. If the Item contains a multi-valued list, then you'll get the first element of the list. If the type you ask for is not compatible with the internal format of the value (e.g., the Item contains a number and you ask for a String), then you'll get a *null* or a 0. If you want the value coerced, it's up to you to coerce it—Java has some great support for that sort of thing.

boolean hasItem(String itemname)

Returns *true* if the specified Item name exists in the Document. This tells you nothing about the type of the Item, or whether it actually contains a value.

void removeItem(String name)

Removes the named Item from the current Document. You must invoke the save() method to have the modification written to disk. All physical Items of the given name are removed, not just the first one. That fact makes this a handy way to, for example, remove all file attachments from a Document, or so you might think. In actual fact, it would be a bad idea to do that. Here's why:

- Removing all $FILE items in this way won't clean up the rich text fields in which the attachment icons are rendered.
- You might be removing attachments that you really don't want to remove, like embedded OLE objects, whose data are also stored as $FILE items.

The right way to get rid of an attachment is through the remove() call on the EmbeddedObject class (see Chapter 4). It does all the right kinds of cleanup.

lotus.notes.Item replaceItemValue(String itemname, Object value)

This is the call to use when you're not sure whether an Item already exists in the Document. Using the appendItemValue() calls can be dangerous, as described above, in cases where the Item name already exists. Using replaceItemValue() instead is safer. It takes as arguments the name of the Item and the new value. For the new value you can pass in any valid Notes data type, or a Vector containing any number of (homogeneous) data values. If the named Item doesn't exist, replaceItemValue() creates it and appends it to the Document.

One point to note is that the value parameter is an Object, so if you want to replace an Item value with a scalar value (such as an integer), you need to convert the scalar to an object. All scalar values have a corresponding object type. For example:

```
replaceItemValue("SomeItem", new Integer(7));
replaceItemValue("AnotherItem", new Double(1.11111));
replaceItemValue("StellaNuthaItem", "literal string");
```

Literal strings will be constructed as objects by the Java compiler anyway, so there is no need to do "new String."

Another point worth noting, although most applications won't ever depend on this feature, is that replaceItemValue() replaces only the value of the named Item (if it exists); it doesn't change the order of Items in the Document's chain.

You can also pass in a DateTime or DateRange instance to set date values. There is a bug, however, in Release 4.6 that makes this unreliable. Instead you should use the Item.setDateTimeValue() call (see Chapter 4).

String toString()

Again, as with many of the other NOI classes, the Document class overrides the Object class's toString() method, returning the Document Universal ID (UNID).

THE LOTUS.NOTES.VIEW CLASS

Views are to Domino/Notes roughly what tables are to a relational database: They are the objects you use to maintain indices, to collect data in a logical way in one place, and to navigate through that data. Views in Notes also have a UI component—they are what you use in order to see your documents, and to make selections and perform various activities on those documents. Unlike a relational database, Notes views can be *flat* (that is, all documents at the same level), or hierarchical (that is, top level documents, indented responses, indented responses-to-responses, and so on, up to around 10 levels deep). In addition, both flat and hierarchical views can be categorized, where groups of documents are sorted together under a single category, or key.

Because Views maintain indices, NOI can implement fast Document lookups. Because Views also maintain a rich nesting relationship among Documents, NOI implements a rich set of navigational methods in the View class. The View class in NOI acts as both a container and as a navigator of Documents.

I've categorized the View calls into four groups:

1. Properties
2. Document searching
3. Document navigation
4. Miscellaneous methods

View Properties

java.util.Vector getAliases()

String getName()

Views can have both names and aliases. When you create or modify a view, bring up the Design Properties box. You'll see that there's an entry for the name, and another for an alias (you can actually enter several aliases, separated by vertical bars). You can specify which character of the name is hot-keyed in the View menu by preceding it with an underscore. For example, if I name a view "Bob's _View", then the V will be underlined in any menu containing a list of view names, and I can just hit **V** on my keyboard to select it. This is a nice feature, but it complicates view name processing. When you look up a View using the Database.getView() call, for example, you might provide the name with or without the underscore in it, and you expect it to match in either case. NOI potentially has to do many lookups:

- First it scans all view names in the database and attempts to match each with the name exactly as you pass it in.
- If that doesn't succeed, then the view names are scanned again and a match is attempted with your String against the view names with underscores removed.
- If that doesn't succeed, NOI takes your String and removes any underscores, then repeats the first two steps again.

The Name property returns the View's name as it is stored in the Database, meaning that if you entered the name with an underscore in it, that's how it will be returned to you when you call getName(). The same is true for aliases, except that there might be more than one, so you get a Vector back instead of a single String.

java.util.Vector getColumns()

Returns a Vector containing lotus.notes.ViewColumn instances. See below in this chapter for a description of the ViewColumn class. The ViewColumn instances are in the Vector in the same order as the columns are defined in the View.

lotus.notes.DateTime getCreated()
lotus.notes.DateTime getLastModified()

Returns DateTime instances, as you'd expect.

lotus.notes.Database getParent()

Returns the View's parent Database instance.

java.util.Vector getReaders()

void setReaders(java.util.Vector names)

Notes lets you attach to a View a list of people who are allowed to access that View. The list is implemented as a simple text list Item attached to the View design document. If you are not in the list (or a member of a group that is in the list), then you will not see the View's name in any menu or navigator, and you will not be able to open that View.

If you can see the View, then you can examine the list, which is returned as a Vector of Strings. Each String is a user or group name. If you have Designer access to the database, then you can set this property as well. The View is updated immediately.

boolean isProtectReaders()

void setProtectReaders(boolean flag)

Let's say you have Designer access to a database, and you want only certain people to use a particular View (maybe it's an administrative view that has sensitive data in it). So you write an application that sets a reader list onto a View using the setReaders() call. You think you're done, but you're not. What's going to happen the next time your database's design is refreshed? Well, Design Refresh is sort of like replication, except that it's one-way: stuff from an updated template (NTF file) is pushed to all databases (NSF files), which "inherit" from it. So if the View that you set the reader list on is updated in the template, a new View design document will be pushed into your database, wiping out your little attempt at access control. Bummer.

Never fear, though. There's a way out: When you set the reader list on the View using setReaders(), all you have to do is call View.setProtectReaders(*true*) as well. This tells the replicator to *not* overwrite your reader list if and when it updates the View design. The "protection" only applies to the reader list, so all other attributes of the View will be updated properly.

String getUniversalID()

Returns the UNID of the View design document.

boolean isAutoUpdate()
void setAutoUpdate(boolean flag)

This property affects the way view navigation behaves in certain cases. Originally (Notes Release 4.0 and 4.1) the View class did not contain this property, which caused some problems, as illustrated by Listing 3.5:

Listing 3.5 File Attachment Example (Ex35AutoUpdate.java)
```
import java.lang.*;
import java.util.*;
import lotus.notes.*;

public class Ex35AutoUpdate
{
    public static void main(String argv[])
        {
        try {
            NotesThread.sinitThread();
            Session s = Session.newInstance();
            Database db = s.getDatabase("", "book\\Ex35.nsf");
            View view = db.getView("Ex35View");
            Document doc = view.getFirstDocument();

            // Loop over all documents, and reset their doc numbers
            while (doc != null)
               {
               int i = doc.getItemValueInteger("DocNumber");
               doc.replaceItemValue("DocNumber", new Integer(i + 10));
```

```
                doc.save(true);
                doc = view.getNextDocument(doc);
                }   // end while
            }   // end try
        catch (Exception e) { e.printStackTrace(); }
        finally { NotesThread.stermThread(); }
        }   // end main
}       // end class
```

Have you spotted the problem yet? Try running this program yourself, using the sample source file and database on the CD. The database (Ex35.nsf) has one view, and the view has one column, which is the document number, sorted in ascending order. I've preloaded the database with five documents, numbered from 1 to 5. The algorithm seems pretty straightforward: Iterate over all the documents in the view from top to bottom, and increment the document number of each by 10.

The problem is that the *while* loop will only execute one iteration. What happens is that the program is modifying an indexed item, and the View's default behavior is to update its index automatically every time that happens. So, we take the first Document (number 1), change the DocNumber Item to 11, and save the Document. The View immediate re-sorts itself so that the newly modified Document is at the end (the highest numbered Document before was only 5). Then we call getNextDocument(), using Document number 11 as the "current" one. Well, there is no Document following number 11 in the View, so the loop terminates.

This isn't a good situation—you could be damaging your database. For example, saving the modified Document might relocate it *higher* in the View, or even lower down, but in the middle of some other Documents. If that were to happen, some Documents would be processed twice, others not at all. Very bad.

Of course, once you know that this is happening (estimate how long it would have taken you to figure it out; I'll wager that the answer is "too long"), it's not too hard to code around it. You can, for example, do the getNextDocument() call *before* you invoke save() on the current Document. That'll work okay. Or, you can use the new (in Release 4.5) setAutoUpdate() call to turn off automatic re-indexing. It might improve your program's performance as well, since you won't be re-indexing at every save().

Turning off AutoUpdate effectively means that while you navigate and (if you like) modify Documents in the View, the View's index (and therefore the contents of the View that you can see) remain static. Changes you make (and changes that other users make too) are not reflected in your in-memory "snapshot" of the View (you'll see changes made to Documents by other users, of course). You can do all your processing, and then tell the View to update itself when you're done (use the refresh() call, below).

AutoUpdate is *true* by default, to make the View class's behavior backwardly compatible with Notes 4.0.

boolean isCalendar()

Returns *true* if the current View is a calendar View. You can still navigate and search as usual.

boolean isDefaultView()

This property returns *true* if the current View is the default View in the Database. The default View is the one that you see by default when you double-click on a Database icon in the UI.

boolean isFolder()

The difference between a View and a Folder is small, but important: Documents are either *in* or *not in* a View based on the View's selection formula. If the formula evaluates to *true* for a given Document, then that Document is in the View; otherwise, it is not. Folders, on the other hand, have no selection formula. They maintain a list of the ids of Documents that are in the Folder. Documents can be added to or removed from a Folder at will, in the UI and also via NOI (see Document.putInFolder() and Document.removeFromFolder() earlier in this chapter).

This call returns *true* if the current View instance is a Folder.

View Document Searching Methods

Whereas Databases have many ways of searching for Documents, a View has only two: full text searching, and searching by key.

void clear()
int FTSearch(String query)
int FTSearch(String query, int maxdocs)

The FTSearch calls in the View class work just like the ones in the Database class, though you don't get as many sorting options, and the search only covers Documents in the View. The results work very differently, however. Recall that the Database.FTSearch() calls return a DocumentCollection instance containing the result set. The View class, however, tries to emulate in NOI what you get when you do a full text search on a View in the UI instead.

When you execute FTSearch on a View, the result is that the View now contains the result set, sorted by relevance score. The "new" View is always flat, even if the original was hierarchical. You navigate the result set just the same as the original View: use the getXXXDocument() calls.

NOI Part 2: Document, DocumentCollection, View, ViewColumn

Some of the navigational calls that apply to hierarchical Views are mapped appropriately when the View is flat. For example, you might use getChild() to get the first child of the current Document in a hierarchical View. In a flat View, getChild() is simply mapped to getNextDocument().

The View.FTSearch() calls return the number of Documents in the result set. You can reset the View to its original contents by invoking the clear() method. As with the Database FT calls, you pass in a String containing the query, and optionally the maximum number of Documents to put in the result set.

lotus.notes.DocumentCollection getAllDocumentsByKey(Object key)

lotus.notes.DocumentCollection getAllDocumentsByKey(Object key, boolean exactmatch)

lotus.notes.DocumentCollection getAllDocumentsByKey(Vector key)

lotus.notes.DocumentCollection getAllDocumentsByKey(Vector key, boolean exactmatch)

lotus.notes.Document getDocumentByKey(Object key)

lotus.notes.Document getDocumentByKey(Object key, boolean exactmatch)

lotus.notes.Document getDocumentByKey(Vector key)

lotus.notes.Document getDocumentByKey(Vector key, boolean exactmatch)

Keyed lookups in a View are pretty fast, and you can specify as many levels of a key as there are sorted columns in the View (only sorted columns are indexed). There are two basic flavors of keyed lookup: one returns all matches (getAllDocumentsByKey), and one returns only the first match (getDocumentByKey). Within each of these two kinds of lookup, the options are essentially the same: You provide a key (single- or multi-valued), and specify whether you want an exact match on that key or not.

In all cases a valid key component is one of the following data types:

- String
- Number
- lotus.notes.DateTime
- lotus.notes.DateRange

The data type of the key component that you supply must match the data type of the column values. If you want to use a single value key (String value is the most common), you can just pass an Object instance of the correct type. For multi-valued keys, you construct a Vector instance, and add the individual values to it. The values in a multi-valued key must be in the same order as the sorted columns in the View.

Set the "exactmatch" parameter to *true* if you want only exact matches on your key. If you specify *false*, then a partial match on string values will succeed (e.g., "A" will match "Alfred" and "Amy" both). All matches are case and accent insensitive.

Of course a View can have sorted columns interspersed with nonsorted columns. For the purposes of key construction, you ignore the nonsorted columns. Let's look at an example.

The database Ex36.nsf (Listing 3.6, as always, on your CD) contains one view named Lookup. The view has four columns: Name, Creation Date, Date, and Sequence. All except Creation Date are sorted. The Date column contains a date range (start/end DateTime pair). Creation Date is just the date that each document was created in the database. We want to first construct a lookup by name only, then do one by a two value key.

Listing 3.6 Multi-Value Key Example (Ex36Lookup.java)

```java
import java.lang.*;
import java.util.*;
import lotus.notes.*;

public class Ex36Lookup
{
    public static void main(String argv[])
        {
        try {
            NotesThread.sinitThread();
            Session s = Session.newInstance();
            Database db = s.getDatabase("", "book\\Ex36.nsf");
            View view = db.getView("Lookup");

            // first try all "A" names
            DocumentCollection dc = view.getAllDocumentsByKey("A", false);
            System.out.println("Found " + dc.getCount() + " matches:");
            int i, j = dc.getCount();
            Document doc;
            for (i = 0; i < j; i++)
                {
                doc = dc.getNthDocument(i);
                System.out.println("\t" + doc.getItemValueString("name"));
                }

            // now let's try for AE Neuman with a date range
            java.util.Vector v = new java.util.Vector(3);
            v.addElement("Alfred E. Neuman");
            DateTime start = s.createDateTime("4/20/52");
            DateTime endt = s.createDateTime("10/12/97");
            DateRange range = s.createDateRange(start, endt);
            v.addElement(range);
            v.addElement(new Integer(2));
            dc = view.getAllDocumentsByKey(v, true);
```

```
                    j = dc.getCount();
                    System.out.println("Found " + i + " multi-key matches:");
                    for (i = 0; i < j; i++)
                        {
                        doc = dc.getNthDocument(i);
                        System.out.println("\t" + doc.getItemValueString("name"));
                        }
                    } // end try
            catch (Exception e) { e.printStackTrace(); }
            finally { NotesThread.stermThread(); }
        }   // end main
}           // end class
```

Let's dissect what's going on here. In the first go around we simply ask for all Documents where the first sorted column (Name) begins with A. By specifying *false* for the *exactmatch* parameter, we're asking for partial matches to be included (this is what you get when you type a string in the view UI, and an edit control pops up. When you hit **Enter**, you get positioned on the first document that matches. The UI only lets you search on the first sorted column, however). The result (using the sample database) is a DocumentCollection containing six matches: three Alfred E. Neumans, two Alfred F. Neumans, and one more Alfred E. Neuman.

Why aren't they in the same order in which they appear in the view? Because DocumentCollections aren't ordered, except in cases where they contain the result of a full text search. If you must get Documents in the order that they appear in the View, you have to use the getDocumentByKey() call to get the first hit, then navigate using the getNextDocument() call. It's then up to you to figure out when to stop.

The next section in the example program builds a Vector containing three key values: "Alfred E. Neuman", a DateRange, and "2" for the sequence number. Note that we're totally ignoring the Creation Date column here, since it isn't sorted, and thus does not participate in the key. This time we call getAllDocumentsByKey() with a *true* for the exactmatch parameter. The result is a new DocumentCollection containing a single Document (the second one in the Lookup view), as this is the only Document that matches all three key values.

Now try an experiment: go into the Ex36 database, edit the Lookup view design. Double-click on the **Name** column to bring up the design properties box, and click on the **Sorting** tab. Make the Name column categorized as well as sorted, and save your changes. Then run the Ex36Lookup program again. Lo and behold, instead of retrieving six Documents for the first search, you only get four, all Alfred E. Neumans. What's up with that? Well, the answer is that keyed lookups will not span category boundaries. The first time, when the view was not categorized, all Documents were basically at the same "level" in the View's index. Once we add categorization to a column, the index is split, and a search can't/won't cross category boundaries. This is a good thing to be aware of when designing fancy lookups.

View Document Navigation Methods

lotus.notes.Document getFirstDocument()
lotus.notes.Document getLastDocument()
lotus.notes.Document getNextDocument(lotus.notes.Document doc)
lotus.notes.Document getPrevDocument(lotus.notes.Document doc)
lotus.notes.Document getChild(lotus.notes.Document doc)
lotus.notes.Document getParentDocument(lotus.notes.Document doc)
lotus.notes.Document getNextSibling (lotus.notes.Document doc)
lotus.notes.Document getPrevSibling (lotus.notes.Document doc)
lotus.notes.Document getNthDocument (int position)

These calls let you spin through a View at any level you wish. For flat Views (where View.isHierarchical() returns *false*) the getChild(), getParentDocument() and getNext/PrevSibling() calls don't have much meaning. They are mapped to the appropriate nonhierarchical call (getNextDocument, getPrevDocument(), respectively).

The getFirstDocument() and getLastDocument() calls are very fast—they just zap to the head and tail of the index. The getNthDocument() call has reasonable performance for small values of "position," but because it always has to start at the top of the index and count every entry, it's slow for large values. The getNext/Prev calls are pretty quick as well, since you provide a current Document each time. Each Document navigated to through a View will know its position in the View. Make sure you don't try to pass in a Document instance that didn't get returned by the current View, because NOI will throw an exception.

Note that for the getNthDocument call, the index is 1-based (the first Document is number 1). All the calls return *null* if the requested Document does not exist.

Navigational behavior is also affected by the AutoUpdate property's setting. If AutoUpdate is on, then the View's index is checked for changes each time you make a navigation call. If the index has been changed, it is automatically refreshed before the operation is completed. For Views that live in Databases on a server, the index could be modified by another user, as the index is always a shared thing. It's not as much of an issue for local databases, where you are the only one who could be making changes (unless you have Agents running in the background).

Note that there's no property or method that tells you how many Documents are in the View. The reason for that is essentially performance and scalability: there might be millions of them, and it would be horrendous to just spin through and count. If you have a case where you *really* need to know, then you have to build a document counter into the View itself.

Note also that the navigation methods say nothing about the non-Document entries in a View. If you have a categorized View, you'll see in the UI that each category has its own line, with the Documents belonging to that category grouped underneath. You might also have subtotal and totals in the View. None of these is retrievable through NOI at the present time (Domino 5.0 may have a new tale to tell—stay tuned). When you navigate through a View (for example, start with getFirstDocument(), and then call getNextDocument() until you get a *null* result), category and other non-Document entries are simply skipped.

The trade-off that was made in the object model design was to favor simplicity over functionality: There would have had to be another class returned by the View navigational methods that encompassed any kind of thing that you might find in a View, only one of which would be a Document. At the time that NOI was first designed, for Release 4.0, this was clearly the correct decision (in my opinion). The object model will clearly evolve over time as more functionality is added.

View Miscellaneous Methods

void refresh()

This method causes the View to refresh its in-memory cache of its index. Any changes (made by you or by any other user) will be reflected. You might have AutoUpdate disabled while you iterate through Documents in a View for a while, then you could call refresh() to update the View's index all at once.

void remove()

Removes the current View from the Database. This change is committed to disk immediately. If you have less than Designer access to the Database, this call will cause an exception.

String toString()

Returns the View's name.

THE LOTUS.NOTES.VIEWCOLUMN CLASS

The ViewColumn class has no methods, only properties, and all of the properties are read-only. You can use the View.getViewColumns() call to get a Vector containing ViewColumn instances in the order in which they were defined in the View.

ViewColumn Properties

String getFormula()

If the column was defined using an @function formula, this property will return the formula that was used.

String getItemName()

If the column was defined as simply the contents of a particular field (item really, but the term *field* is used in this context in the UI) in a Document, then this property returns the name of the item. All columns have an item name property, but the name is automatically generated for formula columns.

int getPosition()

This represents the column's position within the View (beginning with 1).

String getTitle()

This represents the column's title, as defined in the View.

boolean isCategory()

Returns *true* if the column is categorized.

boolean isHidden()

Returns *true* if the column is hidden.

boolean isResponse()

Returns *true* if this column is set to show only responses.

boolean isSorted()

Returns *true* if the column is sorted.

String toString()

Returns the column title.

THE LOTUS.NOTES.DOCUMENTCOLLECTION CLASS

The DocumentCollection class is a strange but useful beast. It isn't a generic collection class, because you can't add and remove things at will. You can only instantiate a DocumentCollection instance by executing some kind of Database level search (formula or full text), by retrieving a Document selection set from the Database class (getUnprocessedDocuments(), for example), or by doing a keyed lookup in a View (getAllDocumentsByKey()).

I've broken up the DocumentCollection calls into three groups: Properties, Navigation, Other.

DocumentCollection Properties

int getCount()

Returns the number of Document instances contained in the collection.

lotus.notes.Database getParent()

Returns the collection's parent Database instance.

String getQuery()

If the DocumentCollection was created as the result of a search, this call returns the actual text of the query, whether it's a formula or a full text query. If the collection was not created from a search operation, this property returns *null*.

boolean isSorted()

Returns *true* if the collection is the result of a full text query, where the Documents are sorted by one of the available criteria (relevance score, date, and so on). Formula search results are not sorted. Full text search results are sorted if the Database contains a full text index (or a multi-database index). Collections containing selected Document lists are not sorted.

DocumentCollection Navigation Methods

lotus.notes.Document getFirstDocument()
lotus.notes.Document getLastDocument()
lotus.notes.Document getNextDocument(lotus.notes.Document doc)
lotus.notes.Document getPrevDocument(lotus.notes.Document doc)
lotus.notes.Document getNthDocument(int position)

These calls do pretty much what you'd expect. They return *null* if the requested Document doesn't exist. The getNthDocument call (as with the method of the same name in the View class) is 1-based. However, the performance characteristics of the navigational calls differ depending on what kind of DocumentCollection you have. This point is worth diving into a bit.

DocumentCollections store essentially two kinds of data structures, depending on how they were created. The *sorted* variety is implemented by storing arrays of data structures. For example, when you get a result set from a full text search that has an index behind it, the Notes API call that DocumentCollection uses gives you back a buffer containing a Note ID and relevance score for each Document. The buffer is sorted by (let's say in this example) relevance score. Because it's an in-memory buffer, there's a practical limit on its size of around 64KB. Thus, full text searches are limited to a result set of 5000 Documents. Multi-database searches contain more information in the buffer for each Document, but the idea is the same.

For nonsorted result sets (e.g., a formula search), the API (different call) gives you back a Notes data structure called an *IDTable*. This is a compacted data structure with its own set of navigational API calls. IDTables can hold hundreds of thousands of entries, and can still be navigated efficiently, especially if you are looking up a particular Note ID.

Knowing this, we can predict which DocumentCollection methods are more efficient for a particular collection:

- Nonsorted collections are best accessed with a call where the Note ID of a reference point is known: getFirstDocument() and getNextDocument(). That's because looking up a given Note ID is very fast, and therefore finding the next one after a known one is also fast. Getting the last Document from an IDTable is slow, because you have to spin through the entire table. This is true also for the getPreviousDocument() call: You have to start at the front of the table and keep going, always remembering the last Note ID until you hit the one you know about. Then you have the previous one. The getNthDocument() call has a similar problem: You have to basically do a getNext() N times.

- Sorted collections are arrays internally, so indexing into the array at any point is okay. All the calls have about the same overhead, though the getNextDocument() getPrevDocument() methods have a tiny bit extra work to do: They have to extract the index of the Document you provide as an argument. No big deal, really.

Note that Document instances are created on the fly as you make the navigational calls. The DocumentCollection class doesn't pre-instantiate each Document and keep a pointer around.

DocumentCollection Other Methods

void FTSearch(String query, int maxdocs)

When you use the Database or View FTSearch() calls, you get back a DocumentCollection instance. In cases where you want to further refine your original search, you can use the DocumentCollection.FTSearch()

call. This method takes the original result set as a starting point, and executes a new full text query on it, replacing the original result set with the new one (the Query property is also replaced, and a new Count is calculated).

You can refine the search as many times as you like. One common occasion for doing this is when an initial query results in a huge result set. Rather than traverse thousands of Documents (because it can get expensive to instantiate a few thousand objects when you don't ever really know when Java's garbage collector will get around to freeing stuff up) and filter one by one, it can be much more efficient to narrow the search criteria, since FTSearch makes use of an index, if there is one.

One problem is that if you end up narrowing the search too far, you can't back up easily, as the last result set is destroyed when a new one is created. There's no undoFTSearch() call.

void putAllInFolder(String foldername)
void removeAllFromFolder(String foldername)

If you know that you want all the Documents in a collection either added to or removed from a particular folder, then these methods are the most efficient way to do that.

void removeAll(boolean force)

If you know that you want to delete all the Documents in a collection from the Database, then this is a very efficient way to handle that task. The force parameter has the same meaning as in the Document.remove() method, but there's no makeresponse equivalent in the DocumentCollection version of this operation.

void stampAll(String itemname, Object value)

Given a DocumentCollection instance, this method provides a way to very efficiently "stamp" a single value into each Document, using the Item name that you supply. You don't have to invoke the save() method on each Document either, since this call commits the changes to disk immediately. This last feature can be a two-edged sword: stampAll() bypasses any in-memory Document information and goes right to the disk. Thus, the following program fragment will lose some of your changes:

```
DocumentCollection dc = db.FTSearch("some query");
Document doc = dc.getFirstDocument();
doc.replaceItemValue("subject", "A new Subject");
dc.stampAll("subject", "A different subject");
doc.save();
```

The problem here is that if doc's subject item is modified in memory, then the DocumentCollection sets the subject item of all contained Document instances (on disk, not in memory) to something. Then doc overwrites the subject set by stampAll() with a save() call. Of course, the save() could have occurred immediately after the replaceItemValue(), but then the stampAll() would have wiped out that value anyway.

The moral of the story is: Know your DocumentCollection.

void updateAll()

When you write an Agent that is set up to run on "all documents that are new or modified since the last time the Agent ran," you must deal with the AgentContext.getUnprocessedDocuments() call (see Chapter 5 for details on the AgentContext class, and see Chapter 8 for more detail on writing Agents), which returns a DocumentCollection. When you have a list of unprocessed Documents, you generally iterate through them, and do something to each (or not, as the case may be). In any case, you must then explicitly tell the AgentContext to remove the Documents you're done with from the list; otherwise, they'll reappear next time you run the Agent, and you almost never want that. Thus, AgentContext has a method called updateProcessedDoc(), which does just that.

Well, 99.9% of the time, you want to remove all the unprocessed Documents from the list, whether you actually do something to them or not. I have yet to come across a case where someone legitimately wanted to have a Document appear in multiple invocations of an Agent. That's why we added this method to the DocumentCollection class in Notes Release 4.5: With a single call you can "mark" all the Documents in the unprocessed collection as "processed," instead of having to remember to code individual calls to AgentContext. updateProcessedDoc().

Summary

You've successfully navigated (and I use the term advisedly) the longest chapter in the book. The next one, Chapter 4, discusses still more NOI classes, with emphasis on data types.

4

NOI Part 3: Item, RichTextItem, RichTextStyle, EmbeddedObject, DateTime, DateRange

This chapter goes into more detail about the classes relating to data values and data types, with a fair amount of attention paid to rich text and embedded objects.

The lotus.notes.Item Class

The Item class is where we really start to get nitty gritty about data values, since it is the set of Items in a Document that really hold all the data. NOI considers an Item's value to be an attribute of the Item, so most of the calls in the Item class are properties. I've arranged the set of properties into two groups: value properties and attributes. You'll see what I mean.

Item Value Properties

These calls are equivalent to the Document.getItemValueXXX() calls.

java.util.Vector getValues()
void setValues(java.util.Vector)

Unlike column values or view lookup keys, Items that contain multiple values are always homogeneous with respect to data type. Thus, an Item that contains a text list cannot also contain a number, and vice versa. The Values property is how you access all the values of an Item at one time. The getValues() call always returns a Vector, even if there is only a single value. The setValues call always takes a Vector as input, even if you have put only one value in it. Use the standard Vector methods to discover how many values there are (Vector.size()), and to iterate through them.

String getValueString()
void setValueString(String text)

These calls allow you to retrieve and set text values for an Item. If you call getValueString() on an Item that contains another data type, NOI will attempt to coerce the value to a String for you. If you call setValueString() on an Item that contains a value of a different data type, then that value is replaced and the type of the Item is changed to text. If there is no value, or if the value cannot be coerced, a *null* is returned.

double getValueDouble()
void setValueDouble(double value)

Like the String version of this property, it attempts to coerce the value type on the read side, and overwrites any existing value type on the write side. If the value type cannot be coerced, a 0 is returned.

int getValueInteger()

void setValueInteger(int value)

As with Strings and doubles, the Integer version of the Value Property coerces on retrieval (if possible). If the value cannot be coerced, a 0 is returned.

lotus.notes.DateTime getDateTimeValue()

void setDateTimeValue(lotus.notes.DateTimeValue)

Notes stores DateTime values internally as numbers, so we added a special property to retrieve a date value as a DateTime object. This is really only useful when you already know that the Item contains a DateTime value, or when you want to set an Item to a DateTime value regardless of what data might have been stored there before. If you ask for a DateTime object from an Item that does not contain a date/time value, then a *null* is returned.

DateTime values are pretty much useless represented as numbers, because unlike in LotusScript, where date values are double precision numbers, Notes uses its own internal format, composed of two 4-byte integer values, one for date and one for time (some of the bits are actually allocated to a Daylight Savings Time flag and to a time zone id).

Item Attributes

lotus.notes.DateTime getLastModified()

Returns the date and time that the Item was last modified within the Document. The Item level information on modification is updated when the Document is saved, not when the in-memory value is modified. Thus the Item's LastModified property can never be later than the Document's, although different Items in the same Document can have different LastModified values. If the Document is new (has never been saved), then this call returns *null*.

This is the property Notes uses to implement field level replication.

String getName()

Returns the name of the Item. All Items have a name.

lotus.notes.Document getParent()

Returns the parent Document of the Item. All Items have a parent Document instance.

int getType()

Returns a constant representing the type of the Item's value. These constants are (as usual) declared *public static final int* in the Item class. Most of the item types listed below are either obsolete (from old versions of the product) or belong to various design elements, and as such are not interesting to most developers. They are all listed here anyway, for the sake of completeness. The possible values are:

- Item.ACTIONCD. Simple action information for Agents.
- Item.ASSISTANTINFO. Agent design data.
- Item.ATTACHMENT. A file attachment. Always named $FILE.
- Item.AUTHORS. Item is of type Text, but the Authors flag has been set. This means that the Item contains the names of users/groups allowed to read and write the Document.
- Item.COLLATION. Special character set collation data.
- Item.DATETIMES. Item contains one or more date/time values.

- Item.EMBEDDEDOBJECT. Item is part of an embedded OLE or other object in the Document. Usually named $FILE.
- Item.ERRORITEM. Error item (obsolete).
- Item.FORMULA. Formula item (obsolete).
- Item.HTML. Item contains raw HTML text, which has also (often, but not necessarily) been rendered into Notes rich text format elsewhere in this Document.
- Item.ICON. Icon item (obsolete).
- Item.LSOBJECT. Item contains LotusScript program data.
- Item.NAMES. The Item is a names Item, containing user and/or group names. If an Item is of type AUTHORS or READERS, it is also implicitly of type NAMES.
- Item.NOTELINKS. Item contains links to other Documents.
- Item.NOTEREFS. Item contains the UNID of Document's parent.
- Item.NUMBERS. Item contains one or more numeric values.
- Item.OTHEROBJECT. Item references an object other than a file attachment or embedded object. Not often seen.
- Item.QUERYCD. Item contains a saved query for an Agent.
- Item.READERS. Item is a names list containing the names of user/groups allowed read access to the Document.
- Item.RICHTEXT. Item contains rich text CD (Composite Document) records.
- Item.SIGNATURE. Item contains a signature. Always named $Signature.
- Item.TEXT. Item contains text (or a text list).
- Item.UNAVAILABLE. Obsolete.
- Item.UNKNOWN. Item's type is unknown.

Chapter 4

- Item.USERDATA. Item is used by an API program (not Notes itself) to store data in a format that Notes does not know about. A "bit bucket" for some application.
- Item.USERID. Item contains a user name from Notes Release 2.
- Item.VIEWMAPDATA. Viewmap design information.
- Item.VIEWMAPLAYOUT. Viewmap design information.

int getValueLength()

Returns the size in bytes of the Item's value. Does not include any overhead for Item level data other than the value.

boolean isAuthors()
void setAuthors(boolean flag)

The Authors property is used to attach a list of users/groups to a Document to provide Document level access control. An Authors Item is usually named $Authors, and contains the list of people allowed to modify the Document.

Setting the Authors property to *true* will set the Names flag as well as the Authors flag on the item. Setting the Authors property to *false* will not clear the Names flag, however.

boolean isEncrypted()
void setEncrypted(boolean flag)

When you encrypt a Document, only the Items marked for encryption actually get encrypted. Use the Encrypted property on the Item class to mark or unmark Items individually.

boolean isNames()
void setNames(boolean flag)

The Names property indicates which Item(s) in a Document contain user/group names. Setting the Authors or Readers property will also set the Names flag on the Item, but you might want to set the Names flag alone. A few places in the Notes UI check for a Names flag on an Item, and will let you do special kinds of address book lookups automatically on the corresponding fields in a form. You can set the Names flag on a form's field in the field property box when you're in form design mode.

boolean isProtected()
void setProtected(boolean flag)

Set this property to *true* if you want only users with Editor (or better) access to be able to modify the Item.

boolean isReaders()
void setReaders(boolean flag)

Similar to the Authors property: defines the list of users/groups who have read access to the Document.

boolean isSaveToDisk()
void setSaveToDisk(boolean flag)

This property is exceptionally useful in those applications where you want to temporarily store data in a Document, but don't want that data written to disk when the Document is saved. The standard mail template uses it extensively for Calendaring and Scheduling.

If the SaveToDisk flag on an Item is *true* (the default), then that Item gets written to disk when the Document is saved. If not, then the Item is simply skipped at Document save() time.

boolean isSigned()
void setSigned(boolean flag)

As with the Encrypted property, when you sign a Document only the Items marked for signing are included in the "digest" of the Document (see the discussion of Document.encrypt() in Chapter 2). Use this property to set or clear the flag for an Item.

boolean isSummary()
void setSummary(boolean flag)

Only Items whose Summary property is set can appear as values in a View, because only Items with their Summary flag set are included in the View's summary data. Author and Reader Items need to have their Summary flags set as well; otherwise, the access control features for which they were designed won't work. Setting either the Authors or Readers property will automatically also set the Names and Summary flags.

Not all Items with the Summary flag set can appear in a View, however. Rich text Items, for example, are explicitly excluded, as are text Items where the length of the text exceeds 15KB. You will also be prevented from setting the Summary flag on any Item whose size exceeds 32KB (the flag is automatically cleared, though no error is raised).

Apart from these restrictions, when you create an Item using NOI, the Summary flag is set for you automatically.

Item Methods

String abstractText(int maxlen, boolean dropvowels, boolean usedict)

This little known method is an interesting way to shrink the contents of a text Item. Users sometimes use it to get around the fact that NOI has a maximum string length of 32,000 characters (64,000 bytes, but when you use Unicode internally it cuts the number of characters you can hold in a 64KB buffer down to 32,000), and many rich text Items contain much more text than that.

The abstractText() call compresses the original text (including rich text) in an Item by optionally dropping all vowels (if you specify *true* for the "dropvowels" parameter), and by attempting to replace words with common abbreviations. It optionally does the abbreviating using a dictionary file, if you specify *true* for the "usedict" parameter. The dictionary file is a simple text file, formatted with each word and its abbreviation on a single line, separated by at least one space. The entries should be in alphabetical order. The file is named "noteabbr.txt" (in lowercase for those operating systems that care), and must be somewhere on your path (your execution path, not the Notes data directory). A sample dictionary is included on the CD, you can add your own abbreviations at will.

AbstractText() also automatically trims whitespace (compressing multiple spaces into a single space, and so on), and trims punctuation where possible.

The method will perform its magic on the first 64KB of text in the Item.

void appendToTextList(String value)

void appendToTextList(java.util.Vector textlist)

This method takes a String, or Vector of Strings, and appends it to the current Item's text or text list. The Item must by of type Text or TextList for this call to work. If the original Item value was only a single String, then this call will convert the Item into a text list. If the original Item contained a String or a text list, then the new String or text list is appended to it.

boolean containsValue(Object value)

Returns *true* if the Item contains the value that you pass in as a parameter. The data type of the object that you pass in doesn't need to be exactly the same as the data type of the Item, but they must be compatible. For example,

- **Text** is compatible with rich text, text, and text list.
- **Number** is compatible with number and number list.
- **DateTime** is compatible with DateTime or DateRange.

The rules for a match vary somewhat with data type:

- **Numbers.** If the Item contains a number, the two must match exactly. If the Item contains a number list, the input argument must be one of the numbers in the list.
- **DateTime.** If the Item contains a DateTime value, the two must match exactly. If the Item contains a DateTime list, the input argument must be one of the values in the list.
- **Text.** If the Item contains rich text, the input String must be a substring in the rich text stream. If the Item contains a single String, then the two must match exactly. If the Item contains a text list, then the input argument must exactly match one of the elements in the list (comparisons are case- and accent-sensitive). One special case: if the Item's Name flag is set (the Item contains one or more user/group names), then the match will succeed if the input argument is a common name that either matches exactly or matches the common part of a distinguished name in the Item. For example, if the Item is a Name Item and contains "CN=Bob Balaban/O=Looseleaf" and I call Item.contains() with an input argument of "Bob Balaban", then the match will succeed.

Note that in Release 4.6 there is a bug which prevernts date-only DateTime values from matching correctly. If, for example, the Item contains the data value for "today," and you pass in a DateTime instance initialized to "today," the call will incorrectly return false.

lotus.notes.Item copyItemToDocument(lotus.notes.Document destination)
lotus.notes.Item copyItemToDocument(lotus.notes.Document destination, String newname)

This method makes a copy of the current Item in the specified Document. The Item's flags (Summary, Name, etc.) as well as its value are copied. By default the new Item will keep the same name as the original, but you can also specify a new name for it. No checking is done to see whether the destination Document already contains an Item of that name. If it does, you will end up with a Document containing multiple Items of the same name which, while okay for things like file attachments, is a definite no-no for data Items.

You may have problems with this call if you use it on a RichTextItem. The problem will arise if the source and destination Documents do not have the same font layouts: The rich text may have different fonts in the destination than it did in the source. The reason for this has to do with the way font information is stored. Each Document has a special Item (named $Fonts) containing a font table. Each font name in the table is associated with a font index, and the table's scope is the entire Document. Any font settings contained in a RichTextItem will contain only the font's index into the table, not the full font information. When you copy a RichTextItem from one Document to another, the $Fonts tables are not merged. Thus, if the destination Document has a different font table layout than the source Document (a likely occurrence, unless you're lucky), the font indices in the copied Item will be wrong. This is a bug that is scheduled to be fixed in Domino Release 5.0. One possible workaround is to explicitly copy the $Fonts Item at the same time. That won't work, though, in cases where the Document has more than one RichTextItem in it.

When you copy a RichTextItem, all of its embedded objects (file attachments, OLE objects) are copied as well.

String getText()
String getText(int maxlen)

The getText() method returns a text version of the contents of the Item. It operates a bit differently from the getValueString() call, however. Both operate the same when the Item contains rich text, but when the Item contains a text list, getValueString() will only return the first element of the list, while getText will return the entire list, with each element separated by the default text list separator (usually a semicolon).

The getText() call also has an option that limits the length of the returned String to a specified maximum. This is particularly useful when you're accessing rich text and only want a small part of what might be a large String. The maximum length is specified in characters (not bytes).

void remove()

Removes an Item from the current Document. If the Item is a multi-part RichTextItem (see the discussion on Document.getFirstItem() in Chapter 3 for details on multi-part Items), all parts are removed.

StringtoString()

Returns the name of the Item.

THE LOTUS.NOTES.RICHTEXTITEM CLASS

The RichTextItem class is the only instance in NOI of class inheritance. RichTextItem extends (the Java term for inherits from) the Item class, meaning that all of the methods and properties that you find in an Item are also available to RichTextItem. RichTextItem also adds some additional methods and properties that are specific to manipulating rich text, and those are what we document in this section.

The RichTextItem class is not as fully functional with Notes rich text as anyone (including the developers of the interface) would like. It will continue to evolve, though, and it does allow you to examine certain aspects of a rich text item, and to add new text, styles, doclinks, and file attachments to it.

RichTextItem Properties

java.util.Vector getEmbeddedObjects()

This is the only property in the RichTextItem class (other than the ones that RichTextItem inherits from Item). The getEmbeddedObjects() call returns a Vector containing all of the embedded objects (including file attachments, OLE/1 objects and OLE/2 objects) in the RichTextItem. Your program does not have to be running on a Windows machine in order to successfully instantiate EmbeddedObjects for OLE objects—it will work on any platform. In LotusScript NOI you do have to be running on a Windows platform in order to activate an OLE object, because in order to run an OLE object the Microsoft OLE libraries have to be available.

Unfortunately, in Java NOI (for Domino 4.6) OLE isn't supported. See the discussion of the EmbeddedObject class later in this chapter for all the gory details.

RichTextItem Methods

void addNewLine()

void addNewLine(int n)

void addNewLine(int n, boolean newparagraph)

This method adds a newline to the rich text stream. You can specify how many newlines to add, and you can also specify (using the *newparagraph* parameter) whether the newline(s) act(s) as a paragraph break or not (the default value for newparagraph is *true*).

Why should you care about the distinction between newlines and new paragraphs? Usually, you won't need to care, but you should also know that Notes does make the distinction, and that a single paragraph in a RichTextItem cannot hold more than 64KB worth of data. If you were to simply append text for a long time either without adding newlines, or adding newlines that were not paragraph breaks, Notes would at some point most likely insert a paragraph break for you, and the resultant rendering for that RichTextItem in the UI might look odd. Or, you might get an exception for the paragraph exceeding 64KB.

Using the addNewLine() call is the recommended way to insert newlines. Explicitly including constructs such as "\n" or "\n\r" in your text stream is not recommended, as these tend to be platform-specific values (a newline in Win95 is not the same as a newline on the Mac, for example). The addNewLine() method is guaranteed to work correctly for all platforms.

void addTab()

void addTab(int n)

This call adds one or more tab characters to the rich text stream. You should use this method instead of explicitly adding constructs like "\t" to your text.

void appendDocLink(lotus.notes.Document doc)

void appendDocLink(lotus.notes.Document doc, String comment)

This call adds a Notes doclink to the specified Document instance to the current RichTextItem. Due to a last minute problem during the development of Domino 4.6 (the developer, yours truly, screwed up a bit), the interface to this method was not correctly specified, and there was no time to correct the error before the product shipped. There should have been three sets of methods here: one each for adding a link to a Document, View and Database. In LotusScript the argument is a Variant, so passing in any of these three object types works. But because Java is strongly typed, there's no way to fool the call into accepting a View or a Database. Sorry.

The doclink is rendered as the standard link icon in the RichTextItem, and contains a server "hint" as well to assist in link resolution later. The server hint is taken from the input Document's parent Database. You can optionally add a comment to the link as well, which displays in the status bar of the UI when you highlight the link.

void appendRTItem(lotus.notes.RichTextItem item)

Use this method to merge a RichTextItem (could be from the same Document or from another one) into the current RichTextItem. Be aware, however, that you may have font problems, as described above in this chapter for the Item.copyToDocument() method.

void appendStyle(lotus.notes.RichTextStyle style)

Adds a new RichTextStyle to the current rich text stream. It allows you to modify the font, color, size, and so on of text as you append it to the RichTextItem. See below for more details on the RichTextStyle class (new in Release 4.6).

void appendText(String text)

Adds text to the current RichTextItem. Text is always appended to the end of the stream—there is no way (currently) to insert or modify text in the middle of the Item. You should not use explicit tabs ("\t") or newlines ("\n" or "\n\r") in the text stream, as they are not always platform portable. Instead use the addTab() and addNewLine() methods.

lotus.notes.EmbeddedObject embedObject(int type, String classname, String source, String name)

Adds an EmbeddedObject to the RichTextItem. EmbeddedObject instances encompass file attachments as well as OLE objects. Unfortunately, OLE doesn't really work with the Java NOI in Release 4.6 (should be fixed in 5.0), so this method in 4.6 is limited to embedding file attachments. See the following section on the EmbeddedObject class for more details on the problems with OLE.

The first argument to the embedObject() call is a constant which specifies the type of embedding you want:

- RichTextItem.EMBED_ATTACHMENT. Embed a file attachment.
- RichTextItem.EMBED_OBJECT. Embed an OLE object.
- RichTextItem.EMBED_OBJECTLINK. Embed a link to an OLE object.

Embedding a file attachment simply means that the file is attached to the document, and an icon for it is rendered into the RichTextItem at the current location. The icon doesn't look exactly the way it does when you attach a file using the Notes UI: You get the same icon, but the name of the file doesn't appear underneath it; you get the name following the icon. The reason for this is that the UI generates the icon/name rendering using a graphical metafile, and the back-end NOI classes don't have the ability to do that. Instead we just stick a generic icon in there and add the name of the file following it.

The difference between embedding an OLE object and embedding an OLE object link is that in the first case the entire object (and all its instance data) is attached to the Document, whereas in the link case only a pointer to a file on disk is stored in the Document. The advantage of a link is that it uses much less space in the Database, however you can't really make use of a link across replicas. Since the link is to a file on disk, everyone who accessed the link would have to have the original file in the same location on his or her own disk, not a very easy setup to maintain.

The "classname" argument is used for OLE objects only. It allows you to specify an application (say, 1-2-3 or Excel) and have NOI create an "empty" embedded object of that class in the RichTextItem. If you don't want an empty embedding, then you specify *null* for the classname, and provide an explicit file path for the "source" argument. The file type is checked against the OLE registry, and if it is a file belonging to a valid OLE application installed on your machine, then OLE will (in a future release of Java NOI, remember, though it does work fine in LotusScript) launch the application, load the file, and re-save it in your Document. You cannot specify both a class name and a source path (when you specify a file, the class is implied).

The third argument, "name," is the name by which you want the embedded object to be known in Domino. This is the name that the UI shows you (right-click on the embedded object in the UI and bring up the Object Properties box), and the name you can use in the getEmbeddedObject() call to retrieve it. It can be any string you like, though the name should be unique within the Document.

lotus.notes.EmbeddedObject getEmbeddedObject(String name)

Locates the EmbeddedObject instance in the current RichTextItem of the name you specify, and returns it. The name should be the user-defined name of the object, which you can specify in the embedObject() call, or edit in the Object Properties box in the UI.

String getFormattedText(boolean striptabs, int linelength, int maxlength)

This method converts a RichTextItem to a text only representation, and allows you to specify whether tabs should be removed (each tab is converted to one space), how long each line should be (newlines are inserted at the end of each line), and the maximum amount of text you want returned. If you specify 0 for the line length, a length of 80 is used.

The maximum length that NOI will return for this call is 32,000 Unicode characters (64KB).

THE LOTUS.NOTES.RICHTEXTSTYLE CLASS

This class is new in Release 4.6, and (finally!) adds functionality to NOI that allows you to manipulate rich text styles when appending text to a RichTextItem. Following the append mode of interaction with RichTextItem, you use the RichTextItem.appendStyle() call to add a style to the rich text stream. All text appended following the style will be rendered with that style.

RichTextStyle has no methods, only properties. All properties are read-write. There are a number of constants that I've documented separately. As usual, all constants are defined as *public static final int* in the RichTextStyle class, so you would reference them using the RichTextStyle. prefix. The reason for using constants for colors and so on (instead of, say, allowing you to specify RGB combinations) is that this was the only way to guarantee platform portability: We wanted you to be confident that you would get the right color on all operating systems.

Can you use any number, or are you just limited to the predefined constants? The actual answer is that, for colors and fonts at least, you are free to use any integer you like. The problem is, though, that only the pre-defined ones are platform portable. Be aware that if you find some color or font that you like to use on, say, Windows, that isn't part of the predefined set, then that's okay, but it might very well display differently on OS/2 or the Mac.

Note that if you set a RichTextStyle into a RichTextItem and then invoke RichTextItem.appendRichTextItem(), the incoming Item (which has its own styles in it) will not be affected by the RichTextStyle.

You instantiate a RichTextStyle object using the Session.createRichTextStyle() call. Style objects are scoped to the Session so that you can reuse them in multiple Databases.

Note that the RichTextStyle class was omitted from the Java Programmer's Guide database distributed with Domino 4.6, but the LotusScript version of the interface is documented in the online help.

RichTextStyle Constants

Color constants are as follows:

- RichTextStyle.COLOR_BLACK
- RichTextStyle.COLOR_BLUE
- RichTextStyle.COLOR_CYAN

Chapter 4

- RichTextStyle.COLOR_DARK_BLUE
- RichTextStyle.COLOR_DARK_CYAN
- RichTextStyle.COLOR_DARK_GREEN
- RichTextStyle.COLOR_DARK_MAGENTA
- RichTextStyle.COLOR_DARK_RED
- RichTextStyle.COLOR_DARK_YELLOW
- RichTextStyle.COLOR_GRAY
- RichTextStyle.COLOR_GREEN
- RichTextStyle.COLOR_LIGHT_GRAY
- RichTextStyle.COLOR_MAGENTA
- RichTextStyle.COLOR_RED
- RichTextStyle.COLOR_WHITE
- RichTextStyle.COLOR_YELLOW

Text effects are as follows:

- RichTextStyle.EFFECTS_EMBOSS
- RichTextStyle.EFFECTS_EXTRUDE
- RichTextStyle.EFFECTS_NONE
- RichTextStyle.EFFECTS_SHADOW
- RichTextStyle.EFFECTS_SUBSCRIPT
- RichTextStyle.EFFECTS_SUPERSCRIPT

Font names are as follows:

- RichTextStyle.FONT_COURIER
- RichTextStyle.FONT_HELV
- RichTextStyle.FONT_ROMAN

Other constants are:

- RichTextStyle.STYLE_NO_CHANGE
- RichTextStyle.YES
- RichTextStyle.NO
- RichTextStyle.MAYBE (equivalent to STYLE_NO_CHANGE)

RichTextStyle Properties

int getBold()

void setBold(int setting)

Retrieves or turns the bold text attribute on or off (use YES or NO), or explicitly carries over the bold setting of the most recent style object added to the rich text stream (use STYLE_NO_CHANGE). Default is STYLE_NO_CHANGE.

int getColor()

void setColor(int color)

Retrieves or sets the current color (use one of the color constants), or explicitly tells NOI to carry over the most recent color setting (STYLE_NO_CHANGE). Default is STYLE_NO_CHANGE.

int getEffects()

void setEffects(int value)

Retrieves or sets one of the special effects settings (use one of the EFFECTS constants), or carries over the most recent setting (STYLE_NO_CHANGE). Default is STYLE_NO_CHANGE.

int getFont()

void setFont(int font)

Retrieves or sets the font that is used for text (use one of the font name constants), or carries over the most recent font (STYLE_NO_CHANGE). Default is STYLE_NO_CHANGE.

int getFontSize()

void setFontSize(int size)

Retrieves or sets the font size (in points) or maintains the most recent setting (STYLE_NO_CHANGE). Default is STYLE_NO_CHANGE. The valid values are between 1 and 250, inclusive.

int getItalic()

void setItalic(int value)

Retrieves or sets the italic property of the text stream (use YES or NO) or maintains the most recent setting (STYLE_NO_CHANGE). Default is STYLE_NO_CHANGE.

int getStrikeThrough()

void setStrikeThrough(int value)

Retrieves or sets the strike-through attribute (use YES or NO) or maintains the most recent setting (STYLE_NO_CHANGE). Default is STYLE_NO_CHANGE.

int getUnderline()

void setUnderline(int value)

Retrieves or sets the underline attribute (YES or NO) or maintains the most recent setting (STYLE_NO_CHANGE). Default is STYLE_NO_CHANGE.

Since this is a new class, let's do a simple example (see Listing 4.1).

Listing 4.1 Rich Text Style Example (Ex41RTStyle.java)

```java
import java.lang.*;
import java.util.*;
import lotus.notes.*;

public class Ex41RTStyle
{
    public static void main(String argv[])
        {
        try {
            NotesThread.sinitThread();
            Session s = Session.newInstance();
            Database db = s.getDatabase("", "book\\Ex41.nsf");
            Document doc = db.createDocument();
            RichTextItem rti = doc.createRichTextItem("body");

            // first style
            RichTextStyle style1 = s.createRichTextStyle();
            style1.setBold(RichTextStyle.YES);
            style1.setColor(RichTextStyle.COLOR_DARK_CYAN);
            style1.setEffects(RichTextStyle.EFFECTS_EMBOSS);
            style1.setFont(RichTextStyle.FONT_ROMAN);
            style1.setFontSize(24);

            // second style
            RichTextStyle style2 = s.createRichTextStyle();
            style2.setBold(RichTextStyle.NO);
```

```
                    style2.setColor(RichTextStyle.COLOR_DARK_RED);
                    style2.setEffects(RichTextStyle.EFFECTS_EXTRUDE);
                    style2.setFont(RichTextStyle.FONT_HELV);
                    style2.setFontSize(18);

                    rti.appendText("First line is default everything");
                    rti.addNewLine();
                    rti.appendStyle(style1);
                    rti.appendText("This text is in style 1.");
                    rti.addNewLine();
                    rti.appendStyle(style2);
                    rti.appendText("This text is in style 2.");

                    // save it
                    doc.save();
                    } // end try
                catch (Exception e) { e.printStackTrace(); }
                finally { NotesThread.stermThread(); }
        }   // end main
}   // end class
```

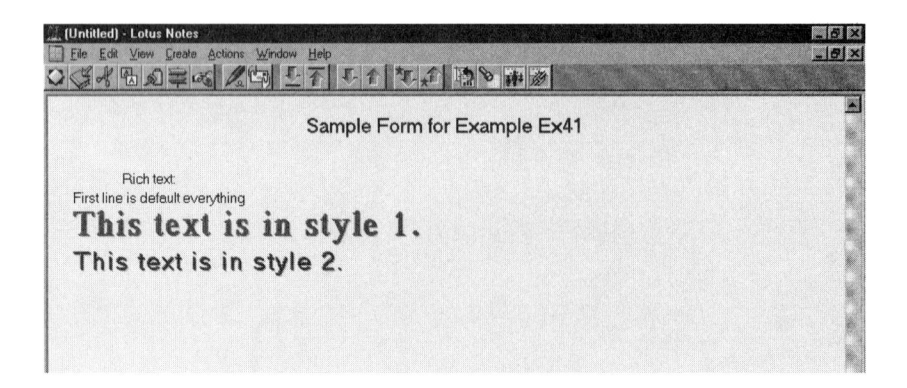

[screenshot: Sample Form for Example Ex41 — Rich text: First line is default everything / **This text is in style 1.** / This text is in style 2.]

If you examine the document created by this program in the Ex41.nsf database on your CD, you'll see that we got what might be some unexpected behavior with respect to special effects. In style1, I turned on the

EMBOSS effect and used that for the second line of text. In style2, I set the effect to EXTRUDE, which you might expect to replace the EMBOSS setting, as they are both set with the same call. However, the third line of text comes out with both EXTRUDE and EMBOSS set (you can verify this by editing the document, bringing up the Text Properties box and moving the cursor between the two lines).

Luckily we can get the behavior we wanted by adding a call to RichTextItem.appendStyle() using a third RichTextStyle instance whose Effects property has been set to EFFECTS_NONE before appending style2.

THE LOTUS.NOTES.EMBEDDEDOBJECT CLASS

As mentioned above, the EmbeddedObject class encapsulates both file attachments and OLE objects. While the Java NOI fully supports manipulation of file attachments through this class, unfortunately (at least in Domino Release 4.6) OLE object activation (required for embedding and activating embedded objects and links) is not supported in Java (it is fully supported via LotusScript). There were two reasons for this limitation in 4.6:

- ❐ OLE requires that each thread on which OLE calls will be made must not only initialize OLE (no big deal there), but each thread must also implement a Windows message pump (usually implemented as a GetMessage()/DispatchMessage() loop). If the message pump is not run on each thread, that thread's message queue can get backed up, and the thread will eventually hang. This is because OLE uses cross-process messaging to communicate between the container program (usually Notes) and the embedded object, especially when the embedded object or control is an EXE ("out of process") application, as opposed to a

DLL ("in process") control or Active/X. This required some nontrivial architectural changes in Notes, and there just wasn't time to complete them before Release 4.6 shipped.

❒ The second reason had to do with the scriptability of embedded OLE objects in Java. With LotusScript, the language has built-in OLE Automation capabilities, just as Visual Basic does. You can get an Automation "handle" (an IDispatch interface, for those of you who know about COM interfaces and OLE) to any embedded object just by "activating" it, which causes OLE to load and run it. Using the Automation handle, LotusScript can transmit commands that are specific to the embedded application (or control) through the IDispatch interface to the object. This allows you a very nice scripting capability directly from LotusScript. Java, however, doesn't have anything like that built in. Even if we had been able to solve the OLE-per-thread problem in time, we would have had to invent an entirely new IDispatch like interface in Java in order for you to be able to manipulate embedded objects. That was just too much work given the time we had, especially since the forthcoming Java Beans/COM Bridge architectures that are coming out soon will solve the Automation problem for us.

Hopefully Domino 5.0 will do a much better job with OLE from Java. In the meantime, some of the methods and properties continue to work in the Java NOI. You create a new EmbeddedObject instance with the RichTextItem.embedObject() call (all EmbeddedObjects live in a rich text item). You can also access existing EmbeddedObjects via the RichTextItem.getEmbeddedObjects(), RichTextItem.getEmbeddedObject() and Document.getEmbeddedObjects() calls.

EmbeddedObject Properties

String getClassName()

Returns the name of the OLE class of the embedded object, if it is an OLE object; it returns *null* for other types of objects. This call works in Java NOI, on any platform, so long as the class is known to Domino.

int getFileSize()

Returns the size of an attached file, in bytes. If you make this call on an EmbeddedObject instance that represents an OLE object, you will probably get misleading results. That's because OLE objects store their data in $FILE Items in a Notes Document, just as file attachments do. The problem is that OLE objects most always use more than one $FILE item, and the getFileSize() call isn't aware of that.

String getName()

Returns the user-defined name of the file attachment or embedded object. Works for OLE objects on all platforms, if a user-defined name was supplied when the object was embedded.

int getObject()

Returns the OLE Automation handle for an embedded OLE object. Does not work in the Java NOI.

lotus.notes.RichTextItem getParent()

Returns the RichTextItem in which the current object is embedded/attached.

String getSource()

Returns the file name of the original file attachment or OLE object. Works on all platforms for OLE objects.

int getType()

Returns a constant representing the kind of object that is embedded/attached, one of: EmbeddedObject.EMBED_ ATTACHMENT, EmbeddedObject.EMBED_OBJECT, EmbeddedObject.EMBED_OBJECTLINK. These constants are identical to the ones described above in the RichTextItem class. They were declared in both classes only for convenience.

java.util.Vector getVerbs()

Returns a Vector containing the list of OLE "verbs" supported by the embedded object. This call has no meaning for file attachments. Because it requires activation of the embedded object, this call does not currently work in the Java NOI.

EmbeddedObject Methods

int activate(boolean show)

Activates an embedded OLE object and returns an Automation handle for it. The argument specifies whether the OLE object should create a separate window to display its UI ("show" set to *true*), or to activate in-place ("show" = *false*).

This method does not currently work in the Java NOI.

void doVerb(String verb)

Execute one of the supported "verbs" in the embedded object (typical supported verbs are Open and Edit). Does not currently work in the Java NOI.

void extractFile(String filepath)

For file attachments only, make a copy of the attachment on disk, at the specified location.

void remove()

Removes the embedded object/attachment from the RichTextItem, including its rendering. Works for OLE objects on all platforms. You must invoke save() on the Document in order to commit the changes to disk.

String toString()

Returns the user-defined name (if any) of the object.

THE LOTUS.NOTES.DATETIME CLASS

The DateTime class represents the internal format of a Notes date value, which includes a date, a time, a time zone and a flag indicating whether daylight savings time is in effect. The methods and properties of this class allow you to do several kinds of date arithmetic (add/subtract months, days, hours, and so on), and to convert between the internal format and Strings, or between the internal format and the LotusScript format.

It seems logical to wonder why there's no conversion between the Notes format and the Java Date class, which actually has a lot of the same functionality (though the Java implementation was kind of buggy, at least in Release 1.1.1). The reason is that the Java date format is an 8-byte integer (a Java *long*), representing the number of milliseconds since 1/1/1970 00:00:00 GMT. There just wasn't time to write a platform portable conversion routine that would handle this data type, which is not native to all platforms supported by Notes. In the meantime, you can accurately convert between Notes and Java native date formats by using Strings.

The LotusScript date format (in case you were curious) follows the BASIC convention. It is a double precision number, where the integer part is the number of days since the reference date (12/30/1899), and the fraction is the ratio of the number of seconds since midnight to the number of seconds in a day. Clearly, this format is not as granular, or as accurate, as either the Java or Notes formats.

Note that as a general rule with this class, all String formatted DateTime values follow the default formatting as set for the current location, and usually include a time zone designation (EDT, EST, whatever). Input Strings should also follow the local format, and can either include or omit the time zone designation.

Notes always converts a DateTime value to GMT for storage internally, though it remembers the time zone in which the original was specified. The value is accessible either in GMT or in the local time zone.

You create a DateTime object using the Session.createDateTime() call.

DateTime Properties

String getDateOnly()
String getTimeOnly()

Returns either the date portion or the time portion of the DateTime in String format.

String getGMTTime()
String getLocalTime()
void setLocalTime(String time)

Returns the current DateTime value in String format for either the GMT or local version of the DateTime value. You can also modify the stored date value using the setLocalTime() call.

Note that if a date value was originally specified in a time zone different from the local time zone, the getLocalTime() and getGMTTime() calls convert that value to their respective zones. To get the DateTime as originally specified, you can use the getZoneTime() call.

int getTimeZone()

Returns the time zone in which the date value was originally specified. The time zone value is usually (but not always) a number of hours plus or minus that you add to the current time to get Greenwich Mean Time (GMT). Some zones have special values, however.

String getZoneTime()

Returns the String version of the DateTime value for the time zone in which it was originally specified. If the original value was not specified with a time zone different from the current zone, then this call is equivalent to getLocalTime().

boolean isDST()

Returns *true* if daylight savings time is in effect for the current DateTime value.

DateTime Methods

void adjustSecond(int value)
void adjustSecond(int value, boolean localzone)
void adjustMinute(int value)
void adjustMinute(int value, boolean localzone)
void adjustHour(int value)
void adjustHour(int value, boolean localzone)
void adjustDay(int value)
void adjustDay(int value, boolean localzone)
void adjustMonth(int value)
void adjustMonth(int value, boolean localzone)
void adjustYear(int value)
void adjustYear(int value, boolean localzone)

The adjustXXX() methods all work essentially the same way: given the current DateTime value, adjust it (plus or minus) by the value provided. Optionally, you can specify that the local time zone should be taken into account in the adjustment. This becomes important when an adjustment (either forward or backward) results in the start and end times being on opposite sides of a Daylight Savings Time boundary. In such a case, if you don't explicitly use *true* for the localzone parameter, you might end up with unexpected results.

For example, if you started with a DateTime of March 15, 1997 2:00:00 PM and adjusted by one month (without taking time zones into account), you'd end with a simple adjustment to the month part of the value: April 15, 1997 2:00:00 PM, even though Daylight Savings Time went into effect during that month.

If, however, you used the version of the adjustMonth() call that lets you specify *true* for the localzone parameter, 3/15/97 2:00:00 PM (implicitly Eastern Standard Time) becomes 4/15/97 1:00:00 PM

Eastern Daylight Time. The second case is more accurate, in the sense that the second date is exactly one month ahead of the first, while in the first case the second date is one month and one hour ahead. There are cases, especially in Calendaring applications, where the distinction is important.

void convertToZone(int newzone, boolean isdst)

Converts the current DateTime value to a new time zone. You can optionally specify whether Daylight Savings Time should be considered.

void setAnyDate()
void setAnyTime()

Notes implements the concept of date and time value *wildcards*, which not all systems do. LotusScript (and VB), for example, make no distinction between a date value with "no time" attached to it, and that same date at midnight (0 time value). Notes does make that distinction, and you can have a date value with no time attached, or a time value with no date attached.

For example, you can create a date-only DateTime object by calling Session.createDateTime("today") (or your local language equivalent keyword). This date value is most definitely not the same as "today 00:00:00" (or any other specific time). Likewise for time values without dates.

You can convert a DateTime value that contains both a date and a time to one that contains only one or the other with these two methods. The setAnyDate() call converts whatever date value is in the current object to "no date," and the setAnyTime() call converts the current time value to "no time." Strings formatted from a DateTime object containing one of these wildcards will simply omit the wildcard portion.

void setLocalDate(int year, int month, int day, boolean isdst)

void setLocalTime(int hour, int minute, int second, int hundredth)

These two calls are not in the LotusScript interface, as LotusScript has built-in functions that do the same thing. They allow you to specify a date and/or time value by providing the components of the value in integer format. The year should be a four-digit year, to avoid unexpected results with Year 2000 default conversions. January is always 1.

void setNow()

Store the current date/time as the value of the object.

int timeDifference(lotus.notes.DateTime t2)

Returns the number of seconds between the current DateTime value and the one provided as an argument (subtracts the value of t2 from the current object's value). The two values are first normalized to a common time zone.

String toString()

Returns the result of the getLocalTime() method.

THE LOTUS.NOTES.DATERANGE CLASS

A DateRange simply represents a pair of DateTime objects, referred to as the start and end times. It provides a convenient way to format ranges as well. You create a DateRange object using the Session.createDateRange() call. If you use the flavor of createDateRange that takes no arguments, you get an "empty" DateRange. If you use the flavor that takes start and end DateTime objects, those objects are linked to the DateRange. If you modify either DateTime object after instantiating the DateRange, the value of the DateRange implicitly changes too. Be careful!

DateRange has no methods.

DateRange Properties

lotus.notes.DateTime getStartDateTime()
void setStartDateTime(lotus.notes.DateTime)
lotus.notes.DateTime getEndDateTime()
void setEndDateTime(lotus.notes.DateTime)

Accepts or returns the starting or ending DateTime object. If you use this technique to set the start and end values, then the DateTime objects are linked to the DateRange. When you (or any NOI method that takes a DateRange as input) accesses the value of the range, the current values for the starting and ending DateTime instances are used. Thus you can change the values of either DateTime object after linking it to the range, and the range's value implicitly changes.

Be sure not to modify the value of the range unintentionally, and also be sure not to make the starting time later than the ending time.

String getText()
void setText()

Sets or retrieves a value for the DateRange in text format. The text format for a date range is two DateTime strings (in whatever local date/time formats are supported), separated by a hyphen.

If you set the value of the range using a String, then any previously linked DateTime objects are unlinked, and new ones are generated. Thus, the following code fragment will correctly modify the ending value of the DateRange:

```
DateRange dr = s.createDateRange();
```

```
dr.setText("1/1/97 12:01 AM - 10/13/97 3:29 PM");
DateTime enddt = dr.getEndDateTime();
enddt.adjustDay(1);
```

String toString()

Returns the value of DateRange.getText().

SUMMARY

That concludes our coverage of the value-related classes. Be joyful, for you have now learned enough of the Java NOI to write interesting programs. Next, Chapter 5 continues with a discussion of still more NOI classes: Agent, AgentContext, International, Form, and Name.

5

NOI Part 4: Agent, AgentContext, International, Form, Name

This chapter discusses the classes relating to the Agent (but see Chapter 8 for a detailed discussion of how Agents are put together), AgentContext, International, Form and Name classes.

THE LOTUS.NOTES.AGENT CLASS

The Agent class represents the programmable aspects of Agents in Domino. You have the ability to locate, modify (to some extent), and execute Agent objects in a Database. See Chapter 1 for an overview of Agents and Chapter 8 for details on how they work.

You can locate Agent instances by using the Database.getAgents() and Database.getAgent() calls.

Agent Properties

String getComment()

Returns the comment string associated with the Agent. A comment can be entered or modified using the Agent Builder UI.

String getOwner()
String getCommonOwner()

Returns the name of the last person to sign the Agent. Agents are signed when they are first saved and whenever they are modified. The getOwner() call returns a fully distinguished (hierarchical) name. GetCommonOwner() returns only the "common" part of the user's name.

lotus.notes.DateTime getLastRun()

Returns a DateTime instance whose value is the date and time the Agent last ran. If the Agent has never run, getLastRun() returns a *null*.

String getName()

Returns the name of the Agent.

lotus.notes.Database getParent()

Returns the Database object in which the Agent lives.

String getQuery()

If a search query was entered when the Agent was created, this call returns it. If there is no query, it returns *null*.

NOI Part 4: Agent, AgentContext, International, Form, Name

String getServerName()

void setServerName(String name)

The ServerName property designates the name of the server on which the Agent is allowed to run. This property is necessary because Agents are design elements, and as such they replicate along with the rest of the Database they reside in. If an Agent was by default allowed to run on any server, a replicated Agent would run on every server to which its Database was replicated, causing all kinds of conflicts and other grief. When an Agent is created, the ServerName property defaults to the current machine. You can edit it to any server name, but only one name is allowed.

As of Domino Release 4.6, you can enter an asterisk ("*") for the server name to indicate that the Agent can run on any server. Be very careful, though, you should be sure that the Database does not replicate to any other server, or you should be sure that you've coded the Agent in such a way that it will never cause replication conflicts. For example, if your Agent only creates new Documents in the Database, you should be okay. If your Agent modifies existing Documents, you are definitely not okay.

If you modify the ServerName property you must invoke the Agent.save() method to commit your changes to disk.

boolean isEnabled()

void setEnabled(boolean flag)

Agents are enabled by default when they are created, if they are set up to run on a schedule (hourly, daily, etc.). The Enabled property has no meaning for Agents that are not scheduled. If you modify the Enabled property you must invoke the Agent.Save() method to commit your changes to disk.

boolean isPublic()

Returns *true* if the Agent is public, or "shared." If the Agent is not public, it can be seen or executed only by the person who created it.

Agent Methods

void remove()

Deletes the current Agent object from the Database.

void run()

Executes the Agent in the foreground. This is a synchronous call and will therefore "block" until the Agent is done. The Agent runs in the current process space, meaning that if you invoke this method from a program running on your workstation, the Agent code will be loaded into your machine's memory (regardless of where the Database containing the Agent lives) and run there. If you invoke this method from a background Agent running on a server, the Agent Manager process will load and execute the new Agent synchronously, suspending execution of the first Agent until the second is done.

Agents invoked this way on a client machine run with the privileges of the current user id. Agents invoked this way from background Agents run with the privileges of the signer, even if the signer of the second Agent is different from the first.

void save()

Saves the current Agent to disk. You must have Designer (or better) access to the Database, or this call will throw an exception.

The Agent is re-signed every time it is saved; therefore, this method will throw an exception if you invoke it from a server-based Agent (can't have just anyone signing Agents with the server's id, right?).

String toString()

Returns the name of the Agent.

THE LOTUS.NOTES.AGENTCONTEXT CLASS

As the name suggests, this class is only available to executing Agents. You get an instance of AgentContext from the Session class's getAgentContext() call (see Chapter 8 for details on how Agents are run by Domino). AgentContext is where all the information about the Agent's location and environment is accessed.

AgentContext Properties

lotus.notes.Agent getCurrentAgent()

Returns an instance of the current Agent object.

lotus.notes.Database getCurrentDatabase()

Returns an instance of the current Database, meaning the Database that the current Agent lives in.

lotus.notes.Document.getDocumentContext()

When an Agent is invoked via the Domino HTTP server, a "context document" is provided, containing the fields in the submitted form, plus a number of other data items (fully described in Chapter 11). The context document is available to the Agent as an instance of the NOI Document class, allowing you to access all the data in the form. You can add to or modify this Document, but the HTTP server ignores any modifications.

If you're writing an API program that uses the C API to execute an Agent, you can supply, as the HTTP server does, an in-memory note handle to the Agent API to serve as the context document. If your Agent adds or modifies Items in the Document, your API program could examine the Document after executing the Agent and make use of those changes.

String getEffectiveUserName()

When an Agent runs in the foreground (or in the background on a workstation), its privileges are those of the current user id. When an Agent runs in the background on a server, its privileges are those of the last signer of the Agent. One exception to this rule is that Agents invoked by the Domino HTTP server can run with the identity of the Web user instead of with the identity of the signer, if the Agent has been set up to do so (on the Agent Design properties box).

The EffectiveUserName property returns the name of the user under whose identity the Agent is running.

int getLastExitStatus()

Returns the status code stored with the Agent from the last time the Agent ran. A value of 0 means that the Agent executed without error.

lotus.notes.DateTime getLastRun()

Returns the date and time the Agent last ran (identical to the Agent.LastRun property).

NOI Part 4: Agent, AgentContext, International, Form, Name

lotus.notes.Document getSavedData()

When an Agent is created, Notes also creates a special Document to go along with it. The purpose of this Document is to allow Agents to store data persistently in the Database across Agent invocations. The "saved data" Document is a design element, not a data element, and so will never appear in any View. It is destroyed whenever its associated Agent is modified or deleted.

The advent of profile documents in Release 4.5 has by and large made use of the saved data document unnecessary. Access to the saved data document is not as efficient (for server Agents) as is access to profile documents, which are cached in the server's memory. Profile documents are saved forever, unlike saved data documents (which are deleted whenever the Agent is modified), making them a bit more generally useful. Saved data documents are also accessible only from their associated Agent (although you could have an Agent store the UNID of its saved data document somewhere, and then use that UNID later to access the saved data document directly), while profile documents are accessible from anywhere. They are still available, however, for compatibility reasons.

lotus.notes.DocumentCollection getUnprocessedDocuments()

The UnprocessedDocuments property is a DocumentCollection containing a set of Documents assembled at run time. The exact contents of the collection depend on how the Agent is configured:

- If the Agent is run from a View action button, and if the Agent is set up to run on "selected documents," then the collection contains the Documents that were selected in the View. You can access the current View by invoking Document.getParentView().

- If the Agent is scheduled and set up to run on "all documents that are new or modified since the Agent last ran," then the collection contains those Documents.
- If the Agent is set up to perform a search, the collection contains the results of the query.

For all other Agent configurations, this property will return an empty DocumentCollection.

AgentContext Methods

lotus.notes.DocumentCollection unprocessedFTSearch(String query, int maxdocs)

lotus.notes.DocumentCollection unprocessedFTSearch(String query, int maxdocs, int sortoptions, int otheroptions)

These calls are identical to the Database.FTSearch() calls, except that instead of operating on the entire Database, they operate only on the UnprocessedDocuments collection. They do not "refine" the UnprocessedDocuments collection by calling DocumentCollection.FTSearch(); instead they create a new collection instance.

lotus.notes.DocumentCollection unprocessedSearch(String query, lotus.notes.DateTime cutoff, int maxdocs)

This call is identical to the Database.Search() call, except that instead of operating on the entire Database, it operates only on the UnprocessedDocuments collection. It does not "refine" the UnprocessedDocuments collection by calling DocumentCollection.FTSearch(); instead it creates a new collection instance.

NOI Part 4: Agent, AgentContext, International, Form, Name

void updateProcessedDoc(lotus.notes.Document)

When an Agent is configured to operate on all Documents that are new or modified since the Agent last ran, the Agent gets a list of Documents called the *left to do list*. This list contains the set of Documents that the Agent has not yet processed. Agents set up this way must explicitly remove Documents from the left to do list; otherwise, those Documents will reappear in the list the next time the Agent runs.

The updateProcessedDoc() call does exactly that for a single Document. Another, often more convenient way to accomplish the same thing is to first get the UnprocessedDocuments collection, then invoke updateAll() on it. This is equivalent to invoking updateProcessedDoc() for every Document in the collection.

String toString()

Returns the effective user name for the current Agent.

THE LOTUS.NOTES.INTERNATIONAL CLASS

Like the AgentContext class, International provides contextual information, in this case about Domino's international settings. Some of the settings are specific to Domino, while others come from the operating system. The International class is composed of read-only properties—there are no methods.

International Properties

String getAMString()
String getPMString()

These strings are used for AM and PM in time formatting.

int getCurrencyDigits()

The number of decimal places used in number formatting.

String getCurrencySymbol()

The character or characters used to denote the local currency.

String getDateSep()
String getDecimalSep()
String getThousandsSep()
String getTimeSep()

The various characters used as separators in dates, times, and numbers.

int getTimeZone()

The current time zone. Might be positive or negative.

String getToday()
String getTomorrow()
String getYesterday()

Returns the strings used in the current language version of Domino for special day names.

boolean isCurrencySpace()

If *true*, indicates that the local currency format uses a space between the currency symbol and the number.

boolean isCurrencySuffix()

If *true*, indicates that the currency symbol follows the number. Otherwise, the currency symbol precedes the number.

boolean isCurrencyZero()

If *true*, indicates that currency amounts between 0 and 1 should have a 0 preceding the decimal point. For example, $0.15, rather than $.15.

boolean isDateDMY()
boolean isDateMDY()
boolean isDateYMD()

These three properties indicate in what order the year, month, and day components of a date are displayed. Only one of these calls will return *true* in any session.

boolean isDST()

If *true*, indicates that the time format reflects daylight savings time.

boolean isTime24Hour

If *true*, indicates that the time format is a 24-hour format.

THE LOTUS.NOTES.FORM CLASS

The Form class allows somewhat limited access to the characteristics of a form. You can create a form instance (though NOI does not currently allow you to create forms programmatically) by using the Database.getForms() and Database.getForm() calls.

Form Properties

java.util.Vector getAliases()

As with Views, a Form can have both a name and one or more aliases. When you create or modify a Form you can specify additional names for it in the Design Properties box. The names are separated from each other by vertical bars. The first name in the list is the name of the Form; the others are aliases. Also as with Views, the names can have underscores in them.

This call returns a Vector containing a String instance for each alias of the Form. If the Form has no aliases, an empty Vector is returned.

java.util.Vector getFields()

Returns a list of field names used in the Form. The list comes from an Item attached to the Form named "$Fields." The contents of this Item are not always up to date, so don't assume that it is always accurate.

java.util.Vector getFormUsers()
void setFormUsers(java.util.Vector users)
java.util.Vector getReaders()
void setReaders(java.util.Vector)

The FormUsers and Readers properties let you control who gets to create Documents using the Form (FormUsers) and who gets to have read access to Documents created with this Form (Readers).

Each property is a list of user and/or group names. If a user is not in the FormUsers list (or in a group that is in the list), then that user will not be able to see the Form name in the Create menu, or otherwise be able to create a Document using the form.

The Readers property works a bit differently. When Documents are created using the Form, the Readers list from the Form gets copied to the Documents as the default $Readers Item. Users who are in the list (or in a group that is in the list) will have Read access to the Document. The Document creator can modify the Document's Readers list in the Document Properties box before saving or sending the Document.

Setting either of these properties causes your change to be committed to disk immediately.

boolean isProtectReaders()
void setProtectReaders(boolean flag)
boolean isProtectUsers()
boolean setProtectUsers(boolean flag)

Setting the ProtectReaders and/or ProtectUsers properties to *true* mark the Readers and/or FormUsers lists as being protected from deletion or modification by the Replicator. Otherwise, it is possible that a new version of the Form will replicate into the database (or be brought in by the Design Refresh operation) and replace your Reader/User lists with its copy.

String getName()

Returns the name of the Form.

boolean isSubForm()

Returns *true* if the Form is a subform.

Form Methods

void remove()

Deletes the Form from the Database.

String toString()

Returns the name of the Form.

THE LOTUS.NOTES.NAME CLASS

The Name class is a nice little utility for parsing distinguished names. You create a Name object using the Session.createName() call, passing a String in as the argument. If the String is a hierarchical name, the Name properties will return various pieces of that name.

A fully distinguished name includes keyword tags designating special parts of the name as meaningful. For example the distinguished name CN=Bob Balaban/O=Looseleaf has two tags in it: the CN= part designates Bob Balaban as the common name, and the O= part designates Looseleaf as the organization. Lots of additional tags are available. For each of the Name properties, I've also provided the distinguished name tag that goes with it.

The Name class has no methods.

Name Properties

String getAbbreviated()

Returns the abbreviated form of the distinguished name. For example, CN=Bob Balaban/O=Looseleaf is returned as Bob Balaban/Looseleaf.

To go from an abbreviated form to a fully distinguished form, use the getCanonical() call.

String getADMD()

Returns the administration management domain name associated with the user name. The tag is A=. If there was no A= tag in the original name, this property returns *null*.

String getCanonical()

Returns the canonical (unabbreviated) form of the name.

String getCommon()

Returns the common part of the distinguished name. The tag is CN=.

String getCountry()

Returns the country part of the name. The tag is C=. If there was no C= tag in the original name, this property returns *null*.

String getGeneration()

Returns the generation part of the name, such as Jr. The tag is Q=. If there was no Q= tag in the original name, this property returns *null*.

String getGiven()

Returns the given name. The tag is G=. If there was no G= tag in the original name, this property returns *null*. There is no reliable way for NOI to parse a given name out of a common name, especially if you consider the international implications. Europeans are used to having a person's given name come first, but in many Asian languages the family name comes first. In the name Yip Wai-ki, for example, the given name is Wai-ki, the surname is Yip.

String getInitials()

Returns the initials belonging to the name. The tag is I=. If there was no I= tag in the original name, this property returns *null*.

String getKeyword()

Returns the part of the hierarchical name known as the *keyword*. The keyword consists of the following pieces of the name, if present, with backslash separators: country\organization\organizational unit 1\.organizational unit 2\.organizational unit 3\.organizational unit 4.

String getOrganization()

The organization, usually the company name. The tag is O=. If there was no O= tag in the original name, this property returns *null*.

String getOrgUnit1()
String getOrgUnit2()
String getOrgUnit3()
String getOrgUnit4()

Returns the specified organizational unit component. An organizational unit is usually a division, department or location identifier within an organization. Lotus, for example, uses office location as an organizational unit in its employees' Notes ids. The tag used for all organizational units is OU=, and you can have up to four of them in a name.

If there was no OU= tag in the original name, these properties return *null*.

NOI Part 4: Agent, AgentContext, International, Form, Name

String getPRMD()

Returns the Private Management Domain part of the name. The tag is P=. If there was no P= tag in the original name, this property returns *null*.

String getSurname()

The surname, or family name. The tag is S=. If there was no S= tag in the original name, this property returns *null*. There is no way for NOI to reliably parse the surname out of the common name.

boolean isHierarchical()

Returns *true* if the Name is hierarchical.

String toString()

Returns the canonical name.

SUMMARY

Whew, we're almost done with the reference part of the book. In this chapter we covered AgentContext, used often when writing Agents; the Agent class, useful for invoking Agents on the fly; and the International, Form, and Name classes, important when you need them and boring otherwise. Next, Chapter 6 concludes our in-depth discussion of NOI with the Registration, Newsletter, and Log classes.

6

NOI Part 5: Registration, Newsletter, Log

This chapter covers three additional utility classes. The Registration class gives you the ability to create and manage Notes id files, while the Newsletter class automates the generation of Documents containing lists of doclinks. The Log class is used to record the activity of LotusScript and Java programs to mail messages, disk files, or Notes databases.

THE LOTUS.NOTES.REGISTRATION CLASS

The Registration class is new in Domino 4.6. It allows you to create certifier, server, and workstation ids, to store them to and retrieve them from a server public address book, to re-certify and cross-certify ids, and to switch id files in the current session. You create a Registration instance with the Session.createRegistration() call.

The philosophy behind doing this class was to support small-to-medium id administration activities. For example, you might populate a Notes database with the names and other vital stats of a bunch of new users, then need an automated (yet customizable) way to generate new ids. You'd use the Registration class in a LotusScript or Java program to spin through the source database and generate an id for each user. The object model is such that this becomes pretty straightforward: you "pre-program" your Registration instance with the invariant information (certifier id, server name, type of id, and so on), then call a method with arguments that are specific to each new id.

There are so many options and "switches" that are relevant to generating a new id that it might be helpful to look at an example before going into the reference material on properties and methods. This example (see Listing 6.1) reads a few names out of a database and generates user ids. The registration server is the place where the public address book gets updated. We want to create new mail files automatically for each person, and add their id file to the address book, as well as have it on disk locally. The certifier id has already been created.

Listing 6.1 Registration Example (Ex61Reg.java)

```
import lotus.notes.*;
public class Ex61Reg
{
    public static void main(String argv¥)
        {
        try {
            NotesThread.sinitThread();
            Session s = Session.newInstance();
            Database db = s.getDatabase("", "book\\Ex61");
            View v = db.getView("New users");
            Document doc = v.getFirstDocument();
            v.setAutoUpdate(false);
```

```
Registration reg = s.createRegistration();

// set up the reg parameters that are always the same
reg.setCertifierIDFile("javatest.id");
reg.setNorthAmerican(true);
reg.setStoreIDInAddressBook(true);
reg.setUpdateAddressBook(true);
reg.setIDType(Registration.ID_CERTIFIER);
reg.setRegistrationLog("book\\certlog.nsf");
reg.setRegistrationServer("");

// expiration date is today + 2 years
DateTime expire = s.createDateTime("today");
expire.adjustYear(2);
reg.setExpiration(expire);

// get each new user document, check "processed"
String last;
String idfile;
String server = new String("");
String first;
String middle = null;
String certpw = "notvalid";
String location = "right here, of course";
String comment = "Created in Ex61Reg.java";
String maildb;
String fwd = null;
String userpw;
String orgunit;
DateTime now = s.createDateTime();

while (doc != null)
    {
    // extract the info we need
    String processed = doc.getItemValueString("processed");
    if (processed.equals("No"))
```

```java
                        {
                        last = doc.getItemValueString("lastname");
                        idfile = new String("c:\\tmp\\" + last + ".id");
                        first = doc.getItemValueString("firstname");
                        System.out.println("User " + first + " " + last +
                                " being processed.");
                        maildb = new String("mail\\" + last + ".nsf");
                        userpw = doc.getItemValueString("password");
                        orgunit = doc.getItemValueString("orgunit");
                        reg.setOrgUnit(orgunit);
                        boolean success = reg.registerNewUser(last, idfile,
                                                        server, first,
                                                        middle, certpw,
                                                        location, comment,
                                                        maildb, fwd,
                                                        userpw);
                        if (success)
                            {
                            // save the date
                            System.out.println("ID created.");
                            now.setNow();
                            Item date = doc.getFirstItem("processeddate");
                            date.setDateTimeValue(now);
                            doc.replaceItemvalue("processed", "Yes");
                            doc.save(true, false);
                            }
                        else System.out.println("Error: id not created");
                        } // end !processed
                    doc = v.getNextDocument(doc);
                    }   // end while
                }   // end try
        catch (Exception e) { e.printStackTrace(); }
        finally { NotesThread.stermThread(); }
        }   // end main
    }   // end class
```

Discussion of Example

This is a somewhat lengthy example, mainly because there are so many registration options to deal with. Let's go through it in some detail so that you get a picture of how it works, and then you can go ahead and browse the following reference material.

The database Ex61.nsf (included in the CD) is used. It contains "new user" records for four people. Each record contains the person's first and last names, as well as his or her organizational unit (a subdivision of the organization; three users are in the "Angels" group, one is in the "Devils" group), and an initial password. Each user will, of course, change her or his password later. Each record also contains a *Processed* keyword field (Yes/No, defaulting to No), and a processed date, which the program will fill in.

Setting up the Registration instance is pretty simple, though the interaction of the various settings can be subtle. Outside the main loop we set up the parameters that don't change from user to user:

- ❐ The certifier id to use.
- ❐ The encryption type.
- ❐ We want to update the server address book with person records for the new users.
- ❐ We want to store the id files in the address book.
- ❐ The id type (flat/hierarchical) is set to whatever the certifier id is.
- ❐ We designate the current machine as the registration server.

Be careful if you use the local machine as the registration server, as in this example: My sample Java program ran under the auspices of my admin id, not under the server id, so the person records contained my name instead of the server's.

We also want to set a rolling expiration date, as opposed to a hardwired one, so we just initialize a DateTime object to "today" and add two years. If we were being good about writing the code so that it would work in any country (believe it or not, "today" is not a universal term), we could create an instance of the International class (Session.createInternational()), and use whatever word was returned by the getToday() call.

Other parameters to the registration method that we'll be calling also don't change per user (certifier password, location, and comment), and these are initialized before the loop as well.

The outer loop in the sample is a simple one: traverse the View for all Documents, and ignore any that have already been processed (contents of the processed Item is not "No"). For each unprocessed Document, we need to extract the per-user information: first and last name, password, and organizational unit. We also construct on the fly an id file name and a mail database name (though we didn't specify that we wanted mail databases to be created, so they won't in this example).

Note that OrgUnit is a property, not a parameter to the registration method; it's the only property that we modify for each user. The registerNewUser() call returns a boolean value of *true* for success. If the id was registered successfully, we want to update that person's record. We update the time stamp in the "now" DateTime instance by calling setNow(), then get the "processeddate" Item from the Document, and modify the Item's value from the DateTime object directly. We could, in theory, have used Document.replaceItemValue and also passed the DateTime object there. After saving the current Document with our modifications, we get the next one in the View.

The program runs just fine from a command line prompt. We supplied the certifier password in the code, so Notes doesn't have to prompt us for it (it does prompt if the certifier id you use requires a password and you didn't specify one in the registration call).

Registration Properties

String getCertifierIDFile()
void setCertifierIDFile(String filepath)

Get or set the location of the certifier id file that you will be using to create new server or user ids. Use either a platform-specific or "canonical" (defined as PC syntax) path name for the certifier id file. The file must be on disk; you can't specify a certifier file that lives in an address book.

boolean getCreateMailDb()
void setCreateMailDb(boolean flag)

Set this option to *true* if you want mail databases automatically created for new user ids at the same time the id is created. The default for this setting is *false*.

lotus.notes.DateTime getExpiration()
void setExpiration(lotus.notes.DateTime date)

Get or set the expiration date for new server or user ids.

int getIDType()
void setIDType(int type)

The id type tells NOI how to generate the names of new users and servers when you create new ids. It is a constant and must be one of the following:

- ❒ Registration.ID_FLAT. Generate flat (nonhierarchical) names.
- ❒ Registration.ID_HIERARCHICAL. Generate hierarchical names.

❏ Registration.ID_CERTIFIER. Generate flat names if the certifier id has a flat name, else generate hierarchical names. This is the default.

int getMinPasswordLength()
void setMinPasswordLength(int length)

Get or set the minimum password length that a user must provide when he or she changes their password. This limit does not apply to the initial password that you can specify when you create a new id using the Registration class.

If you don't specify a minimum length, NOI uses the certifier's minimum password length. You can specify 0, but it isn't recommended.

String getOrgUnit()
void setOrgUnit(String name)

Get or set the organizational unit part of the new id's name. This is the "OU=" part of a distinguished name. The organization part of the id ("O=") will, of course, come from the certifying id.

String getRegistrationLog()
void setRegistrationLog(String dbname)

Query or specify the name of the database used to log registration information. If you specify this property, you must specify the name of a database that was created from the certlog.ntf template. NOI adds entries to this database whenever you create new id files.

To be honest, I've never been able to get this property to do anything. It's an open problem report at Iris. We hope it'll be fixed in a point release.

String getRegistrationServer()
void setRegistrationServer()

Specify or query the name of the server whose public address book will be updated as a result of creating new user or server ids. If you are running your program on the server that you want to be the registration server, just specify "" for this property. If the registration server is another server, and that server is not available when you run your program or Agent, then NOI will throw an exception.

boolean getStoreIDInAddressBook()
void setStoreIDInAddressBook(boolean flag)

The default behavior is to create an id file on disk, at a location that you specify. Set this property to *true* if you also want newly created ids to be stored in the registration server's public address book. The id will still be created on disk too.

Note that setting this property to *true* has no effect unless you also set the UpdateAddressBook property, because unless a record is created in the database, there's no place to attach the id file.

boolean getUpdateAddressBook()
void setUpdateAddressBook(boolean flag)

Set this property to *true* if you want id creation to automatically update the registration server's public address book when new certifier, server, or user ids are created. A new person/server/certifier record is added to the database.

boolean isNorthAmerican()

void setNorthAmerican()

If this property is *true* (the default), then a North American id will be created. Otherwise, an international id is created. The difference is primarily in the length of the encryption keys used: North American ids have 64 bit keys, while international ids have smaller keys. The international version of Domino/Notes requires the use of international ids, because of United States Department of Defense restrictions on the export of encryption software (write your Senator or Congressperson!).

Registration Methods

boolean addCertifierToAddressBook(String idfile)

boolean addCertifierToAddressBook(String idfile, String password, String location, String comment)

Adds the specified certifier id file to the server's public address book, using the RegistrationServer property to figure out which server to use. If you don't supply a password and the id file requires one, then NOI will prompt you at run time.

If you have set the StoreIDInAddressBook property (and the UpdateAddressBook property), then NOI will attach the id file to the new record in the address book. Returns *true* if successful.

boolean addServerToAddressBook(String idfile, String server, String domain)

boolean addServerToAddressBook(String idfile, String server, String domain, String password, String network, String adminname, String title, String location, String comment)

This method takes an existing server id and creates a new entry for it in the registration server's public address book, using the RegistrationServer property to figure out which server to use. If you don't supply a password and the id file requires one, then NOI will prompt you at run time.

If you have set the StoreIDInAddressBook property (and the UpdateAddressBook property), then NOI will attach the id file to the new record in the address book. Returns *true* if successful.

void addUserProfile(String username, String profilename)

Given the name of a user who already has a Person entry in the server public address book (NOI uses the RegistrationServer property to select which server to check), this call adds the name of a user profile to that person's record. The "profile" name should in no way be confused with "profile documents" referenced elsewhere in this book (see, for example, the Database.createProfileDocument() call in Chapter 2). It refers instead to a "setup profile," stored by name in the server's public address book. The content of a setup profile is a subset of the fields in the Person record. You can use setup profiles to create standard user configurations, and not have to manually add each field for each user.

Adding a profile name to a Person record copies the data from the profile entry to the user's entry in the address book.

boolean addUserToAddressBook(String idfile, String fullname, String lastname)

boolean addUserToAddressBook(String idfile, String fullname, String lastname, String password, String firstname, String middle, String mailserver, String mailfile, String fwdaddr, String location, String comment)

This method takes an existing user id and creates a new entry for it in the registration server's public address book, using the RegistrationServer property to figure out which server to use. If you don't supply a password and the id file requires one, then NOI will prompt you at run time.

If you have set the StoreIDInAddressBook property (and the UpdateAddressBook property), then NOI will attach the id file to the new record in the address book.

boolean crossCertify(String idfile)

boolean crossCertify(String idfile, String certpw, String comment)

The crossCertify() call adds a cross certificate for the specified id file to the registration server's public address book. If the server's certification id requires a password and you do not supply one, NOI will prompt for it at run time.

void deleteIDOnServer(String username, boolean isserverid)

Deletes the id file attachment from the record (either a user or a server) belonging to the name you provide. If the name is a user name, set the "isserverid" parameter to *false*. You must have Editor access to the registration server's public address book. The rest of the record is not modified, only the id file attachment is deleted.

void getIDFromServer(String username, String filepath, boolean isserverid)

If the registration server's public name and address book contains a record for the name you specify (either a user or a server name), and if that record contains an id file attachment, this call will extract the id file to the specified disk location on the current machine. Use *true* for the "isserverid" parameter if the name you pass in is a server name. Use *false* if the name you provide is a user name.

NOI Part 5: Registration, Newsletter, Log

void getUserInfo(String username, String mailserver, String mailfile, String maildomain, String mailsystem, String profile)

Embarrassingly, this call does not work at all in the Java NOI (but at least it doesn't crash). The point of it (and it does work in LotusScript) was to return information from the registration server's public address book on the specified user entry, using a very efficient lookup mechanism. The fact that this routine didn't work didn't come to light until late in the release cycle for 4.6. It will be fixed in a future point release.

A perfectly good workaround (though a bit less efficient) is to go to the registration server's address book directly (names.nsf), get the People view, and use View.getDocumentByKey() to find the correct record. Then just get the data directly from the appropriate Items.

boolean recertify(String idfile)

boolean recertify(String idfile, String certpw, String comment)

This call re-certifies an expired id file, using the certifier id specified in the CertifierIDFile property. If the certification id requires a password, you can either provide one in the expanded version of this call, or let Notes prompt you for it when you run the program. Set the new expiration date using the Expiration property.

boolean registerNewCertifier(String org, String idfile, String password)

boolean registerNewCertifier(String org, String idfile, String password, String country)

This call creates a new certifier id file. You must specify the RegistrationServer property, this is the server whose public address book will be updated. If you want a new entry made for this new id in the address book, set the UpdateAddressBook property to *true*. If you want the certifier id file attached to the certifier record, set the StoreIDInAddressBook property to *true* also.

The "org" parameter is required, and represents the organization name ("O=" part of a distinguished name) for the id. All user and server ids created with this certifier will have the same organization, if the ids are hierarchical. The organization name must be at least three characters. The "idfile" parameter specifies a disk location for the new id file, it is a required argument. The password is optional, but highly recommended.

This call always creates a hierarchical certifier. If you really want a flat certifier (not recommended), you have to do it through the Notes UI.

The return value will be *true* if the call was successful.

boolean registerNewServer(String server, String idfile, String domain, String password)

boolean registerNewServer(String server, String idfile, String domain, String password, String certpw, String location, String comment, String network, String adminname, String title)

The registerNewServer() method creates a new server id. The "server" (server name), "idfile" (disk location to write the id file) and "domain" (domain name) arguments are required, the others are all optional (though it is highly recommended that you always supply a password too). The "location," "comment," "network," "adminname" (administrator's name), and "title" simply go into the appropriate fields of the server record in the registration server's public address book (if you turn on the UpdateAddressBook property). If you set the StoreIDInAddressBook property to *true*, then the new id file is attached to the server record as well as being written to disk.

If you have not set the RegistrationServer or CertifierIDFile properties, an exception is thrown. If the certifier id requires a password, you can either supply it in the registerNewServerCall() or let Notes prompt for it at run time. The type of id generated (flat or hierarchical) is controlled by the setting of the IDType property (default is TYPE_CER-TIFIER, which follows the id type of the certifier id).

The return value is *true* if the call is successful.

boolean registerNewUser(String lastname, String idfile, String server)

boolean registerNewuser(String lastname, String idfile, String server, String firstname, String middle, String certpw, String location, String comment, String maildbpath, String fwdaddr, String password)

The registerNewUser() method creates a new user id. The "lastname," "idfile" (disk location to write the id file) and "server" (server name) arguments are required, the others are all optional (though it is highly recommended that you always supply a password too). The "firstname," "middle" (middle name/initials), "location," "comment," and "fwdaddr" (forwarding address) simply go into the appropriate fields of the person record in the registration server's public address book (if you turn on the UpdateAddressBook property).

If you set the StoreIDInAddressBook property to *true*, then the new id file is attached to the server record as well as being written to disk. If you turn on the CreateMailDb property and supply a location for the "maildbpath" parameter, then a new mail database will automatically be created (on the server specified in the "server" argument) when the id is generated.

You must supply the CertifierIDFile and RegistrationServer properties. If the certifier id requires a password, you can pass it in in the registerNewUser() call, or let Notes prompt for it at run time. Note that the registration server is not necessarily the same as the user's default server. The registration server is the one where the public address book (typically the master address book for the domain) lives, the "server" argument in this call only specifies where the user's mail database lives (although the argument is required even if you aren't creating a mail database for the user, because the user's "home" server information is needed in the public address book).

The type of id generated (flat or hierarchical) is controlled by the setting of the IDType property (default is TYPE_CERTIFIER, which follows the id type of the certifier id).

The return value is *true* if the call is successful.

String switchToID(String idfile, String password)

The switchToID() call has only one required argument, the disk location of the id file to which you want to switch the current session. If that id file doesn't require a password, or if you want Notes to prompt for the password at run time, use "" for the "password" argument.

The following steps are performed:

- ❐ Locate the new id file, read it into memory.
- ❐ Validate the input password. If it is missing or incorrect, prompt for a password.
- ❐ Close all server and database connections for the current id.
- ❐ Make the new id the current one

The return value of the call, if successful, is the name associated with the new id.

THE LOTUS.NOTES.NEWSLETTER CLASS

The Newsletter class is used to format a collection of Documents in a couple of different ways. You create a Newsletter instance with the Session.createNewsletter() call, passing in a DocumentCollection instance (required). The Newsletter instance then operates on that collection. The two methods on this class both return new Document instances, one with a rendering of the specified Document in the input collection, the other containing a doclink for each of the Documents in the collection. The Newsletter properties control the selection and formatting of the output.

If you refer back to Chapter 2, where we discussed full text searching on a Database, you'll recall that the DocumentCollection returned by a full text search on a single Database and the one returned by a search on a multi-database index are somewhat different. The first simply contains a list of note ids for all the Documents, which are all in the same Database. The second kind contains the equivalent of a doclink for each Document in the collection, because each could be in a different Database. If you instantiate a Document from a collection resulting from a multi-database search, you might be incurring a lot of extra overhead, because the referenced Database might not be open yet.

Believe it or not, there's actually a reason for bringing this up now: If you create a Newsletter instance with a DocumentCollection that contains the results of a multi-database search, you get very high efficiency when you generate a *newsletter* Document from it (see below). The reason is that the *doclinks* in the collection are simply transferred to the newsletter; the referenced Documents (and Databases) do not have to be opened. All the information needed to generate the Newsletter is contained in the DocumentCollection.

Newsletter Properties

String getSubjectItemName()
void setSubjectItemName()

When you create a *newsletter* (Document containing doclinks for each input Document in the collection), you don't want just a row of doclinks, you need some kind of tag line for each one. And, of course, you'd like each link's tag line to come from the individual Document.

This property tells the Newsletter class which Item on the Document to use for the tag line (for single-database result sets). It should be the name of an Item that contains text (or something that can be coerced to text), and the Item should (ideally) be present in all Documents in the collection. That isn't always possible, though, because the Documents resulting from a full text search might very well come from different Views, and be created using different forms. If the specified tag Item is not found for a given Document, the link is still included, but the tag line will be empty.

This property is ignored when the input collection is the result of a multi-database search. In that case the tag line is formatted automatically (see the description of formatMsgWithDoclinks(), below).

boolean isDoScore()

void setDoScore(boolean flag)

If this property is *true*, the relevance score associated with each Document in the result set is displayed in the newsletter. Be aware, however, that the relevance score is only included in the results of a full text search when the Database on which the search was performed has a full text index. Otherwise the score will always be 0. The default setting is *true*.

boolean isDoSubject()

void setDoSubject(boolean flag)

The property controls (for single-database searches) whether or not a tag line will appear for each doclink in the newsletter. For multi-database search results, the tag line always appears. The default setting is *true*.

Newsletter Methods

lotus.notes.Document formatDocument(lotus.notes.Database destination, int index)

This method takes a single Document in the collection of search results (specified by the *index* parameter, which is a 1-based index), and essentially sets up a new Document instance with the contents of the source Document rendered in it, similar to what you get when you do a Forward operation on a mail message. The steps that this method goes through are:

- ❏ Create a new Document instance. If a "destination" Database was passed in, the new Document is created in that Database. Otherwise the new Document is created in the current user's default mail Database. This can be a problem for background Agents, because (a) you might not want the new Document created in the *signer's* mail Database, and (b) the default mail Database might be on a different server from the one where the Agent is running, and the Agent will therefore be unable to open it (this is a security restriction on background Agents). It is recommended (for performance if nothing else) that you always supply a Database. If you're going to invoke send() (without saving) on the resulting Document, then it really doesn't matter which Database it's created in anyway.
- ❏ Create a new RichTextItem named "Body" on the new Document.
- ❏ Use the Document.renderToRTItem() method to render the source Document into the new RichTextItem on the destination Document.

The new ("destination") Document is returned if the call is successful.

lotus.notes.Document formatMsgWithDoclinks(lotus.notes.Database destination)

This is the method that creates a newsletter containing a tag line and a doclink for each Document in the collection of search results. The format of the output Document depends on what type of search was done (single- or multi-database), and on how you set up the Newsletter properties.

For single-database queries, you have the option (see the description of Database.FTSearch() in Chapter 2) of sorting the result set by relevance score or by date. The DoScore property controls whether this column will appear in the output Document. Relevance scores will always be 0 if the source Database does not have a full text index. If the Documents are sorted by date, the creation date is used.

If the DoSubject property is set and an Item name was provided in the SubjectItemName property, then the contents of that Item (if it exists on the Document) are used as the tag line. If the Item does not contain text, the contents of the Item are converted to text for you automatically.

For multi-database search results, the sort key column and the tag line column are always displayed. The sort key column is the same as that which exists for single-database searches (either the relevance score or the Document creation date). The tag line is the "summary" line stored for the Document in the multi-database index, if one can be found. There are cases where the Document has no summary line. For example, the current user's access to the Database where the Document lives was less than Reader, or the Database had no designated default View. In that case, the name of the database (in parentheses) where the Document lives is used as the tag line.

It all sounds kind of confusing, but let's do two examples (one single-database search and one multi-database), and show you some screen shots of how the output is formatted.

The first example (Listing 6.2) takes a simple discussion database, does a search on it, and formats a newsletter with doclinks to the results.

Listing 6.2 Newsletter Example (Ex62News1.java)

```java
import lotus.notes.*;
public class Ex62News1
{
    public static void main(String argv¥)
        {
        try {
            NotesThread.sinitThread();
            Session s = Session.newInstance();
            Database db = s.getDatabase("", "book\\Ex62.nsf");
            DocumentCollection dc = db.FTSearch("java", 0,
                                Database.FT_SCORES,
                                Database.FT_STEMS+
                                Database.FT_THESAURUS);
            Newsletter nl = s.createNewsletter(dc);

            // store results in another db
            Database output = s.getDatabase("", "book\\Ex62output");

            // pick an item in both main and response docs
            nl.setDoSubject(true);
            nl.setDoScore(true);
            nl.setSubjectItemName("newslettersubject");
            Document result = nl.formatMsgWithDoclinks(output);

            // add the query and form name as separate items
            result.appendItemValue("query", "java");
            result.appendItemValue("form", "newsletter");
            result.save(true, false);
            } // end try
        catch (Exception e) { e.printStackTrace(); }
        finally { NotesThread.stermThread(); }
        }  // end main
}  // end class
```

Chapter 6

The output newsletter is saved in a different Database (Ex62output.nsf, also on the CD). The newsletter is in Figure 6.1.

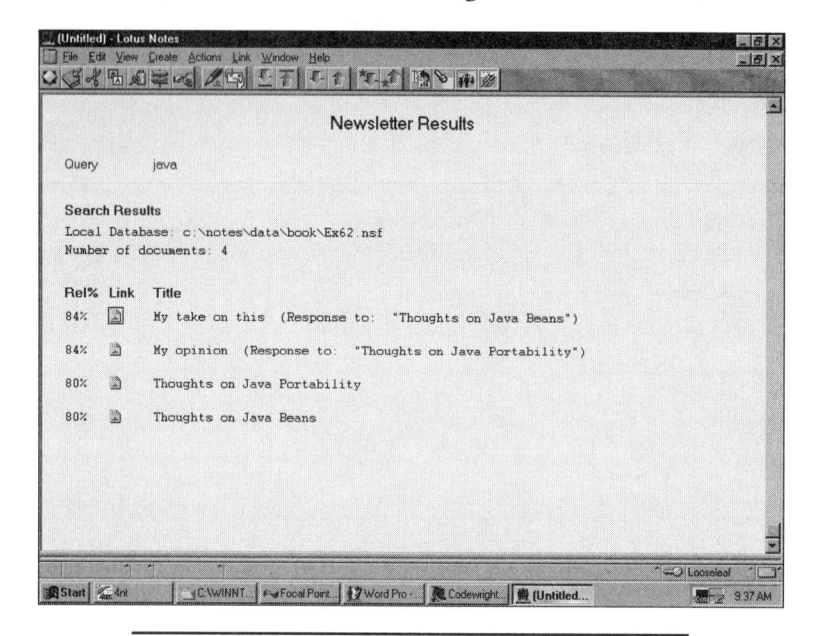

Figure 6.1 Newsletter result from single database search.

Figure 6.2 shows what happens when we do a similar thing, but use a multi-database index instead.

Listing 6.3 Multi-Database Newsletter Example (Ex63News2.java)

```
import lotus.notes.*;
public class Ex63News2
{
    public static void main(String argv¥)
        {
        try {
            NotesThread.sinitThread();
            Session s = Session.newInstance();
            Database db = s.getDatabase("", "book\\Ex63.nsf");
```

```
            DocumentCollection dc = db.FTSearch("java", 0,
                           Database.FT_DATE_ASC,
                           Database.FT_STEMS+
                           Database.FT_THESAURUS);
            Newsletter nl = s.createNewsletter(dc);

            // store results in another db
            Database output = s.getDatabase("", "book\\Ex62output");

            nl.setDoScore(true);
            Document result = nl.formatMsgWithDoclinks(output);

            // add the query and form name as separate items
            result.appendItemValue("query", "java");
            result.appendItemValue("form", "newsletter");
            result.save(true, false);
            } // end try
        catch (Exception e) { e.printStackTrace(); }
        finally { NotesThread.stermThread(); }
        } // end main
    } // end tclass
```

You'll notice two differences in the output of this example (Figure 6.2): The doclinks are sorted by date instead of by relevance score (that's not an accident—we requested it that way in the second Java program), and the tag lines are different. Instead of some text from the subject item in each Document, the multi-database search results Newsletter shows only the name of the Database in which each Document lives, in parentheses. That's because in each case the matching text (the text that's indexed) is contained in a RichTextItem, not in a plain text Item. Thus, it can't be stored in the search site index. Instead we just get the Database name.

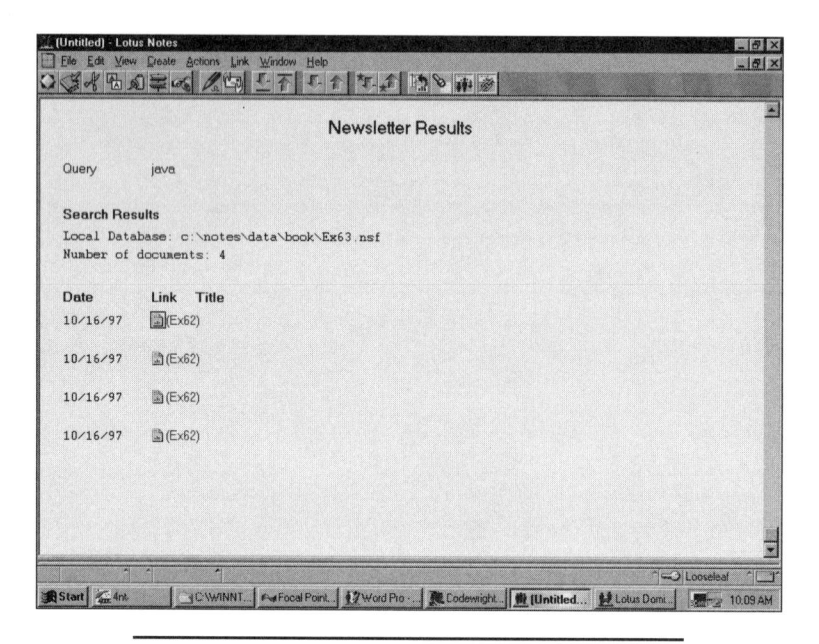

Figure 6.2 Newsletter result from multi database search.

The multi-database (or "search site") index is contained in the Database Ex63.nsf. I went through my *site* (the example databases I put together for this book) and marked a bunch of the databases as "include in multi-database indexing" by bringing up the Database Properties box, selecting the Design tab and checking off the option. Then I created a "Search Scope Configuration" document in the multi-db index database (Ex63.nsf) and set it to index all relevant database on the server. Then I just created the full text index on Ex63, and ran my Java program.

There is another significant difference between the single- and multi-database search Newsletters: In order to create the single search doclinks, each Document is opened and queried for the relevant information, especially for the tag line. In the multi-database search case, all the information needed to create the Newsletter entry is stored in the search results; the Documents are not opened Thus, multi-database newsletters are faster to generate than single-database newsletters. Go figure.

THE LOTUS.NOTES.LOG CLASS

The Log class is another bundle of utilities, this time aimed at allowing you to conveniently log "actions" and "errors" during the execution of a program. You specify whether you want your log output to go to any of:

- A Notes database
- A mail message
- A disk file
- A network message queue
- The current Agent's log

You create Log instances using the Session.createLog() method, optionally passing a *program name*, basically any string by which you want the Log identified. The program name is prepended to all output messages.

Any Log instance can support multiple simultaneous output streams. You can, for example, invoke openFileLog(), openMailLog(), and openNotesLog() all on the same instance. Each logAction() or logEvent() call will then write output to three streams. No outputs are open by default.

Log Properties

int getNumActions()
int getNumErrors()

Returns the number or errors or actions that have been logged so far.

String getProgramName()
void setProgramName(String name)

Retrieve or reset the program name associated with this Log instance. The name can be set at Log create time in the Session.createLog() call, or can be set/overridden using this property. The program name is prepended to all output messages.

boolean isLogActions()
void setLogActions(boolean flag)
boolean isLogErrors()
void setLogErrors(boolean flag)

These properties control whether errors and actions are actually logged. If they are on, then all calls to logAction() and logError() will result in messages being output. If they are off, then calls to logAction() and logError() are ignored. Useful for turning logging on and off dynamically during a program's execution. Both are on by default.

boolean isOverwriteFile()
void setOverwriteFile(boolean flag)

When you call the openFileLog() method you specify the file that will receive the output messages. If a file of the same name already exists, this property will control whether that file is overwritten, or appended to. The only time this property's setting has any meaning is when the openFileLog() method is called, so make sure you set it first. The default value is *false*.

Should this option have been an argument on the openFileLog() call instead of a separate property? Yeah, probably.

Log Methods

void close()

Closes the Log and flushes all output. The instance is not destroyed when you do this, so you can reuse the Log by invoking any of the open methods again.

void logAction(String message)

void logError(int code, String message)

Logs actions and errors to the Log instance's output stream or streams. The message can be any String. The error code can be any integer. You can, for example, use the text and error code contained in a NotesException instance that you *catch*. No translation of the error code is done, it is logged as a number.

void logEvent(String text, String queue, int event, int severity)

This method is not often used, but can be useful in certain cases. For one thing, it only works on servers where event reporting is enabled. Secondly, you have to know the name of a relevant event queue when you write the program, or else acquire it somewhere at run time.

When you log an *event* you specify the text of a message, as with actions and errors. You also supply the name of an event queue on which to place the event, and event and severity codes. The valid event codes are:

- Log.EV_ALARM
- Log.EV_ COMM
- Log.EV_ MAIL
- Log.EV_ MISC

- Log.EV_ REPLICA
- Log.EV_ RESOURCE
- Log.EV_ SECURITY
- Log.EV_ SERVER
- Log.EV_ UNKNOWN
- Log.EV_ UPDATE

There is no checking done to to verify the event code you use (so long as it is one from this list), it's pretty much up to you. Make sure that you use something that's reasonable and understood by your intended recipient.

The valid severity codes are:

- Log.SEV_FAILURE
- Log.SEV_ FATAL
- Log.SEV_ NORMAL
- Log.SEV_ UNKNOWN
- Log.SEV_ WARNING1
- Log.SEV_ WARNING2

void openAgentLog()

This call is only valid when the current program is an Agent with a valid AgentContext. If you invoke it from any other kind of program, NOI will throw an exception. If the openAgentLog() call is made on a Log instance, all logged errors and messages will be appended to the Agent's log, which you can view by selecting the **Agent** in the Agent View UI, then selecting **Agent/Log** from the menu.

This call can be made in either foreground or background Agents. The output stream is flushed when the Agent terminates, or when you invoke the close() method.

void openFileLog(String filespec)

This method causes action and error output to go to the specified disk file. If, when you invoke openFileLog(), a file of the same name already exists on disk, then the behavior of this method is controlled by the OverwriteFile property:

- If OverwriteFile is *true*, the existing file is overwritten
- If OverwriteFile is *false*, new output is appended to it.

This method cannot be used from a background Agent running on a server unless the signer of the Agent is designated to have "unrestricted" privileges in the server's entry in the public address book. Restricted Agents are not allowed to access disk files.

The output stream is flushed either when the close() method is invoked, or (if the Log instance is used in an Agent) when the Agent terminates. If you are using the Log instance from an Application, the output stream is flushed when the Session's NotesThread instance terminates.

void openMailLog(java.util.Vector recipients, String subject)

This method tells the Log instance to create and keep track of a Document instance that will be used to collect all output messages. The message text is appended to a RichTextItem named "Body."

You must supply a recipients list when you invoke this method, because there is no way for you to add one later (you never get to see the mail Document). The recipients list is stored in the SendTo Item for later mailing. You can optionally supply a String that is stored in the Subject Item. This is the line that is typically displayed in most mail database Inbox views.

Output to the Document is flushed either when the close() method is called or when the Session's NotesThread instance terminates. The Document is mailed at that time also. There is no way to cancel mailing of the Document created by openMailLog() once you've called this method.

void openNotesLog(String server, String database)

This method causes output to go to the specified Notes database. Each message (action or error) causes a new Document to be created in the database, and the message is split up into multiple Items in each Document.

There is a standard template (alog4.ntf) that you can use to create databases that are suitable for this kind of output. The template contains one view and one form, named "Log Entry". The Items that are written to this form by the Log class are:

- A$LOGTIME. The date/time the message was logged.
- A$PROGNAME. The program name.
- A$USER. The user id.
- A$ACTION. The action message, if any.
- A$ERRCODE. The error code, if any.
- A$ERRMSG. The error message, if any.

You can, of course, have Notes database output go to any database, it's just more convenient to use one generated from the template, or to copy the form from that database to another one that you want to use.

String toString()

Returns the Log instance's program name.

SUMMARY

Congratulations! You've made it all the way through the play by play (blow by blow?) on all 23 Domino classes. Smile! The next chapter talks about how to write Java applications using NOI, and Chapter 8 tells you how to write Agents using NOI.

7

WRITING NOI APPLICATIONS

If you've been checking out the examples in all the previous chapters, you've already become familiar with how to write a Java program that runs from your command line and manipulates Notes objects. We'll review the basic techniques again in this chapter, then go on to show how to write interesting multithreaded Applications. This chapter sticks to topics having to do with writing Applications, while Chapter 8 covers the technology specific to Agents.

SINGLE-THREADED APPLICATIONS USING NOI

A single-threaded application is easy—all the examples up until now have been such. The only thing you need to remember is to initialize and terminate the current thread in your class's *main* function using the static NotesThread calls sinitThread() and stermThread() (the latter should be invoked from a *finally* block for maximum safety). Listing 7.1 is a skeleton NOI application that does nothing but start up, print a message, and shut down:

Listing 7.1 Skeleton Single-Threaded Application

```
import java.lang.*;
import java.util.*;
import lotus.notes.*;
public class Skeleton1
{
    public static void main(String argv[])
       {
       try {
           NotesThread.sinitThread();
           System.out.println("Hello World!");
           }
       catch (Exception e) { e.printStackTrace(); }
       finally { NotesThread.stermThread(); }
       } // end main
} // end class
```

Naturally in this example the NotesThread init/term calls are completely unnecessary since we haven't created any Notes objects. Still, this very simple example has a few points worth emphasizing, even if you're familiar with Java, so that the topics we cover later are more comprehensible:

- ❐ This is a true application, as distinct from Agent, applet, or servlet. Its *main* function is invoked directly from the Java interpreter, and you start it by typing *java Skeleton1* on the command line.

- ❐ The import statement for java.lang.* is redundant, because Java always gives you those classes anyway. The import statements for java.util.* and lotus.notes.* are most definitely *not* redundant; you need them in order to use any of the java.util classes (most notably Vector, but there are others that are pretty useful) or any of the Notes classes.

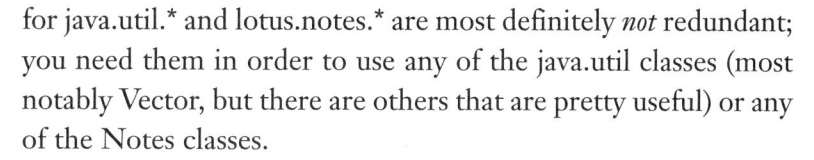

- ❐ The *main* function has to be *static*, meaning that no instance of the Skeleton1 class exists when Java runs the program. We'll see what effect this has on us later.

- ❐ The input argument to *main* is reminiscent of C, except that there's just an argv, no argc. You don't need the argument count as a separate parameter, as you do in C, because all arrays in Java have a built-in *length* field you can use to query the size of the array. Argv will contain any input arguments from the command line, always passed in as Strings.

- ❐ The Notes initialization and termination that we're doing are only valid for the current thread, the one on which *main* is invoked.

- ❐ The System.out stream is predefined and set up by Java. We can write to it and not really care where it goes. In the case of a command line program such as this, it goes to the window that launched the program. Likewise, we can read from the "console" window using System.in.

- ❐ When the *main* function ends, the current (and only) thread terminates, and you're back in the console window staring at a "Hello World!" message.

In a real application you'd replace the System.out.println call with all of your program's logic, probably complete with manipulation of other classes, including possibly some NOI classes. The Skeleton framework, however, is still good enough to get you going in all cases, so long as you only ever need one thread.

Skeleton Multithreaded Program

But what if you want to (or like to) use more than one thread to execute your Application's logic? There are lots of reasons why you'd want to do that: You can achieve greater parallelism by executing two or more tasks simultaneously, especially when one or more of them is subject to long delays waiting for network or disk i/o. Any program that accesses the Internet, for example, is subject to delays while it waits for a response from some distant and overloaded server. Even if your Application is just doing a lot of disk i/o, you'd be surprised how much of the total run time your program spends waiting for the disk to spin to the proper location so that the magnetic head can catch a few bytes of data at a time.

Multithreaded programming is one of the really strong points of Java; the language has lots of built in constructs and utilities that make it pretty simple to deal with. Let's do another skeleton, this time with the basics for a multithreaded NOI Application.

Listing 7.2 Skeleton Multithreaded Example Using NotesThread

```
import java.util.*;
import lotus.notes.*;
public class Skeleton2 extends NotesThread
{
    public static void main(String argv[])
       {
       try {
           Skeleton2 s2 = new Skeleton2();
           s2.start();
           s2.join();
           }
       catch (Exception e) { e.printStackTrace(); }
       } // end main
public void runNotes()
```

```
        {
        System.out.println("Postcard from Another Thread");
        }
}  // end class
```

The most interesting part of this version of Skeleton is that our *main* program creates an instance of the class that it is declared in, then calls the *start* method on it. The Skeleton2 class extends (inherits from) lotus.notes.NotesThread, not java.lang.Thread. The reason for this is simple: Notes is not completely (or even mostly) implemented in Java, although it is a product that runs portably on many different operating systems. It requires some setup and shutdown *per thread*, not just per process. The best way to both ensure that this happens and that it isn't too inconvenient for you, the NOI programmer, was to invent the NotesThread class. It handles the per-thread initialization and teardown of Notes for you, and in all other respects is exactly like java.lang.Thread, which it extends.

One difference, though, is in the way that you use NotesThread, versus the normal way of using Thread. When you have a class that extends Thread, you implement your logic in a method named *run()*. When you use NotesThread you implement your logic in a method named *runNotes()* instead. In fact, if you tried to write something like Skeleton2 and implement a run() method, you'd get a compile time error, because NotesThread implements run() as a *final* method; you can't override it.

Why have this difference? The reason is that NotesThread needs to be sure that it gets invoked *before* any code in your class can possibly run on the thread, so it can do you the favor of initializing Notes, and your NOI objects will work as advertised. NotesThread also needs to be sure that it does the right per-thread shutdown of Notes when your program (or at least this thread in your program) is done. If you didn't do the setup, the first time you tried to use an NOI object you'd probably crash. If you didn't do the teardown then when your last NotesThread instance was done your program would hang. That wouldn't be too cool, so here's the order in which you want things to happen when you run Skeleton2:

1. You type "java Skeleton2" on the command line. The Java Virtual Machine (VM) is started in your current process space.

2. Java creates a Thread instance, loads and verifies Skeleton2, and calls the static main() function. No instance of Skeleton2 has been created yet. We'll call this *thread1*.

3. The main() function does a *new* on Skeleton2, so Java creates an instance of it. Skeleton2 inherits from java.lang.Thread. Note that we didn't provide a constructor for Skeleton2. Doesn't matter, Java will create a default one (no arguments) for us.

4. main() calls start() on s2. It then (while step 5 proceeds on another thread) immediately calls s2.join(), which just waits for s2's new thread to complete.

5. Java creates a new execution thread, let's call it *thread2*, transfers control to it and, using that new thread, calls the run() method, which was declared *final* in NotesThread. We've started executing on *thread2* now.

6. The NotesThread run() method makes sure that the required Notes libraries are loaded, and calls an exported C routine to initialize Notes for the current thread (*thread2*).

7. If step 6 goes well, NotesThread.run() next invokes the runNotes() method.

8. Because Skeleton2 has a runNotes() method and is the last extended class in the inheritance chain, its method gets invoked, still on *thread2*. If we had omitted a runNotes() method from Skeleton2, the one in NotesThread (the next class up the inher-

itance chain) would get called (all Java methods are *virtual* in the C++ sense). In that case there's no problem, since NotesThread has a default runNotes() implementation, just in case. It doesn't do much, just returns.

9. Skeleton2's runNotes() method is called. It sends a string to the system output stream (Java's version of *stdout*), then returns.

10. We're back in NotesThread.run(). Even if Skeleton2's runNotes() (or something it called) had thrown an Exception, we'd still get back to NotesThread.run()because the call to runNotes() is in a *try* block, and following that is a *catch* that does nothing but print a stack trace (for your debugging convenience). Following the *catch* block is a *finally* block, which Java guarantees to execute after the *try* is done, regardless whether it exits normally or because of an exception. The finally block simply calls Notes again to shut down the current thread, then it exits.

11. NotesThread.run() returns to java.lang.Thread.start(), which kills the system thread.

12. *Thread2* is gone now, so back on *thread1* our main() function returns from its call to s2.join(), then exits.

13. Java shuts down *thread1*, and having nothing else to do, exits. The Java process terminates, and control returns to your console window.

Note also that we didn't need to use the static NotesThread.sinitThread() and stermThread() calls in this version of main(). It's still a static method run on a thread created by the Java VM, but since we didn't create or use any Notes objects in main(), no initialization of Notes was required.

So there you have it, a basic multithreaded Java application all set up for NOI. Before going on to show you how to do really interesting things with multithreaded NOI applications, let's take a quick look at another way to set up a multithreaded skeleton.

Listing 7.3 Skeleton Multithreaded Example Using Runnable

```
import java.util.*;
import lotus.notes.*;
public class Skeleton3 implements Runnable
{
    public static void main(String argv[])
        {
        try {
            Skeleton3 s3 = new Skeleton3();
            NotesThread thread1 = new NotesThread(s3);
            thread1.start();
            thread1.join();
            }
        catch (Exception e) { e.printStackTrace(); }
        }
    public void run()
        {
        System.out.println("Hello from Skeleton3");
        }
}   // end class
```

Skeleton3 illustrates the other common way to launch threads. Sometimes you just can't have your class extend NotesThread. Maybe it already needs to extend some other class, and Java only allows single inheritance (we could have had Skeleton3 extend some other class in this example). Maybe your application is such that you want to manage NotesThread instances instead of instances of other classes. In any case, you can set it up this way just as easily and effectively as the way we did in Skeleton2.

The second standard option for multithreading (the one that we use in Skeleton3) is to create an instance of NotesThread directly, and pass to its constructor an instance of your class. Your class can inherit from anything, but it must implement the Runnable interface. *Implements* simply means that your class has in it all the methods that are defined in the interface. The Runnable interface has only a single method: run(), so (unlike with Skeleton2, where we were prohibited from implementing a run() method) Skeleton3 *must* implement a run() method. This is the method that NotesThread will invoke for you.

Here are the steps that take place when the Skeleton3 program runs.

1. Java invokes Skeleton3's main() function.
2. main() instances a Skeleton3.
3. main() creates an instance of NotesThread, passing the Skeleton3 instance in as an argument. NotesThread saves s3 away for later.
4. main() calls NotesThread.start().
5. Java creates a new thread and invokes NotesThread's run() method.
6. NotesThread.run() does its Notes setup *shtick*, then invokes the run() method on the reference to s3 that it saved away in its constructor.
7. Skeleton3.run() is invoked, prints out a message, and returns.
8. NotesThread has the same logic following its call to Skeleton3.run() as it did following its call to Skeleton2.notesRun(): a *finally* block where Notes is terminated for the current thread.
9. NotesThread returns to Thread.start(), which kills the thread and returns to main().
10. main() has been waiting on a join() call in its original thread. It now continues, and exits.

11. Java shuts down its process, returning to the console window.

Thus the actual differences in the two techniques can be summarized in a small table.

Table 7.1 Two Techniques for Multithreading an Application

Extend NotesThread	**Implement Runnable**
main() instances your class only	main() instances your class and NotesThread
main() calls YourClass.start()	main() calls NotesThread.start()
NotesThread calls YourClass.runNotes()	NotesThread calls YourClass.run()

MULTITHREADED APPLICATIONS USING NOI

The same techniques that we applied above to generate one additional thread can be used to generate any number of them. Any thread that is an instance of NotesThread can be used to manipulate NOI objects. Let's do an example where we share a Database instance across a few threads. This one, and the accompanying database, are on the CD.

Listing 7.4 Example Multithreaded Application (Ex74Multi.java)

```
import lotus.notes.*;
import java.util.*;
public class Ex74Multi extends NotesThread
{
    private int index;
    private Database db;
    public static final int n_threads = 5;

    public static void main(String argv[])
        {
        try {
```

Writing NOI Applications

```
            NotesThread.sinitThread();
            Session s = Session.newInstance();
            Database db = s.getDatabase("", "book\\Ex74.nsf");
            Ex74Multi array[] = new Ex74Multi[n_threads];
            for (int i = 0; i < n_threads; i++)
                {
                array[i] = new Ex74Multi(i, db);
                array[i].start();
                }

            System.out.println("All threads started");

            // now we wait
            for (int i = 0; i < n_threads; i++)
                {
                array[i].join();
                System.out.println("Thread " + i + " is done");
                }

            System.out.println("All threads done, exiting");
            }
        catch (Exception e) { e.printStackTrace(); }
        finally { NotesThread.stermThread(); }
        }   // end main
public Ex74Multi(int i, Database d)
    {
    this.index = i;
    this.db = d;
    }

public void runNotes()
    {
    try {
        this.sleep(500);
        System.out.println("Starting thread " + index);
        Document doc = db.createDocument();
```

```
                doc.appendItemValue("index", new Integer(index));
                DateTime dt = db.getParent().createDateTime("today");
                dt.setNow();
                doc.appendItemValue("creation time", dt);
                doc.save(true, false);
                System.out.println("Thread " + index + " exiting");
            }
        catch (Exception e) { e.printStackTrace(); }
        }
} // end class
```

Discussion of Ex74Multi

Let's analyze this one a little and dissect a couple of interesting aspects of it. First of all, notice that the Ex74Multi class extends NotesThread, so that we can conveniently use the NOI objects. But then why does main() use the explicit static init/term calls to NotesThread (sinitThread and stermThread)? Remember that main() is *static*, and is invoked directly from the Java interpreter; no instance of the class has yet been created, and so no NotesThread initialization code has been called for main(). We could have coded this differently by having main() do nothing but create an Ex74Multi instance, then call start() on it, putting the multithreaded logic into runNotes() instead. But then we would have most likely wanted to create a second class to do what we now do in runNotes(), and that seemed like too much work. Later we'll be doing stuff that way.

The main() function does all the setup: gets a Session, opens the Database for this example, and then creates an array of Ex74Multi instances, so we can keep track of them. As we create an instance, we pass in two arguments: the instance's index (place in the array) and the Database instance. The class constructor does nothing but cache the arguments in some member variables. Then, after constructing each instance, main() invokes start() on it.

The start() method in java.lang.Thread creates a new thread and (via NotesThread) invokes our runNotes() method. When main() is done with object creation, it prints a message and enters a second loop, wherein it waits for each thread in turn to complete. When each thread is done, it prints another message. Note that calling join() in sequence to make sure all the threads are done is okay, but not the greatest technique in the world. It's safe, because calling join() on a thread that has already terminated is a no-op. The issue is that you don't really know which thread will end first, but in this case we really don't care. Later we'll see other ways of doing this that are more appropriate to the real world.

When all threads have finished, main() cleans up and exits. Meanwhile, what about runNotes()? This is where the meat of the program really is: Each thread adds a single Document to the Database. Note that because of the way we set up our constructor, each thread is operating on the *same* Database instance, although each is creating its own Document and DateTime instances.

The first thing each thread does is sleep for half a second. Why? Well, there are a couple of reasons why you would consider explicitly slowing down each thread like this:

- ❐ All user threads (NotesThread is always a user thread, as opposed to a system thread) run at the same priority, and all user threads run at a higher priority than the garbage collection (gc) thread. If you run a big program with a lot of threads where each thread is (albeit temporarily) consuming resources and never "yielding," then the gc thread never gets a chance to run. You could run out of memory, or file handles, or some other system resource, even though you coded your program to reuse object references, and so on. Yielding allows the gc thread a chance to free up memory that is now unused. This technique isn't guaranteed to work, and different VM implementations on different platforms might respond differently. Your other alternative is to explicitly call System.gc(), which fires off a garbage collection cycle synchronously (don't do it too often!!).

❒ Another reason for doing it in this example was to randomize the order of completion a bit. I wanted to show that just because the threads started in order 0 through 4, and just because they all executed exactly the same code path didn't mean that they would necessarily complete in order. Adding a sleep() call was one way to break up the order of execution a bit. I haven't proved one way or the other whether it really had an impact.

The next thing runNotes() does is print out a message using its current index value. Then it creates a Document in the Database, adds the index value and the current DateTime value to the Document, saves it, and prints another message. The following output reproduces one of the runs of this program on my machine:

```
[d:\lotus\work\wordpro\book\ java Ex74Multi
All threads started
Starting thread 0
Starting thread 1
Starting thread 2
Starting thread 3
Starting thread 4
Thread 2 exiting
Thread 1 exiting
Thread 3 exiting
Thread 0 exiting
Thread 4 exiting
Thread 0 is done
```

```
Thread 1 is done
Thread 2 is done
Thread 3 is done
Thread 4 is done
All threads done, exiting
```

Note that main()'s messages are all in order (no surprise, as they are printed out from *for* loops), but the threads themselves exited in an unexpected order: 2-1-3-0-4. If you look in the sample database for this program (Ex74.nsf, on the CD) you'll see that I've set up the view to sort by creation date, and that indeed, even though all the Documents were saved within one second, they sort in (almost) the same order as the exit messages. Note that while Thread 0 claimed to have exited ahead of Thread 4, in the database Thread 0 sorts below Thread 4. The explanation is that Notes's DateTime granularity is one hundredth of a second, and if two Documents' sorting values are both within the same .01 second, then the sort order is unpredictable.

Is this program thread safe? What does *thread safe* mean? Both good questions. Chapter 10 addresses the issue of thread safety in much more detail, but for now I'll just point out a few relevant facts:

1. Java has a great language construct called *synchronize*. When you synchronize a method or block of code, Java guarantees that no two threads will ever execute that method (or block of code) on the same object instance at the same time. It essentially creates a *semaphore*, or critical section lock, or whatever you're used to calling it, around that code, and invisibly stores that semaphore in the object instance. If you declare a method as synchronized, the entire method is a critical section. The best thing about synchronize is that when you use it Java cleans it up for you: no matter how you exit a synchronized block of code (return statement in the middle, fall out the bottom, throw an exception, call

something else that throws an exception), Java cleans up the semaphore for you. A big win for ease-of-coding.

2. All NOI classes are synchronized on all their methods. This means that even though two threads might be simultaneously attempting to execute the Database.createDocument() call on the same Database instance (as in Ex74Multi), only one can get there first, and the other has to wait until the first one is done. This doesn't prevent a thread from calling createDocument() on a different Database instance, of course.

3. Synchronizing all the methods isn't enough, however. What happens when two different threads try to save two different Document instances to the same Database at the same time? Sure, Document.save() is synchronized, but here we have two different Document instances—synchronization doesn't apply. This is a perfect example of a fairly common case where two independent operations (saving two different Documents) have a hidden synchronization requirement: Few file systems allow you to actually write to the disk in the same file at the same time from two different threads. It's for this reason that the code in Notes that handles updates to databases is (and has always been) internally semaphored, or synchronized.

4. All the built-in Java library calls that share resources (System.out.println, for example) are synchronized as well, so that we don't get two threads trying to write two messages simultaneously to System.out, and having the text of both intermingled on the screen. Does this slow things down? Of course. The whole point is that you trade off local (per thread) throughput for two things: correctness of operation (you don't get garbled messages) and higher global (program wide) throughput. If this trade-off doesn't work for you (either because the result isn't correct anyway or because global performance isn't better), then

you should rethink whether your programming task is suitable for a multithreaded solution.

A MULTITHREADED WEB CRAWLER

Let's use the techniques covered so far, plus some very nice built in Java classes, to write a simple Web crawler. The idea of a Web crawler is that, starting on a given page, you find all the links on that page, and recursively travel each link, to a preset depth. We'll do a very simple one that only goes a couple of levels deep (see Listing 7.5). We'll create a Document in a Database for each link we find, and make each link Document a response to its parent link. When we're done we'll have a Database that represents in document/response format a hyperlinked subset of the Web.

Listing 7.5 Web Crawler Example (Ex75Crawl.java)

```
import lotus.notes.*;
import java.util.*;
import java.net.*;
import java.io.*;
public class Ex75Crawl extends NotesThread                        5
{
    // members
    private Database theDb;
    private Document myParent;
    private URL theUrl;                                           10
    private InputStream theIstream;
    private int myDepth;
    protected static final int MaxDepth = 3;
    protected static final int MaxLinks = 5;
                                                                  15
    public static void main(String argv[])
```

```java
    {
    // Print "usage" message if no argument passed in
    if (argv == null || argv.length == 0 || argv[0] == null)
        {
        System.out.println("Usage: java Ex75Crawl <URL>");
        return;
        }

    // Construct a URL for the initial page
    try {
        System.out.println("D0: Opening page " + argv[0]);
        URL url = new URL(argv[0]);
        InputStream istr = url.openStream();

        // if we're still here, set up the Database
        try {
            NotesThread.sinitThread();
            Session s = Session.newInstance();
            Database db = s.getDatabase("", "book\\Ex75.nsf");
            Ex75Crawl highest = new Ex75Crawl(0, null, db, url, istr);
            highest.start();
            highest.join();
            }
        catch (Exception e) { e.printStackTrace(); }
        finally { NotesThread.stermThread(); }
        }
    catch (Exception e) { e.printStackTrace(); }
    }   // end main

// constructor for this class
public Ex75Crawl(int depth, Document parent, Database db, URL url,
                 InputStream istr)
    {
    this.theDb = db;
    this.theUrl = url;
```

```
        this.theIstream = istr;
        this.myDepth = depth + 1;
        this.myParent = parent;
        }                                                           55
// main logic for Ex75Crawl
public void runNotes()
    {
    int linkcount = 0;                                              60
    DateTime dt;
    Document doc = null;

    // are we too deep?
    if (this.myDepth > MaxDepth)                                    65
        return;

    try {
        this.sleep(100);
        doc = this.theDb.createDocument();                          70

        // top level doc has different form
        if (this.myDepth == 1)
            doc.appendItemValue("Form", "WebURL");
        else doc.appendItemValue("Form", "WebURLR");                75

        doc.appendItemValue("URL", this.theUrl.toString());
        doc.appendItemValue("Depth", this.myDepth);
        dt = this.theDb.getParent().createDateTime("");
        dt.setNow();                                                80
        doc.appendItemValue("StartCrawl", dt);

        // make this document a response to its parent
        if (this.myParent != null)
            doc.makeResponse(this.myParent);                        85

        // make sure the page is html
        String type = this.theUrl.openConnection().getContentType();
        doc.appendItemValue("ContentType", type);
```

```
            if (!type.equalsIgnoreCase("text/html"))          90
            {
               doc.replaceItemValue("Comment", "Link is not html");
               return;    // goes to "finally"
            }
                                                              95
         // save the doc, else there's no UNID that children
         // can use to make themselves responses
         doc.save(true, false);

         // parse the input stream for links, create new object for each
         BufferedReader reader =
            new BufferedReader(new InputStreamReader(this.theIstream));
         String line;
         while ((line = reader.readLine()) != null)
            {                                                 105
               doc.replaceItemValue("Comment", "Read line: " + line);

               int index = line.indexOf("HREF=");
               if (index < 0)
                  continue;   // no more links                110
               index += 6; // move past the starting dbl-quote
               int index2 = line.indexOf("\"", index); // find 2nd quote
               if (index2 < 0)
                  break;
               String newUrl = line.substring(index, index2);   115

               // validate this url, have we seen it before?
               Item links = doc.getFirstItem("Links");
               if (links != null && links.containsValue(newUrl))
                  continue;                                   120
               System.out.println("D" + this.myDepth + ": Opening page"
                     + newUrl);

               // Append this link info to our doc, then crawl the link
               URL u = new URL(this.theUrl, newUrl);          125
```

```
            if (linkcount == 0)
               {
               linkcount = 1;
               doc.appendItemValue("LinkCount", 1);
               doc.appendItemValue("Links", u.toString());        130
               }
            else {
                 if (++linkcount > MaxLinks)
                    {
                    doc.replaceItemValue("Comment",               135
                                     "Max link count exceeded");
                    return;
                    }
                 doc.replaceItemValue("LinkCount",
                                  new Integer(linkcount));        140
                 Item item = doc.getFirstItem("Links");
                 item.appendToTextList(u.toString());
                 }
            InputStream is = u.openStream();                      145
            Ex75Crawl inst = new Ex75Crawl(++myDepth, doc, this.theDb,
                                     u, is);
            inst.start();   // but don't wait for it
            } // end while
      } // end try                                                150
catch (Exception e) { e.printStackTrace(); }
finally {
         // add stop time, save again
         try {
              if (doc != null)                                    155
                 {
                 dt = this.theDb.getParent().createDateTime("");
                 dt.setNow();
                 doc.appendItemValue("StopCrawl", dt);
                 doc.save(true, false);                           160
```

```
                    }
                }
                catch (Exception e) { e.printStackTrace(); }
            } // end finally
        } // end runNotes                                              165
} // end class
```

DISCUSSION OF THE WEBCRAWLER

This program actually does quite a lot in its 170 or so lines. I've numbered the listing for convenient reference, and we'll go through it in some (but I hope not excruciating) detail.

First, we have to import more than the usual number of classes, because we're using some i/o stream classes and some network classes that we haven't so far seen here. Next note that the Ex75Crawl class extends NotesThread, but that main() still does a static NotesThread init/term sequence, because we want to instantiate (and open, which is an expensive step) our Database only one time, and then share it across all threads.

There are two constants that we define at compile time (lines 13 and 14): one for the maximum recursion depth (this isn't really a recursive program, though the term is still a good one for this application), and one for the maximum number of links per page that we'll retrieve. Students of the unintended side effects of combinatorial explosion will understand why I set these limits so low.

The program expects a URL on the command line, which it uses as the starting page. The full URL syntax must be provided (although we could have coded around that easily enough), such as http://www.lotus.com. Leaving off the http:// part will cause a malformed URL exception. At line 26 main() prints a progress message (D0 refers to the depth level of the current thread), and instantiates a URL instance. We open an input stream on it, just to make sure that it really exists and can be connected to. Some of the Web sites I tried this with (notably both www.lotus.com and www.microsoft.com) refused to let my program connect, probably because they want to shut out all nonbrowser traffic. I found that my Domino site provider let me in, however.

> **NOTE** Please don't try this using my site provider's URL because too many hits from programs like this can effectively be a denial-of-service attack, which is certainly unethical and probably illegal.

If we don't experience an exception so far, then we go ahead and create a Database instance for Ex75.nsf (it's on the CD). Then (line 36) we instantiate the highest level instance of Ex75Crawl, passing into its constructor our current level (0), the Document instance at the current level (there isn't one yet, so *null*), the Database instance, the URL to crawl, and the input stream instance from that URL. Then main() starts that instance and waits for it to finish (line 38). It probably would make no difference if main() didn't wait, even though it goes on to do a NotesThread.stermThread(). Any other Ex75Crawl instances that are busily out there crawling away are, by definition, on different threads, and so have their own init/term logic. Even if main() exits before the other threads are done, Java lets the other threads keep going. The interpreter exits when the last thread is finished.

Following the code for main() is the class constructor, at line 47. All it does, as in the previous example, is stash away the arguments in instance variables. Further along, at line 59, is the real meat of this class, the runNotes() method. All the rest of the logic is in this one method.

The first thing runNotes() does is check for its depth exceeding the maximum "recursion" level. If we didn't have this check in here, the program would run forever, almost guaranteed. Why do I say "guaranteed"? Because, lots of sites have links back to their home pages from down within a "deeper" page. If the crawler were to hit one of those sites, it would go into an infinite loop, always cycling back to the home page. Even if that weren't the case, a given thread would only stop when it hit a page with no links on it. How many of those are there? Not many.

At line 69 the program sleeps for 0.1 second, in case the Garbage Collector thread is desperate to run. At line 70 runNotes() creates a new Document instance in the current Database. Notes likes it better if top-level and response Documents don't share the same form, so we assign the "Form" Item a value based on our depth (lines 73–75). After that, we add the current URL, depth, and the time we began crawling to the Document. If a parent Document was passed in, we make the current Document a response to it (line 84).

The next thing to do is to make sure that the current URL is actually something we can parse, that is, an HTML page instead of something else, like a GIF file. We get the "content type" from the URL, and store that in the Document as well, then check for the type being "text/html" (the specified MIME encoding for an HTML page). If the current page is not HTML, we add a comment to that effect to the Document, and bail out. Note that we don't call save() before the return statement at line 93. We don't have to, because the return will actually branch down to the finally block following the current *try* block, at line 152, where the save() will happen.

The next thing we have to worry about is that we might be starting a new "recursive" thread real soon, and that thread is going to want to make the current thread's Document a parent to the child thread's new Document. It won't be able to do that unless our current Document has a Universal ID (UNID), so we need to save() the current Document at this point. That automatically gives it an UNID, and the child Document (if any) will put that UNID in an Item named $REF, thereby making itself a response Document (that's what the Document.makeResponse() call does).

Now (line 100) we can go ahead and start scanning the current page for links. Links in HTML are encoded as an HTML tag that looks something like:

```
<A HREF="[some URL]"><IMG SRC="/eapps/nocgism.gif" Border=0> </A>
```

where "[some URL]" is where the actual URL spec would be. So, we scan the page line by line, using a nice Java class called BufferedReader, to find a substring "HREF=". If we find one (the value returned by String.indexOf() is greater than or equal to 0, at line 109) we skip ahead to the first double quote, then scan the string for the closing double quote, and make a new String instance out of what's in between (lines 111–115).

At line 118, we try to figure out whether or not we've ever seen this same URL on this page already, because if so, then we want to skip it. That turns out to be pretty easy, because we already save every link we find on the page in a text list on our current Document instance. All we have to do is find the Item, and invoke the containsValue() method. If it returns *true*, we just skip to the next line in the page. If this really is a new URL (at least on the current page), then we print out a little message, including the current recursion depth (line 121), create a new URL object, bump the page's link counter, and add the new URL to our text list (lines 125–130). If the link counter for the page exceeds our limit, we bail. (I admit that I did not code this optimally: the limit test should be *after* we process a link, which would save us reading lines that we know we aren't going to care about. Why don't y'all go in and fix it up?)

If we're not above our limit, then (line 145) the program opens an input stream on the new URL, creates a new Ex75Crawl instance, and spawns a new thread. Note that we don't wait for the new thread at all. The next thing that happens is that we add the end-of-crawling date/time to the Document (lines 157–160) and save() the Document again; then runNotes() exits.

In order to keep the length of the example within reason, I didn't make the URL parsing as robust as it would be for a production program. For example, the code assumes only one HREF per line of HTML, with no spaces around the "=". Even more importantly, we've ignored the possibility of a BASE tag on the HTML page, which (if present) changes the meaning of each URL on that page.

You can see the results of my test run in the database Ex75Crawl, on the CD. Again, please *do not* try to repeat my experiment using the same URL that I did—pick another one—there are lots to go around.

SUMMARY: MULTITHREADED NOI APPLICATIONS

I hope this chapter has given you a good grasp of how you can write standalone NOI applications that do interesting and powerful things. I especially hope that you have gained some appreciation for the subtleties and power of multithreaded programming. This combination of the power of Domino/Notes and the power of Java are why I come to the conclusion over and over again that the combination of the two is enormously important, and interesting, to us developer types.

Coming up next, Chapter 8 goes into great and gory detail on how to write Domino Agents in Java, including multithreaded Agents. Chapter 9 tells you how to debug Agents, given that Notes does not (in Release 4.6 anyway) include an integrated Java development/debugging environment. Chapter 10 will consider some additional issues with sharing NOI objects across threads.

8

WRITING NOI AGENTS

In Chapter 7 we covered a lot of aspects of using Java and NOI to write applications; could writing Agents be very different? The answer is both yes and no. The basics are definitely the same, particularly the use of the NOI classes. There are some differences that are worth exploring in detail, however:

1. The Agent execution environment is worth understanding in some detail because there are benefits and gotchas that you should know about concerning identity, security, timeouts, and so on.
2. Agents get to use the AgentContext class.
3. There are some important special considerations when writing multithreaded Agents.

Each of these points is considered in detail in this chapter.

AGENT INFRASTRUCTURE: THE LOTUS.NOTES.AGENTBASE CLASS

None of the preceding chapters on the NOI interfaces talks about this class, primarily because you never use it directly, unlike the other classes. It is, however, very important to you if you're writing Java Agents for Domino: All Agent programs must include a class that extends AgentBase; this is the *main* class for the Agent.

AgentBase does a lot of work for you:

- It extends NotesThread, so your Agent class is all set up and initialized for Notes.
- AgentBase creates a Session instance and pre-loads it with an AgentContext instance all set up for the current Agent.
- It creates a java.lang.ThreadGroup instance to which all threads spawned by the Agent automatically belong. This is used for shutting things down when the Agent terminates (see below).
- AgentBase also creates a timer thread to monitor the progress of the Agent. If the Agent exceeds the administrator-set time limit for background Agents, the Agent can be killed (the technical term for this is "terminated with extreme prejudice").
- AgentBase handles redirection of the standard Java output streams System.out and System.err to the Notes log and to the Java console. Notes does the same for LotusScript (except that there's no Java console), so that, for example, output from the MsgBox and Print statements are redirected.
- It creates a special output stream using the standard Java class java.io.PrintWriter. This stream is used when an Agent is invoked from the HTTP server. Text output to this stream is cached by the Agent and is returned to the HTTP server as the

result of running the Agent. It typically is served back to a browser.

❏ Finally, AgentBase invokes your class's NotesMain() function, which is where you write your program.

Okay, so why another method (NotesMain) that you have to keep track of for Agents? Mainly because AgentBase itself extends NotesThread, and therefore must implement its own startup and shutdown logic in a runNotes() method. Because we have to be absolutely sure that AgentBase's own runNotes() method gets called from NotesThread, and not your class's, runNotes() is declared *final* in AgentBase. AgentBase's runNotes() method calls NotesMain(), which is where you implement your Agent's logic.

Let's look at a simple example of a single-threaded Agent. This Agent is meant to be run from a View Action on Documents that have been selected in the view. It uses the Newsletter class to format a Document containing doclinks to each of the selected Documents, and mails it to the Agent's author (the person who signed it).

Listing 8.1 Simple Agent Example (Ex81Agent.java)

```
import java.lang.*;
import java.io.*;
import lotus.notes.*;

public class Ex81Agent extends AgentBase
{
    public void NotesMain()
        {
        try {
            Session s = this.getSession();
            AgentContext ctx = s.getAgentContext();
            Database db = ctx.getCurrentDatabase();
            DocumentCollection dc = ctx.getUnprocessedDocuments();
```

```
                System.out.println("Found " + dc.getCount() + " selected docs");
                Newsletter nl = s.createNewsletter(dc);
                nl.setSubjectItemName("Subject");
                Document doc = nl.formatMsgWithDoclinks(db);
                doc.send(ctx.getEffectiveUserName());
                System.out.println("Newsletter sent to " +
                                ctx.getEffectiveUserName());
            }
        catch (Exception e) { e.printStackTrace(); }
        }
} // end class
```

Pretty simple for an interesting piece of functionality, no? We're getting lot of leverage out of AgentBase and AgentContext here:

- ❒ The Session has been set up for us, including the AgentContext instance.
- ❒ We can get the "current" Database (the one the Agent lives in) from AgentContext.
- ❒ We can also get the list of Documents selected in the view from AgentContext.
- ❒ System.out.println() is automatically redirected to the Java Console.
- ❒ AgentContext also includes the name of the "effective" user, in this case the signer of the Agent.
- ❒ If we needed to know something about the current View (from whence the selected Documents came), we could get it from any of the Documents contained in the collection, by using the Document.getParentView() call. This would require instantiating at least one Document, though.

How did we set this Agent up in the Notes UI? Domino 4.6 does not, unfortunately, include an integrated Java development environment (it's scheduled to appear in Domino 5.0). I wrote the code for Agent using my standard editor, then compiled it using the Java Development Kit (JDK) I downloaded (free! and legal!) from the JavaSoft Web site (http://java.sun.com). From that point I just used the Notes Client to create an Agent in my Ex81.nsf database (select **Create Agent** from the menu). From there, follow these steps:

1. Type in the Agent's name. You can make it either shared or private.
2. Set the Agent to run "manually, from the menu."
3. Set the Agent to run on "selected documents."
4. Select the Java radio button (see Figure 8.1 for a screen shot of the setup)
5. Click on the **Import class files** button, select the **.class file** (or files) that the Java compiler produced for you.
6. Save the Agent. Notes will sign it with the current id.
7. Go into view design for the View from where you want to run the Agent.
8. Create a View Action. Pick the **Add Action** button.
9. For the type of action, select **Run agent**, and specify your new Agent.
10. Save the View.

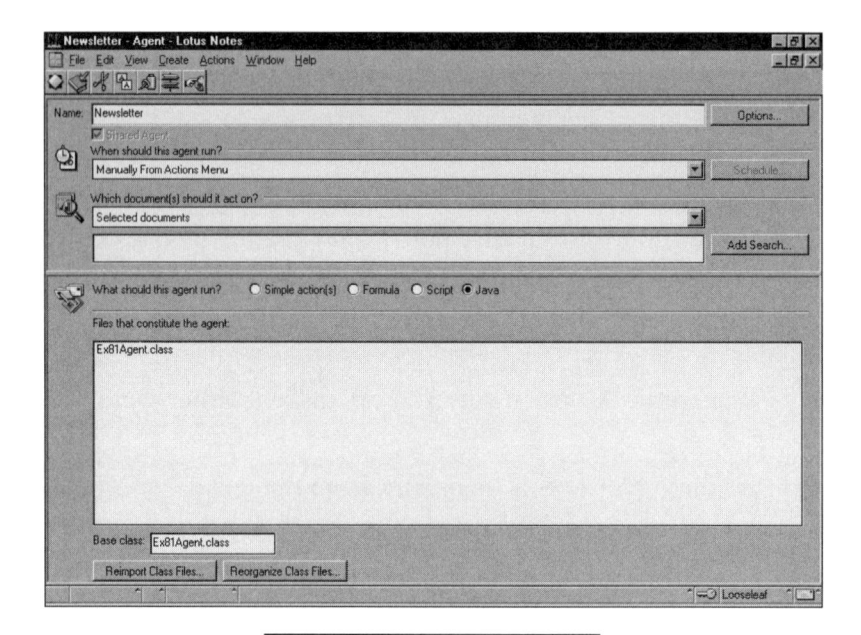

Figure 8.1 Setting up a Java Agent.

At this point you can go into the View and select any number of Documents, then click on the action button at the top. The Agent runs, and the set of selected Documents is delivered to it in the AgentContext.unprocessedDocuments property. The first time you run an Agent like this in a session it will take a little extra time, as Notes has to start up an instance of the Java Virtual Machine (VM). Agents run in this way from the Notes Client will run synchronously, meaning that you can't do anything else in the UI while the Agent is executing. You can interrupt the Agent by hitting **Ctl-Break** on the keyboard.

The last thing the Agent does when it runs is send mail to the author (or last modifier) of the Agent (the *effective user*). See Figure 8.2 for an example of the View and the Java Console on top. See Figure 8.3 for a screen shot of the resulting Newsletter.

Writing NOI Agents

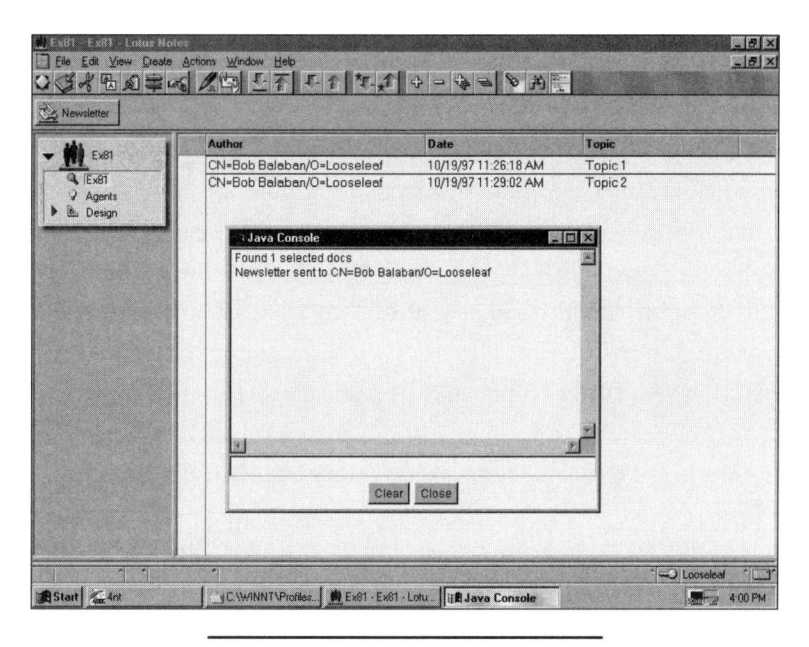

Figure 8.2 Notes view and Java console.

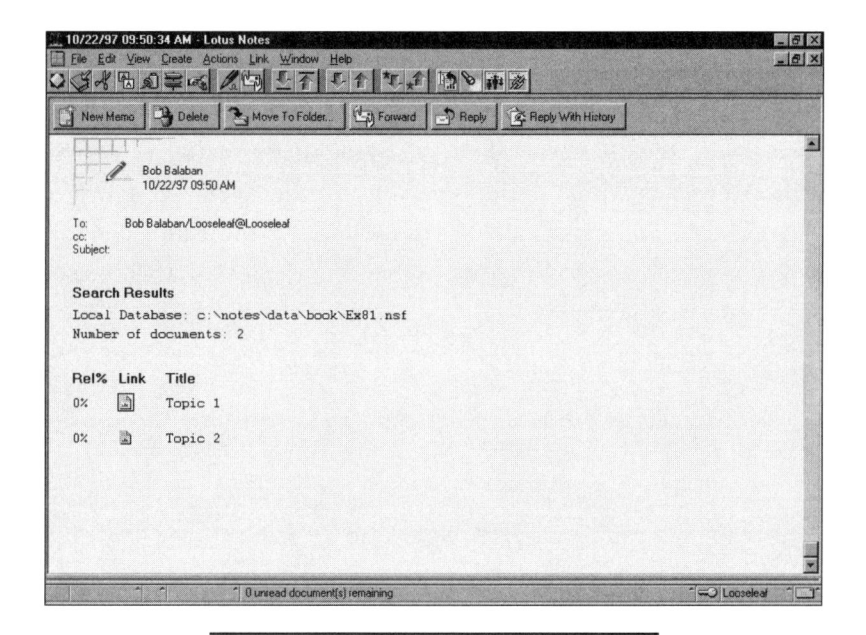

Figure 8.3 Newsletter Created By Ex81Agent

AGENT IDENTITY

We keep referring to the Agent's effective user name. As we described back in Chapter 5 in the section on the Agent and AgentContext classes, background server Agents (those triggered on a scheduled basis, by a new-mail or new/modified Document event, or by a URL via the HTTP server) run with the privileges of the last signer of the Agent. Thus, the Agent, when it runs, assumes the identity of the signer, not of the current Notes id, which in the case of a server based Agent is the server's id. To do otherwise would be a security violation: an Agent running with the server's privileges when the creator of the Agent has (most of the time) fewer access rights would cause big problems.

Thus, the *effective use*r is the one whose identity the Agent is temporarily assuming. The Agent cannot do anything on the server that the user herself could not do, in terms of creating or deleting databases, opening databases, creating/deleting/modifying Documents, and so on. There is one additional wrinkle here: When you create an Agent that is meant mainly for Web-based applications (meaning that the server will be accessed from a Web browser, using the HTTP server module, which itself can trigger Agents), you have the option for each Agent of declaring that it will run *either* with the signer's identity *or* with the Web user's identity. You select which option you want in the Agent Design properties box. Go to the Agent View in your database, and right-click on the Agent, then select **Agent Properties**. See Figure 8.4 for a picture of the Agent Properties box.

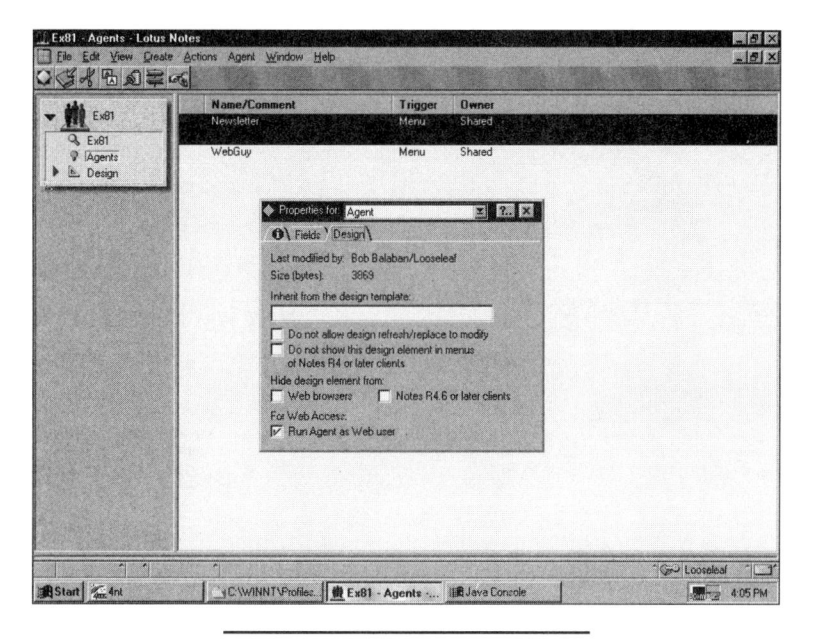

Figure 8.4 The Agent properties box.

There are several choices worth exploring here, but the **Agent identity** option is the last one on the Design tab. What would happen if we made just this one change to the Agent, and then access the database from a browser? The answer is: Nothing, because View Action buttons aren't supported by the Domino HTTP server. We could, however, create a slightly different Agent that better illustrates some of the ways you'd take advantage of the HTTP server (see Listing 8.2).

Listing 8.2 Web Browser Agent Example (Ex82Browser.java)

```
import lotus.notes.*;
import java.util.*;
import java.io.*;

public class Ex82Browser extends AgentBase
{
```

Chapter 8

```
    public void NotesMain()
    {
    try {
        Session s = this.getSession();
        AgentContext ctx = s.getAgentContext();
        PrintWriter output = ctx.getAgentOutput();
        String st = new String("Hello " + ctx.getEffectiveUserName());
        output.println"<B>"(st);
        System.out.println(st);
        }
    catch (Exception e) { e.printStackTrace(); }
    }
}
```

Note that we write out two messages here: one to the special PrintWriter stream, which goes back to the invoking browser, and one to System.out, which goes to the system log file, and (if we run the Agent from the Notes UI) to the Java Console window. I created a new Agent in the Ex81.nsf database, called "WebGuy, " and imported the Ex82Browser.class file. Leaving the design properties untouched for the moment, I started my Domino/HTTP server, brought up the Internet Explorer browser, and typed the following URL for my new agent: http://localhost/Ex81.nsf/webguy.

"Localhost" is just a special TCP/IP name for the current machine, so that you can access your Domino server from the same machine that it is running on (my laptop, for example) without the machine having to be connected to a real network. Figure 8.5 shows the result in the browser.

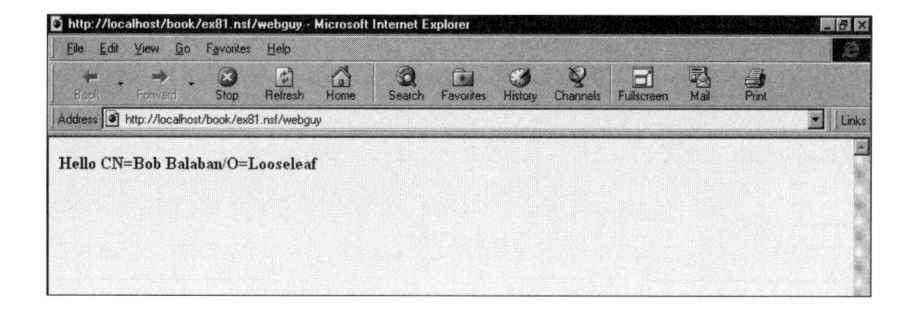

Figure 8.5 Result of running Webguy Agent.

Note that we didn't see the default Agent Done response, we saw the message I sent. And what's more, it came out in a bold font. That's because in the output to the PrintWriter stream I prepended a "<B>" HTML tag, so that the text that followed was made bold by the browser. This is an important point: It shows that you can write a Domino Agent to format rich text output for the browser which invokes it, using simple HTML commands. You use standard Java output primitives on the special stream to buffer the stuff up, and Domino serves it all up to the browser when the Agent terminates. Because the returned Agent output is stored in a single hunk of continuous memory, you want to make sure that you don't let it get bigger than 64KB. That should be plenty, however, for a single page.

Okay, now let's go and check off that **run as web user** option in the Agent's design properties, and refresh from the browser. Figure 8.6 shows the result.

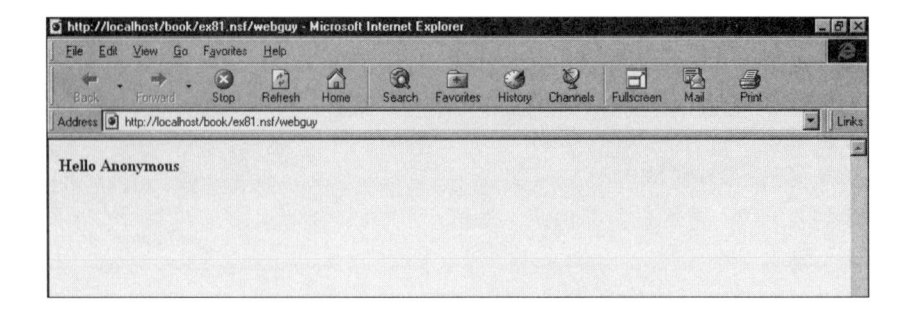

Figure 8.6 Running Webguy as the Web user.

Note that this time the user name that the Agent operated under was "Anonymous." That's because I set up my server to allow anonymous access and gave everyone in the world the right to run Agents on my machine (I edited the server record in the public address book and entered the hierarchical user name wildcard for everyone, "*" in the **can run restricted agents** field.

When the browser accessed the server and caused the HTTP server to run the Agent, HTTP assigned the name "Anonymous" to my connection, because my user session was not authenticated. Authentication can happen either from a browser using *Secure Sockets Layer* (SSL), or by logging in in response to a Domino username/password prompt, neither of which I turned on for my laptop's server. Thus, I received the default user name. I also had to give an appropriate level of access to the Ex81.nsf database via its ACL.

AGENT SECURITY

This joke was popular when we started developing agent technologies for Notes Release 4.0 several years ago: What do you call an Agent that has no security controls on it? Answer: a virus.

Sad but true, there are lots of products out there that make a big deal out of having *mobile Agents*, *intelligent Agents* and *wizards* of all kinds, but when you ask if these beasties are digitally signed, you usually get "Oh, we're addressing that." Or if you ask how much control the server administrator has over these things, the answer is usually something like, "Yes, we'll have that in our next release."

Domino implements two basic security principles that apply to Agents:

1. Agents can run either in the foreground or in the background, but in no case will an Agent have greater access to a server or a database than does the person who created or last modified it.

2. Agents running on servers are subject to control by the system administrator so that the running of Agents is not allowed to consume the server machine entirely.

This seems obvious, but you'd be surprised how often these tenets are overlooked in other products. Let's delve into how Domino accomplishes both of these goals in more detail.

Agent Access Control

The two cases (foreground/background) are quite distinct. Agents running in the foreground are being used from a Notes Client, where there is a user id in force. The Agent might be invoked directly by the user (from the Agents View, from an Action button, from a button on a form, etc.) or indirectly because of, for example, a LotusScript program attached to some event (Database or Document open, maybe) that fires off an Agent. In all cases, however, the Agent is being run because of some explicit action performed by the user, and the Agent is always operating under the auspices of the user's id. Thus, if the Agent tries to go out to some server and modify the public address book, it will only succeed if the user has the authority to do that operation.

Background Agent execution can take place either in the Notes Client or on the server. In the Client case, as with foreground operation, the Agent is running under the authority of a user id, and can do anything the holder of that id can do. When an Agent runs in the background on a server, the only id that is present is the server's id, and we almost never want Agents to operate as the server. Instead, server Agents operate with the privileges of the person who created or last modified the Agent (except when they are triggered by the HTTP server and are set up to run with the identity of the Web user, as shown above, which is a special case).

How do we know who an Agent should run as? There's a digital signature attached to every Agent when it is created or modified. If for some reason the signature is missing or can't be verified (someone tampered with the Agent record in the database, or the signature has no certificates in common with the server where it is being verified), the Agent won't run. All databases that the Agent accesses when run on a server are opened with the privileges of the user whose name is in the signature (the Replicator does something similar when it synchronizes two databases). Unfortunately, the API technique used to enforce selective privileges on a database only work on databases local to the machine where the program (the Agent) is being run. Therefore, server Agents are prohibited from accessing databases on machines other than the one on which they are running. This restriction may be resolved in Domino Release 5.0.

Agent Administration

Database access is, however, only one aspect of Agent security. How do we ensure that Agents don't bring the server down by making it run out of disk space, or by consuming lots of system resources? To prevent this sort of thing, Domino gives the server administrator all kinds of control over how and when Agents execute.

Figure 8.7 shows a screen shot of the Agent Manager section of a typical server record in a public address book.

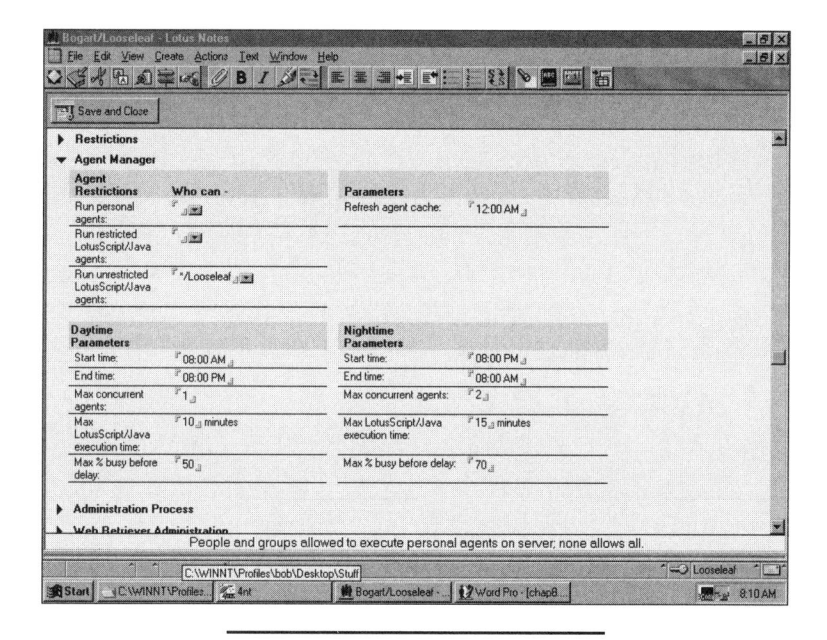

Figure 8.7 Agent Manager parameters.

These are the basic "throttles" that a system administrator can use to control how and when Agents execute on a server.

❑ **Who can run personal Agents?** If this field is empty, no one can run personal (private) Agents. The ability to *create* personal (or shared) Agents is controlled per database in the access control list, but this field controls whose Agents will actually execute on a server. Shared agents are not affected by this field.

- **Who can run "restricted" Agents?** Restricted Agents have fewer privileges on a system than do unrestricted Agents (see below in Table 8.1 for a list of all the things restricted Agents can't do). The restrictedness of an Agent does not belong to the Agent itself, however, but to the signature on the Agent. At run time the Agent Manager checks an Agent's signature against the contents of this field and decides whether the Agent is restricted.

- **Who can run "unrestricted" Agents?** If an Agent's user (or group containing the user) name is not in either the Restricted or Unrestricted field, then the Agent will not run. Putting a name in both fields is redundant—you can't be both restricted and unrestricted at the same time. If a name is in both fields, it is considered unrestricted.

- **Refresh Agent cache.** Specifies the time of day (or night) at which the server record is re-read by the Agent Manager, and all in-memory Agent data is flushed and recomputed. This is done so that changes to scheduling parameters and access are revalidated once a day. Changes to individual Agents are picked up right away by the Agent Manager, because it is monitoring changes to Agent records in all databases.

- **Start time.** Agent Manager execution parameters are divided into two groups: daytime and nighttime, allowing for different server loadings depending on whether lots of users are expected to be logged into a server. This field specifies at what time to transition from nighttime to daytime, or vice versa.

- **End time.** Together with the Start Time field, defines the span during which the server uses daytime or nighttime parameters.

- **Maximum concurrent Agents.** The maximum number of Agents that will be allowed to run concurrently. The default is one during the day and two at night, but you can put in whatever you think appropriate. The Agent Manager consists of one overall "supervisor" process, plus one "executive" process for each possible concurrent Agent. So if you specify that up to five Agents should execute concurrently on a server, then you'll actually have a total of six Agent Manager processes in memory.

- **Maximum execution time.** The Agent Manager will "time out" Agents that exceed this execution limit. The limit is in clock time, not CPU time. Agents that time out are made to cease execution, and an entry is made in the server log to that effect. There are some special considerations having to do with time outs and multithreaded Java Agents (see below).

- **Maximum Percentage Busy.** As Agents execute on a server, the Agent Manager keeps track of how much of the CPU is being consumed by Agents. If the percentage exceeds the value entered in the server record, the Agent Manager will delay executing Agents until the number falls to acceptable levels. It was discovered late in the release cycle of Domino 4.6 (too late to do anything about it) that the calculation used to compute the percentage of CPU taken up by Agents did not properly account for multi-CPU computers. The error was fixed for Release 4.61, but for 4.6 you should adjust this value appropriately for SMP machines. If you want the maximum percentage to be 25% and you have a two-processor machine, set the value to 50%.

Table 8.1 Restricted Agent Operations

	Unrestricted	**Restricted**
Disk i/o	Yes	No
Network i/o	Yes	No
Embed OLE objects	Yes	No
Attach files	Yes	No
Detach files	Yes	No
Modify environment variables	Yes	No
Read system variables	Yes	No
Access system clock	Yes	No
Modify Thread Group	No	No
Install a Class Loader	Yes	No
Create Subprocess	Yes	No
Call System.exit()	No	No
Load DLL	Yes	No
Define lotus.notes classes	No	No

Agent Latency, Or, Why Won't My Agent Run?

A very important design consideration for the Agent Manager was that it should not consume the resources of every server on which it runs. You've seen one outcome of that above in the kinds of controls that a server administrator can exercise over it. Another issue concerns the actual throughput and performance of the Agent Manager implementation itself. In order not to cycle endlessly and suck up all the CPU cycles on the machine, the Agent Manager has several built-in delays, many of which are controllable via "environment variables," values that are maintained in the machine's notes.ini file. For example, when you set an Agent to be triggered by new mail arriving in a database, Agent Manager doesn't run the Agent every time new mail arrives. It waits a small interval of time, in case a few new messages arrive close together, then starts the Agent and gives it the entire list, which is much more efficient.

Here are some of the environment variables you can control to tune Agent Manager behavior. In order to add an environment variable to your NOTES.INI file, just use a text editor. (Figure 8.8 shows a screen shot of a typical NOTES.INI file.)

- **AgentManagerSchedulingInterval.** Valid values are 1 minute to 60 minutes. Default is 1 minute. Specifies the frequency with which the Agent Manager runs a scheduling cycle, meaning, how often it searches its internal queues looking for something that's ready to run.
- **AMGR_UntriggeredMailInterval.** Valid values are 1 minute to 1440 minutes. Default value is 60 minutes. Sometimes Agents that should be triggered by new mail arriving just aren't. This parameter tells the Agent Manager how often to check for that situation.
- **AMGR_DocUpdateAgentMinInterval.** Valid values are 0 to 1440 minutes. Default value is 30 minutes. Specifies how long to wait between execution of the same Document Update Agent. When a document update event is posted to the Agent Manager it checks update Agents to see when they last ran. If the interval is less than this parameter, the Agent(s) are not run.
- **AMGR_NewMailAgentMinInterval.** Valid values are 0 to 1440 minutes. Default value is 0. Specifies the minimum interval to wait between executions of a new mail Agent (as distinct from a document update Agent).
- **AMGR_DocUpdateEventDelay.** Valid values are 0 to 1440 minutes. Default value is 5 minutes. Specifies the amount of time the Agent Manager will wait between receiving a document update event and starting execution of any update Agents. This is done so that a rapid series of changes can be batched up and processed by the Agent all at one time.

- **AMGR_NewMailEventDelay**. Valid values are 0 to 1440 minutes. Default value is 1 minute. Specifies the amount of time the Agent Manager waits between receiving a new mail notification and starting execution of any new mail Agents.

- **DEBUG_AMGR.** This parameter, if set, turns on debug reporting to the server console (and therefore to the server log) by the Agent Manager. Several settings are possible here, depending on what kind of information you want. The valid values for this variable are: "*" for all options; "r" for Agent execution events; "s" for Agent scheduling events; "l" for Agent loading events; "m" for Agent memory warnings; "p" for Agent performance statistics; "c" for Agent control parameters; "v" for all other options, such as reporting of database searching and updates to internal queues. You can specify as many individual debug codes as you want. For example, "DEBUG_AMGR=pcr".

- **DominoAsynchronizeAgents.** The Domino HTTP server typically wants to be multithreaded, so that it can handle multiple incoming HTML requests simultaneously. But because these incoming requests can sometimes involve the execution of Agents on the server, a parameter is provided to control whether HTTP Agent execution should also be multithreaded. If this parameter is set to "1", then Agents invoked this way will run concurrently. If it is set to "0", Agent execution will be serialized when invoked from HTTP (only one Agent can execute at a time). You might want to serialize Agents on a server if the Agents are calling out to some back-end API that might not be thread safe. Early versions of LS:DO (the LotusScript classes for ODBC) had problems with this, although these problems have been largely resolved in Domino 4.6. The default value is 0.

Writing NOI Agents

```
100: COMPANYNAME=Looseleaf Software, Inc.
101: MTATEMP=C:\TEMP
102: NOTESPROGRAM=c:\notes\
103: OldRegKey_MAILTO="c:\notes\notes.exe" =C:\WINNT\notes.ini %1
104: WWWDSP_SYNC_BROWSERCACHE=0
105: WWWDSP_PREFETCH_OBJECT=0
106: ScriptFont=Helv,A000000
107: BCASEWINDOWSIZE=16 23 420 288
108: ADMINWINDOWSIZE=32 46 326 453
109: $BPCOMP=Looseleaf Software, Inc.
110: $BPTITLE=President & Janitor
111: $DriveLetter=G
112: $EnableAlarms=0
113: NetWareSpxSettings=0,0,0,0,0,3,24581
114: EmptyTrash=0
115: WeekStart=1
116: SDI_WINDOW=0
117: DisableImageDithering=1
118: $BPMAILADD=Bob Balaban/Looseleaf @looseleaf @Notes Net
119: NewMailSeqNum=26
120: JavaDlgSettings=*.class!*.jar,*.cab,*.zip!*.jpg,*.gif,*.au!*.java!0
121: NewMailInterval=5
122: DominoEnableJavaServlets=1
123: JavaUserClasses=c:\notes\data\domino\servlet;f:\jserv\lib\classes.zip
124: ServletLocation=c:\notes\data\domino\servlet
125:
```

Figure 8.8 NOTES.INI file.

In addition to the delays enforced above, Agent Manager has a built-in delay in its main processing loop, the infinite (until it's shut down) outer loop that checks for tasks to perform. It runs a few iterations, then sleeps for about a minute. Again, this is to make sure the process is not compute bound.

With all this, there's probably an absolute minimum delay for event-triggered Agents of between 1 and 2 minutes. This is okay for most applications, but it doesn't work well for new mail Agents in applications where it is a hard and fast requirement that the Agent get first crack at incoming mail before a user could possibly see it. Because new mail Agents never execute synchronously on delivery of messages (it would slow down the Router too much), there is always a race condition, a window of 1 or 2 minutes between when the mail arrives and when the Agent will process it, during which a user could get in there first using the Notes Client. Look for this problem to be addressed in Domino 5.0.

Other Interesting Environment Variables

There are some additional environment variables in NOTES.INI that affect Java execution.

- **JavaUserClasses.** Normally when Domino executes a Java Agent (foreground or background), it uses its own internal CLASSPATH setting to locate predefined Java classes (for example, those belonging to the Java run-time system, and those in notes.jar). Sometimes it is really necessary for you to modify the CLASSPATH Domino uses to add one or more additional directories. If this variable is set, it is prepended to the internal CLASSPATH value.

- **JavaMaxHeapSize.** The Java Virtual Machine maintains its own memory heap, and sometimes it runs out of memory (especially if the garbage collector doesn't get to run very often). The default maximum heap size is 64MB, but you can make it larger (or smaller, I suppose) be setting this variable. The value of the variable is in bytes.

- **JavaStackSize**. The default VM stack size is 400KB—you can make it larger with this variable. The value is in bytes.

MULTITHREADED AGENTS

There are a couple of references above to the fact that multithreaded Agents require something special in order to function properly. The reason for this is yet another Agent security consideration, something new to the Java environment that was never a problem with LotusScript, since LotusScript is not a multithreaded language.

Consider a background server Agent written in Java that spawns multiple threads. What happens if the main Agent terminates (or times out), but the child threads do not? What if there are 300 child threads, each of which purposely goes into an infinite loop, and the Agent runs every half hour? Well, the answer is that this would be a bad thing—the server would eventually be brought to its knees. This is often called a "denial of service attack," because the malicious (or just stupid, which sometimes amounts to the same thing) Agent is consuming system resources, and thus preventing others from utilizing them.

For this reason, Domino terminates all child threads belonging to an Agent when the Agent's *main thread* (the one explicitly launched by Domino on which your NotesMain() method is called) terminates. The server keeps track of all threads spawned by a given Agent by keeping them all in the same ThreadGroup (a standard Java class for managing threads). When the Agent's NotesMain() call ends (and we always know when that happens, because it's invoked from NotesThread, remember), the ThreadGroup is terminated as well.

This means that you want to be very careful how you code a multi-threaded Agent: You want the NotesMain() thread to hang around long enough for all child threads to complete, yet you want this to happen in a "system-friendly" manner, where you don't use up too many resources just checking child thread status. The technique used in Chapter 7, Listing 7.4 (Ex74Multi.java) where the main line thread does a sequential series of join() calls, one on each child thread, works okay, but isn't as elegant or efficient as we might like. In Listing 8.3, we recode it to do a better job. At the same time, we'll change it to be an Agent instead of an Application.

Listing 8.3 Waiting For Child Threads (Ex83Multi.java)

```
import lotus.notes.*;
import java.util.*;
public class Ex83Multi extends AgentBase
{
    public static final int n_threads = 5;
```

```java
public void NotesMain()
{
    int i;
    Object waitSem = new Object();      // used for wait/notify

    try {
        Session s = getSession();
        AgentContext ctx = s.getAgentContext();
        Database db = ctx.getCurrentDatabase();
        Log alog = s.createLog("Ex83");
        alog.openAgentLog();
        Ex83Child array[] = new Ex83Child[n_threads];
        for (i = 0; i < n_threads; i++)
            {
            array[i] = new Ex83Child(i, db, alog, waitSem);
            array[i].start();
            }

        alog.logAction("All threads started");

        // now we wait
        boolean foundone = true;
        while (foundone)
            {
            // wait to be pinged by a child
            try {
                synchronized(waitSem) { waitSem.wait(); }
                }
            catch (InterruptedException iex) {}

            foundone = false;

            // see who it was that notified us

            for (i = 0; i < n_threads; i++)
                {
                if (array[i] != null && array[i].isDone())
```

```
                    {
                    System.out.println("Child " + i +
                                            " reporting done.");
                    array[i] = null;
                    }
                else if (array[i] != null)
                    {
                    foundone = true;
                    alog.logAction("One or more threads still active");
                    }
                }   // end for
            }   // end while
        alog.logAction("All threads done, exiting");
            }
        catch (Exception e) { e.printStackTrace(); }
        }   // end NotesMain
}  // end Ex83Multi

/*** Now the child  class that does the work ***/
class Ex83Child extends NotesThread
{
    private int index;
    private Database db;
    private Log alog;
    private boolean done;
    private Object waitSem;

    public Ex83Child(int i, Database d, Log l, Object sem)
        {
```

```
            this.index = i;
            this.db = d;
            this.alog = l;
            this.done = false;
            this.waitSem = sem;
            }

    public synchronized boolean isDone()
        {
        return this.done;
        }

    public void runNotes()
        {
        try {
            this.sleep(500);
            this.alog.logAction("Starting thread " + index);
            Document doc = db.createDocument();
            doc.appendItemValue("index", new Integer(index));
            DateTime dt = db.getParent().createDateTime("today");
            dt.setNow();
            doc.appendItemValue("creationtime", dt);
            doc.save(true, false);
            this.alog.logAction("Thread " + index + " exiting");
            }
        catch (Exception e) { e.printStackTrace(); }
        finally {
                synchronized (this) { this.done = true; }
                // notify the parent thread
                synchronized (waitSem) { waitSem.notify(); }
                }

        }
} // end class
```

Writing NOI Agents

The following code shows the contents of Ex83Multi Agent Log after executing:

```
Started running agent 'Ex83 Multi-threaded' on 10/20/97 11:08:44 AM
Running on new or modified documents: 5 total
Found 5 document(s) that match search criteria
10/20/97 11:08:44 AM: All threads started
10/20/97 11:08:45 AM: One or more threads still active
10/20/97 11:08:45 AM: One or more threads still active
10/20/97 11:08:45 AM: One or more threads still active
10/20/97 11:08:45 AM: One or more threads still active
10/20/97 11:08:45 AM: One or more threads still active
10/20/97 11:08:45 AM: Starting thread 0
10/20/97 11:08:45 AM: Starting thread 1
10/20/97 11:08:45 AM: Starting thread 2
10/20/97 11:08:45 AM: Starting thread 3
10/20/97 11:08:45 AM: Starting thread 4
10/20/97 11:08:45 AM: Thread 1 exiting
10/20/97 11:08:45 AM: Thread 3 exiting
10/20/97 11:08:45 AM: Thread 2 exiting
10/20/97 11:08:45 AM: Thread 0 exiting
10/20/97 11:08:45 AM: Thread 4 exiting
10/20/97 11:08:45 AM: All threads done, exiting
Ran Java Agent Class
Done running agent 'Ex83 Multi-threaded' on 10/20/97 11:08:46 AM
```

The Ex83Multi Agent differs from the original Ex74Multi Application in several interesting ways:

- ❒ Since it's an Agent, we can use AgentContext and Agent log features to simplify the coding a bit, and to keep the Agent's debug output attached to the Agent itself.

- ❒ Ex83Multi uses a separate class to do the per-thread work. Ex83Child inherits from NotesThread, whereas Ex83Multi inherits from AgentBase. We probably could have left it all in one class, but spinning off multiple AgentBase instances is heavier weight than we need.

- The loop that checks all the child threads for termination actually queries each child class instance to see if the "done" flag has been set internally. Note that the isDone() call is synchronized, because there's a place in Ex83Child's logic where we set the value of the flag. That logic too is semaphored, using a synchronized block. This avoids a race condition where a caller is querying the isDone() call on one thread at the same time that the instance is setting the value of its local variable on another thread.

- The loop that searches for a "done" child thread is not a continuous loop, because to just continuously execute the *for* loop over and over would waste compute cycles. Instead we use the wait/notify feature of Java to good advantage. As with *synchronized*, the wait() and notify() calls need an object instance to operate on, so we create a variable of class Object to serve that purpose. Its only function is to be the hook for the wait/notify sequencing. The parent thread calls wait() on it at the beginning of each *while* loop iteration. That effectively puts the parent thread to sleep until a notify() happens on that same object. The waitSem object is passed to each child thread in its constructor, and when a child is done, it calls notify() on the semaphore object. That causes an InterruptedException to be thrown, which the parent catches. The child threads are in effect "pinging" the parent, waking it up each time. Because the semaphore object is shared, access to it must also be synchronized. The wait() and notify() calls are not declared *synchronized*, so we have to do that explicitly.

❐   Note that all the threads in this Agent share not only the Database instance (as in the previous example), but the Log instance as well. Several of the threads can be calling logAction() at the same time, and (because the call is synchronized) they don't step on each other.

SUMMARY OF AGENT OUTPUT OPTIONS

As you've seen in the preceding examples, Agents have a few different ways of sending output to the outside world, for logging or debugging purposes. Table 8.2 summarizes them.

Table 8.2 Agent Output Options

	Foreground Agent	**Background Agent**
System.out	Java console	Server console, server log
AgentBase.getAgentOutput()	(nowhere)	Browser (HTTP agent only)
Log.openAgentLog()	Agent log	Agent log

SPECIAL FUNCTIONALITY FOR WEB AGENTS

We've already mentioned that you can invoke a LotusScript or Java Agent from a Web browser via the HTTP server. We've also mentioned that when you submit a form from a Web browser to an Agent, the AgentContext.getDocumentContext() call will return a Document instance that contains all the fields from the form.

What wasn't mentioned before is that the AgentContext.DocumentContext property also provides you with a number of metadata about the way the Agent was invoked. If you're a CGI programmer, then you're already familiar with the concept of *CGI Variables*. If not, read on.

There are a number of parameters that the Domino HTTP server automatically sets into the context Document before invoking the Agent. They are all listed and described in the Domino online help database, so I'll just summarize them here (all values are of type String):

- **Auth_Type.** Authentication method used to validate the user. Often missing.
- **Content_Length.** Length of the content as provided by the client. Often missing.
- **Content_Type.** When there's attached information (e.g., for POST and PUT), this is the data content type (e.g., "text/html").
- **Gateway_Interface.** CGI version number for the server. Often missing.
- **HTTP_Accept.** The MIME types that the client accepts.
- **HTTP_Accept_Language.** The two letter language code (e.g., "en" for English).
- **HTTP_Referer.** The URL of the page from which the user arrived. Sometimes missing.
- **HTTPS.** "ON" if SSL mode is enabled, otherwise "OFF".
- **HTTP_User_Agent.** The name of the user's browser. The values here are not as straightforward as you might expect. When I dump the value for Internet Explorer version 3.02, I get this string: "Mozilla/2.0 (compatible; MSIE 3.02; Windows NT)". Isn't Mozilla that big dinosaur the Japanese are so fond of? Go figure.
- **Path_Info.** The part of the URL following the database name with which the Agent was invoked.

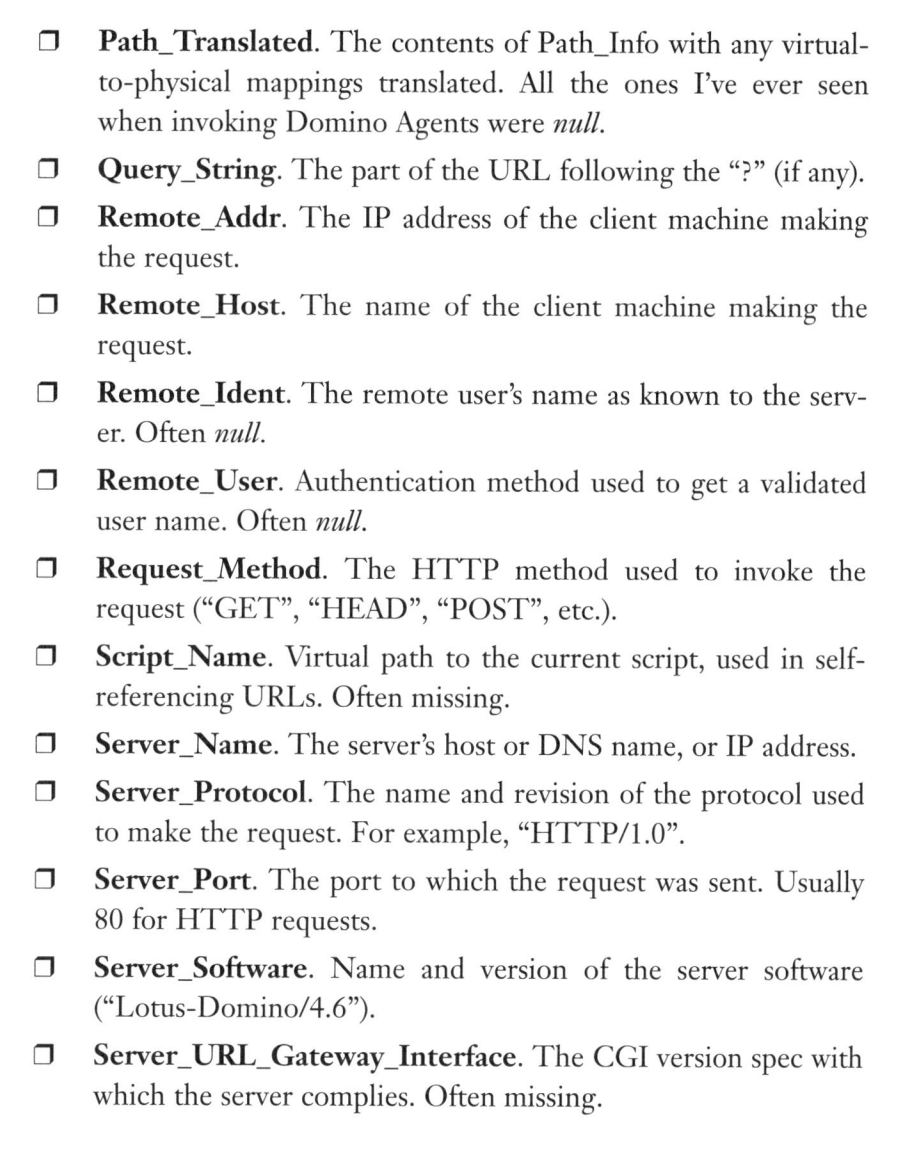

- **Path_Translated**. The contents of Path_Info with any virtual-to-physical mappings translated. All the ones I've ever seen when invoking Domino Agents were *null*.
- **Query_String**. The part of the URL following the "?" (if any).
- **Remote_Addr**. The IP address of the client machine making the request.
- **Remote_Host**. The name of the client machine making the request.
- **Remote_Ident**. The remote user's name as known to the server. Often *null*.
- **Remote_User**. Authentication method used to get a validated user name. Often *null*.
- **Request_Method**. The HTTP method used to invoke the request ("GET", "HEAD", "POST", etc.).
- **Script_Name**. Virtual path to the current script, used in self-referencing URLs. Often missing.
- **Server_Name**. The server's host or DNS name, or IP address.
- **Server_Protocol**. The name and revision of the protocol used to make the request. For example, "HTTP/1.0".
- **Server_Port**. The port to which the request was sent. Usually 80 for HTTP requests.
- **Server_Software**. Name and version of the server software ("Lotus-Domino/4.6").
- **Server_URL_Gateway_Interface**. The CGI version spec with which the server complies. Often missing.

There may also be other Items in the ContextDocument whose names begin with HTTP_ or HTTPS_. Some that I've seen are HTTP_CONNECTION, HTTPS_KEYSIZE, HTTP_HOST, HTTP_UA_CPU, HTTP_UA_OS, HTTP_UA_COLOR, and HTTP_UA_PIXELS.

Chapter 8

Let's do a quickie Agent (Listing 8.4) that dumps the contents of the context Document. This Agent is on the CD in source form and is also contained in Ex84.nsf.

Listing 8.4 CGI Variable Dumper (Ex84CGI.java)

```java
import lotus.notes.*;
import java.util.*;
import java.io.*;

public class Ex84CGI extends AgentBase
{

    public void NotesMain()
    {
    try {
            Session s = this.getSession();
            AgentContext ctx = s.getAgentContext();
            Document doc = ctx.getDocumentContext();
            PrintWriter pw = this.getAgentOutput();

            if (doc == null)
                pw.println("No context document");
            else
                {
                java.util.Vector v = doc.getItems();
                pw.println("Found vector with " + v.size() +
                        " elements<BR>");
                int i;
                for (i = 0; i < v.size(); i++)
                {
                Item item = (Item)v.elementAt(i);
                pw.print("Item " + i + ": ");
                if (item == null)
                    pw.print("NULL");
                else pw.print(item.getName() + " / " +
```

```
                                    item.getText());
                pw.println("<BR>");
                }
            }// end else
        }
        catch (Exception e) { e.printStackTrace(); }
    }
}
```

We'll use this later in Chapter 11 as the foundation for an Agent/Servlet adapter. Figure 8.9 shows some of the output of the Agent in a browser window.

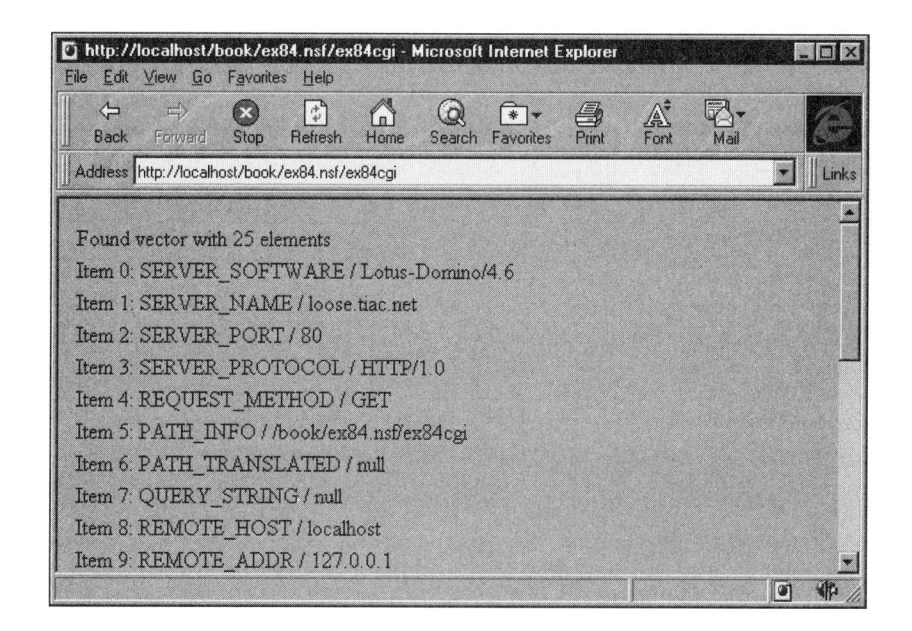

Figure 8.9 Output of Ex84CGI Agent.

Figure 8.10 Shows the output of the same URL with some query parameters added.

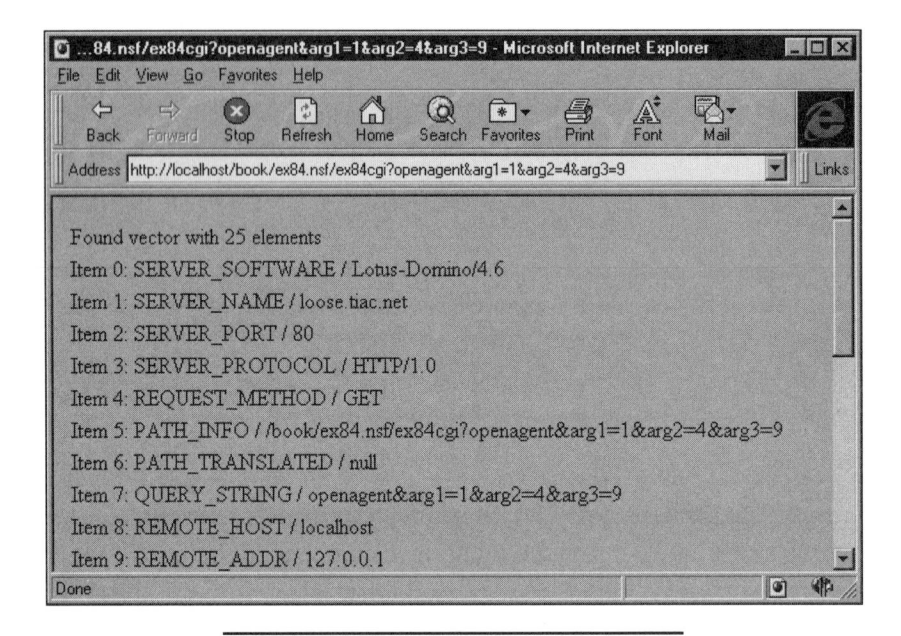

Figure 8.10 Ex84CGI Agent output with query.

SUMMARY

We've seen in this chapter how to write single- and multithreaded Agents for NOI. We've also seen how Agents can be triggered from the Domino HTTP server, and how to pass CGI variables through to an Agent. In the next chapter, we consider some of the problems with debugging Domino Java Agents.

9

DEBUGGING NOI AGENTS

Those of you who have used LotusScript to create Agents or event handlers in the Notes user interface are by now familiar with the LotusScript Integrated Development Environment that comes with the Notes Client. You get a LotusScript editor and debugger all in one. Unfortunately, Domino 4.6 does not include an IDE for the new Java interface. As you saw in Chapter 7, creating Java applications that use NOI is not really a problem: You're writing a standalone program, and you can use whatever development tools you like, so long as the Notes libraries and jar files that you need are available. In Chapter 8 you saw that Java Agents for Domino are developed outside the Notes Client and imported into a database using the Import Class Files button in the Agent Builder UI.

You can certainly use a third-party development tool to create your Java Agent: You do the type-compile-fix cycle until you get a clean compile, then you're ready to import the class(es) into Domino. But how do you debug it? Your Agent has no main() function, so you can't run it from the command line, and no third-party tool will have a clue as to how to deal with an Agent either. Only Domino can launch a Java Agent with the proper context all set up, but Domino doesn't (yet) provide a debugger for Java. What's a frustrated developer to do? There are some obvious choices:

1. Use lots of System.out.println calls to trace the execution of the Agent. This is fine for small programs, but if you're going to use this technique (which harks back to the early days of C programming, when the only debuggers available were at the assembly language level, if you were lucky), you have to put in a compile time "isDebug()" call around each println so that later, when you switch over to production mode, your users aren't staring at all your debug messages. Then you have to recompile the Agent before deploying it, to reset your internal debug flag. This is definitely a suboptimal solution.

2. Write your Agent so that it can be used two different ways: as a real Agent, or as a standalone program. The advantage of this approach is that you can use a real Java debugger. The problem with it is that you can't debug the Agent the way it will be really working: complete with Agent context.

The approach I'm going to suggest here is a refinement of option 2: You can code your Agent so it operates as a standalone program so that you can use a real debugger; you can also *fake* the context part by writing just a bit of extra code. It is possible to write an Agent that, in a sense, has multiple personalities. It has a main() method so it can run as a standalone program, and it extends AgentBase and has a NotesMain() method, so it can be a real Agent ("it's a floor wax *and* a dessert topping"). As a standalone program it can also have a hard-wired Agent

Sample Debuggable Agent

Original Agent

Let's start by reprinting a sample Agent from Chapter 8 in Listing 9.1, then we'll rewrite it a bit to be debuggable. The Agent is real simple, but this technique can be applied to a program of any complexity. This Agent was originally Ex81Agent.java.

Listing 9.1 Original Sample Agent (Ex81Agent.java)

```java
import java.lang.*;
import java.io.*;
import lotus.notes.*;

public class Ex81Agent extends AgentBase
{
    public void NotesMain()
        {
        try {
            Session s = this.getSession();
            AgentContext ctx = s.getAgentContext();
            Database db = ctx.getCurrentDatabase();
            DocumentCollection dc = ctx.getUnprocessedDocuments();
            System.out.println("Found " + dc.getCount() +
                                        " selected docs");
            Newsletter nl = s.createNewsletter(dc);
            nl.setSubjectItemName("Subject");
            Document doc = nl.formatMsgWithDoclinks(db);
            doc.send(ctx.getEffectiveUserName());
```

```
                System.out.println("Newsletter sent to " +
                                ctx.getEffectiveUserName());
            }
        catch (Exception e) { e.printStackTrace(); }
        }
} // end class
```

Okay, now how do we give this a main() so that it can be invoked from the command line, or from a Java development tool? In order to do that, we need to write a main() and have it initialize Notes properly. But if that's all we do, the program will never run. Why? Because the first thing the NotesMain() method (normally the place where the Agent is first invoked by the AgentBase base class) does is call AgentBase.getSession() to retrieve a Session instance. If we run from the command line, AgentBase hasn't been set up as it normally would be by Domino, so there will be no Session instance, and our program will bomb out with a NullPointerException right away.

Never fear though, we can code around that by creating a new constructor for our Agent class that takes a Session instance as an argument, and by then overriding AgentBase's getSession() call to return the right thing (see Listing 9.2). I've added a main(), changed the name of the class, and added a new constructor. This is an intermediate form of the Agent we're working toward, so it isn't included in the CD (the final version is included).

Listing 9.2 First Revision of the Agent

```
import java.lang.*;
import java.io.*;
import lotus.notes.*;

public class Ex90Agent extends AgentBase
{
    private Session my_session;
```

Debugging NOI Agents

```
public static void main(String argv[])
    {
    try {
        NotesThread.sinitThread();
        Session temp = Session.newInstance();
        Ex90Agent agent = new Ex90Agent(temp);
        agent.NotesMain();
        }
    catch (Exception e) { e.printStackTrace(); }
    finally { NotesThread.stermThread(); }
    }  // end main
public Ex90Agent() { super(); }
public Ex90Agent(Session s) { this.my_session = s; }
public Session getSession()
    {
    if (this.my_session == null)
        return super.getSession();
    else return this.my_session;
    }

public void NotesMain()
    {
    try {
        Session s = this.getSession();
        AgentContext ctx = s.getAgentContext();
        System.out.println("User is " + ctx.getEffectiveUserName());
        Database db = ctx.getCurrentDatabase();
        DocumentCollection dc = ctx.getUnprocessedDocuments();
        System.out.println("Found " + dc.getCount() + " selected docs");
        Newsletter nl = s.createNewsletter(dc);
        nl.setSubjectItemName("Subject");
        Document doc = nl.formatMsgWithDoclinks(db);
        doc.send(ctx.getEffectiveUserName());
        System.out.println("Newsletter sent to " +
```

```
                                    ctx.getEffectiveUserName());
            }
        catch (Exception e) { e.printStackTrace(); }
        }
} // end class
```

Our new main() is pretty standard: initialize Notes, create a Session, create an instance of our class (passing the session into the constructor). Then, instead of calling agent.start() as we normally would, we call agent.NotesMain() directly. Why can't we still call agent.start(), and just have NotesMain() run on another thread? Because in "debug mode" we're entering our Agent program through main(), not through AgentBase, and when we do that our AgentBase instance is not properly initialized (it is normally initialized from Notes when an Agent is started). Were we to call agent.start(), we'd get a NullPointerException somewhere in AgentBase at the point where the code accesses a member variable that it expects to be there, but in this case is *null*.

Note also that we now provide a nondefault constructor for the Ex90Agent class, so that our main() can pass a Session instance in to it. And, having written a nondefault constructor, we have to write a default constructor as well.

The next piece of code we rewrote was to implement a getSession() override. Normally our NotesMain() method just calls the getSession() that's implemented in AgentBase, and we get the Session instance that has been all set up with an AgentContext for us. This version of getSession() is designed so that it will work equally well in both our standalone/debug case and in the "real Agent" case. All it does is return the cached Session instance if there is one (debug case), or else call the method we would normally call anyway in AgentBase to get the Session (that's the line "return super.getSession();").

So what happens when we actually run this from the command line? Let's step through it so far.

1. We type *java Ex90Agent* in a command window.
2. Java invokes our main() procedure.
3. main() initializes Notes, then creates a Session instance as you normally would for a standalone Application.
4. main() creates an instance of Ex90Agent, passing in the Session instance. The Ex90Agent constructor saves the Session instance in a private member variable.
5. main() invokes NotesMain() on Ex90Agent.
6. NotesMain() calls this.getSession(), which returns the Session cached in step 4.
7. NotesMain() calls Session.getAgentContext() and then AgentContext.getEffectiveuserName().
8. At this point, Java raises a NullPointerException, because the kind of Session that we created (using the static call Session.newInstance()) doesn't contain any Agent context information. Only Sessions created by AgentBase can contain a real Agent context.

Still, not to worry, we're making real progress here. The next thing we need to do is to fake up some Agent context. To do that we have to create our own versions of the Session and AgentContext classes. And what better way to do that, given that we're using a great object-oriented language here, than to simply "specialize" the existing classes by inheriting from them?

Debug Class Extensions: DbgSession

We'll make our two new classes *public*, meaning that they each have to be coded in their own file. We could have made them private to the Ex90Agent class, but that would really limit their reusability. If we make them first-class objects, then we can use them for all our Agent debugging needs without recoding them each time. See Listings 9.2 and 9.3, and the corresponding files on the CD. The versions here (so far) are skeletons, to which we'll be adding more methods in just a bit.

Listing 9.2 Extended Session Class (DbgSession.java)

```
import lotus.notes.*;
public class DbgSession extends lotus.notes.Session
{
    private Session s;
    private DbgAgentContext context;
    public DbgSession() throws NotesException
        {
        super(1);  // any number will do
        // get a "real" session to redirect calls to
        this.s = Session.newInstance();
        }
    public AgentContext getAgentContext() throws NotesException
        {
        // return one of our debug versions
        if (this.context != null)
            return this.context;
        return new DbgAgentContext(this.s);
        }
} // end class
```

The only method we're overriding (so far) in this class is getAgentContext(). We want to return our debuggable AgentContext instance, not the normal NOI one. Our debuggable Session class acts as a wrapper for the real Session class, and we can redirect calls to our instance to the real one as needed. That way we don't have to re-implement all the logic of the Session class ourselves. Because DbgSession is also a Session (it inherits from Session, therefore it is one) we don't have to change any of the declarations in the main() function (or anywhere else for the most part) that use Session; assigning an instance of DbgSession to a variable declared as Session is perfectly kosher.

You'll note, however, that DbgSession both inherits from Session and creates a real Session instance that it can redirect calls to. What gives with that, why do both? The answer lies in the interface from the Java NOI classes to the C++ implementation in the Notes code.

Normally each NOI Java object instance, of whatever class, is really acting as a wrapper for a C++ class implemented inside Notes core. The Java instances keep track of pointers to C++ objects and redirect all the method invocations into the Notes code. When we create our DbgSession instance, we use the constructor you see above. It has to call its base class constructor (in the Session class). Were we to call the default Session class constructor we'd hit a safety check in all the NOI classes. Since the Session class was originally designed to be instantiated only by the static newInstance() method, the default constructor for Session makes a call to System.exit() to terminate the current process. Looking back, I wish we'd done it differently, because it would have made writing this chapter on debugging Agents a bit easier. However, as it stands in Domino 4.6, you can't call the default constructor of any of the NOI classes, as each was meant to be strictly contained by a parent object (with the exception of Session, which has a static creation method).

So, to make a long story short, we have to use a nondefault Session base class constructor from DbgSession, one which expects a handle to a C++ object as an argument. Of course, we have no such C++ handle to give it, so we make up a number (1 in this case; any number will do). That works okay, but we now have to be absolutely sure that we never invoke a method on our DbgSession instance that will go to our base class instance and try to invoke a C++ call on a handle that we've phonied up. If we do, it's guaranteed to crash.

That's why, even though our DbgSession instance is also a Session (which gives us the convenience of not having to redeclare stuff) it isn't a real Session that we can invoke real Session methods on. We can, however, override certain Session methods to suit our own purposes, and, in cases where we want to use the real Session methods, we've also generated a real Session instance on the side to which we can redirect calls. You'll see how we need to override additional Session methods below, as we refine the example.

Debug Class Extensions: DbgAgentContext

Now let's look at our debuggable version of the AgentContext class (see Listing 9.3).

Listing 9.3 Extended AgentContext Class (DbgAgentContext.java)

```
import lotus.notes.*;
public class DbgAgentContext extends lotus.notes.AgentContext
{
    public DbgAgentContext(Session s) throws NotesException
        {
        super(s, 1);  // use any number here
        }
    public String getEffectiveUserName()
        {
        return new String("Bob Balaban");
        }
}  // end class
```

Nothing too controversial here, really. As with DbgSession, we have to call the base class constructor with a C++ handle (we lie and say "1"). We also have to provide a Session instance, and we're going to use the one passed in by DbgSession in its getAgentContext() call, which is going to be the real Session instance to which we redirect calls.

One interesting thing is that we've overridden the getEffectiveUserName() method to return a hardwired string. This is the way we'll get around not having a real Agent context to work with: We'll fake one for the caller. We'll add some more overrides to AgentContext later.

Further Revisions to Ex90Agent

Now let's recode our Agent's main() function slightly to create a DbgSession instead of a regular old Session and try it again. The only change we need to make is to call "new DbgSession();" instead of "Session.newInstance()". Of course we have to have compiled our new Dbg classes too.

What happens? We get a NullPointerException in the Session's constructor. Something it needs isn't initialized. Again, that's because the Session class wasn't designed to handle this sort of situation; the first ever instantiation of a Session instance in our program is being forced to take an unexpected code path (because we're calling a Session constructor that we're really not supposed to be using). Had we world enough and time before Domino 4.6 shipped, certainly we would have cleaned this up for you. But never fear, we're nearing the end of most of the bad hackery, and once you get set up to debug Agents this way, you won't have to worry about it again. So onward.

We need to, in our Agent's main() method, initialize a dummy Session object just to get the whole system in gear, then we can get rid of it. So we'll just add a call to Session.newInstance() before the "new DbgSession()" call (the version of Ex90Agent.java on the CD has all these changes in it, don't worry).

Let's recompile and run it again. This time our Agent's NotesMain() method does get a valid (well, our invented one) AgentContext instance, and we see a message with a user name: so far so good. Then the program crashes because we invoked AgentContext. getCurrentDatabase(). The DbgAgentContext class has no implementation of this method, so Java directed the call to the AgentContext base class, which does have one. That call then got tossed over to Notes with a totally invalid C++ handle ("1"), and Notes croaked. Not to worry, though. All we need to do is continue to hardwire some additional AgentContext methods to return something valid, so the program can keep going. To avoid torturing you by continuing to go step by step with this, let's look ahead and see what other classes we're going to have to create wrappers for.

First we need DbgAgentContext to return some kind of Database instance for the getCurrentDatabase() call. Can we use a real Database instance (easy to get, just pick a database), or will we have to extend the class? In this case we can just use a real Database instance that getCurrentDatabase() can pick. I just used the Database that goes with the original Ex81Agent sample.

The next thing in our NotesMain() function that we need to worry about is the getUnprocessedDocuments() call on AgentContext. Again that's no real problem, we just have to implement a getUnprocessedDocuments() call in DbgAgentContext that uses the current Database to create some kind of collection for us. I decided to use FTSearch() to find some Documents in the Database.

Looking again at NotesMain(), we see that there's a call to Session.createNewsletter(). That's one that we'll have to override in DbgSession, so that the call gets redirected to the real Session object.

From there on out we don't have to do anything special. Listing 9.4 shows all the code for Ex90Agent as modified, plus the full listings of DbgSession and DbgAgentContext (all are also on the CD).

Listing 9.4 Debuggable Agent Plus Debug NOI Classes

```
/*** Class Ex90Agent ***/
import java.lang.*;
import java.io.*;
import lotus.notes.*;

public class Ex90Agent extends AgentBase
{
    private Session my_session;

    public static void main(String argv[])
        {
        try {
            NotesThread.sinitThread();
            Session temp = Session.newInstance();
            temp = new DbgSession();
            Ex90Agent agent = new Ex90Agent(temp);
            agent.NotesMain();
            }
        catch (Exception e) { e.printStackTrace(); }
        finally { NotesThread.stermThread(); }
        }   // end main

    public Ex90Agent() { super(); }
    public Ex90Agent(Session s) { this.my_session = s; }
    public Session getSession()
        {
        if (this.my_session == null)
            return super.getSession();
        else return this.my_session;
        }

    public void NotesMain()
        {
        try {
            Session s = this.getSession();
```

```java
            AgentContext ctx = s.getAgentContext();
            System.out.println("User is " + ctx.getEffectiveUserName());
            Database db = ctx.getCurrentDatabase();
            DocumentCollection dc = ctx.getUnprocessedDocuments();
            System.out.println("Found " + dc.getCount() +
                                        " selected docs");
            Newsletter nl = s.createNewsletter(dc);
            nl.setSubjectItemName("Subject");
            Document doc = nl.formatMsgWithDoclinks(db);
            doc.send(ctx.getEffectiveUserName());
            System.out.println("Newsletter sent to " +
                                    ctx.getEffectiveUserName());
            }
       catch (Exception e) { e.printStackTrace(); }
        }
}  // end class

/*** Class DbgSession, override of lotus.notes.Session ***/

import lotus.notes.*;
public class DbgSession extends lotus.notes.Session
{
    private Session s;

    public DbgSession() throws NotesException
        {
        super(1);   // any number will do

        // get a "real" session to redirect calls to
        this.s = Session.newInstance();
        }

    public AgentContext getAgentContext() throws NotesException
        {
        // return one of our debug versions
        return new DbgAgentContext(this.s);
        }
```

```java
    public Newsletter createNewsletter(DocumentCollection dc)
            throws NotesException
        { return this.s.createNewsletter(dc); }

} // end class

/*** Class DbgAgentContext: override of lotus.notes.AgentContext ***/

import lotus.notes.*;
public class DbgAgentContext extends lotus.notes.AgentContext
{
    private Session session;
    private Database currentdb;

    public DbgAgentContext(Session s) throws NotesException
        {
        super(s, 1);   // use any number here
        this.session = s;
        }

      public String getEffectiveUserName() throws NotesException
        { return new String("Bob Balaban"); }

      public Database getCurrentDatabase() throws NotesException
        {
        Database db = this.session.getDatabase("",
"book\\Ex81.nsf");
        this.currentdb = db;
        return db;
        }

    public DocumentCollection getUnprocessedDocuments()
                throws NotesException
        { return this.currentdb.FTSearch("Balaban", 0); }
} // end class
```

So, are we done? In fact, so far as this particular Agent is concerned, we are. You can run this Agent now from the command line, like any application. Any Java development tool that handles Java 1.1.x code will be perfectly happy to let you debug this program. You can also import it into a Notes Database and let it run as a real Agent, though if you leave it unmodified you'll have to import the DbgSession and DbgAgentContext class files also, because they are explicitly referenced.

How does the code know the difference between the two situations? Simple, when you run it from the command line, code starts executing in the Ex90Agent's main() method. Alternatively, when you let it run as a real Agent (either foreground or background), code execution starts in NotesMain(), invoked from AgentBase. In that code path the getSession() call returns the real AgentContext instance set up by AgentBase, because there's no cached DbgAgentSession instance.

If you wanted to save a bit of space in the database, you could—when you're ready to go to production mode with your Agent—comment out the main() method. Then you wouldn't have to import the debug class files at all. Alternatively, you could code the main() function slightly differently. Instead of

```
temp = new DbgSession();
```

you could do it this way:

```
temp = Class.forName("DbgSession").newInstance();
```

This is the only line of code in the Agent class that explicitly references any of the debug classes. If we change it to remove the load time "link" to our debug classes, we can import just the one Agent class into our database. Using Class.forName() to load the DbgSession class and Class.newInstance() to create an instance of it accomplishes exactly that. This way the only time that the debug classes are required is when our main() function is called, which it never would be from Notes. This technique works because the compile time reference to the debug class no longer appears in our Agent's compiled code, and the Java class loader no longer knows at load time that the class is referenced.

What other modifications might you have to make if you re-use these debug classes yourself? Essentially you just have to add more methods to DbgSession and DbgAgentContext as needed: Any Session or AgentContext method that your Agent uses must be overridden in the debug extensions, otherwise your program will crash Domino.

So, how bad a hack is this, really? My own opinion (although I admit to being prejudiced) is that it's in the neighborhood of slightly grungy but not too bad. The business of having to wrapper real objects with debug objects and the strange constructor limitations are slightly repellent, and that's something that could and should definitely be cleaned up in NOI. The idea of extending NOI classes to do debug type activities is perfectly normal in an object-oriented world, and one of the things that Java actually tries to be good at, so no problem there. The NOI classes were explicitly and purposely not declared *final* to allow just this sort of extension by anybody at all.

SUMMARY

Debugging Java Agents in Domino 4.6 is not as simple an undertaking as we'd like. Still, with a bit of effort, as you've seen in this chapter, it is possible to recast an Agent program slightly so that it can be debugged using any Java 1.1 compatible development tool.

Chapter 10 goes into still more detail about how objects can be shared across multiple threads in a Java NOI program.

10
SHARING OBJECTS ACROSS THREADS

We've seen in the earlier chapters on multithreaded Agents and applications that NOI objects can be used (shared, in a sense) by more than one thread in a program. How does that work? It certainly isn't obvious that it should work, and it isn't always obvious when and why you'd want to do it. This chapter delves a bit into these issues.

WHY SHARE OBJECTS ACROSS THREADS?

Let's assume you've made the decision to write a multithreaded application or Agent, and that you already know that one or more of the threads you're going to create will use NOI objects. You've gone through an analysis that concluded something like, "We have multiple, independent tasks that need to be completed, and each task is subject to significant i/o or network delay. Therefore our program will benefit from a multi-threaded architecture."

Are there cases where you'd want to access one or more NOI instances on more than one thread at a time? Quite possibly. Some examples might include:

1. Multiple threads creating Documents in a single Database (as in samples Ex74Multi and Ex75Crawl from Chapter 7). There's no reason to create a Database instance for each thread.
2. Multiple threads each conducting a different search on a single Database.
3. More than one thread needing access to an AgentContext instance.
4. Lots of threads making use of a single Session instance.

You can probably come up with numerous scenarios in which you'd want to have a common resource operated on by more than a single thread at a time. Databases certainly fall into this category, but so do Sessions, Documents, DateTime objects, and others. Pretty much any time you want threads to share some kind of application context you'll be confronted with the sharing issue.

NOI AND THREAD SAFETY

Is the Java NOI thread safe? What does *thread safe* mean? We started to address this question in Chapter 7, but now it's time to look at the problem more closely. I'll propose the following criteria for whether or not a program is thread safe:

1. **Stability.** Threads can share objects by invoking methods on those objects and the program will not crash.

2. **Data reliability.** A thread storing data to or retrieving data from an object instance must be sure that the data are internally consistent. Another way of putting this is to say that a data put or get operation on an object by a single thread must be *atomic*; that is, all the data you store in the object are stored at the same time, and all the data you get from the object are retrieved at the same time. No other thread can modify the data in the object during your store or retrieve operation.

One could propose more criteria, and books are constantly being written on the topic. I claim that these are the two most important criteria for using the Java programming interface to Notes. If you'd like to pursue the general design issues of multithreaded programming in Java, one book I like is *Concurrent Programming in Java*, by Doug Lea (Addison-Wesley, 1997).

By these criteria, the Java NOI is indeed thread safe. Any of the objects (with one exception, which we'll get to) can be used simultaneously by any number of threads (as long as each thread is a NotesThread instance). All NOI methods are *synchronized*, meaning that no two methods on an NOI object can be invoked by more than one thread at a time. This in and of itself is not enough, as we'll see, but it is required; it's the only way to ensure that one thread isn't reading a piece of data while another is writing the same piece.

As I mentioned, synchronization of Java methods is necessary but not sufficient to provide thread safety in NOI. It would be if all of NOI were implemented purely in Java, but we know all too well (especially if you read Chapter 9) that most of the real functionality is implemented in C and C++ in the Notes/Domino core. Each Java object instance is really a wrapper for a corresponding C++ object instance, and lots of state data are maintained in the C++ layer. That state data need to be thread safe as well, naturally.

You might suppose that synchronizing all the Java methods might still be enough to protect the internal C++ state data. After all, if only one call at a time can get through to the C++ layer, where's the conflict? The answer is that there is still a great potential for conflict because of the side effects of calling a method on an object. Let me illustrate it this way:

1. You instantiate a Database instance, and do a lookup on a note id to get a Document.
2. You pass the Document to a second thread, to do some manipulation on it.
3. Back on the first thread you continue to look up Documents in the Database.
4. The second thread decides to delete the Document, removing it from the Database.

Removing a Document from a Database on one thread while the Database is in use on another thread poses a potential problem for the Database class. The searching operations that your first thread executes are all synchronized calls to a Database instance. But the Document.remove() method is a synchronized *Document* class call, and the *semaphore* used by Java to implement method synchronization won't prevent the remove() call from executing concurrently with a Database search call. That's because the semaphore (or "lock, which prevents simultaneous access from multiple threads") is on the object instance that owns the method, and in our example here we're calling two methods on objects belonging to two different classes. While two Database or two Document calls *would* be synchronized, when you make one call on each object the two calls are *not* synchronized with each other.

It matters because the remove() call on the Document must cause the Document instance that's going away to be removed from the list of

Documents maintained by its parent Database. Thus a call to a Document method will cause an indirect invocation of some code in the Database class, and the list of Documents belonging to the Database must therefore also be protected by a semaphore. If it weren't, you could easily have a situation where Database.FTSearch() is locating a Document instance and returning it while Document.remove() is in the middle of deleting that Document. The Database instance's internal data structures would get out of synch and you'd have a problem somewhere down the road—maybe a crash, maybe a search result set full of already deleted Documents.

So, the point is that all the NOI objects that maintain state data that might be modified through calls to other (related) objects must be made explicitly thread safe in the C++ code, through the use of semaphores.

There's an interesting distinction that should be made here, and one which I think the Java mechanism of synchronization blurs a bit: It is always the case that when writing code that is meant to be thread safe, you must worry about what data structures need to be protected by semaphores, not what code needs to be protected. This might sound subtle, and it is, but it's very important, and if you can grasp the distinction and take it to heart you'll end up writing better code.

Let's take the Database object's list of child Documents as an example. Each Database instance will have its own list, of course. Each Database instance can be invoked from multiple threads, both directly (via calls to Database methods) from Java and indirectly (via calls to methods on child Document instances, for example) from C++. Because the contents of the Document list must retain integrity, any operation that adds a Document to the list or removes a Document from the list must be atomic, that is, it must be guaranteed sole access to the list during the lifetime of the add/remove operation. It would clearly be a big problem if a piece of code was attempting to add a new element to the end of a linked list at the same time that another piece of code was doing the same thing: Someone somewhere is bound to come up with an invalid pointer. Thus we semaphore (protect) the list. The code that wants access to the list must obtain a lock, guaranteeing sole access, before modifying the list, and it must release the lock when done. But it's always the list, not the code that is being protected.

Another wrinkle which Notes deals with very nicely internally, and Java doesn't, is the distinction between read locks and write locks. To continue our Database list example, if you only have one kind of semaphore (as Java does), then readers and writers of the list both have to try to get the exact same lock before they can access the list. But it is also true that we can achieve greater overall program concurrency if we allow multiple simultaneous readers. There's no reason to make two threads who both just want to scan the list for a matching Document wait for one another; they can both read the list at the same time without doing any damage.

One issue (I won't say problem) with Java is that there is only one kind of semaphore built into the language, and it makes no distinction between reading and writing. Of course, you can write your own semaphore class that does all the right things for distinguishing between readers and writers, but that's a lot of work (check out the section on "Readers and Writers" in Chapter 5 of *Concurrent Programming in Java*). Maybe someday they'll add something to the language to support that.

In the meantime, Notes has some great internal semaphoring capabilities, including read-write semaphores. The logic of a read-write semaphore is roughly as follows:

- Permit any number of readers to obtain a lock as long as there is no writer.
- Permit only one writer at a time to obtain a lock.
- If a writer holds the lock, no readers may obtain a lock.

❐ If any readers hold the lock, no writer may obtain a lock.

The advantage of using a scheme like this is, as I mentioned above, that you get greater concurrency (fewer readers of a data structure have to wait per session overall) and therefore better throughput. The overall point here is that not only are the Java NOI classes thread safe (with a couple of restrictions mentioned below), but that the internal mechanisms by which they are made thread safe are optimized for performance.

WHAT *ISN'T* THREAD SAFE?

There are three topics worth mentioning here: (1) restrictions on multithreaded use of the lotus.notes.DbDirectory class, (2) a warning about algorithms (as opposed to classes) that aren't thread safe, and (3) restrictions on memory management and the use of the Session class.

Multithreading Restrictions on DbDirectory

The DbDirectory class is mostly used to locate and get Database instances on a server. You can use DbDirectory to iterate through all the Databases of a particular type (NSF, NTF, replicas, etc.) on a specified machine (see Chapter 2 for a writeup of all the DbDirectory methods). Typically, you do an iterative search by first calling DbDirectory.getFirstDatabase(), then successively calling getNextDatabase() until a *null* is returned, indicating the end of the list.

Unfortunately, the Notes APIs that the DbDirectory class uses to implement an efficient search of Databases is not completely thread safe. This means that you can't, for example, call getFirstDatabase() on one thread and then call getNextDatabase() on the same DbDirectory instance from another thread. It won't crash if you do (DbDirectory keeps track of which thread getFirstDatabase() was called on), but it'll throw an exception. Unfortunately there's no way around this in Domino 4.6, but in practice you shouldn't ever be seriously inconvenienced.

There is absolutely no problem with using DbDirectory on a single thread. Likewise there is no problem in reusing a DbDirectory instance on a second thread: The only restriction is that if you make a getFirstDatabase() call on a given thread, then all subsequent getNextDatabase() calls must also be made on that thread. You are free to call getFirst/NextDatabase() on one thread, then reuse the same instance on another thread to do a new getFirst/NextDatabase() sequence. There's no particular advantage to doing so, however. You can always just create a DbDirectory instance for each thread that needs one, and never share them.

This is the only restriction like this in all of the Java interface (so far as I know). All other objects may be freely used from as many threads as you like.

Thread Unsafe Algorithms

Regardless of how thread safe the actual NOI code and data structures are, there will always be algorithms that are inherently unsafe when used in a multithreaded environment. You should be aware of this as you code your Agents and applications.

Let's take an example from the Notes UI that many people have come across. We'll postulate two users, UserA and UserB, both remotely accessing the same document in the same database on the same server. Here's the sequence of steps:

1. UserA opens the document, reading it into her workstation's memory.

2. UserB opens the document, reading it into his workstation's memory.

3. UserA and UserB both make changes to the document while its contents are still in their respective workstations' memory.

4. UserA saves her version of the document back into the database on the server.

5. UserB attempts to save his version of the document back into the database, but gets an error saying that the document was modified since the time UserB last read it.

There's no way for Notes to prevent this sort of conflict, given the nature of the beast as a multi-user groupware product. No amount of data structure semaphoring will circumvent this problem. The only thing you (the application developer) can hope to do is detect the conflict and warn the user appropriately, or take corrective action.

The same is true for programs using NOI: You have to be aware of when you might be building multithreading conflicts into your algorithms. For example, the following program (Listing 10.1) is likely to cause problems:

Listing 10.1 Multithreading Conflicts Example (Ex101Conflict.java)

```
import lotus.notes.*;
public class Ex101Conflict
{
    public static void main(String argv[])
        {
        try {
            NotesThread.sinitThread();
            Session s = Session.newInstance();
            Database db = s.getDatabase("", "book\\Ex101.nsf");
            Document doc = db.getDocumentByID("20FA");
```

Chapter 10

```
                // start 2 threads, one to modify doc, one to delete it
                Ex101Modify mod = new Ex101Modify(doc);
                Ex101Delete del = new Ex101Delete(doc);
                mod.start();
                del.start();
                mod.join();
                del.join();
                }
        catch (Exception e) { e.printStackTrace(); }
        finally { NotesThread.stermThread(); }
        } // end main
} // end class

class Ex101Modify extends NotesThread
{
    private Document my_doc;

    public Ex101Modify(Document doc)
        { my_doc = doc; }

    public void runNotes()
        {
        try {
            System.out.println("Modifying Document " +
                                this.my_doc.getNoteID());
            sleep(500);
            for (int i = 0; i < 100; i++)
                this.my_doc.replaceItemValue("item2", new Integer(i));
            sleep(500);
            this.my_doc.save(true, false);
            System.out.println("Modified document saved");
            }
        catch (Exception e) { e.printStackTrace(); }
        } // end runNotes
} // end class
```

```
class Ex101Delete extends NotesThread
{
    private Document my_doc;
    public Ex101Delete(Document doc)
        { this.my_doc = doc; }

    public void runNotes()
        {
        try {
            System.out.println("About to delete document " +
                                this.my_doc.getNoteID());
             this.my_doc.remove(true);
            }
        catch (Exception e) { e.printStackTrace(); }
        }
} // end class
```

I created the Ex101 database (available on the CD) with a single document in it, then used the Document Properties box to get its note id. The main() program navigates its way to that Document instance in the Database, then starts two threads, passing the Document to each. One thread iterates over a loop updating (in memory) the contents of one of the Items in the Document. Meanwhile the second thread is deleting the Document. I know that (for pedagogical purposes) the delete thread will complete first, because I've added some sleep() calls to the modify thread to slow it down.

If you want to try this out for yourself, you have to add a document to the database, then get the note id and use it in the main() function instead of "20FA", and finally recompile the sources. To get the note id for any document, select that document in a view, or open it. Then bring up the Document Properties box; right-click on a selected document, or use the **File/Document Properties** menu command. The information tab on the properties box contains a long ID string, with colons separating it into sections, as in Figure 10.1. The last part of the ID, beginning with the characters "NT" is the eight-character note id (not including the "NT"). You can use this eight-character string in the Database.getDocumentByID() call (you can also skip any leading zeros).

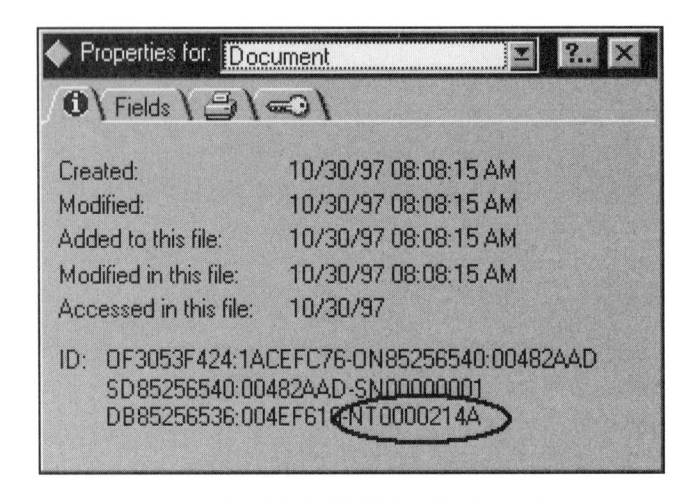

Figure 10.1 Document Properties box.

When I ran it, I got a NullPointerException on the replaceItemValue() call where it calls an internal routine named NotesBase.CheckObject(). The purpose of the CheckObject() routine is to detect conflicts such as the one I've manufactured here: Somehow between the time a Document instance is created and a call on one of its methods is made, the Document has been deleted. CheckObject() notices during one of the replaceItemValue() calls that the object is no longer valid, and throws the exception.

Now, you can argue, as I do, that both the program and the Notes classes are thread safe, because no data is corrupted, and the program doesn't crash. It's the algorithm that's problematic, not the code. It's NOI's job to make sure that the objects behave as advertised, and to let you, the programmer, know when you have a conflict. It's your job to anticipate the conflicts that might legitimately arise and to account for them in the code. For example, now that you know about the CheckObject() call, you could add it explicitly into the program, so that you check an object before invoking a method on it. Or, you could catch exceptions as we already do in the example, but make the logic a bit more interesting than just printing a stack trace and bailing out. You could recover in some way to preserve your thread's data: take the contents of the field that you're trying to replace and write it to a new Document, or some such technique.

Memory Management and lotus.notes.Session

One final issue that all Java NOI developers should be aware of has to do with the relationship between instances of the Session class and threads.

First a little background. We've said a few times in this book that the NOI classes comprise a *strict containment hierarchy*, which simply means that every object (with the exception of Session, which is the root object in the containment hierarchy) is contained by a parent object (Documents by Database, Items by Documents, and so on). No object is ever instantiated via the Java *new* operator. The root object (Session) is instantiated via a static method, and all other objects are instantiated by a method on their container (Session.getDatabase(), Document.createRichTextItem(), and so on).

The reasoning behind imposing this design constraint on you was straightforward: In the real Notes implementation, no object can be free-floating; all objects have a container of some sort to provide context. To have a Document exist without a Database to give it context is meaningless in the Domino/Notes world.

The corollary to saying that all objects have a container is that if a container object goes away, then all its subsidiary objects must also go away. In LotusScript, objects that go out of scope in a program are automatically destroyed, because LotusScript maintains a reference count for all object instances and keeps track of everything. Java works a little differently: When an object reference goes *out of scope* (meaning that the object is no longer pointed to by any other objects and is no longer in the current execution scope) the object is "available" for deletion. It isn't actually destroyed until the Java VM's garbage collection thread gets around to "collecting" the storage belonging to that object.

The effect is the same, however, in that when a container object is destroyed (meaning that the object in memory is destroyed, *not* that the actual Notes object that the Java object represents is deleted) all objects belonging to that container must also be made to go away. In a Java program, we're never sure if or when the garbage collection thread (affectionately known as the gc thread) will get around to cleaning up memory, and we do know that any given Java program that makes heavy use of NOI can in practice create numerous object instances, which can really run up the memory usage bill. If the gc thread takes its sweet time (remember, the gc thread runs at a lower priority than any thread you create, so it can often get "starved") coming around to clean up, we can end up with hundreds or thousands of objects lying around, unreferenced and useless in memory. For example, consider the following code fragment (Listing 10.2):

Listing 10.2 How to Use Up Memory

```
Document doc = SomeView.getFirstDocument();
while (doc != null) doc = SomeView.getNextDocument(doc);
```

Seems innocent enough, right? Wrong. In LotusScript you'd be fine, because each time you assign a new Document instance to the "doc" variable, LotusScript would destroy the old (now unreferenced) instance automatically. Java, however, simply marks the old instance as unreferenced, and it doesn't get cleaned up until the gc thread comes around, which might be seconds, minutes, or hours later. Or never, because if there were 100,000 Documents in the View (a not unheard of situation), you'd run out of memory before the gc thread ever got to do its thing. The only way around this is to explicitly call System.gc(), which causes the garbage collector to run synchronously on the current thread. Not the greatest solution, but better than nothing. My own opinion is that it would be nice if JavaSoft were to provide some way for a user program to set the priority of the gc thread.

To help work around this problem, the Java implementation of NOI associates each Session instance with the thread instance on which it was created. Each Session object is simply tagged with the id of the thread that was running when the object came into being. When that thread terminates (and you'll remember from our discussion of NotesThread way back in Chapter 2 that we always know when a NotesThread instance terminates), any Sessions created on that thread are explicitly destroyed. What I really mean by "destroyed" in this case is not the Java notion of just setting everything to *null* so that it can be garbage collected later. I mean that the C++ object for which the Session instance is really just a proxy, or wrapper, is deallocated in Notes memory. This is done so that memory gets cleaned up for you more often than Java might be able to do it. Of course the memory that gets released is C++ memory, not Java memory, as there is no way for any Java program to explicitly force the destruction of any Java object. Still, C++ is where most of the memory in an NOI program is consumed.

The implications of this are important to anyone doing multi-threaded programming with NOI: When a NotesThread instance terminates, any Session object created on that thread is killed, and (because of our strict containment rule) therefore *all objects created in that Session's context are also destroyed.*

Take, for example, our little conflict program in Listing 10.1 (Ex101Conflict.java). You'll see that the main() function explicitly waits for each of the two child threads to complete before exiting. I have to do that, because it passed an object (Document) to each of those threads, and that object was created (indirectly) from a Session instantiated on the main() thread. If main() were to exit before both of the child threads terminated, the Session instance, and the Database and Document instances that came from it, would all be destroyed while still in use on the other threads. By waiting, we ensure the integrity of the Session and all its children.

We could, of course, have coded it differently so that main() would not have to wait. We could have had each child thread create its own Session instance, and navigate to the Document individually. That's the trade-off you have to consider when designing a multithreaded program using NOI: Would you rather have the thread that created the container object hang around and wait until everyone who shares that container (and all objects instantiated from the container) is done? Or would you rather not share objects across threads as much, and have each thread potentially duplicate some code (and take some time) to instantiate its own objects.

My inclination is to lean toward sharing objects where it makes the most sense to do so. If you find that you're stretching the code in some way just so that you can share an object across threads, it probably isn't a good idea. If your algorithm requires (for functional reasons, or for performance reasons, or even just for convenience of coding reasons) that an object be shared by more than one thread, go ahead and do it, no need to be afraid. Just be aware of which threads are using which objects, and which threads are using objects created by which other objects, and make sure that the right threads hang around the right amount of time. To the extent that you can, without violating good design practice, keep the use of an object single threaded (create it, use it, and forget it all on one thread)—your life will be a bit simpler.

Summary

I've tried in this chapter to explore some special issues with respect to multithreaded NOI programming. While most people using the Java NOI for run of the mill applications or Agents won't run into serious trouble, it helps to understand how the underlying system is really put together when you need to develop a large, production quality piece of code. To sum up, here's my recommended do's and don'ts:

1. Do use multithreading to improve overall application throughput when you can. If your code is doing a lot of i/o (disk or network), consider how you might structure your algorithm to allow several threads to perform independent tasks simultaneously.

2. Do be aware of memory usage issues at all times (the Java hype says you never have to worry about memory management, but you do). Use the System.gc() call judiciously, if necessary.

3. Do share Notes object instances across threads if it makes the overall operation of your program simpler.

4. Do think in advance about how your program will operate in a multi-user world.

5. Do test your multithreaded programs at least twice as much as you do your single-threaded programs.

6. Don't use threads in your program just for fun. If you can't explain to someone else why you need multithreading, you probably don't need multithreading.

7. Don't build conflicts into your multithreaded algorithms and then spend eternity semaphoring them. If the algorithm is broken, no amount of code will fix it.

8. Don't let your Session instance die before you're done with all child objects created (directly or indirectly) from that Session instance.

The next chapter talks about programming Servlets with Domino, and tells you how you can convert an existing Servlet into a Domino Agent (and it also tells you why you might want to do that).

11

UPGRADING SERVLETS TO AGENTS

This chapter is designed especially for two groups of people: (1) Those interested in learning more about the relationship of Servlets to Agents; and (2) those of you who have a non-Domino Web server (shame on you!), have Servlets in production, and are interested in learning how to convert those Servlets to Domino Agents. People that have installed Lotus Go and are upgrading to Domino, for example, should read on if they have any Servlets that they want to enhance and preserve. I'll show you how you can write an Agent/Servlet Adapter that allows your existing Servlets to be turned into Domino Agents.

WHAT IS A SERVLET?

A Servlet is kind of a cross between an Applet and a CGI/bin program. It's like an Applet in that you write it in Java, and it typically inherits from a base class such as javax.servlet.GenericServlet (you can alternatively implement one or more of the standard interfaces in your own class). It's like a CGI/bin program in that it sits around on a server machine waiting to be invoked, usually via some URL syntax. Unlike CGI/bin programs, though, the server doesn't have to start up a new process each time a Servlet is invoked—all Servlets run in the server's Java VM process, and the VM will cache Java classes for a period of time, which is a big performance win.

The Servlet class is not part of the standard Java language. It's considered an extension, which is why the package name is "javax.servlet" instead of "java.servlet". You can download a free copy of the Java Servlet Development Kit from the JavaSoft Web site (http://java.sun.com), and a copy of the Java Servlet Development Kit is included on the CD for this book.

Unlike Applets, Servlets don't have any user interface, because they run on server machines where there's usually no one present to enjoy it anyway.

Why would you use a Servlet? There are lots of things a Web-based application wants to do that are best done on the server machine, as opposed to from the browser. Anything you'd have previously torn your hair out to write as a CGI/bin program or Perl script can be done (more easily, in my opinion) in Java as a Servlet: connections to back-end relational database systems, redirection to other servers, and, of course, Domino applications (although I'll try to convince you later in this chapter that Domino Agents offer advantages over Servlets that you should seriously consider if you're starting from scratch).

SETTING UP DOMINO TO RUN SERVLETS

This section might appear out of order in the chapter, but if you want to try out any of the samples on a Domino server, then you'll have to do a

Upgrading Servlets to Agents

couple of things to set it up first. For other kinds of servers refer to the provider's documentation.

Servlet support is by default disabled in Domino 4.6, so you need to do a couple of things. First of all, add the following lines to your server's notes.ini file:

```
DominoEnableJavaServlets=1
JavaUserClasses=c:\notes\data\domino\servlet; f:/servlet/lib/clas
```

Of course you would use the correct path names for your mac
needed to create the servlet subdirectory under the domino direc
wasn't created by default at install time. The first line tells the
server to initialize the Servlet Manager (you'll see a message abo
in the server console when HTTP starts up). The second line ac
directory where you'll place your compiled Servlet code, so th
Servlet Manager can find it. You can use any directory you lik
putting it under \notes\data\domino is convenient. You also need the servlet runtime support classes on your classpath (these are part of the Servlet Development Kit).

Next, make sure that HTTP is running in your Domino server. If your notes.ini includes HTTP among the tasks that the server always runs (look for the "Servertasks=" line), then you're all set. If you want to start it up manually, then type "load http" in the server console window.

The next thing you need is a Servlet configuration file. This file tells the Servlet Manager how to map URLs to .class files for running Servlets. Here's one I'm using to run some sample Servlets that Sun has on their Web site:

```
#Servlet configuration
Servlet HelloWorldServlet {
}
Servlet SnoopServlet {
}
```

```
Servlet DateServlet {
}
Service HelloWorldServlet  /servlet/HelloWorldServlet
Service SnoopServlet  /servlet/Snoop
Service DateServlet  /servlet/Now
```

The servlet.cnf file goes in your Notes data directory and must be named servlet.cnf. A sample servlet.cnf is included on the CD. This one, for example, maps the URL "http://<server>/servlet/now" (note that the names are not case sensitive) to the DateServlet.class file, located in the Domino HTTP server's "/servlet" directory.

Finally, just put some Servlet .class files in the specified directory, bring up a browser, and type a URL to invoke one of the Servlets. The Servlet sends back an HTML response which you see in your browser. The Java Servlet Development Kit which I mentioned above contains the sample Servlets (including source code) referenced in this servlet.cnf sample file.

Figures 11.1 and 11.2 show what I got when I ran the sample DateServlet and HelloWorldServlet programs from my browser using Domino.

If you also want to be writing your own Servlets, you need to add the location of the classes.zip file installed from the Java Servlet Development Kit to your CLASSPATH variable.

Upgrading Servlets to Agents

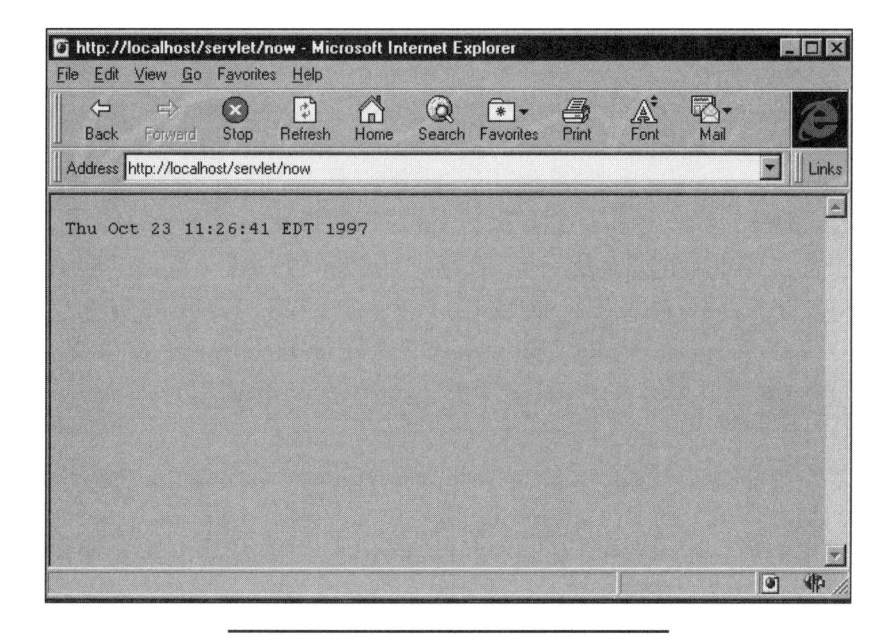

Figure 11.1 Running the DateServlet sample.

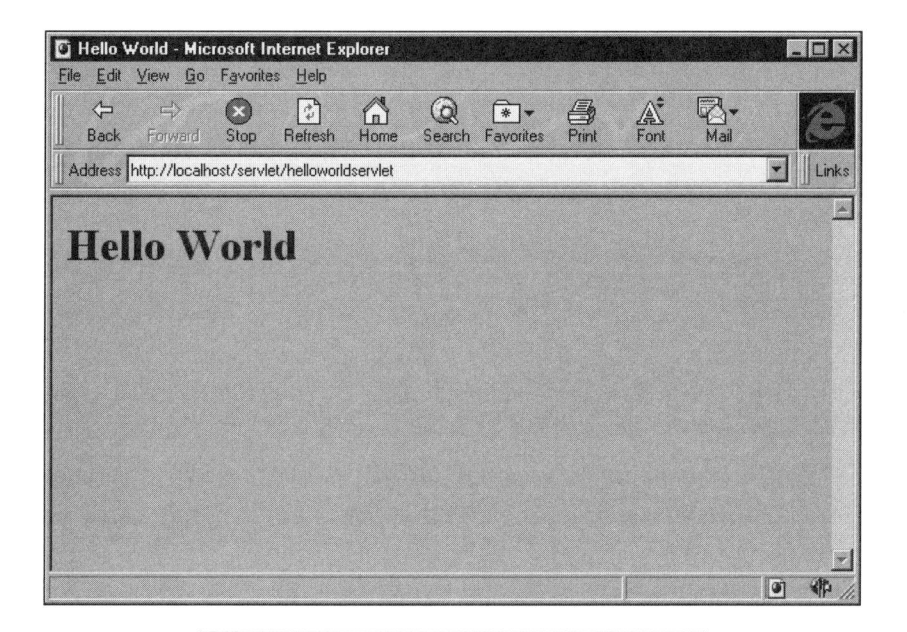

Figure 11.2 Running the HelloWorldServlet sample.

WRITING A SERVLET

The javax.servlet package is pretty straightforward—there are only a few classes and interfaces that you need to deal with for a simple Servlet:

- **javax.servlet.http.HttpServlet**: This is a basic framework for a Servlet implementation. It implements the javax.servlet.Servlet interface, and adds specialization for handling HTTP requests to the more general javax.servlet.GetnericServlet class. Most of the time you can write a class that extends either HttpServlet or GenericServlet and go from there.

- **javax.servlet.http.HttpServletRequest**: This is an interface that is used to package up all the incoming information that a Servlet needs to do its job, including information about the invoking URL and about the current execution context (meaning essentially, information about the HTTP server that is invoking the Servlet). You can use (or extend) a class that JavaSoft provides that implements this interface called sun.servlet.http, but I prefer to avoid any classes that are not part of the "java" or "javax" packages. As you'll see in the examples coming up, it isn't very hard to implement your own class for this.

- **javax.servlet.http.HttpServletResponse**: This is also an interface, and it is used to collect the Servlet's output and transmit it back to the user's browser session. The typical way of doing that is to write output to the output stream maintained by the HttpServletResponse instance. As you'll see below, you can get an instance of the javax.servlet.ServletOutputStream class by calling HttpServletResponse.getOutputStream(). Again, you can use the sun.servlet.http.HttpResponse class if you like, but I prefer not to.

❒ **javax.servlet.ServletConfig, javax.servlet.ServletContext**: We'll use these when we write our Servlet-running Agent in the next section of this chapter. For now, you can think of these interfaces as providing a Servlet with information about its initialization parameters (ServletConfig) and about its current execution context (ServletContext). You get a ServletContext instance from a ServletConfig instance, and the Servlet gets a ServletConfig instance passed to it at initialization time.

The Servlet paradigm is pretty simple: You invoke it with a URL, as in the above examples, and you can pass input (or "request") parameters as part of that URL. Everything following the Servlet's name is parsed into parameter input for the Servlet. For example, the URL

```
http://LocalHost/servlet/SnoopServlet/foo/bar?a=z
```

invokes the Servlet SnoopServlet with a path parameter of "/foo/bar" and a query string of "a=z".

The Servlet gets a special object instance of the class javax.servlet.ServletRequest (or one of its derivatives) containing all the input parameters, if there are any. The Servlet also gets an instance of the javax.servlet.ServletResponse class (or one of its derivatives), which it uses to format its output. The contents of the ServletResponse instance are transmitted back to the browser.

I started with one of Sun's standard Servlet examples and modified it in Listing 11.1.

Listing 11.1 Sample Hello World Servlet (HelloWorldServlet.java)

```
import java.io.*;
import javax.servlet.*;
import javax.servlet.http.*;

public class HelloWorldServlet extends HttpServlet
```

```
{
    public void doGet (HttpServletRequest req, HttpServletResponse resp)
    {
     try {
         resp.setContentType("text/html");

         ServletOutputStream out = resp.getOutputStream();
         out.println("<html>");
         out.println("<head><title>Hello World</title></head>");
         out.println("<body>");
         out.println("<h1>Hello World, from Looseleaf" +
                                 "Software, Inc.</h1>");
         out.println("</body></html>");
         }
    catch (Exception e) { e.printStackTrace(); }
    }

    public String getServletInfo()
    {
     return "Servlet to say hi, from Looseleaf Software";
    }
} // end class
```

Note how similar this is to a server Agent that formats HTML output and sends it back to the browser, as in the Ex82Browser example in Chapter 8 (except that with Agents we use a java.io.PrintWriter stream and a different call to get it). If you compile this code and install it in your domino\servlet directory, you should be able to invoke it (assuming you've set up the servlet.cnf file as I showed above) from a browser. This is a pretty simple one, as it takes no input arguments and does nothing of much interest.

If you're using Domino to run Servlets and you're in a develop/test/fix cycle, you'll have to shut down and restart the HTTP server task (not the whole Domino server) to get it to reread the Servlet's .class file. You can do that by going to the Domino console window and

Upgrading Servlets to Agents 321

typing "tell HTTP quit," then after you get the shutdown message, type "load http." This is a bit of a pain, but actually is better for run-time performance: The Servlet Manager caches Servlet .class files in its Java VM for a while, and therefore doesn't have to reload them from disk on every invocation. The only way to "flush" them, htoug, is to restart the http process.

Now let's add some NOI calls to this Servlet. Listing 11.2 adds the name of the current Notes id. Observe that I didn't say "effective name," because that is only available to Agents. This call (from the Session class) will return the actual id in force when the program is run.

Listing 11.2 HelloWorld Example Modified For NOI (HelloNOIServlet.java)

```java
import java.io.*;
import javax.servlet.*;
import javax.servlet.http.*;
import lotus.notes.*;

public class HelloNOIServlet extends HttpServlet
{
    public void doGet (HttpServletRequest req, HttpServletResponse resp)
    {
     try {
            NotesThread.sinitThread();
            resp.setContentType("text/html");
            Session s = Session.newInstance();

            ServletOutputStream out = resp.getOutputStream();
            out.println("<html>");
            out.println("<head><title>Hello World</title></head>");
            out.println("<body>");
            out.println("<h1>Hello World, from Looseleaf"
                                    "Software, Inc.</h1>");
            out.println("Current user name is: " + s.getUserName());
            out.println("</body></html>");
```

```
      }
      catch (Exception e) { e.printStackTrace(); }
      finally { NotesThread.stermThread(); }
   }

   public String getServletInfo()
   {
      return "Servlet to say hi, from Looseleaf Software";
   }
}  // end class
```

Figure 11.3 shows the output of this Servlet (don't forget that you have to add an entry in servlet.cnf and restart the HTTP server for this to work).

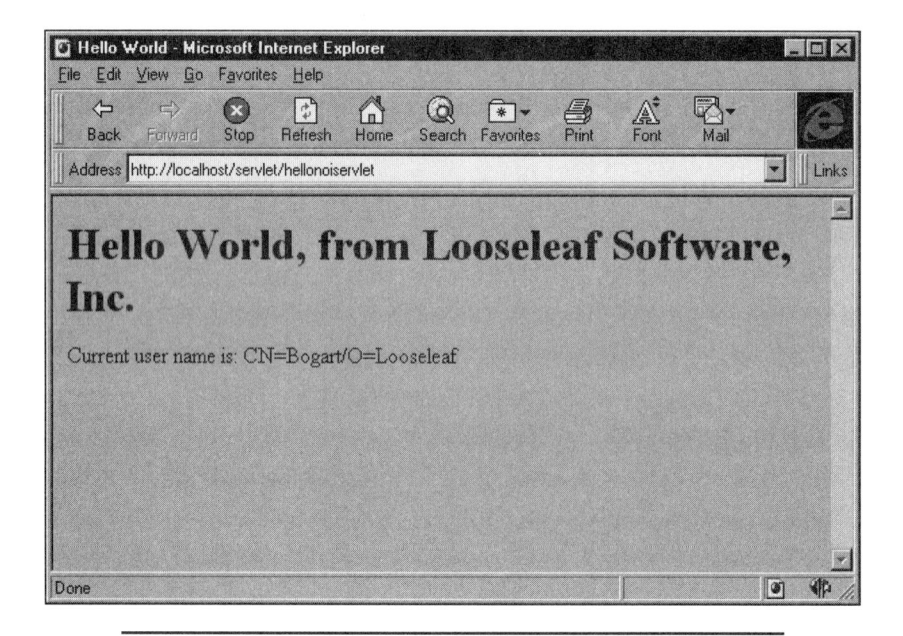

Figure 11.3 Output of the HelloNOI Servlet (HelloNOIServlet.java).

Here's a real-life case where we really need to use the static NotesThread init/term calls. We can't have the Servlet extend NotesThread, because it has to extend one of the Servlet classes. Note also that even though the Servlet is being run by a Domino task, we still have to explicitly initialize and terminate the thread for Notes if we want to use any of the NOI objects. Note that the id in effect is the server's, so watch out!! All servlets run under the auspices of the server's ID. We could have created a multithreaded Servlet which spawned a NotesThread instance to do the work and avoided the static NotesThread calls, but this way seemed much simpler.

Now that you know how to set up Servlets in general and also know how to make them NOI-aware, you're all set to write that killer Servlet for Domino. Actually, if you don't mind that all Servlets that use NOI run with the server's id, then you can write NOI Servlets for any HTTP server, not just Domino.

TRANSFORMING SERVLETS TO AGENTS: THE SERVLET/AGENT ADAPTER

Let's say you've been using Servlets and now you're interested in seeing how to better integrate them with Domino. You can, of course, continue to use them as is on a Domino machine, as we've seen above. You can even enhance them to interact with NOI, as I've shown. No big deal there, why would you want to "transform" a Servlet (especially one that already works!) into a Domino Agent? Well, to paraphrase every real estate broker you've ever talked to, "Security, security, security," and "convenience, convenience, convenience."

That's not to say that Servlets enforce no security at all, because you do have to get a server administrator to install the .class or .jar file on the server and update the servlet.cnf file. Depending on the temperament of your server administrator, this can be either relatively painless, or it could be worse than getting a root canal. If you find yourself in the latter category, imagine further what it will be like when you decide, after deploying your Servlet for a while, that you want to enhance it—every month.

The big advantages of Agents over Servlets are:

- Agents are part of the database design in which they reside. You can update them remotely from a Notes Client, and they replicate around with the rest of the database.
- Agents are signed and can be selectively set to run with the privileges of the signer (the default) or (when invoked via the HTTP server) with the privileges of the Web user (and Domino will authenticate the Web user for you as well).
- Agents can be restricted further in their access to system resources (see the discussion of restricted and unrestricted users in Chapter 8). Servlets have godlike access to the system's resources, including network and disk.

There are no real drawbacks to using Agents instead of Servlets (that I could think of, assuming you're using Domino 4.6, of course). All the argument passing features are available to Agents as well, as you'll see.

If you already have a production environment that makes significant use of Servlets, and you'd like to migrate them as painlessly as possible into a Domino environment, you have three choices:

1. You can just install them on the Domino machine as is, set up a servlet.cnf file to tell Domino's HTTP task where they live and what they should be called, and you're done. Of course you don't get any of the advantages of Agents this way.
2. You can recode each Servlet as an Agent. This option isn't too terrible, unless you have lots and lots of working Servlets. You

have to make AgentBase the base class, instead of Servlet or HttpServlet, and you have to access any CGI variables through the Document returned by AgentContext.getDocument Context().

3. I've saved the best for last. You can use the Agent-to-Servlet Adapter that we discuss in the following sections. It's an Agent that can parse URL arguments and run any Servlet whose .class file it can find.

Servlet-Running Agent

The basic approach here is to write a Java Agent that knows how to load and run Servlets (which, after all, are just Java programs), passing through any arguments that it can parse out of the invoking URL. You've already seen in Chapter 8 how easy it is to parse CGI variables out of a URL using the AgentContext.getDocumentContext() call (Ex84CGI.java). Now let's enhance that basic program to pull out a Servlet name, load, and run it.

We'll adopt a convention that the URL should contain a parameter called "DOMINO_SERVLET", and that the value of the parameter is the name of the Servlet to run. We'll also assume that the Notes environment variable "JavaUserClasses" is set up to point to the directory where not only our Servlet class(es) lives, but where any other supporting classes (such as all the classes used in the Agent) reside. This is an important point, because the HTTP server's Java Virtual Machine (VM) doesn't have a class loader that knows how to pull .class files out of a Notes database, as the Agent Manager does. Thus, because our Servlet is using some of our supporting classes directly (such as AgentRequest and AgentResponse, discussed below), they have to be available. If these new classes were part of the lotus.notes package, we wouldn't have to worry about it.

This first version of the Agent will ignore parameters beyond the Servlet name. We'll name the Agent RunServlet and store it in the database Ex11.nsf.

A word of caution: Dipping our toes into this kind of technology is, so far as I can tell, pretty pioneering of us. We're writing a Domino Agent that, in fact, implements part of the functionality of an HTTP server, in that it locates and loads Servlet programs, as well as provides context for them. There is very little documentation on how to do this correctly, other than the specification on the classes themselves (which only tell you what the API looks like, not how to use it).

To implement this Agent I had to create some support classes that implement some required interfaces (all the source code for these classes is on the CD):

- **AgentCGIEnumerator**. Implements java.util.Enumeration for the CGI items in an Agent context Document. Called from AgentServletConfig and AgentRequest.
- **AgentRequest**. Implements javax.servlet.http.HttpServletRequest. Provides the API so that a Servlet can query the contents of the context Document, which contains the standard CGI variables.
- **AgentResponse**. Implements javax.servlet.http.HttpServletResponse. This interface exists mostly to allow the Servlet to get an output stream to write to.
- **AgentServletConfig**. Implements javax.servlet.ServletConfig. You need one of these in order to load a Servlet. Provides an alternative API to access the CGI variables.
- **AgentServletContext**. Implements javax.servlet.ServletContext. You need one of these in order to implement a ServletConfig. It gives the Servlet access to information about the network context, and a way to log messages.

- **AgentOutputStream**. We needed something that could extend the ServletOutputStream class (the stream that the Servlet uses to write its output; it comes from the response object) to accommodate the Agent's java.io.PrintWriter stream (set up by AgentBase for exactly the same purpose). Unfortunately, although the PrintWriter and ServletOutputStream classes both make use of java.io.OutputStream to do their thing, you can't cast a PrintWriter instance to ServletOutputStream, as they don't have a common ancestor. Writing a class that extends ServletOutputStream allows us to wrapper a PrintWriter instance and redirect calls to it. This helps ensure that Servlets won't have to be recoded when they get run by our Agent.

The main class for this Agent is RunServlet. All the classes are loaded into the RunServlet Agent in Ex11.nsf. The URL we'll use to try it out is:

```
http://localhost/book/Ex11.nsf/RunServlet?OpenAgent&DOMINO_SERVLET=
HelloNOIServlet2
```

Note that this time we need an explicit "?OpenAgent" action directive, because we want to add some "query arguments" afterwards. If you don't have query arguments and the Agent name is the last thing in the URL, then the ?OpenAgent directive is implied. If you do have arguments following the Agent name, you need an explicit ?OpenAgent directive. You can have as many argument name/value pairs as you like, as long as you start each with an "&" and separate the name from the value with an "=".

Listing 11.3 shows the code for the RunServlet Agent.

Listing 11.3 Simple Agent/Servlet Adapter (RunServlet.java)

```
import lotus.notes.*;
import java.util.*;
import java.io.*;
```

```java
import javax.servlet.*;

public class RunServlet extends AgentBase
{
    public void NotesMain()
      {
      try {
          Session s = this.getSession();
          AgentContext ctx = s.getAgentContext();
          Document doc = ctx.getDocumentContext();
          PrintWriter pw = this.getAgentOutput();

          if (doc == null)
             {
             pw.println("No context document");
             return;
             }

          // create request/response objects
          AgentRequest req = new AgentRequest(doc, s);
          AgentResponse resp = new AgentResponse(doc, s, pw);

          /* We have some context, look for the servlet name.
             One of the arguments to the agent is supposed to
             be &DOMINO_SERVLET=xxx. It appears in the QUERY_STRING
             CGI parameter, but we need to parse it out. An easy
             way to do that is to use the request object's getParameter()
             call, which does the parsing for us */

          String servname = req.getParameter("DOMINO_SERVLET");
          if (servname == null || servname.length() == 0)
             {
             pw.println("Invalid Servlet name<BR>");
             pw.println("Query string was: " + req.getQueryString() +
                                       "<BR>");
             return;
             }
```

```java
/* Load the servlet into the VM. We assume that the Classpath
   is set up correctly */

Servlet servlet = null;
try {
    Class cls = Class.forName(servname);
    if (cls == null)
        {
        pw.println("Servlet " + servname + " not found <BR>");
        return;
        }

    Object obj = cls.newInstance();
    if (obj == null || !(obj instanceof javax.servlet.Servlet))
        {
        pw.println("Invalid Servlet class " + servname +
                                "<BR>");
        return;
        }

    servlet = (Servlet)obj;
    }
catch (Exception e)
    {
    e.printStackTrace();
    pw.println("Servlet " + servname + " not found <BR>");
    return;
    }

// we need a ServletConfig instance for the servlet
ServletConfig config = new AgentServletConfig(s, doc);

// init the servlet
System.out.println("Initializing Servlet " + servname);
servlet.init(config);

// send the request, get the response
System.out.println("Invoking Servlet " + servname);
```

```
                servlet.service(req, resp);

                // all done, destroy it
                System.out.println("Destroying Servlet " + servname);
                servlet.destroy();

                }    // end try
            catch (Exception e) { e.printStackTrace(); }
            }    // end NotesMain
    }    // end class
```

Discussion of the RunServlet Agent

Most of what this Agent does is not rocket science. It's a regular old Agent that looks for the name of a Servlet on the URL with which it was invoked, loads the corresponding Servlet class file, and runs it. Actually, it isn't quite that simple, mostly due to the fact that if we want to support argument passing (and we do), then we have to deal with the fact that all our CGI arguments are in a Notes Document instance, not in some stream managed by the server. The "adapter" implementation I'm presenting here is really a skeleton, it doesn't handle a bunch of the options (POST requests, for example) that you'd want from a production piece of code. Still, you could take what I'm giving you here and enhance the heck out of it pretty easily.

The Agent starts out normally, getting the Session, AgentContext, context Document, and output stream objects. We want to pass the standard PrintWriter stream to the Servlet in the response object, because that's the stream that Domino will serve up to the client's browser as the result of running the Agent. The response object will make the PrintWriter instance look like a ServletOutputStreamInstance by using the AgentOutputStream class.

Next we create the request and response objects. The JavaSoft-supplied classes sun.servlet.http.HttpRequest and sun.servlet.http.HttpResponse, while part of the Servlet Development Kit, are not part of the javax package. Instead they belong to the package sun.servlet.http, which means that not all versions of Java are guaranteed to include them, so we try to avoid using those classes here. Aside from that, the standard request and response object interfaces (javax.servlet.http.HttpServletResquest and javax.servlet.http.Http ServletResponse) that the Sun classes implement don't give you any way to tell these objects what output stream to use, nor where to get their input parameters, which is another reason for writing our own code.

So, for all those reasons, I had to create my own request and response objects (implementing the standard interfaces). I called the new classes *AgentRequest* and *AgentResponse*. The code for these two classes is on the CD, but not here in the text, mainly because they're a bit long and tedious: They take the information they need as arguments to their constructors and implement all the methods to get CGI variables and HTTP headers, and so on. The big difference between these objects and the ones in the kit are that they know how to get the parameters and headers from the Agent's context Document. If you're interested in the details, go ahead and plow through the code on the CD. You'll find that much of the standard functionality is not implemented yet, but there's enough there to get some sample Servlets running.

One of the nice things that the request object does is parse through the CGI QUERY_STRING variable for you and pull out the various argument names and values (if any). So rather than parse through the query string ourselves, we let AgentRequest do it. That gives us the name of the Servlet (case sensitive, as all Java class names are) to run.

The next thing we have to do is get the class for the Servlet loaded into the VM. The Servlet Development Kit contains a sun.servlet.ServletLoader class, but I didn't want to use it because it's not part of the javax package (it belongs to the sun.servlet package). So I just used the static method Class.forName() to load the Servlet's .class file (it has to be on the Classpath). That call returns an instance of the java.lang.Class class, which you can then use to create an actual instance of the class that you just loaded. Note that only Unrestricted Agents are allowed to do this.

Once we have an object instance for the Servlet's class, we can use the *instanceof* operator to verify that it really is an instance of javax.servlet.Servlet. Assuming all is well to this point, we can generate a configuration object (our own AgentServletConfig class) and use that to initialize the Servlet. Then all we need to do is invoke the Servlet.service() method, passing in the request and response objects we generated earlier. The Servlet will use the request object to get all its parameters, and will use the response object to write out its results. The base class implementation of service() (in the javax.servlet. http.HttpServlet class) figures out the type of request we're making, and dispatches the call appropriately. Our example Servlets will use the doGet() method to respond to GET requests.

When we return from the service() call, we clean up the Servlet, and then we're done. If we were writing a real Servlet manager, we probably would invent a Servlet management scheme that allowed us to initialize and destroy Servlet instances only once, rather than every time they were invoked. That exercise is left to the reader.

I modified the HelloNOIServlet code a bit to take advantage of being run from an Agent. Listing 11.4 shows the revised code, and I've renamed it HelloNOIServlet2 (original, huh?), so that the files on the CD wouldn't conflict.

Listing 11.4 The HelloNOIServlet2 Example (HelloNOIServlet2.java)

```java
import java.io.*;
import javax.servlet.*;
import javax.servlet.http.*;
import lotus.notes.*;

public class HelloNOIServlet2 extends HttpServlet
{
    public void doget(HttpServletRequest req, HttpServletResponse resp)
    {
     ServletOutputStream out = null;
     System.out.println("From Servlet HelloNOIServlet: doget() invoked");

     try {
            resp.setContentType("text/html");
            out = resp.getOutputStream();
            Session s = ((AgentRequest)req).getAgentSession();

            out.println("<html>");
            out.println("<head><title>Hello World</title></head>");
            out.println("<body>");
            out.println(
                "<h1>Hello World, from Looseleaf Software, Inc.</h1>");

            AgentContext ctx = s.getAgentContext();
            out.println("Current user name is: " +
                            ctx.getEffectiveUserName());
            out.println("</body></html>");
            }
     catch (Exception e) { e.printStackTrace(); }
     }

     public String getServletInfo()
     {
         return "Servlet to say hi, from Looseleaf Software";
     }
} // end class
```

Discussion of HelloNOIServlet2

The entry point where we locate our logic is still the doGet() method. As I stated above, the base class implementation of the service() method that our Agent invokes sees that our request is an HTTP GET, and calls the Servlet's doGet() method.

There's a debug message that will go to the server console. The next line is identical to the original Servlet, it gets the output stream to use for returning a result to the browser. The stream that's returned in this case, though, is really an AgentOutputStream (but because it extends ServletOutputStream we can treat it as such with no casting). All calls to "out" will be redirected by AgentOutputStream to the PrintWriter stream belonging to the Agent.

The next thing the Servlet does is cast the input request object (of class HttpServletRequest) as an AgentRequest instance, and use a new method on that class to get the Agent's Session. In the old version of the program we just did Session.newInstance(), which would also work here, but we'd lose all of the Agent's context. Using the correct Session is much better, as you'll see.

The next few lines are identical to the original, except that behind the scenes they're really printing to a PrintWriter instead of to a ServletOutputStream.

Then we get the Session's AgentContext instance, and print out the "effective" user name. This also is different from the original, where we printed out the result of the Session.getUserName() call, which is always the server's id. By getting the effective user name, which is only available to Agents, we can get the name under whose privileges the Agent is running: either the signer or the Web user. The rest is, as they say, history. We left out the NotesThread init/term calls that were in the original, because we know we're being invoked by an Agent, and so we don't need them.

So, as I said before, we could have run the original Servlet code unmodified from the RunServlet Agent. The small changes I did make were to take advantage of additional Domino functionality.

Figure 11.4 Shows you what happens when we run the Agent from the browser with the URL above. In the first run, the Agent is set up to run with the identity of the Web user.

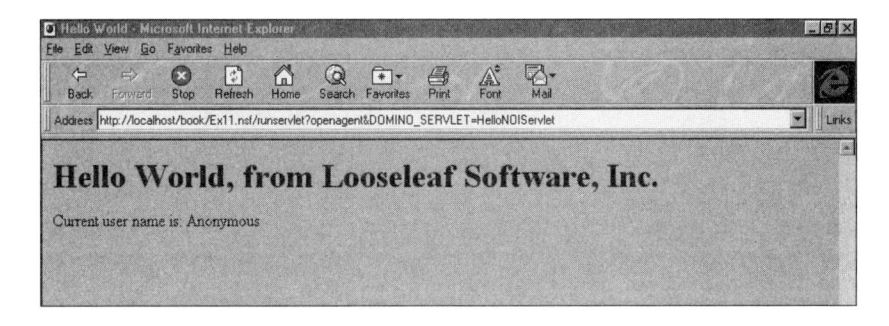

Figure 11.4 Running a servlet from an agent (Web user).

Note that the user's name is Anonymous, because the Web user was not authenticated by the HTTP server. Now let's change the Agent's properties to run with the identity of the signer. Figure 11.5 shows the output for that.

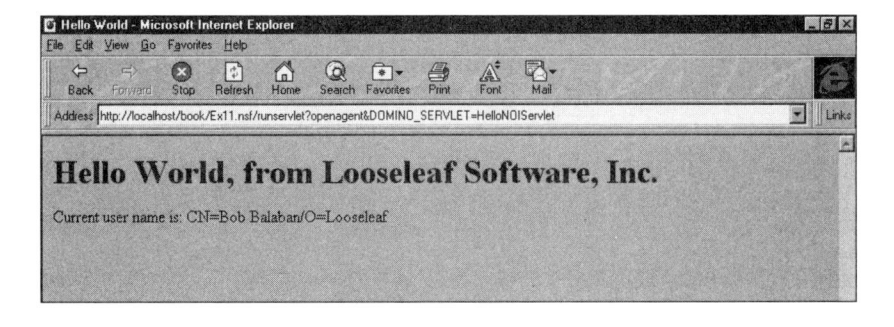

Figure 11.5 Running a servlet from an agent (signer).

Now the user is yours truly, the signer of the Agent. Is this cool, or what? I didn't have to modify a single line of code to make that change, just bring up the Agent Properties box for the RunServlet Agent, uncheck the "run as Web user" box, and save it (sometimes these things just work out). The Agent's and Servlet's debug messages (System.out.println) all go to the server console and to the server log as is usual for an Agent.

PROCESSING OPTIONAL ARGUMENTS

Our HelloNOI Servlet examples didn't use any input arguments at all. The RunServlet Agent looks for a single argument in the QUERY_STRING parameter, "DOMINO_SERVLET=", to get the name of the Servlet to run. There's no reason, however, that we couldn't add more parameters to the query string (delimited by "&"), and have the Servlet look for them in the standard way.

For example, we could take our original URL above, and add another parameter for the HelloNOIServlet program to parse:

```
http://localhost/book/Ex11.nsf/RunServlet?OpenAgent&DOMINO_SERVLET=Hel
loNOIServlet2&optional=howdy
```

In the Servlet's doGet() method, all we have to do is invoke the request getParameter() call, passing the parameter name in ("optional" in this case). The String value of the parameter is returned, if it is found in the query string. The parameters can come in any order, and even the DOMINO_SERVLET parameter doesn't have to be first.

SUMMARY

So, to wrap up, what can we say about Servlets and Agents? I think the following points are key:

1. Agents offer advantages over Servlets in terms of security, control over use of system resources, and deployment.

2. If you don't want to use Agents, you can still make use of Domino's Java NOI by using the Notes classes from your existing Servlets.

3. If you're upgrading to Domino from a server environment where you have lots of Servlets already, I've shown you a way to seamlessly integrate your existing Servlets into the Domino framework, without recoding the Servlets. Servlets that are run this way inherit all the security and context features of Agents, which (I claim) makes them much more interesting.

Coming up next in Chapter 12: NOI and Java Beans. Are they really good for your heart? Stay tuned.

12

NOI AND JAVA BEANS

You've probably heard about Java Beans by now, but unless you're actually developing some, you're also probably not quite sure precisely what a Java Bean is. That's not too surprising, since tracking down an authoritative definition isn't easy. Beans are not like applets or servlets: A given Java class is an applet if it extends java.applet.Applet, or it's a servlet if it extends javax.servlet.Servlet. There is no prescribed base class for Beans.

If you download and install a recent copy of the Java Development Kit (JDK) from Sun's Web site (http://java.sun.com), you'll find that there is in fact a class called java.beans.Beans; however, a Java class that wants to be a Bean would probably never actually extend this class. There are several characteristics that seem to be included in most people's definitions of Java Beans. If your Java class includes these, it can be considered a Bean:

1. Must have a default constructor (one that takes no arguments).
2. Method names must follow the Beans naming conventions.
3. Classes should be serializable, but it's not required. *Serializable* means that objects of the class support having their content being serialized on a data stream. More on this in the following section.
4. Class can optionally implement events in a standardized way.
5. Classes can optionally support a java.beans.BeanInfo interface.
6. Class can optionally support a java.beans.Visibility interface.

The Java Beans specification is freely available from the JavaSoft Web site, and goes into each of these points in some detail, so I won't try to duplicate that here. What follows in this chapter is a brief examination of where the Java NOI conforms to these characteristics and where it departs from them, and why.

BACKGROUND: WHAT ABOUT BEANS?

One way to look at what Java Beans are about is to think of them as Java's answer to Microsoft's OCX and Active/X component technology. People who early on jumped on the downloadable Java applet bandwagon found that their development efforts suffered from the lack of standardization around code reuse and event propagation. Tool builders in particular found themselves blocked in their ability to develop high level development environments for Java applets by the fact that it was relatively hard to read any random .class file and figure out what the code did.

JavaSoft answered these concerns in their Java 1.1 release by incorporating several new technologies directly in the language: a component model, an event model, standardization of method naming conventions, serialization and "introspection" capabilities, among others. All of these are discussed more below.

The current level of Bean technology in Java has largely been driven by the needs of the tool builders: the Borlands and Symantecs and IBMs of the world who have been building sophisticated development environments for other languages (C, C++, even SmallTalk) for years are now doing the same for Java. Their early efforts were hampered because it was so hard to write a tool that could figure out what a given Java class was all about just from its compiled byte codes (not impossible, just hard). The common goal of these tool builders was to make the language support the right set of features, to enable them to create development tools that could, for example, allow a user to drag icons representing individual Java classes onto a palette, and "wire" them together into a complete working applet, all without making the user write a line of Java code.

There are now a number of tools which in fact support this level of capability: IBM's Bean Machine, Borland's JBuilder, and Symantec's Visual Cafe (among others) are all aimed at this kind of functionality, and all make heavy use of the Beans technologies listed above. This focus has tended (in my opinion) to skew the discussions and developmental efforts around Java Beans toward an applet-centric and user-interface-centric view of the Java component world. The Java Notes Object Interface, on the other hand, is (at least in its Domino 4.6 incarnation) very much oriented toward development of server-based applications and Agents. That's not to say that the currently available visual builder tools are not appropriate for use with NOI, only that the strengths of each do not necessarily mesh well (yet).

Let's delve briefly into the important new Beans-oriented technologies in the Java 1.1 release, and also consider how NOI deals (or doesn't deal) with each.

Java Beans Technologies

Method Naming Conventions

Although Java makes no explicit distinction between the methods and properties of a class, other languages do, and people often find tools that present these distinctions more approachable. If you associate properties with object attributes (blue, bold, x pixels wide by y pixels high), and methods with object behaviors (start, stop, move to a new location on the screen), you have a nice division of the object's interface.

The Java Beans spec gives you some standard patterns for naming the methods on a class so that pairs of set/get methods can be collected into single properties by a process of induction. Take, for example, these two methods from the lotus.notes.View class (see Chapter 3 for the details):

```
java.util.Vector getReaders()
void setReaders(java.util.Vector names)
```

This pair of methods is expressible as a single read/write property: Readers, and a good builder tool can present just the one property name in a list of properties for the class, hiding the fact that there are really two methods that implement the property. The pattern here is expressible as follows:

```
<DataType> get<PropertyName>()
void set<PropertyName>(<DataType>)
```

Another example of a property pattern is:

```
boolean is<PropertyName>()
void set<PropertyName>(boolean)
```

Any pair of methods on a class that fit one of these two patterns qualifies as a Java Beans read/write property. If only the "get" call of the pair exists, then the property is read only. You can see why this is nice for builder tools: They can present an object's properties in a nice user interface and allow users to specify at design time that certain "event triggers" should cause certain properties to be set to certain values. This allows the tool to take on the work of writing the actual Java code to implement that logic.

Methods are a bit more eccentric in this world—they can have any number of arguments and return any type of result, or none at all. Whereas properties lend themselves to visual "wiring" (*get* properties take no arguments and return a single value; *set* properties return nothing and take only a single value), methods are trickier, and typically require the user to deal with Java syntax a bit more. Furthermore (again this is my own opinion), a heavy reliance on exposing the functionality of a class as properties is much more consistent with UI objects than with server objects. Users have no trouble visualizing what will happen when an event trigger causes a message to be sent to an object on the builder's palette causing that object to change some UI characteristic (size, color, position on the screen, and so on). It's a bit more difficult to figure out how to represent in a nice visual fashion how an event should cause a *method* requiring two or three arguments (a Database open, for example) to get executed. We'll see some of the implications of this below.

The Java NOI classes all conform to the Beans naming conventions, as described in Chapter 2.

Event Model

Before the release of Java 1.1, events were confined to Java's Abstract Windowing Toolkit (AWT) subsystem. The Java Beans specification says that *any* class can be an event source or an event handler. Without going into all the details of all the various ways events can be implemented between classes, you can use the new Beans classes to rather flexibly implement any set of events for a class that makes sense to you. A class might be only a source (emitter) of events, only a handler (catcher) of events, or it might do both. Classes that receive event notifications might act on those notifications by changing one or more of their attributes, by emitting additional events of their own, or by ignoring them. A class might *source* an event which constitutes a notification to the world that it is about to do something, and then listen for a response to see if any objects out there want to veto the action.

Parenthetically we should note that Lotus's own InfoBus technology, which lets Java Beans embedded in an applet page "find" each other and exchange event notifications and data, has been adopted by JavaSoft and will soon appear as part of the language specification.

Currently, NOI does not support events. The NOI classes neither source nor listen for any Java events. This is one of the areas of what one might refer to as the *cognitive dissonance* between the very UI/Client-oriented view of Java Beans and the very "invisible"/Server orientation of NOI for Domino 4.6. There simply is no server analog (at this time, anyway) to the applet "page" on which multiple Beans might be embedded, and within which they might want to communicate with each other.

We can envision such a setup, of course, perhaps in terms of collections of Agents or servlets that watch for events of various kinds and use InfoBus (or something) to talk to each other. That technology is not yet here, though. For one thing, both the Domino Agent framework and the usual HTTP servlet architecture assume a predefined triggering of Agents and servlets: You specify a schedule or pick one of a limited set of events to trigger an Agent, or you invoke a servlet via a URL. Servlets and Agents are loaded into memory and run when invoked. Neither architecture currently supports the idea of an Agent or servlet that sits in memory all the time, "listening" for one or more event notifications, upon receipt of which it does something.

Given the current state of the art, though, it made no sense for the Domino 4.6 NOI to support event handling on the server, so none was implemented. Chapter 14 comes back to this topic in the context of future directions for NOI.

Introspection and BeanInfo

Introspection is the ability of a program (typically a builder tool, but it could be any program) to glean from a Java class the exact methods, properties, and events that the class implements. You can see why a builder tool would need that information: It has to present a class's interface in a nice way to a user who may not know how to write a line of Java code. The best and most reliable way to receive that information is to somehow get it from the class in question itself. Parenthetically, I have no idea why the term introspection was chosen for this technology. Seems to me it really should have been "extrospection," or "inspection," instead; the class isn't analyzing itself after all.

Before Java 1.1 was released, the only way to introspect a Java class was to read the Java byte codes from the .class file and parse them yourself. Of course you'd also have to look for and parse the class's superclasses, if there were any.

Java 1.1 has a new class that handles all this for you, called java.beans.Introspector. It reads a Java class file from disk and figures out who its superclasses are (if any), and what methods, properties, and events those classes implement. It returns an instance of a descriptor class, called java.beans.BeanInfo, which you can interrogate to get the exact signatures of all public methods, properties, and events.

Sometimes, though, a Bean developer wants to hide certain aspects of the Bean. Perhaps a method was declared public because it gets called by other classes with which the Bean has a special relationship, but the method shouldn't be called by the builder tool, or by the end user at all. Or perhaps there's more than one form of some method or property, and only one of the variants is the one that should be used. In such cases the developer of a Bean is free to implement her or his own BeanInfo class (java.beans.BeanInfo is an interface, so any class can implement it). The way you associate a BeanInfo class with the class which it describes is simply by name: If your class is named lotus.notes.Session, for example, then the associated BeanInfo class must be named lotus.notes.SessionBeanInfo.

When the java.beans.Introspector class is asked to parse a Java class, it first looks for a BeanInfo for that class. If it finds one, it has only to instantiate it and invoke the descriptor methods to get all the information about that class which the developer wants known. If no BeanInfo class is found, then the Introspector actually reads the byte codes for the target class to get the information (this process is called *low level reflection*).

Because the Java NOI for Domino has no hidden methods or properties, there are no explicit BeanInfo classes for it. One could argue that certain methods that appear in the output generated by the javadoc utility should either not have been *public* or should be hidden by use of a BeanInfo class. The GetCppObject() call (present in all of the NOI classes) is one example. It is used internally to get the handle of the C++ object for which the target Java instance serves as the wrapper. It probably should either have been declared *protected* instead of public, or it should have been hidden with a BeanInfo. Fortunately the call is pretty harmless.

Visibility

There's another Beans interface called java.beans.Visibility. This interface is optional for Java Beans, and was added late in the development cycle of Java Beans 1.0. It was, in fact, added at the explicit request of

Lotus and Iris to handle the fact that the NOI classes present no user interface whatsoever (JavaSoft readily agreed that it was useful).

The Visibility interface is meant to handle two different situations:

- ❒ A smart builder tool needs to know whether or not any given Bean requires a user interface.
- ❒ A Java Bean needs to know at any given time whether or not it is okay to present a user interface.

In the first case, the tool can inquire of any Bean that implements the java.beans.Visibility interface whether it requires a user-interface capability via the needsGui() call. In the second case, a tool (or an applet, more likely) can tell a Bean either that it's okay or not okay to put up a user interface via the dontUseGui() and okToUseGui() calls.

All the NOI classes implement the Visibility interface, and all return *false* for the needsGui() call. Unfortunately, I suspect that most builders (and applets) pretty much ignore this interface. But I could be wrong about that; there are tools that deal just fine with *invisible* Beans, such as those that play sound clips only. Still, there's an important difference between "invisible" and "has no UI". Watch out for subtle problems in this area when using builder tools together with the NOI classes.

Serialization

Serialization is the process by which an object instance is written to an output stream for persistent storage or transmission over a network. The reverse of serialization is called deserialization, which is the process by which an object previously serialized is brought back into memory and re-instantiated with the same state it had before.

In order for a class to be serializable, it must implement the interface java.io.Serializable. This interface has no methods at all—it simply "marks" a class as one which can be serialized (and, implicitly, deserialized).

Why is this particularly relevant to Java Beans? The answer is that Beans, as components in a larger applet or application, might very well be given state at design time, and be expected to know about that state later, at run time. Suppose, for example, that you had a Java Bean which simply displayed a colored square on the screen, let's call it BobsShape. BobsShape has (for the purposes of this example) the following properties:

- Height (in pixels)
- Width (in pixels)
- Location (x/y coordinate of the upper-left corner)
- Color

You might go through the following steps when embedding that Bean in an applet you were constructing:

1. Start the builder tool (JBuilder, Bean Machine, whatever), and create your basic layout for the applet.
2. Explore a palette of available Beans, including BobsShape. Each available Bean presents a design time icon to the builder, and that's the icon you see for it.
3. You select the icon for BobsShape, and drag it onto the palette at a specific position. You now see a square of default size and color.
4. Behind the scenes, the builder tool creates an in memory instance of the BobsShape class, and sets the Location property of that instance to the point to which you dragged it.

5. You then stretch the lower-right corner to enlarge the square. The tool sets the Width and Height properties appropriately.
6. You use the tool's UI to select a different color for the square, the tool sets the Color property of the BobsShape instance.

Now comes the fun part: You want to actually generate the applet and save it in a jar file so that it can be downloaded to someone's browser, whereupon they'll see a square of correct size and color on the applet's page in the correct position. There are two different ways the builder tool could handle this:

1. It can write out a bunch of Java source code for the applet that has hardwired in it the parameters for the Bean: color, size, position. At applet initialization time, the Java code would create a new instance of BobsShape on the fly, then set its parameters appropriately. The shape would then appear on the page where it was supposed to.
2. A more elegant way to handle this would be to have at applet generation time each embedded Bean serialize itself to an output stream. The stream would contain, for each embedded Bean, a binary representation of each of the Bean's persistent properties (color, size, etc.). The stream would be written to a .jar file, which would also contain the actual applet code. When the .jar file got downloaded to someone's browser, the applet would start up, deserialize all its components, and be off and running.

In the second mechanism, each Bean saves its own state onto some output stream. At run time, the browser or the applet is responsible for noticing that there is some serialized information in the .jar file. It can then use Java's deserialization mechanism to (a) construct each object instance that is required, and (b) tell each instance to deserialize itself (load its individual property values) from an input stream.

The default behavior for serialization of an object is that all member variables in the object instance are written to the output stream, unless they are declared *transient*. Transient variables are skipped. Scalar values are simply written out. Object references are recursively serialized. If an object needs control over how one or more of its members is serialized, it can implement a writeObject() and a readObject() call to customize the serialization and deserialization behavior. Still more control is offered by the java.io.Externalization interface.

Serialization is a terrific piece of functionality for a few reasons. First, it is useful in many situations, not just in the applet builder scenario. Objects can be serialized for persistent storage to disk (or to an object database), or for transmission across a network (when you make a remote call with an object reference as an argument). Serialization has to handle not just the storage of a single object, but must operate recursively as well, serializing all objects to which a given object refers. While doing that, serialization has to also maintain the integrity of all object references, so that if (for example) two objects both refer to a third, the third object is not serialized more than once. If it were, then when the stream was read back in and deserialized, you'd end up with two instances of a class, whereas you only had one to begin with.

To invoke serialization you simply write an object to a special stream, of class java.io.ObjectOutputStream. The writeObject() method on that class inspects the target object to see if the Serialization or Externalization interfaces are implemented. If neither interface is present, an exception is thrown.

When you deserialize objects, you simply read them off an instance of the class java.io.ObjectInputStream. The readObject() call figures out what the next object in the stream is, invokes its default constructor, and then tells the object (which we already know is serializable) to read its members from the stream itself. The object emerges fully constructed (possibly invoking readObject() recursively, if it has object member variables).

You can see why this approach is attractive: there is much less code for tool developers to write, and it provides a very nice general purpose mechanism for persistent storage of all kinds, that any class can use. There's even a way you can do implicit version control (of a limited sort), so that if you save an object to a stream, modify the object's implementation by adding an additional member variable, and then read the older version of the object back off an input stream, it will work (see the documentation on java.io.ObjectStreamClass. getSerialVersionUID()). Of course, the new member variable's data will be missing in the input stream, and you have to account for that in your code.

Domino's Java NOI, however, does not make use of serialization at this time. There are a couple of reasons for this, both historical, and functional:

❐ Serialization requires that each class have a default constructor. As we've mentioned before, none of the NOI classes has a default constructor that is really usable, because of the requirements of a strict containment hierarchy. At the time that this particular design decision was locked down (i.e., coded) there were no real Beans-aware builders to work with (the Beans spec had just been released). Thus, there was really no way to test out (in time) whether having a default constructor for each class could be made to work, given the design constraints imposed by the back-end Notes code (especially the one that says you can't have free-floating objects).

❐ It was never clear that any builders could really make effective use of the NOI classes anyway, partly because the ones that we knew about in those early days were so applet centric, and partly because they were all very property centric, whereas NOI makes heavy use of methods to do things like instantiate child classes.

❏ The Java 1.1 software that incorporated robust object serialization wasn't available early enough for us to be able to come to grips with it in time for the 4.6 release.

As a result, none of the NOI classes implements either the Serializable or the Externalizable interfaces. Furthermore, all member variables in all the NOI classes are declared *transient*. This means that, at this time anyway, you can't use a builder tool to set an NOI object's initial state at design time, save the object in a .jar file, and have it "remember" that state later at run time.

Furthermore, any builder tool that relies on being able to instantiate an NOI object at design time using its default constructor had better be able to trap a System.exit() call, as that's what the default base class constructor for NOI does (remember, no one is supposed to call it). The developers of IBM's BeanMachine discovered this quirk in time to deal with it, but I don't know if any of the other vendors have done so.

NOI AND BUILDER TOOLS

I've experimented using two different Java development environment products with the Domino Java NOI: Borland's JBuilder and Symantec's Visual Cafe. I picked these two to try out because they are popular tools from reputable vendors (this isn't a product review or endorsement; I just wanted to share a bit of experience with you about how NOI works in these kinds of environments). There are other tools that are (I'm sure) perfectly good too, I didn't try out every one.

One tool that I know will *not* work with Domino NOI is Microsoft's Visual J++. The problem with VJ++ is that Microsoft never adopted the standard Java Native Interface (JNI) architecture. JNI is the specification which allows Java code to call into C or C++ modules, an important requirement for using the Notes classes.

The choices for Java development tools range from the simple (any text editor for typing in Java code, command line Java Development Kit compiler and interpreter from JavaSoft) to the fully featured (syntax driven editor, source code debugger, performance profiler). For Java Beans, which tend to the, shall we say, "rich" end of the functional spectrum, the full-featured development environments are a big plus, especially when it comes to debugging. If the application or Agent you're writing is small and simple, a few System.out.println() calls and a decent Java Console (as in the Notes client) are about all you need. For an event-driven, embeddable component with heavy user-interface requirements involving hundreds of lines of code, a real debugger is a big win.

Some of the new Java development tools also offer features like source code versioning and archiving. Anyhow, I picked these two products to try out, and was pleased with the results, once I got them set up and operational.

Borland's JBuilder is strong in its handling of Java Beans: Borland has really gone to town with its exploitation of the Beans introspection and event-handling features (no surprise there—they contributed to the original Beans specifications). I was hoping they would figure out (as the Bean Machine developers did) that the Domino NOI classes could really be treated as Beans, but for the lack of default constructors. Unfortunately, JBuilder refused to recognize all but a few of the NOI classes as Beans when I tried to load them onto the components palette (see Figure 12.1).

Symantec's Visual Cafe likewise refused to treat any of the NOI classes as Beans. Both, however, did a fine job of debugging the samples. Figure 12.2 shows Visual Cafe in debug mode on the sample debuggable Agent Ex90Conflict, from Chapter 9, and Figure 12.3 shows approximately the same code in the JBuilder debugger. Of course I had to debug the Agent as a standalone program.

Chapter 12

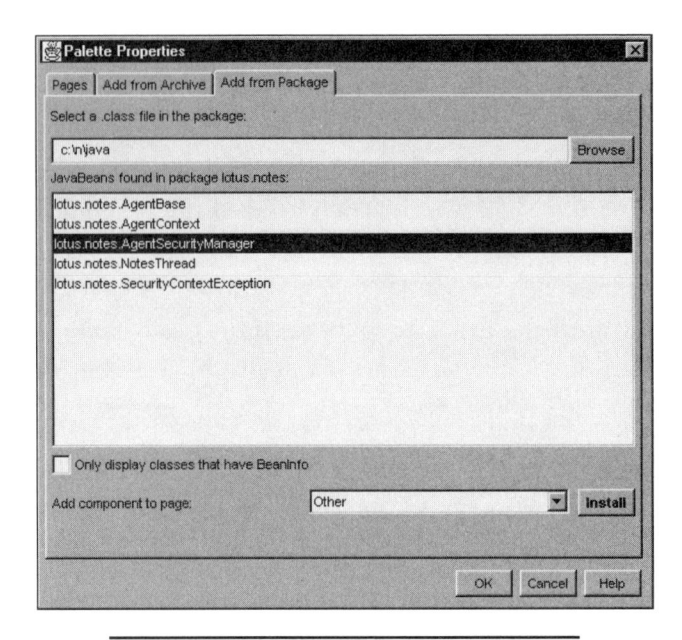

Figure 12.1 JBuilder's reaction to NOI as Beans.

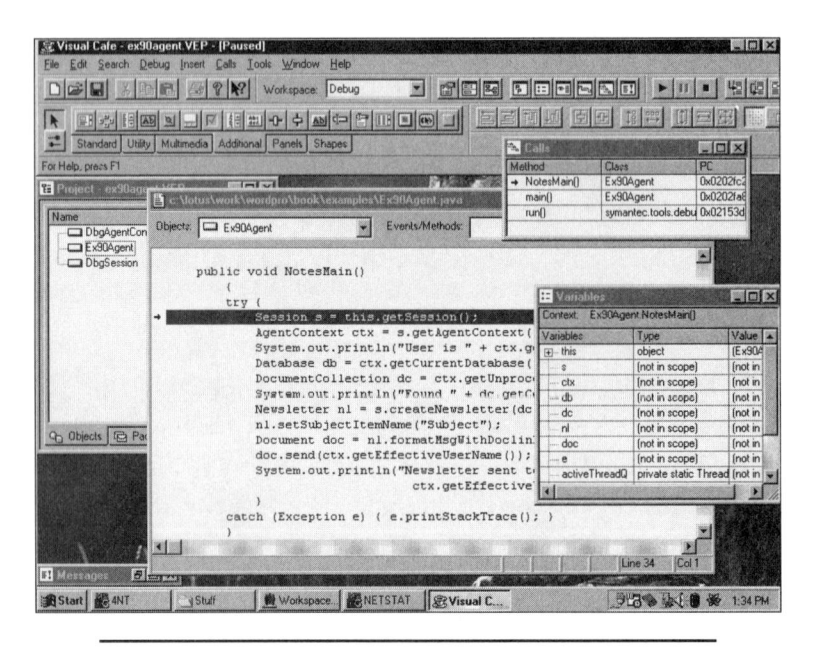

Figure 12.2 Debugging the Ex90Conflict Agent with Visual Cafe.

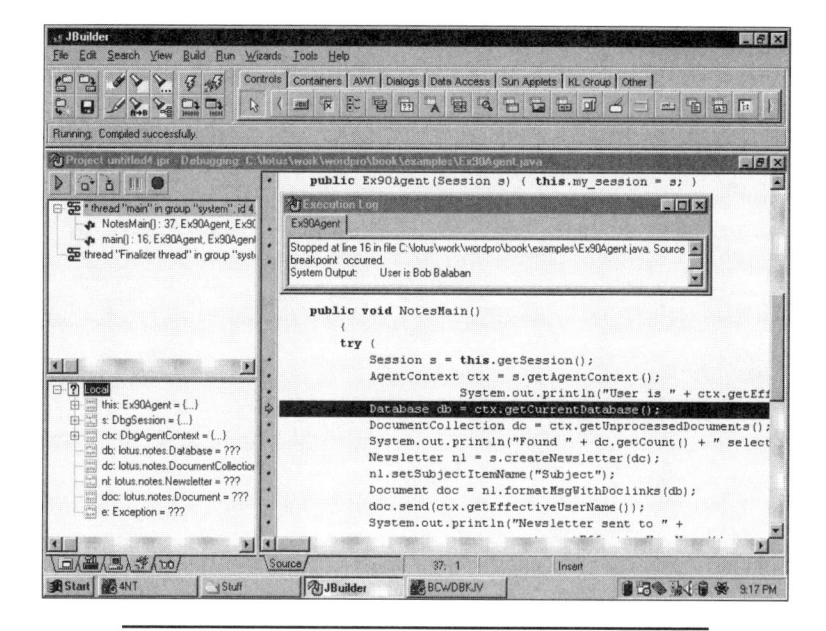

Figure 12.3 Debugging the Ex90Conflict Agent with JBuilder.

SUMMARY: ARE NOI OBJECTS JAVA BEANS?

The answer to whether or not the NOI objects are "real" Beans is probably debatable. If you agree that serialization is an option, not a requirement, then the only reason you wouldn't be able to consider the NOI classes to be true Beans is that they don't support a real default constructor (which could in all likelihood be fixed in a future Domino release). If you feel strongly that serialization is a required trait, then you'll argue that they aren't real Beans at all. If you take the pragmatic approach and say that they're not Beans because two builder tools won't treat them that way, then I really can't disagree too much.

In the end I'm not sure it matters very much one way or the other, at least not right now, given the current UI centric focus of Beans development. When more vendors and tools start focusing on using Java Beans as a component technology aimed at *server* Application development, then I think Domino NOI will have a strong role to play. Besides that, whether the NOI classes are "real" Beans or not doesn't seem to affect our ability to use different development tools to create and debug interesting Java programs that make use of Domino objects, as you've seen with both JBuilder and Visual Cafe.

In the next chapter, we'll take a look at how to use yet another Java API together with the Java NOI to access relational databases.

13

JDBC AND NOI

We've seen in the earlier chapters of this book how to use the Notes Object Interface (NOI) from Java programs (applications, Servlets, and Agents) to manipulate Domino objects to our advantage. In this chapter, we'll look at how to integrate the use of NOI with other Java APIs, specifically the one from JavaSoft known as JDBC (Java Database Connectivity). Combining NOI for Notes database access with JDBC for relational database access opens up some very interesting possibilities for application developers.

WHAT IS JDBC?

The Java Database Connectivity library is a set of Java classes written by JavaSoft (and rewritten by various tool vendors according to the JavaSoft spec) that provide a database independent way of accessing relational data. It provides a relational database object model, and as such may not be appropriate for access to nonrelational databases (though some nonrelational databases do allow you to treat them as relational databases using adapter interfaces such as JDBC, Notes for one, using the NotesSQL ODBC driver). If you're familiar with the ODBC classes (known as LS:DO, for LotusScript:Data Object) that have been shipping with Domino since Release 4.0, you can think of JDBC as a Java API, which more or less accomplishes the same thing.

The Java classes can be found in the package java.sql, and JavaSoft's implementation can be downloaded for free from their Web site (other vendors also give you their implementations for free). The Java classes are really a "driver manager" layer on top of a set of database "drivers," where each driver knows how to access a particular vendor's relational database system (dBase, Informix, Oracle, DB2, Sybase, etc.). Your Java program specifies a URL-like connection string specifying the data source to which you want to connect. The java.sql layer tries to find a driver that is compatible with that data source. If it can find one, it loads it and passes the connection information (database name, and optionally a user name and password) off to that driver, which makes the actual connection. Then SQL queries can be passed through the driver to the back-end database system, possibly over a network, and the results come back and are retrieved via a "result set" class.

This whole system was modeled fairly closely after Microsoft's ODBC (Open Database Connectivity) APIs, which have been in widespread use for years. Notes has provided a set of LotusScript classes for interfacing to ODBC ever since Notes Release 4.0.

JavaSoft (and some of the other tool vendors) provide a couple of ways of implementing drivers for individual databases: You can write the entire driver in Java, or you can write a Java driver which in turn passes requests off to an existing ODBC driver. This is known as the *JDBC/ODBC Bridge*. Further information on how the drivers work follows in the next section.

WHY DO WE CARE ABOUT JDBC?

A large percentage of the world's data lives in computer-based databases. Production databases at even medium-sized companies routinely grow to sizes exceeding 4 or 5 terabytes (1 terabyte is 1000 gigabytes, or 1,000,000,000,000 bytes). While Notes can in general only sustain good performance on databases in the gigabyte range (plus or minus), it has proven a fantastic tool for "front-ending" serious database applications and workflow applications based on large databases. Data can be accessed on the fly from Notes, and used to populate forms and views. Notes databases can be used as "staging areas" for aggregated data from a back-end database, and from there replicated around the world.

More recently, developers are discovering the possibilities for Web-based applications using Domino. As more companies begin to seriously invest in applications that can be run from a client browser, Domino is proving to be an excellent tool for grabbing data from legacy systems and presenting it on an inter/intranet via HTTP, as well as for collecting user submissions and updating back end storage. Agents play a particularly important role in this kind of system integration, allowing for customized data validation, user authentication, interactivity, and workflow triggering.

I predict that Domino/Notes integration with legacy database systems (relational and others) will be one of the biggest growth areas for Domino application developers, and that JDBC (or its successors) will play a very important role.

Chapter 13

LAYER UPON LAYER

As I stated above, JDBC gives you two options for connecting to a database: the "pure" Java approach, where a vendor has supplied you with a JDBC driver written entirely in Java that talks to the back-end database API; or the JDBC/ODBC Bridge technique, where a small Java driver itself loads and communicates with an existing ODBC driver for the target database.

Of course, the JDBC or JDBC/ODBC driver itself is implemented typically on top of some database vendor's APIs to the real database system. Let's take a look at the actual architecture of a Domino Java NOI Agent that also uses JDBC to retrieve and/or store data in a legacy database system. Figure 13.1 shows the "pure Java" setup, and Figure 13.2 shows the JDBC/ODBC hybrid approach.

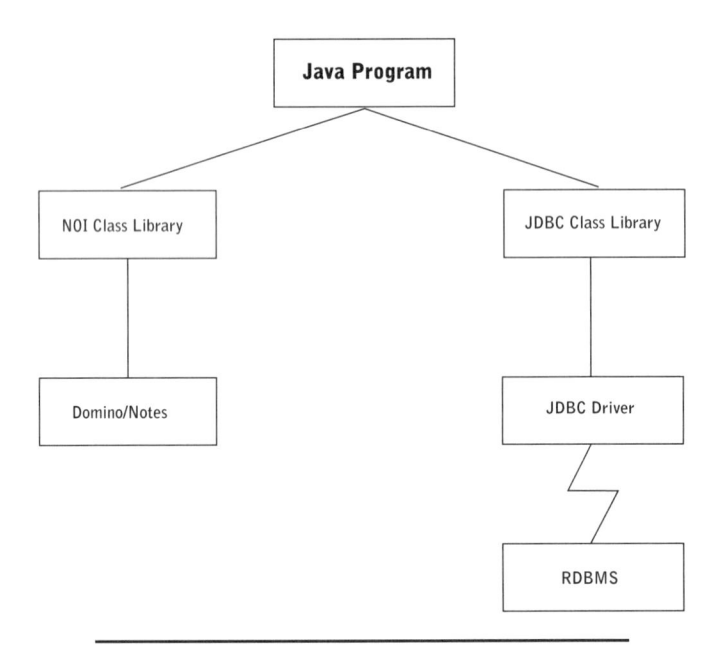

Figure 13.1 Architecture of NOI With Pure Java JDBC.

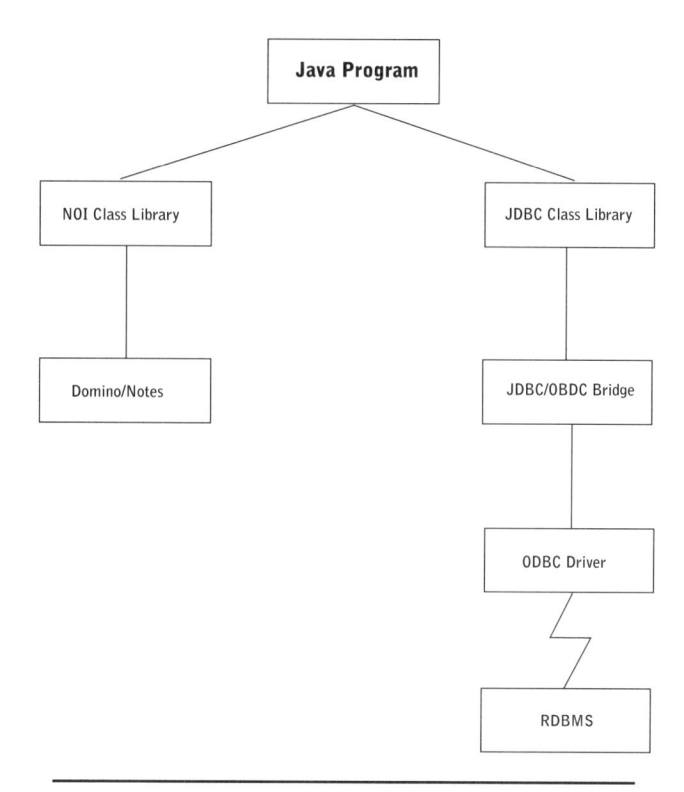

Figure 13.2 Architecture of NOI With JDBC/ODBC Bridge.

The java.sql classes that make up the Java part are specified by JavaSoft, but any vendor can supply a conforming implementation. Regardless of whose java.sql classes you use, any vendor can supply any of the other components: JDBC drivers, ODBC drivers, or the JDBC/ODBC Bridge. That's the beauty of software API standards (when they work); you can mix and match as you like.

Note that a Domino server that uses ODBC or JDBC to communicate with a back-end database system will usually also include a setup for the database vendor's "client API" software. This is the code that the JDBC or ODBC driver calls to actually talk to the DBMS, which is typically not located on the Domino machine, but elsewhere in the network. It's possible, of course, that a pure Java JDBC driver uses the database system's networking protocol to communicate directly, without going through the Client API layer. ODBC drivers typically do not do that. Ask your vendor how their drivers were implemented.

Which way should you go if you're looking at implementing a Domino/JDBC application? Fortunately you can pick on a per-Agent (or application) basis which driver architecture you will use, because the database URL syntax controls the driver protocol, as we shall see. Here are some points to consider:

- **Performance**. In general, the pure Java JDBC driver will be a better performer than the hybrid JDBC/ODBC architecture, mainly because there is one fewer layer for data to be translated across. This is a rule of thumb, however, not a law graven in stone. Ask your vendor for performance benchmarks, specifically for benchmarks using JDBC. Many driver sets are available for free "on trial" for some amount of time from their vendor. You can write your own benchmark, try out a couple of different vendors' drivers, and make up your own mind, if performance is a key consideration for you.
- **Availability**. There are dozens of choices out there for ODBC drivers for every conceivable database system. There are fewer choices for pure Java JDBC drivers, at least at this time, because the technology is newer. If the target database you want to support does not have an available pure Java driver, then you'll probably have to go with a hybrid JDBC/ODBC solution.
- **Reliability**. A hybrid JDBC/ODBC solution from a vendor that you know and trust could well be better than a pure Java driver from a startup whose code robustness is unproven, or even known to be buggy.

- **Thread safety**. While writing thread safe code is easier in Java than in C or C++, having a JDBC driver written purely in Java is still no guarantee that it is thread safe. As we've seen in earlier chapters of this book, Web-based applications triggered through Domino's HTTP server are generally required to be thread safe. I've shown you how to write thread safe applications and Agents that use NOI, but of course you have no control over the code in a JDBC or ODBC driver you purchase from a third party. Furthermore, you also have no control over the "Client API" layer supplied by the database vendor, if there is one.

The bottom line on this is that you should test the heck out of any JDBC application before deploying it, especially if it needs to be thread safe. Pure Java implementations are not automatically guaranteed to work better than hybrid JDBC/ODBC solutions.

TESTING STRATEGIES

Luckily it is possible to do significant testing of multiple vendors' drivers without rewriting lots of software. Because the JDBC interface is standardized (the whole point of it, really), the Agent or application needs to be written only once (but of course you'd want to make sure to test it with a few different back-end databases, if your production environment will require that your code be used that way). Because the connection URL in your Java code accesses a "data source," not an actual database, by name, the driver (be it JDBC or ODBC) is responsible for resolving the data source name to a real database. Thus you can point the Agent at different databases simply by changing the JDBC or ODBC configuration information. Of course, if you do that you have to be sure that all the databases have the same schema, otherwise your code won't work.

For Web-based applications you can also switch Domino between single- and multithreaded execution of Domino Agents. You can set the **DominoAsynchronizeAgents** environment variable in your server's NOTES.INI file to control this feature (see Chapter 8 for more details). Setting the variable to 1 lets the HTTP server run Agents in a multi-threaded way, improving overall throughput. If you set it to 0 (the default), Domino will serialize all Agent execution (only one Agent will run at a time; all others will wait until the currently executing one is done). If you find that your Web-based JDBC or ODBC application is crashing, and you suspect that the culprit might be some code that isn't thread safe, you can set DominoAsynchronizeAgents to 0 (you have to restart the HTTP server for it to take effect). If the crash goes away, then you likely have a thread safety problem.

INSTALLING JDBC AND ODBC

Installing the JDBC *driver manager* is easy, or even trivial. This is the code that belongs to the java.sql package, and could well be included in current releases of the Java Development Kit. If so, there's nothing you have to do. If not, you can download the JDBC code from JavaSoft's Web site for free. Then you just need to be sure that the JDBC .class files are on your CLASSPATH.

If you purchase JDBC database drivers from a third-party vendor, you'll need to follow their instructions for installation. Sometimes the drivers also come with the vendor's own java.sql implementation, which you can use instead of JavaSoft's if you wish (check the vendor's installation instructions, they might *require* that to use their drivers you also have to use their driver manager, or they might not).

If you use the JDBC/ODBC bridge, you'll have to make sure that you have the ODBC manager and driver set installed as well. My laptop's Microsoft Windows95 did not come with ODBC, but my desktop's

Windows NT had an ODBC manager and a few drivers included. Again, when you purchase a driver set from a vendor it often comes with its own ODBC manager, which when you install the drivers might replace the one on your system. Make sure that your version of JDBC includes a JDBC/ODBC Bridge if you want to use your ODBC drivers (JavaSoft's does).

Whether you're using JDBC alone or in combination with ODBC, you'll have to configure one or more data sources in order to actually access any databases. Think of a data source definition as your system's local name for some remote database. It specifies what driver can be used with the database, the database's "real" name (possibly including remote network information), and so on. This configuration information is used by the Driver Manager to select a driver for the data source whose name you specify in your Java program (if you don't specify a particular driver explicitly), and by the driver to locate the actual database and open a connection to it. Because each vendor's setup procedure is different, I won't detail how to do all that here. Read your vendor's install instructions carefully. For Windows, all the ODBC software I've ever used added an icon to the Control Panel at install time. Clicking on the icon brings up the ODBC Manager belonging to the last one I installed. From there I could select either a driver or a data source to configure, or add a new data source.

To prepare a JDBC example for this chapter I went to the Intersolv Web site (this doesn't constitute a particular endorsement of their software; I chose it because I had used it before and was familiar with it) and downloaded a free trial copy of their DataDirect ODBC manager/driver package, as well as their JDBC/ODBC Bridge software (Intersolv and JavaSoft jointly developed the Bridge). I installed the software, and configured a data source for a *comma delimited* text file that I created as a small sample database (a comma delimited file is one of the database types for which Intersolv supplies an ODBC driver). Apart from the actual download, the setup took about half an hour.

Note that the JDBC/ODBC Bridge does not work with Microsoft's VJ++ development environment. (Microsoft has refused to implement JavaSoft's Java Native Interface - JNI - specification for calling out to C from Java, and JNI is required for the JDBC/ODBC Bridge. The same holds true for the Domino Java NOI, which is why VJ++ can't be used as an NOI development environment.)

JDBC Example

I won't go into deep detail on how JDBC's classes actually work. There are excellent white papers and even a tutorial for JDBC available on the JavaSoft Web site (http://developer.javasoft.com/developer/ onlineTraining/jdbc/index.html and http://java.sun.com/products/ jdbc). A very good article called "Getting Started With JDBC" by John Papageorge is also available at http://developer.javasoft.com/ developer/readAboutJava/jpg/startjdbc.html. The HTML documentation that comes with the software is pretty good too. You can also find electronic versions of these (and other) links on the CD in the database References.nsf.

Driver and Database Selection

The java.sql.DriverManager is the class responsible for selecting and loading database drivers at connect time. You specify a URL syntax particular to JDBC to tell the DriverManager how to connect to the database you want. The basic layout of a JDBC URL is as follows:

```
jdbc:<subprotocol>:<subname>
```

The first part ("jdbc:") is just the protocol specifier, like "http" or "ftp". The "subprotocol" is the name of either a specific driver (must be a pure Java driver), such as "dbaw" for Symantec's dbANYWHERE, or the special "connectivity mechanism" name "odbc". The latter is used when you are using the JDBC/ODBC Bridge; it tells JDBC to load an ODBC driver specific to the data source name that comes next. The driver manager then has to look up the data source configuration with the ODBC Manager to figure out which driver to load.

The third part of the URL is the data source specification. For an ODBC name, it must be one of the configured data sources. For a Java JDBC driver, it can include a host name and port, such as:

```
jdbc:dbaw://localhost:9988/xyzzy
```

In this case the database server machine name is "localhost", and the requested port number is 9988, followed by the database name. Here's an ODBC example:

```
jdbc:odbc:Employees
```

In this case "Employees" must be a known ODBC data source name.

The JDBC documentation says that the subprotocol can also be a remote naming service, such as "dcenaming." A *remote naming service* is some piece of software that you have access to (locally or over a network) that maps names (in some canonical format) to network addresses. Common naming services include DNS (Domain Naming Service), Novell's NDS (Netware Directory Service), and Sun's NIS (Network Information Service). The JDBC documentation tells you how to register your own subprotocol.

The JDBC-style URL is used in the DriverManager.getConnection() call to establish a connection with a database. An instance of the java.sql.Connection class is returned. Once you have a Connection instance you can send off SQL queries in various forms (including parameterized queries), using the java.sql.Statement class. When you execute a query you typically get back an instance of the java.sql.ResultSet class. You use ResultSet methods to iterate through the returned data, usually row by row.

The Code

I created the following simple example using (with permission) a sample program named SimpleSelect included with Intersolv's trial version of their JDBC software. I modified it to use the ODBC data source I have set up on my computer (the source "database" is a comma delimited text file named TABLE1.TXT and is included on the CD) named Employees. I also modified the logic that writes out the result set, in a vain attempt to make the column headers and the fields in each row line up nicely. I added some new code to also add the data to a Notes database (Ex13.nsf, also on the CD).

I say "vain attempt" because I wasn't particularly successful. This is a good example of where behavior in "ODBC land" is not always the same from driver to driver. The Intersolv text file driver apparently trims leading zeros from numbers and trailing spaces from strings in a result set (whether you want it to or not). If you develop a nice way of doing that, please let me know.

Listing 13.1 shows you the source code for the simple application I used. It does nothing more than connect to the database, retrieve all rows from a single table, and print out all the rows to the screen. For each row, I create a new Document in the sample Database. In each Document, I use the column name (referred to as the column "header" in the sample code) as the Item name for each column value.

Listing 13.1 JDBC Data Retrieval Example (Ex13Select.java)

```
//
// Copyright:    1990-1996 INTERSOLV, Inc.
//               This software contains confidential and proprietary
//               information of INTERSOLV, Inc.  You may study, use, modify
//               and distribute this example for any purpose.  This example
//               is provided WITHOUT WARRANTY either expressed or implied.
```

JDBC and NOI

```java
//      This program was modified by Bob Balaban to load the
//      retrieved data into
//      a Notes database. Modifications Copyright 1997 Looseleaf
//      Software, Inc.
//

import java.net.URL;
import java.sql.*;
import lotus.notes.*;

class Ex13Select
{
    public static void main (String args[])
    {
    // The following code will enable JDBC logging and send all
    // logging information to a file named 'jdbc.out'
//      try {
//          java.io.OutputStream outFile = new
//                  java.io.FileOutputStream("jdbc.out");
//
//          java.io.PrintStream outStream = new
//                  java.io.PrintStream (outFile, true);
//
//          DriverManager.setLogStream (outStream);
//          }
//      catch (java.io.IOException ex) {
//          System.out.println("Unable to set log stream: " +
//                  ex.getMessage());
//          }
        String url    = "jdbc:odbc:Employees";
        String uid    = "";
        String pwd    = "";

        String query = "SELECT * FROM Table1.txt";
        boolean startedNotes = false;
```

```java
try {

    // Create a JDBC driver object from our
    // JDBC to ODBC Bridge in order to register it
    // with the system

    java.sql.Driver d = (java.sql.Driver) Class.forName (
        "sun.jdbc.odbc.JdbcOdbcDriver").newInstance ();

    // Register the driver

    DriverManager.registerDriver (d);

    // Attempt to connect to a driver.  Each one
    // of the registered drivers will be loaded until
    // one is found that can process this URL

    Connection con = DriverManager.getConnection (
                url, uid, pwd);

    // If we were unable to connect, an exception
    // would have been thrown.  So, if we get here,
    // we are successfully connected to the URL

    // Check for, and display and warnings generated
    // by the connect.

    checkForWarning (con.getWarnings ());

    // Get the DatabaseMetaData object and display
    // some information about the connection

    DatabaseMetaData dma = con.getMetaData ();

    System.out.println("\nConnected to " + dma.getURL());
    System.out.println("Driver       " + dma.getDriverName());
    System.out.println("Version      " + dma.getDriverVersion());
    System.out.println("");

    // Create a Statement object so we can submit
    // SQL statements to the driver
    Statement stmt = con.createStatement ();
```

```
            // Submit a query, creating a ResultSet object
            ResultSet rs = stmt.executeQuery (query);

            // Display all columns and rows from the result set
            // need to init Notes here
            NotesThread.sinitThread();
            startedNotes = true;
            String dbServ = "";
            String dbName = "book\\Ex13.nsf";
            dispResultSet (rs, dbServ, dbName);

            // Close the result set
            rs.close();

            // Close the statement
            stmt.close();

            // Close the connection
            con.close();
            }
     catch (SQLException ex)
            {
            // A SQLException was generated.  Catch it and
            // display the error information.  Note that there
            // could be multiple error objects chained
            // together
            System.out.println ("\n*** SQLException caught ***\n");

            while (ex != null) {
                  System.out.println ("SQLState: " + ex.getSQLState
());
                  System.out.println ("Message:  " + ex.getMessage
());
                  System.out.println ("Vendor:   " + ex.getErrorCode
());
                  ex.printStackTrace();
                  ex = ex.getNextException ();
                  System.out.println ("");
```

Chapter 13

```
                }
            }
        catch (java.lang.Exception ex)
            {
            // Got some other type of exception.  Dump it.
            ex.printStackTrace ();
            }
        finally {
              if (startedNotes)
                NotesThread.stermThread();
            }
        }    // end main
//-------------------------------------
// checkForWarning
// Checks for and displays warnings.  Returns true if a warning
// existed
//-------------------------------------
      private static boolean checkForWarning (SQLWarning warn)
             throws SQLException
      {
      boolean rc = false;

      // If a SQLWarning object was given, display the
      // warning messages.  Note that there could be
      // multiple warnings chained together

      if (warn != null) {
          System.out.println ("\n *** Warning ***\n");
          rc = true;
          while (warn != null) {
              System.out.println ("SQLState: " + warn.getSQLState
());
              System.out.println ("Message:  " + warn.getMessage
());
```

```
                System.out.println ("Vendor:    " + warn.getErrorCode
());
                System.out.println ("");
                warn = warn.getNextWarning ();
                }
            }
        return rc;
    }

    //————————————————————————
    // dispResultSet
    // Displays all columns and rows in the given result set
    //————————————————————————

    private static void dispResultSet (ResultSet rs, String dbServ,
                                       String dbName)
        throws SQLException
    {
    int i;
    Session s = null;
    Database db = null;
    Document doc = null;

    // Get the ResultSetMetaData.  This will be used for
    // the column headings
    ResultSetMetaData rsmd = rs.getMetaData ();

    // Get the number of columns in the result set
    int numCols = rsmd.getColumnCount ();
    String headers[] = new String[numCols];

    // Display column headings, save them
    String colHdr;
    for (i=1; i<=numCols; i++)
        {
        colHdr = rsmd.getColumnLabel(i);
        if (i > 1)
```

Chapter 13

```
                System.out.print("  ");
        System.out.print(colHdr);
        headers[i-1] = colHdr;
        }

    System.out.println("");

    // Display data, fetching until end of the result set
    // We'll create a new Document in the Database for each row,
    // using the column headers as the Item names.

    try {
        s = Session.newInstance();
        db = s.getDatabase(dbServ, dbName);
        }
    catch (Exception e)
         {
        System.out.println("Couldn't open Notes database " +
dbName);
        e.printStackTrace();
        s = null;
        db = null;
        }

    boolean more = rs.next ();
    if (!more)
        System.out.println("No rows were retrieved");

    try {
        while (more)
             {
            // Loop through each column, getting the
            // column data and displaying it
            // create new document
            if (db != null)
                doc = db.createDocument();

            String value;
```

```
                    for (i=1; i<=numCols; i++)
                        {
                        value = rs.getString(i);
                        if (i > 1) System.out.print(" ");
                        System.out.print(value);

                        // add the value to the document
                            doc.appendItemValue(headers[i-1], value);
                        } // end for

                    System.out.println("");

                    // Fetch the next result set row, save the document
                    more = rs.next ();
                    doc.save(true, false);
                    }      // end while
            }   // end try
        catch (Exception e) { e.printStackTrace(); }

        }  // end dispResultSet
    } // end class
```

Figure 13.3 shows the output to the command window, and Figure 13.4 shows the resulting records in the Notes database's view.

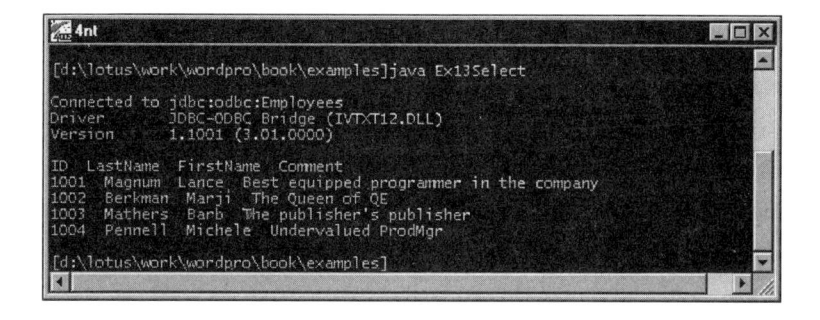

Figure 13.3 Ex13Select output to command window.

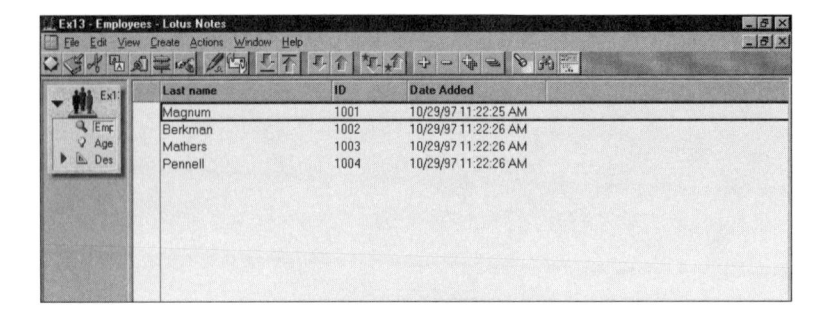

Figure 13.4 Ex13 Database view.

Discussion of Data Retrieval Example

Note that this is a single-threaded example, so we have to do the static method Notes initialization thing before we call the subroutine (dispResultSet) that creates the Notes Documents. The NotesThread.stermThread() call is in the last *finally* clause of the main program. We had to also use a boolean to tell us in the *finally* whether or not Notes was ever actually initialized, because an exception occurring before the init call would always end up in the *finally* logic, and if we try to terminate a Notes thread that was never initialized, there'll be trouble. Another way of doing that would be to use nested *try* blocks, with a *finally* on the inner one where the NotesThread.sinitThread() call is made.

Other than that there isn't too much to say about this example. The usage of the JDBC classes is quite ordinary and straightforward. You (especially you SQL heads out there) should be able to follow it easily.

The only slightly out of the ordinary thing about it is the registration of the JDBC/ODBC Bridge class (sun.jdbc.odbc.JdbcOdbcDriver), using the Class.forName() call to load the .class file into the Java VM. The Class instance returned from forName() is used to create an actual instance of the class in the newInstance() call. That instance is passed to DriverManager.registerDriver(), another static method invocation. The driver is registered as the handler for the "odbc" subprotocol, so that when our URL ("jdbc:odbc:Employees") is processed by the DriverManager.getConnection() call, the correct driver is used.

You've seen me state elsewhere in this book that I prefer to avoid using classes from the "sun" package, and that I like to stick to classes in the java or javax (or lotus.notes) packages. Why, then, are we using sun.jdbc.odbc.JdbcOdbcDriver? Because this is a vendor-specific software configuration, that is, the JDBC/ODBC driver implementation is not "standard" in the way that the classes in java.lang or javax.servlet are. And the reason that we use Class.forName() to load the bridge class instead of just saying *new jdbc.odbc.JdbcOdbcDriver()* is that we want to defer the class lookup on the computer to run time. Because the class is nonstandard, we can't be sure that every machine will have it lying around. Thus we would rather not have the class loaded when the program is loaded, but when the Class.forName() call is actually executed. This gives us an opportunity (of which I have, alas, not availed myself in this particular example) to do better error recovery.

A Word on Agent Security

As we've discussed elsewhere in this book, Agents come in two flavors: restricted and unrestricted. Restricted Agents cannot make use of as many server resources as can unrestricted Agents. One of the things restricted Agents can't do is load DLLs (other than the Notes DLL which implements NOI, of course). Because "pure" JDBC only causes Java classes to be loaded, there are no problems with security. Restricted Agents, however, will not be able to use the hybrid JDBC/ODBC Bridge configuration as virtually all ODBC drivers are implemented in C or C++.

You might want to consider this limitation if you're implementing background Agents that need to use JDBC.

SUMMARY

Relational database connectivity for Notes/Domino is, in my opinion, both one of the most powerful and also the most often overlooked capabilities among groupware developers. Combining NOI with JDBC gives you the power to move all kinds of data between Notes databases and any other database system that supports SQL queries.

You can, for example, write a multithreaded Java Agent that is invoked from a browser via the Domino HTTP server, and which collects user input using a simple Domino form. The Agent can then perform multiple queries on a remote database system, format the results as HTML output, and send it back to the browser, possibly updating a Notes database as well. Updating the Notes database can, in turn, trigger a workflow application, such as serial approval, email notification, inventory restocking, or almost anything else.

I'd say that the only area of database connectivity where Domino/NOI is weak involves moving around binary data (sometimes called *BLOBs*, for *Binary Large OBjects*). The NOI object model does not (yet) support binary data (and neither do lots of JDBC/ODBC drivers, by the way). As this kind of functionality becomes more popular (especially for Web-based applications such as video streaming), I'm sure you'll see it added to NOI, making it even more powerful.

Domino's ability to use Java to integrate these various back-end tools is unmatched by any other product.

Coming up in Chapter 14 is a prognostication of where some of the NOI-related technologies could go (and we hope will go) with the next release of Domino.

14

A Look Ahead to Domino 5.0

We'll wrap up the book by summarizing the major advances in programmability featured in Domino 4.6, and do a bit of crystal ball gazing about where some of these technologies might be headed in the next major feature release, Domino 5.0.

> **NOTE** Aside from a personal involvement with the early development of some CORBA prototypes during my tenure at Iris Associates, I have no personal knowledge whatsoever of specific product plans for Domino 5.0 beyond what has been publicly announced by Lotus. What follows stems from my own opinions and research, and is in no way based on any inside information. I have not asked anyone at Lotus or Iris to comment on specific product plans for this book.

Domino 4.6 Programmability: Summary

I'm biased, of course, but I'd rate the following as the major advances in programmability for Domino 4.6:

1. Notes Object Interface Java binding.
2. Java Agents for Domino.
3. Java Servlets for Domino.

Virtually all the new functionality is more relevant to the Domino Server product than to the Notes Client product, although you can run Java Agents in the Client as well as on a server.

Java NOI

Some people have asked me if the Domino 4.6 Java interface was "ported" from the LotusScript classes. The answer is emphatically no. There was some effort made to keep the Java APIs as close in feeling to the LotusScript classes as possible, but no code was ported from one to the other. Both interfaces (or "bindings" as we sometimes call them) are thin layers on top of a common set of C++ classes that make up the Notes LSX (which stands for LotusScript eXtension module). The behaviors that are the real class implementations are thus common to both LotusScript and Java (and to the OLE Automation interface as well, for that matter). The fact that the architecture still bears the name "LotusScript" is only an historical artifact at this point.

At one level, having the Java binding to the Notes Object Interface in Domino 4.6 is simply a way of allowing people to write standalone API programs using Java instead of C or C++. Java applications as we've described them in this book are really no different from any C API program, other than in the language of implementation. One advantage of using Java over C is that you get all the nice object-oriented constructs. An advantage of using Java over the C++ API is that with Java you can compile a program on one platform and have it run unmodified and without recompiling it on another, even when the operating systems are different. There are, though, differences in the kinds of functionality covered by the Java class library and the other APIs. Being newer, the Java interface (and LotusScript too because remember, they rest on exactly the same code) does not yet have all the functionality of the C API (the lowest level and in most ways most functional API for Notes), but eventually it will. The rule of thumb is, if the Java API gives you the functionality you need to accomplish your task, then use it. If not, consider using a hybrid approach: Java for the functionality that you can implement using Java, and call-outs to C or C++ code for the rest.

I predict (and hope) Lotus will begin some serious investment in broadening the coverage of both the Java and LotusScript interfaces.

In sum, the overall Notes Object Interface represents the programmable face of the product. You get to manipulate real Notes/Domino objects, and without having to go through a user interface. You can automate and schedule behaviors that you invent or customize. The fact that there is now a Java binding to that object interface gives you both more choices and more functionality: you can make use of nice built-in features of the Java language, and integration with other Java technologies (Servlets, for example) becomes much simpler.

Java Agents

LotusScript Agents have been a fixture of Notes programmability since Release 4.0 in January 1996 (that's about a decade in Web years). The Agent Manager module in the Domino server handles schedule-triggering as well as event-triggering of Agent programs, and together with the NOI infrastructure manages Agent identity and security. Without the

NOI classes they wouldn't be able to do much, of course, which is why so much of this book focuses on the functionality and interface of the object model.

The new Java Agent functionality in Release 4.6 is best described this way: Anything you could do with a LotusScript Agent you can now also do with a Java Agent. What could be simpler? Naturally you also get to take advantage of features in Java that aren't in LotusScript, such as easy network access and multithreading.

JAVA SERVLETS

The Java Servlet interface is a relatively new and as yet under-explored technology from JavaSoft. The basic idea is very simple though: You can write CGI (Common Gateway Interface) programs in Java, have them triggered by your Web server via a URL, and you can pass parameters to them as well.

I've tried to make the point in this book that Agents are better than Servlets for use in production server-based applications, particularly where security and server administration and control over resources is a concern. I've also offered those of you with working Servlets who want to integrate them with the Domino Agent subsystem with a minimum of pain some source code (Chapter 11) for an Agent that knows how to load and run Servlets. This gives you the best of both worlds: no need to rewrite a line of code in an existing Servlet, but all the security and identity features of an Agent.

This little technique would be impossible without the Java NOI and Agent capabilities. It's an example of how using Java opens up possibilities for the integration of Domino with other useful technologies.

OVERVIEW OF FORTHCOMING ENHANCEMENTS

So what's my best guess for the future of Domino as it relates to Java, NOI, Agents, and so on? I think that there are some obvious areas where these things can (and probably will) be extended:

1. Java IDE.
2. Remote Object Access: Domino server Object Request Broker (ORB) and NOI for ORB clients. Remote Method Invocation (RMI).
3. Java classes for other standard protocols: LDAP, IMAP, etc.

The following sections discuss each in some detail.

JAVA DEVELOPMENT ENVIRONMENT

There are two large holes in the Java offerings in Domino 4.6: There's no Integrated Development Environment (IDE) for Java, and none of the Notes Client user interface scripting features that you get with LotusScript are available for Java.

I hope (though I don't *know*) that both of these will be addressed in Domino 5.0. The biggest need is for an integrated Java debugger so that the contortions you have to go through now (described in detail in Chapter 9) to debug Java Agents will no longer be necessary.

The next thing that Domino customers will demand is the ability to script the Notes Client with Java (currently you can only do it with LotusScript or @function formulas). Once there's a Java IDE in place, it should be possible (I can say this because I'm not responsible for implementing it) to hook up all the UI events in the current Visual Basic-like model to Java. Java itself, as we've discussed in Chapter 12, has no real event model; you have to use Java Beans to accomplish serious event processing. So perhaps what we'll see will be akin to what we now have with Agents: You'll write a Java Bean that implements a specified interface (or extends a specified lotus.notes class) that allows it to hook into all the Notes Client event processing. That would be, as they say, way cool.

REMOTE ACCESS TECHNOLOGIES FOR DOMINO NOI

I've made the point throughout this volume that in Domino 4.6 the Java NOI APIs are only available on a machine that has Domino installed. There's a lot you can do with that: Agents, Servlets, Applications, and so on. But you can't do Applets. Domino has all kinds of Applet support built in (you can embed Applets in a Notes document, you can have the Domino server serve up an Applet over HTTP, and you can even have Applets invoke Domino Agents with URLs and parse through the HTML response), but you can't write an Applet that will get downloaded to someone's browser and have that Applet use any of the NOI classes.

The reason is simple: NOI requires that a bunch of Notes DLLs (or the platform equivalent) be present on the machine; all the real object behaviors are implemented in the Notes core code. You, the Applet author, have no idea whether anyone downloading your Applet has Domino installed. Furthermore, even if they did, most browsers won't let an Applet load a DLL into memory because that would be a potential security violation.

There are other techniques available for communicating between Applets and Domino:

- ❒ You get two programmable "events" that Domino automatically supports via the HTTP server: document open and document

A Look Ahead to Domino 5.0

save. You can designate Agents that the server will run when these events are triggered from a client's browser.

❒ You can cause an Agent to be run on the server by invoking it with a URL. The Agent can format HTML output that gets returned to the client, and there's no law that says that HTML has to be displayed. It could simply be parsed by the Applet code as returned data.

These techniques, while useful, are not optimal (to say the least) for serious client/server development efforts.

There are, however, some object remoting technologies out there that will probably be making an appearance in Domino 5.0. The primary one, in which a lot of effort has already been invested at Lotus, is called CORBA, which stands for Common Object Request Broker Architecture. CORBA is a specification, not a product. It is "owned" by a consortium called the Object Management Group (OMG). Any vendor is free to implement a conforming Object Request Broker (ORB) however they like. The purpose of CORBA implementations is to allow objects that reside on a server to have their methods invoked remotely, from one or more client machines. It's a bit like Remote Procedure Call (RPC) mechanisms (which is how the Notes Client talks to the Domino server today), although it was designed from the beginning to be used in object oriented systems.

The next couple of sections go into more detail about CORBA and Domino, and what you will probably see in Release 5.0 in this area, and how it applies to Applets.

Another object remoting technology called Remote Method Invocation has been invented by JavaSoft, and released as part of Java 1.1. RMI is a lot like CORBA, but it is more tightly tied to Java. I don't expect to see any official support for RMI in Domino, but as you'll see in the section below on this topic, it won't be very hard for you, if you need it, to write an RMI server that front-ends the Domino classes.

Finally, no discussion of remote object technology would be complete without at least a mention of Microsoft's DCOM.

CORBA and Domino

CORBA is very interesting in the context of Domino: it provides a way for developers to write programs that either live on or are downloaded to a client machine which use a standard on-the-wire network protocol to access objects that live on a server somewhere, and invoke their methods and have results returned to them. Moreover, because the client and server communicate via a standardized protocol (called IIOP, which stands for Internet InterORB Protocol), the client and server can be implemented in different programming languages.

The details of how CORBA works are way beyond the scope of this chapter (and of this book), but there are plenty of published works on it (see the database of useful links on the CD, references.nsf). I'll just give you the basics here.

On the server side, you have a bunch of object classes. You also have an Object Request Broker (ORB), which is a program written in any language you like (C++ is common, but there are Java ORBs available now too). The ORB is itself a server process—it listens for object requests on a TCP/IP port and dispatches any that come in to the object(s) in question. A request is formatted using the rules of the IIOP protocol: It contains an object reference, a method identifier, and (optionally) a bunch of arguments. The ORB passes the method invocation request along to the referenced object, which executes the request. The results, if any, are returned to the client by the ORB, again using the IIOP protocol.

The object interfaces are specified on the server using a language-independent syntax called IDL (Interface Definition Language). You use IDL to define the methods and properties that each object supports. You then use an IDL compiler to translate your language-independent specification into a set of implementations in a specific target programming language. The IDL compiler generates source code for classes (or whatever it can generate for target languages that aren't object oriented) that implement "skeletons" in the target language (C++, Java, whatever). You (the server object developer) take those skeletons and use them as the basis for implementing your object behaviors. The object definitions also get stored in something called the Interface Respository (IR). The IR can (if the server ORB supports this functionality) be used by client programs to dynamically find out what the interfaces for a given object class look like.

The IDL compiler and server ORB come with (if you buy a commercially available one, if not you write all this yourself) a runtime support library for the server which handles all the IIOP protocol translation and method invocation dispatching. The ORB also handles various "services" such as security (though there are all kinds of different schemes, from SSL to Kerberos), naming, and location (finding out what machine a particular object class might reside on). See the OMG specs at http://www.omg.org if you need the details.

The most common way you would make use of server objects from a client is to get a copy of those object's IDL definitions. You can then use an IDL compiler (doesn't have to be the same one that was used to create the server objects) to create client-side "stub" classes. These are very lightweight objects whose only purpose is to serve as "proxies" on the client machine for the "real" objects that live on the server. Each defined server class has an identical looking proxy class on the client side, with the identical set of methods and properties. The job of the proxy class when invoked from a client program is to collect the method arguments (if any), package them up as an IIOP request, and ship them off to the server. The proxy then waits (most of the time, there are options supported by some IDL compilers that allow for asynchronicity on the client) for a response from the server. It takes the returned IIOP packets and formats them as returned values to the caller.

The language generated by the IDL compiler for the client stubs must match the language used for the client program, but it can be a totally different language from the one the server skeletons use. That's because the CORBA and IIOP specifications tell you exactly what data types are allowed and how to format them for language-independent processing. The ORBs on both the client and server sides handle any required data format translations.

That's the simple explanation. There's one additional important wrinkle: If your client-side stub objects are implemented in Java, then they can be downloaded to the client machine at runtime, and don't need to be permanently installed there. This works because Java has sophisticated dynamic class loading capabilities. The stub classes (together with their underlying runtime support classes that handle sockets, IIOP, and so on) can be packaged together in a .jar file and await your pleasure on some HTTP server somewhere. *Voila:* Applets that can be downloaded to any browser and use IIOP to talk back at an object-to-object level to the server from whence they came.

Domino Server ORB

Domino 5.0 is expected to ship with an ORB, possbly one developed by IBM, Lotus's parent company or possibly another one. I'm not aware of (and Lotus isn't talking publicly about it yet) what arrangements they plan to make for security (though SSL support would be a good bet), naming services, and so on. The existing LSX architecture fits nicely into the CORBA scheme: Each NOI class already has a C++ implementation; all you'd need is an interface layer for the ORB to dispatch method invocations to (big hand wave here, there are many details that make it a bit less than the slam-dunk I'm portraying).

I would expect to see all the NOI classes available for remote use via CORBA. I also hope Lotus/Iris will decide to publish the actual IDL definitions for the interfaces. Will the remote interface to the Domino

NOI look the same as the current LotusScript and Java bindings? It could, but there are some good reasons why it shouldn't.

The easy implementation (I know, because I prototyped one when I worked at Iris) would be to take the existing interface for either Java or LotusScript, and translate it directly into IDL. From there, you can generate the C++ skeletons that get bolted onto the Notes LSX, and you're pretty much done (there are some issues with data type translation and persistent object references, but we'll hand wave that, too, for now). Then you could take the same IDL and use another IDL compiler to generate client-side Java stubs. Those stubs can then be used from remote machines in either Applets or applications to talk to NOI objects on a Domino server using IIOP. So far so good.

The problem with this model is that the network performance of this implementation would be pretty bad. Each method/property invocation has to make a round trip from the client to the server and back. For example, let's count the number of trips to the server that the following few lines of client code would have to make:

```
Session s = Session.newInstance();
Database db = s.getDatabase("names.nsf");
View v = db.getView("People");
Document doc = v.getDocumentByKey("Balaban");
String name = doc.getItemValueString("lastname");
```

I count five, one for each line. The one nice optimization that you get for free here is that the View.getDocumentByKey() call does all its work on the server, but this program would perform rather poorly in terms of network i/o, especially if we were doing something like coding a loop over a thousand Documents in a View.

The solution (assuming that we're optimizing for network traffic, which might or might not be the right decision in all cases) is to modify the interface to do as much work as possible on the server. That means changing the object model somewhat, and implementing some different code on the server side. In the Document iteration case, for example, you might want an interface that lets you get a big chunk of data all at once, maybe 10, 20, or 100 Document's worth in one round trip. Then you'd cache all those bytes on the client, making for better access times and user interaction response overall.

Such a redesign is a two-part effort. First, you need to redesign (or add on to one) the existing server interfaces to be more optimized for network traffic. Second, you need to do some work on the client side, which is covered in the next section. I expect some changes along these lines in Domino 5.0.

Applet Access to Domino Server ORB: NOI for ORB Clients

On the client side, the simple thing to do would be, as above, to just compile the objects' IDL into Java stubs, and write Applet programs on top of that interface. But as I just said, this will result in poor performance, especially over the Web, which has relatively high messaging latency (meaning, it's slow).

The real idea is to write a set of Java classes that can be downloaded for Applet use, but which is more optimized for networking. They would sit atop the default set of stubs generated from the IDL (you still need those) and do some intelligent caching of data, along the lines of the 100-Document chunks example above. This would not only reduce overall network traffic, but also improve user response time, which is particularly important for an Applet.

These new client-side classes might well have a significantly different interface from what we now see in NOI, but they might not. One advantage in this sort of architecture is that the client classes don't need to be constrained by what you can implement using IDL: They're a *real* set of Java classes that know how to talk to the IDL-generated stubs.

One disadvantage is that doing it this way increases the number of bytes of Java code that have to be downloaded before you can run your applet. You need to pull down the actual applet code, the client-side classes, the IDL stubs, and all the required IIOP and networking runtime support code. This situation can be improved somewhat by using .jar files (especially compressed ones); we'll have to see how it goes.

Regardless of the exact implementation that Lotus/Iris settles on, you can expect that in Domino 5.0 you'll be able to write applets in Java that are stored on a Domino server and downloaded to any Web browser, and that you'll be able to write those applets to include NOI-like calls to server objects. The possibilities for such an enabling technology are truly wide open. You can imagine, for instance, that people somewhere at Iris and/or Lotus are busily writing some Java Beans that implement slices of Notes Client functionality. There's no reason why these Beans shouldn't be usable by downloadable applets.

One could also picture the Lotus eSuite components (a set of Java Beans designed from scratch to be used by downloaded applets that implement utility functions such as spreadsheets, word processing, and charting) gaining remote NOI capabilities and talking directly to Notes databases on Domino servers using IIOP. The Domino server could become not only an application platform and data server, but a true object server as well.

On the server side, it would be awfully nice to be able to write your own server objects, register or install them in some way on the Domino server, and have the Domino ORB handle remote access to them automatically. I don't know if this will happen in Domino 5.0, as there are significant architectural hurdles that need to be overcome beyond what it will take to support just the NOI classes remotely.

Remote Method Invocation (RMI)

CORBA isn't the only remote object manipulation architecture out there. JavaSoft has released a set of classes in the java.rmi package that essentially do the same sort of job that CORBA does, though it's for Java only and uses a different networking protocol.

RMI is a "lighter weight" technology than CORBA in a couple of ways: It is much easier to install and set up (it comes with the Java Development Kit); it is easier to develop remotable interfaces; and there is a smaller networking footprint for applets because less code has to be downloaded.

If you have some existing classes for which you want to develop a remote interface, it's pretty easy to do using RMI (see the RMI documentation for the details on http://java.sun.com/products/jdk):

1. Create a remote interface for each class. Your interface must extend the java.rmi.remote interface, which has no methods. This "marks" your class as being available for remote invocation.

2. For each method in your class, decide whether you want it to be remotely invoked. If you do, add it to your remote interface. Modify your class to *implement* your new interface.

3. Use the RMI compiler (the rmic utility comes with the JDK) to process your remote classes. RMIC generates both skeletons and stubs, along the lines of the CORBA model.

4. Write an RMI server. Unless you need a lot of control over how it works, you can do this very easily by just writing a Java application (with a static main() method) and extending the java.rmi.RemoteServer class. Your server will field remote method calls and dispatch them to the proper classes on the server. See the RMI documentation for details on registration and so on.

5. Write the client program. The client-side code will use the stubs generated by RMIC, which are (as in CORBA) remoted versions of the server-side implementations. You essentially have, for every server class, a remote client proxy class (they have to have different names, unfortunately). Your client code must reference the proxy classes, each of which has the same method signatures as its corresponding server class.

6. The client program can be a downloadable applet, no problem there. In fact, the amount of code that needs to get downloaded to the client browser is smaller for RMI than for CORBA, because a bunch of the RMI code is already installed on the client as part of the base Java classes (assuming you have a browser that supports a version of Java that contains RMI; not all of them do yet).

7. The client proxies and the server communicate using a private wire protocol, also called RMI.

Can the RMI server classes use NOI? Yes they can, so long as you have Domino installed on the server machine. Does this mean you can write applets that talk remotely to the Domino 4.6 Java NOI using RMI? Yes, but you have to write the RMI server yourself; Lotus doesn't provide one.

So which is better, CORBA or RMI? "Better" being a slippery concept sometimes, I'll offer the following pros and cons of each:

- **CORBA pros:** Supports multiple languages. Can (in theory) mix and match different vendor client and server ORBs, because all support IIOP for data and object transfer. Robust set of services available (though it varies from vendor to vendor). Well understood technology, it has been around for many years. Lots of production systems in existence, fairly large community of practitioners available for assistance and support.

- **CORBA cons:** Not the easiest technology to bring into a production environment, there's a fairly steep learning curve to climb before you're up and running. It is even more difficult to implement your own ORB (though most people never need to). Each vendor's ORB will have different integration techniques for remoting your object classes. This means that you can't count on easily switching vendors for server-side ORBs. Unless you have an ORB implemented in Java, and unless your server objects are also implemented in Java, you can't count on being able to switch platforms easily. It can sometimes be hard to translate your application's data types into the base types supported by IDL.

- **RMI pros:** Very easy to get something working. Everything is in Java, so there's less code overhead, smaller footprint on the client and over the network (in terms of how much code has to be downloaded). No IDL to deal with, all native Java data types are supported. Works on all platforms that can run a Java VM.

- **RMI cons:** It isn't a "standard" in the way that CORBA is. The technology belongs to Sun/JavaSoft, and is controlled by them. You're reliant on a single vendor for technical support and bug fixes. There is not yet a large community of RMI users on which to lean for assistance. When I implemented an RMI prototype for Notes in 1996 (using JDK 1.02, before the newer 1.1x became available), I found that I wasn't able to get all the information I needed on the server's multithreading behavior. RMI only works for Java; if you have classes implemented in some other language, you either have to use "native" calls from Java to C or invent some other solution.

In the end, my own opinion is that Lotus made the right decision by going with CORBA over RMI, mainly because of issues like openness and standardization.

DCOM

Microsoft has, of course, a competing technology for remote object access. Anyone who has done any OLE programming in the past few years is intimately familiar with COM, Component Object Model. COM is the technology Microsoft invented to let objects present interfaces to the world, to have those interfaces be standardized and discoverable at run time. COM is itself intimately tied up with C++, but it is a powerful framework. Given a pointer to any COM object, you can find out what interfaces it supports. The object does not necessarily have to implement all its interfaces itself, it can contain child objects and use a delegation model to present contained objects' interfaces as its own.

DCOM simply stands for Distributed COM, and is meant to be the machine-to-machine version of COM, where the invoker of an interface's method does not have to reside on the same machine as the implementor of the interface. OLE already handles a form of remote method invocation: You can invoke a method on an OLE interface from a "container" object's process and have the "server" object which implements the method be in a different process with its own address space. OLE handles the proxying, marshalling, and de-marshalling (packing and unpacking buffers full of argument data) involved in remoting calls across the process boundary, something that is ordinarily fairly difficult to do. DCOM is (at least conceptually) just an extension of that technology from cross-process to cross-machine, using a network as the link.

DCOM comes for free with Windows NT 4.0, and is supported by a bunch of new classes in the Microsoft Foundation Classes (MFC) framework. DCOM uses YAWP (Yet Another Wire Protocol, an official Looseleaf acronym) to communicate DCOM messages across a network link.

Microsoft has positioned DCOM as a direct competitor to both CORBA and RMI, and can give you chapter and verse on why DCOM is the superior technology (I myself don't necessarily believe that it is superior, as I probably use a definition of the term somewhat different from Microsoft's.) Since I'm not an expert on DCOM I can neither confirm nor deny Microsoft's claims. I do, however, question their motives in conducting what at times looks like a food fight.

A couple of points I will make, however: If you adopt DCOM you pretty much tie yourself to both C++ (Microsoft's version of it) and Windows NT operating systems. I wouldn't be surprised to see Microsoft come out with a Java interoperability story for DCOM (they may already have done so for all I know), making it a direct competitor to RMI. At this point all I can say is that, like RMI, DCOM is a fairly new technology, and the issues pro and con need some time to settle out.

Summary: Whither Remote Objects for Domino?

I suppose I could descend into punditry and position this section as a "Who will win?" discussion, but I won't. The real question of interest here is: What makes the most sense for Domino, and what are we likely to see in the next revision?

Again, not having any inside information to draw on, I can only make observations from what I know and what I've seen in the press. I know for sure that both a server ORB and some kind of remote client Java classes extending NOI are in the works for Domino Release 5.0. I don't know exactly what they'll look like, but the ORB will most likely conform to all the relevant standards. The new downloadable Java classes will most likely bear some resemblance to the 4.6 Java NOI, but will probably include some differences as well. They'll be tuned for network performance, and they will be be programmed on top of the "bare" IDL-generated stubs.

Somewhere around the release of Domino 5.0 I would expect to see some cool Java Beans that use the remote interfaces to do interesting bits of Domino functionality within applet frameworks. Since Beans are mostly self-contained, they don't have to depend on features in the base product, and could ship independently.

Will Domino support either DCOM or RMI? I doubt that we'll see an officially supported RMI in Domino, but I wouldn't be surprised to see some kind of DCOM support. Notes has always been an excellent OLE container, and the expertise within the organization on COM goes fairly deep. There have been rumblings in the press about this too. The issue for Iris and Lotus is likely to be more one of engineering resources and product ship deadlines than one of remote object religion. If they can get the code done in time, they probably will do it (again, just my opinion).

The big issue around supporting multiple remote object technologies for the customer is likely to be one of installation and deployment. There are currently very few network firewalls that will allow IIOP, DCOM, or RMI to pass through; most are programmed to allow HTTP only. This means that if you want to allow users outside your firewall to download applets that remotely manipulate server objects using one of these protocols, you might have to convince your network administration bureaucracies to allow some new stuff through the firewall. This is usually not an easy task. No problem if you're just doing your deployment within a corporate intranet, though, as there's usually no firewall involved. Another possibility is to use ORB (or whatever) software that tunnels its protocol through HTTP. There are ways to take (almost) any network protocol and wrapper it with HTTP so that a firewall will let it through. The downside of doing this is that it puts more of a burden on both the server and the client software (they have to catch HTTP requests and responses, decode from them the real protocol, and then dispatch that message). Furthermore, if everyone starts tunneling all kinds of protocols through HTTP, the firewall vendors will make their firewalls smart enough to figure out what's really going on, and then they'll start refusing tunneled protocols as well. We'll be right back where we are now.

This is not an easy problem, and I expect that real and practical solutions will take a bit of time to emerge.

OTHER PROGRAMMABLE INTERFACES FOR DOMINO

The other big news relating to Domino 4.6 besides the Java NOI (okay, okay, but that's how I see it) was that the Domino server now supports standard Internet application protocols such as Lightweight Directory Access Protocol (LDAP) and Internet Mail Access Protocol (IMAP). LDAP support in the server means that any client who also knows the protocol can gain access to the Domino directory: browse user entries, look up mail addresses, and so on. IMAP support allows clients to read and create mail messages. Thus the two protocols work together so that, for example, from a Web browser you can use a Domino server to create new mail documents, complete type-ahead on recipient names, and send the messages.

These interfaces are both programmable today, in the sense that you can write a Java (or C++) program on a client machine that opens a socket to the LDAP or IMAP port on a Domino machine, and talks to it using the standard protocol. What would be much nicer, though, would be to have some Java class libraries that handle all the grungy bit packing and communications back and forth for us.

JavaSoft has announced that they are working on a mail package for Java, but design and development are still in progress, and there isn't much we can say about it at this stage. Java support for LDAP is somewhat further along, though, so we can talk a bit about the Java Naming and Directory Interface (JNDI).

JNDI is, as of this writing, in beta. you can download a published specification and pre-release software from http://java.sun.com/products/jndi. JNDI is meant to cover a wide range of naming and directory service functionality, and to do much more than just LDAP, though LDAP is one of the protocols that JNDI will support.

The basic idea of the Naming and Directory Interface is to provide a one-size-fits-all API for network based naming and directory services. The API is defined in two packages: java.naming and java.naming.directory. There are several interfaces that would be used by implementors to expose support for a given naming or directory service. One could, for example, use the naming package interface to implement a service that finds, say, printers on the local network. You'd write a class that *implements* the java.naming.Context interface, and have the Context.lookup() call return objects of class Printer. Other methods on the Context interface allow you to iterate through names that the context knows about, and to define new bindings of names to objects.

The java.naming.directory.DSContext is a special case extension of the java.naming.Context interface. It deals specifically with directory objects and their attributes. The set of attributes belonging to a directory entry is arbitrary: Each attribute has a name and a value. Sounds just like a Notes Document, doesn't it? You'd implement a class using the DSContext interface for each kind of directory you wanted to support, and LDAP could (and probably will) be one of them.

If the API sounds kind of vague (I've left out a bunch of the details, but the JavaSoft spec is pretty complete), that's because JavaSoft wanted the interfaces to be completely general purpose; their aim is to eventually provide implementations of the interface (and allow other vendors to write them as well) that wrapper all kinds of naming and directory services: CORBA, Novell NDS, Sun's NIS, DNS, as well as LDAP. Support for each kind of naming or directory service is "plugged in" to the architecture (JavaSoft's beta release contains support only for LDAP and NIS) by writing classes that implement the required interfaces.

This is a great overall architecture, it's open in the sense that we (the masses of software developers) are not dependent on JavaSoft to support our favorite naming or directory service. We can write our own, and it works in the overall framework just fine, assuming that the design of the basic object model is flexible enough to handle the idiosyncrasies of our particular product.

So, what does this mean for Domino? For one thing, it means that when JNDI is released, you'll be able to browse and update Domino directories from a Java program via LDAP, with no enhancements required on the server side (it already supports LDAP in Release 4.6). There could also be a native Domino implementation of JNDI, but it's probably too soon to say whether there would be significant functional advantages to doing it that way. The same is most likely true of the forthcoming Java mail APIs: I suspect that an early release of whatever JavaSoft defines will support the IMAP protocol, and you'll therefore be able to use Domino mail services that way. Still, you have a choice: You can code to the "raw" protocols, or use a nicely packaged class library instead.

Of course you can also use the lotus.notes package to do anything with Domino that you can do via either LDAP or IMAP, without having to deal with a generic interface that may not support all the functionality of the underlying product. Choice is the name of the game these days, and you can pick the interface that suits your needs best; that's why Domino supports the appropriate Internet standards (such as LDAP and IMAP) in the first place.

SUMMARY

If the past is prelude, then I think we can reasonably expect Domino/Notes to continue to evolve as a product for a long time to come. The trends in the programmability area will almost certainly continue toward more openness in several areas:

- More and more of the functionality of the product will become available to developers as Java (and LotusScript) interfaces. The direction toward making as much of the functionality of the older C API available through NOI will continue.

- The Internet standard protocols that Domino already supports will become conveniently programmable over time, and new standards and interfaces will emerge. The synergy between Lotus and JavaSoft may well grow as Domino continues to support protocols and JavaSoft continues to develop standardized Java interfaces to those protocols.

- New remoting technologies such as CORBA and RMI will also continue to evolve. Domino will become tightly integrated with some or all of them, beginning with Release 5.0. Initially we can expect to be able to use CORBA/IIOP to remotely program Domino objects. Future releases are likely to add even more functionality by supporting technologies like automatic failover, naming and server location services, and so on.

- Integrated Java development environment. Badly needed, almost certain to get done one way or another.

- Some of the current Notes Client functionality will very likely be made available in the form of a library of Java Beans. A "Bean-ized" version of the Notes Client view interface is one obvious possibility. These Beans would be available for use in downloadable applets as embeddable user interface widgets that know how to talk directly back to the Domino server, using the CORBA/IIOP communications facility that we know is already in the works. The nice thing about this is that it gives third-party developers the opportunity to embed slices of the Notes Client user experience into the browser environment with minimal effort.

Chapter 14

That about wraps up my list of speculations and prognostications for what's coming in Domino Release 5.0 and beyond. Of course it could all be different next year as the world continues to change at accelerating speed. That's the exciting (and sometimes bewildering) thing about the software industry these days.

BIBLIOGRAPHY

Here's a not-quite-random collection of articles and books that you might find interesting. The references in this bibliography are not available on the Web. Take a look at Appendix A for Web links. The contents of both this bibliography and Appendix A are in a database (References.nsf) on the CD.

"What's New with LotusScript in Notes 4.5", by Bob Balaban. *The View* vol. 2 No. 6, November/December 1996, Wellesley Information Services.

> This two-part article—part 2 appeared in the January/February 1997 issue (Vol. 3 No. 1) describes new classes for LotusScript in Notes 4.5.

"Creating Powerful Compound Documents and Applications with OLE, LotusScript and Notes", by Bob Balaban. *The View* vol. 2 no. 5, September/October 1996, Wellesley Information Services.

How to use the OLE Automation features of Notes and LotusScript to do interesting things.

"This is Not Your Father's Basic: LotusScript in Notes Release 4", by Bob Balaban. *The View* vol. 1 no. 5, November/December 1995, Wellesley Information Services.

An overview of all the LotusScript classes in Notes Release 4.0.

"CGI Programming with the Domino Web Server", by John T. Chamberlain. *The View* vol. 3 no. 4, July/August 1997, Wellesley Information Services.

Great overview of CGI programming using Domino. Covers CGI basics and how-tos using LotusScript

"An Introduction to the New Notes Object Interface for Java", by Bob Balaban. *The View* vol. 3 no. 5, September/October 1997, Wellesley Information Services.

Overview to the Java NOI. If you read this book, you don't need the article. But tell your friends.

"A Test Drive of the New Web Development Features in Notes Designer for Domino 4.6", by Chris Reckling. *The View* vol. 3 no. 5, September/October 1997, Wellesley Information Services.

Covers all the new Web design stuff in Domino 4.6: Java Applets, adding Web-only elements to Notes forms, how to use hide-when formulas, etc etc

Java Design, by Peter Coad and Mark Mayfield, 1997, Prentice-Hall. ISBN 0-13-2711494

Good set of design principles for Java programming.

Design Patterns, Elements of Reusable Object-Oriented Software, by Erich Gamma, Richard Helm, Ralph Johnson and John Vlissides, 1995, Addison-Wesley. ISBN 0-201-63361-2

>Good design frameworks for Java.

Concurrent Programming in Java, Design Principles and Patterns, by Doug Lea, 1997, Addison-Wesley. ISBN 0-201-69581-2

>Great discussion of all the nuances of multithreaded programming in Java.

Web Server Technology, by Nancy J. Yeager and Robert E. McGrath, 1996, Morgan Kaufmann Publishers. ISBN 1-55860-376-X

>Ever wondered how HTTP, firewalls and reflected IP addressing really works? Get this book.

Java in a Nutshell, by David Flanagan, 1996, O'Reilly & Associates. ISBN 1-56592-183-6

>Good book for C++ programmers who want to learn Java.

CORBA Fundamentals and Programming, by Jon Siegel (ed.), 1996, John Wiley & Sons. ISBN 0-471-12148-7

>Hefty, but it covers pretty much everything you need to know to start doing CORBA programming.

Client/Server Programming with Java and CORBA, by Robert Orfali and Dan Harkey, 1997, John Wiley & Sons. ISBN 0-471-16351-1

>Good info on how you can write Java ORBs.

Hacking Java, the Java Professional's Resource Kit, by Mark Wutka, 1997 Que Corp. ISBN 0-7897-0935-x

>Lots of tips and tricks for doing cool stuff with Java.

60 Minute Guide to LotusScript 3 Programming for Lotus Notes 4, by Robert Beyer, Roland Houle, Jr., and Robert Perron. 1996, IDG Books. ISBN 1568847793

The first (and still one of the best) guides to LotusScript programming and to the Release 4.0 Notes classes. Doesn't include enhancements made since Release 4.0, however.

A

Useful Links and References

The information in this APPENDIX is reproduced from the References.nsf database on the CD.

Agents

URL: http://www.notes.net/Today.nsf/cbb328e5c12843a9852563dc006721c7/349c511a459c22ae852564ff0071f677?OpenDocument

Title: "Controlling the Agents in Your System"

Great article by Julie Kadashevich on how to tune the Domino Agent Manager.

URL:	http://www.notes.net/Today.nsf/cbb328e5c12843a9852563dc006721c7/06b61d2bc44aced68525643a00705cdd?OpenDocument
Title:	"Creating Agents in the Personal Web Navigator"
	Good description by Teresa Deane on how to create LotusScript Agents that do interesting Web things.
URL:	http://www.notes.net/Today.nsf/cbb328e5c12843a9852563dc006721c7/9ce517d127d4550785256505006a1b92?OpenDocument
Title:	"Running Java Agents in Domino"
	Great overview by Russ Lipton on how to work through the user interface of the Notes Client to create and run Domino Agents.
URL:	http://www.notes.net/Today.nsf/cbb328e5c12843a9852563dc006721c7/06f0b77f66d5528d85256522005be3de?OpenDocument
Title:	"Tips on Debugging Java Agents"
	This is a more limited version of what you have already read in Chapter 9 of this book. But I included it anyway.
URL:	http://www.notes.net/Today.nsf/b1d67fedee86c741852563cc005019c5/4501ebd065a0759e8525654000641bef?OpenDocument
Title:	"When Will My Agent Run?"

Excellent article by Julie Kadashevich describing how the Agent Manager decides when to run an Agent. It isn't as simple as you might think.

CORBA

URL: http://www.omg.org

Title: Object Management Group

The home page for the Object Management Group. Full of links to CORBA and IIOP specs, success stories (no failure stories I could locate), and other reference material. Has a very nice area called "CORBA for Beginners. I particularly like their "CORBA the Geek" motif.

URL: www.iona.com

Title: ORB Vendor

Iona is one of the best known commercial ORB vendors. Their product is called Orbix.

URL: http://www.visigenic.com

Title: ORB Vendor

One of the best-known commercial ORB vendors. Netscape distributes their ORB.

Domino Publications

URL:	http://www.advisor.com
Title:	Notes & Domino Advisor
	One of the best known publications and conference organizers in the Notes industry.
URL:	http://www.wellesleyinfo.com
Title:	Wellesley Information Services
	Home page for the publisher of *The View* and other magazines.

General Notes Info

URL:	http://www.notes.net/Today.nsf/cbb328e5c12843a9852563dc006721c7/590f92c029bed834852564680050adaf?OpenDocument
Title:	Bob Balaban Interview
	This is an interview done in March of 1997, when I worked at Iris.
URL:	http://www.keysolutions.com/NotesFAQ/ lotus-notes.html
Title:	KeySolutions Notes FAQ page
	A good source of info on Notes/Domino from a Lotus Business Partner.

URL:	http://www.notes.net/Today.nsf/cbb328e5c12843a9852563dc006721c7/950678b4b3ec0c2c8525645300514b99?OpenDocument
Title:	"The Future of Domino and Java"
	An article I wrote for the Iris Web site in the Spring of 1997

HOME PAGES

URL:	http://www.ibm.com
Title:	IBM Home Page
	IBM's home page. Lots of links to hardware info, software products, and so on.
URL:	http://www.notes.net
Title:	Iris Home Page
	The main Iris Web site. Contains areas for downloading software, discussions on current releases, and a "Webzine" with articles on current topics of interest.
	You can post questions here for Iris developers to answer.
URL:	http://java.sun.com
Title:	JavaSoft Home Page
	The JavaSoft home page. From here you can get to pretty much anything to do with Java.

URL:	http://www.looseleaf.net
Title:	Looseleaf Home Page
	The home page for Looseleaf Software, Inc. Not a whole lot there yet, but I'm soliciting feedback on the book, so vote early and vote often.
URL:	http://www.lotus.com
Title:	Lotus Home Page
	The Lotus home page. Links from here to developer pages, Business Partner pages, and so on. Updated product downloads and trial versions, etc.

IMAP

URL:	http://www.notes.net/Today.nsf/cbb328e5c12843a9852563dc006721c7/74b8753859bedea6852565050072da7c?OpenDocument
Title:	"Getting More Out of Internet Mail with IMAP"
	Nice article by Mark Gordon, about how IMAP works.

JAVA BEANS

URL:	http://java.sun.com/beans/index.html
Title:	Java Beans Specs
	The specs on Beans, plus how to download the BDK (Bean DevKit)

URL:	http://developer.javasoft.com/developer/onlineTraining/newbeans/index.html
Title:	Online tutorial on Beans
	Part of JavaSoft's Developer Connection site.

JAVA DEVELOPMENT

URL:	http://java.sun.com/products/api-overview/index.html
Title:	Java API Page
	A page that keeps track of Java API releases and tells you how to get the latest JDKs
URL:	http://java.sun.com/nav/developer/index.html
Title:	JavaSoft Developer's Page
	The main page on JavaSoft's site for developers. You can join the Developer Connection (free), and get to the download and documentation pages from here.
URL:	http://java.sun.com/products/index.html
Title:	JavaSoft Products
	A list of all the JavaSoft products, with links to product specific info and doc.

JDBC AND ODBC

URL:	http://developer.javasoft.com/developer/readAboutJava/jpg/startjdbc.html
Title:	"Getting Started With JDBC"
	Good article by John Papageorge, on the JavaSoft Developer Connection site.
URL:	http://www.intersolv.com/datadirect/data-jdbc_njet.htm
Title:	Intersolv JDBC tools
	Good free trial download links here.
URL:	http://java.sun.com/products/jdbc
Title:	JavaSoft JDBC Page
	The main page in JavaSoft's site for info on Java database connectivity
URL:	http://developer.javasoft.com/developer/onlineTraining/jdbc/index.html
Title:	JDBC Short Course
	A nice on-line tutorial on JDBC by the Mage Lang Institute.
URL:	http://www.intersolv.com/datadirect/data-odbc.htm
Title:	Intersolv ODBC tools
	You can download a free trial copy of the Intersolv ODBC drivers here.

LDAP

URL:	http://java.sun.com/products/jndi/index.html
Title:	JavaSoft JNDI Page

The JNDI white paper and specs. You can also download software here.

OTHER TOOLS

http://www.lotus.com/developers

URL:	http://193.164.160.162/ldw.nsf/WizSectionSearch?SearchView&Query=([a]+co+16)+AND+([n]+co+1)&a=16&t=LSXToolkit
Title:	LSX Toolkit page

The LSX Toolkit helps you build your own classes for Domino using C++. These classes can then become part of the Domino environment in both LotusScript and Java. The toolkit can be downloaded for free. This link may be volatile, as the Lotus site changes frequently. If you can't get to it, try http://www.lotus.com/developers and then navigate to the LSX Toolkit info, or do a site search.

RMI

URL:	http://java.sun.com/products/jdk/rmi/index.html
Title:	JavaSoft RMI Page

Base page for information about Remote Method Invocation, specs and so on. The software is included in the Java 1.1.x release, so you don't need to get RMI separately.

SERVLETS

URL:	http://webreview.com/97/10/10/feature/index.html
Title:	Articles on Servlets

An issue of a webzine called WebReview featuring articles on Servlets.

URL:	http://java.sun.com/products/java-server/servlets/index.html#sdk
Title:	JavaSoft Servlet Page

This is where you can go to get the Servlet Development Kit and documentation.

WEB SERVER

URL:	http://www.notes.net/Today.nsf/cbb328e5c12843a9852563dc006721c7/89fb100bf3d93ec68525645200615a95?OpenDocument
Title:	"Architecture of the Domino Web Server (1)"

Part 1 of a 2-part article on the Iris site by Richard Schwartz.

URL:	http://www.notes.net/Today.nsf/b1d67fedee86c74 1852563cc005019c5/79abe7c0a013769985256465 0057702a?OpenDocument
Title:	"Architecture of the Domino Web Server (2)"
	Second part of Richard Schwartz's article.

B

NOTES OBJECT INTERFACE CLASS DIAGRAM

They say a picture is worth 10**3 words. Figure B.1 is a simplified class-name-only picture of how the Java NOI classes relate to each other. When I say *relate*, I mean *by containment*. If you'll indulge me for a moment, lots of books and articles make a big deal about inheritance hierarchies. I've always thought that containment was much more interesting to the journeyman programmer: you want to know how to navigate to the object that you need to do your job, not worry about how beautiful some idealized *IsA* layout is. That's just my opinion, of course.

Anyway, Figure B.1 shows how the classes relate to each other in terms of containment, and there is (as a bonus for the OO fanatics) one instance of inheritance as well. The pull-out poster included with this book gives you, at the expense of some real estate, the same picture, plus all the methods associated with each class.

Appendix B

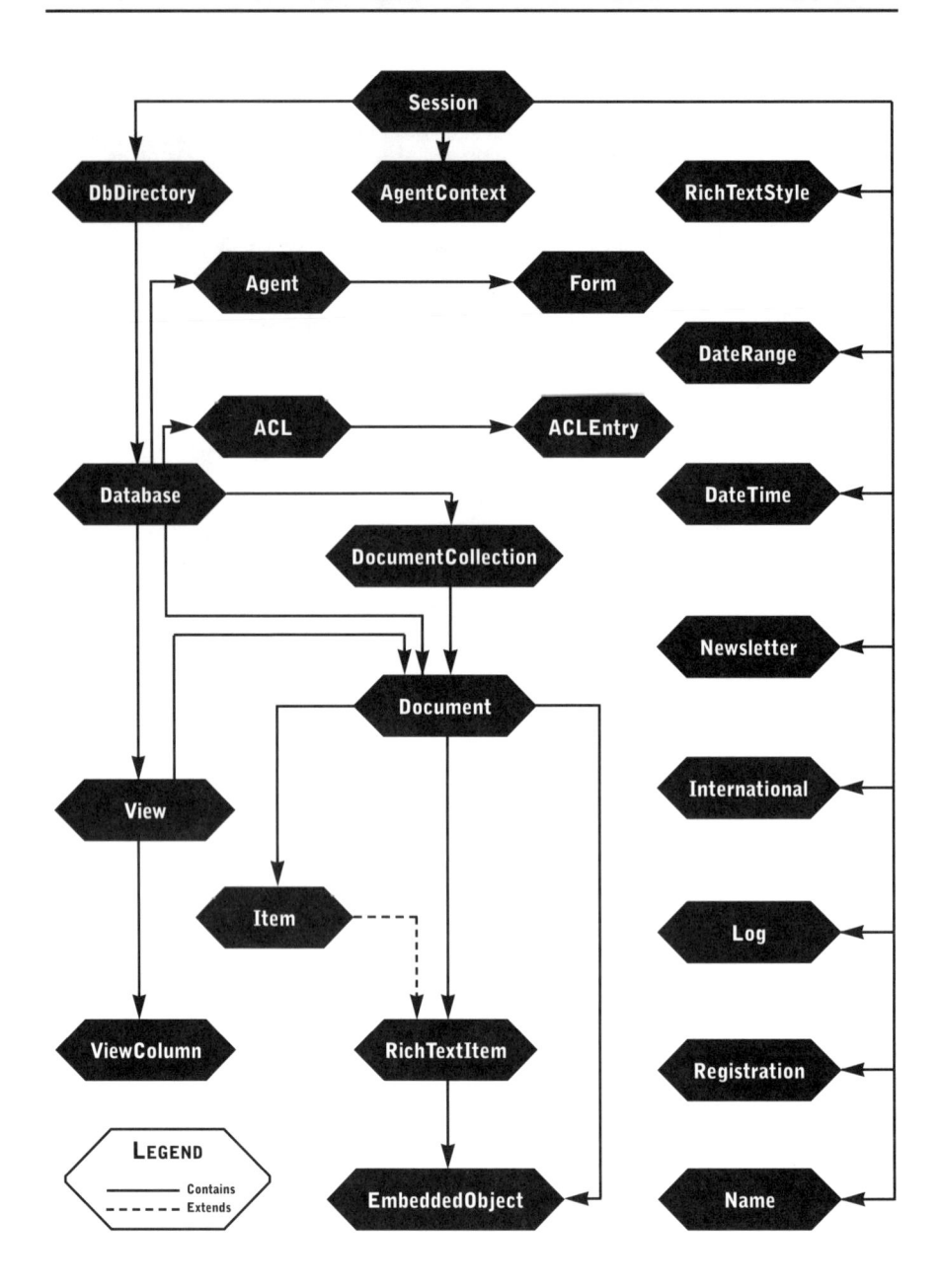

```
                    Session
                   /   |    \
         DbDirectory  AgentContext  RichTextStyle
              |
              |  Agent ──→ Form
              |
              |  ACL ──→ ACLEntry           DateRange
              |
           Database                         DateTime
              |    \
              |   DocumentCollection
              |         |
              |      Document               Newsletter
              |       /   \
            View   Item  (extends)          International
              |       \
         ViewColumn  RichTextItem           Log
                         |
                   EmbeddedObject           Registration

                                             Name
```

LEGEND
— Contains
- - - Extends

C

DOMINO SETUP FOR WRITING JAVA PROGRAMS

Given that you have an installed and running Domino server or Notes Client, you're all set as far as *running* Java Applications or Agents that use the Notes Object Interface. But you'll need to do a bit of extra setup if you want to *write* any Java programs for NOI. Let's go over the basic system requirements.

SYSTEM REQUIREMENTS

You must use an operating system that supports Java, meaning one for which a Java Virtual Machine has been released. There are some Domino platforms for which no VM has yet been released, and there are others for which you can find a VM, but it has not been "certified" for Domino. The lack of certification shouldn't necessarily deter you, as I'll explain shortly.

Table C.1 summarizes the status of Java programming for each of the Domino platforms. Domino is compatible with Java version 1.1 and above only. Java 1.02 will not work with Domino NOI, although 1.02 Applets do work in the Notes Client and can be served up by the Domino HTTP server.

Table C.1 Java Availability For Domino 4.6 Platforms

Operating Platform	Java VM Available?	Java Certified for Domino?	Java Built for Domino?
Windows 32-bit (Win95 and NT; Intel only, not Alpha)	Yes	Yes	Yes
Windows 16-bit (Windows 3.1)	No	No	No
Mac	Yes	No	No
NLM	No	No	No
Solaris (SPARC)	Yes	Yes	Yes
Solaris (Intel)	Yes	No	No
HPUX	Yes	Yes	Yes
AIX	Yes	Yes	Yes
OS/2 v 2.2 and later	Yes	No	Yes
AS400	Yes (1998)	Yes	Yes
OS390	Yes (Domino V5)	Yes	Yes

Just because there's no certified support for Java on a particular platform doesn't necessarily mean you can't use Java to program NOI on that platform. Usually certification of a feature on a platform simply means that Lotus has tested the feature on that platform and believes that it is working properly. It also means that Lotus provides technical support for that feature on that platform and will accept (and ultimately fix) problem reports.

Some of the UNIX platforms were built with all the Java support code included, but no formal testing was done. If you're willing to experiment and do without official tech support, there's no reason why you shouldn't try using NOI on a uncertified system. If, however, the Java support code was not built for a given platform (e.g., Macintosh, Win16), NOI won't be available on that platform, even if a Java VM is available from the system vendor. You won't kill your system by trying it; at worst, you'll get some error messages.

But, you ask, isn't Java a cross-platform language? Why can't I take the notes.jar file from a supported platform and use it on another one, as long as there's a Virtual Machine to run it in? You can try, but it won't work because the Java code in the NOI classes (distributed in a single jar file called notes.jar) all make use of calls in to C and C++ code in the Notes core. If the C/C++ interface wasn't built for a given platform, there's just no way to call into Notes from Java.

DEVELOPMENT TOOL OPTIONS

You can use all kinds of development tools to write Java programs that use the NOI classes, ranging from the free and basic to the expensive and sophisticated. The only tool that I've come across that I know *won't* work, for reasons explained elsewhere, is Microsoft's Visual J++. For purposes of illustration, I'll mention three tools that I have used.. My mention of a particular tool does not constitute an endorsement of that tool or of that tool's vendor. I haven't made an exhaustive study of all the tools that are available, either.

The most basic, and in some sense the most authoritative, Java development tool is JavaSoft's Java Development Kit (JDK), available for free from the JavaSoft Web site (http://java.sun.com, see the References.nsf database on the CD-ROM for this and other links). It contains a compiler, an interpreter, the classes you need at runtime, and not much else. Additional tools, such as the Bean Development Kit (BDK), the Servlet Development Kit, and a kit for RMI are separately available as well, and they are also free (the Servlet Development Kit is also on the CD for this book).

If you use the JDK as the basis for your Java programming, you must supply your own text editor to type in the Java source code. Then you use the JDK tools (typically from a console window command line) to invoke the compiler and to run your program (unless it's an Agent, in which case you use Notes/Domino to run the program, as described in Chapters 8 and 9). A debugger comes with the JDK, but most people find it useless (I sure did). Still, the JDK is the authoritative, "reference" implementation of the language (on Win32 and Solaris, the platforms for which it's officially available from JavaSoft:), and code compiled using the JDK will (at least in theory) run in any other vendor's VM.

Two other development environments I've used are Borland's JBuilder and Symantec's Visual Cafe. Both provide approximately the same features: multiwindowed development and debugging environment; project orientation; code generation wizards to help you get going, particularly with Applet programming; and libraries of useful widgets. SunSoft also has an Integrated Development Environment (IDE) for Solaris, although I haven't tried it.

With a full-blown IDE, you typically use a wizard to generate the basic code for your program, or you can bring up an editor window and type some in yourself (or take some existing code and add it to your current project). Then, entirely from within the tool's user interface, you can compile, run, and debug your Application or Applet. The debuggers are pretty nice. They allow you to step through your program line by line, set breakpoints and examine variables, and browse class hierarchies. Debugging Agents, of course, is another matter, as the Notes runtime has to be involved (see Chapter 9 for tips on how to debug Agents).

All of these tools require some tweaking before you can use them with Domino's NOI classes.

PATH AND CLASSPATH SETUP

Most people are familiar with the concept of a search path for executable programs: you can define an environment variable on most kinds of systems that contains a list of directories that the system will search for executable programs. This environment variable is usually called "PATH". For the Java interpreter a similar environment variable, called "CLASSPATH", tells it where to look for Java classes that it might need to find and load. Each tool has its own way tospecify these variables. The following sections describe how to set up each of the three tools I've mentioned to work with NOI. The exact representation of these environment variables is platform specific, so check the exact syntax ("CLASSPATH" vs. "classpath," for example) for the system you're using.

Note that Domino usually does not require you to add the Notes executable directory to your PATH, but you should do so for all systems on which you will be running Java applications. The reason is that Java, when running a Domino NOI program, needs to find and load the Notes DLL (or platform equivalent) into which the Java classes want to call. If your Java program is not located in the Notes executable directory (the directory where most of the Notes files are installed), Java will be unable to run your program.

JDK

For the JDK, you simply set the CLASSPATH environment variable to include the notes.jar file. The installation instructions for the JDK will tell you how to set up the initial CLASSPATH. For example, on Windows 95 systems, you might add the following line to your autoexec.bat file:

```
set classpath=.;c:\jdk11\lib\classes.zip;c:\notes\notes.jar
```

The "classes.zip" file is a container file that has in it all the standard Java runtime packages (java.lang, java.util, java.io, etc.). You simply append the Notes container file, which includes lotus.notes package.

For Windows NT you could accomplish the same result by going to the control panel, bringing up the System tool, and selecting the **Environment** tab. Then you would enter the above line into either the System Variables section (if you wanted it to apply to all users of the machine) or in the personal section for the current user.

The initial "." in the example classpath above tells the VM to search the current directory for classes that need to be loaded. If you use this technique, you can use any directory on your system to develop your Java code. Or, you can name your Java source directory explicitly.

JBuilder

When you install the JBuilder tool, it sets up its own CLASSPATH setting and will ignore your CLASSPATH environment variable, if you have one. That's because JBuilder, like most Java development tools, comes with its own copy of the Java VM and runtime classes. Therefore it wants to maintain its own CLASSPATH variable.

To use JBuilder successfully with NOI, you have to tell it where the Notes classes are. To do that, you can just edit the Jbuilder.ini file that lives in the JBuilder\bin subdirectory. There's a line in there for ClassPath and also one for IDEClassPath. I couldn't find any documentation of how the two differ, but I just appended my notes.jar path to both. Also, because I stored all the Java source files that I used for my samples (they're all on the CD) in a single directory on my system, I appended that directory as well. That way I could "add" my source files to a JBuilder project and compile and debug them without having to store them in a JBuilder subdirectory. For the IDE to find my source files, I also had to modify the SourcePath entry.

The modified IDEClassPath and Classpath entries in my JBuilder.ini file look like this:

```
IDEClassPath=..\lib\jbuilder.zip;..\lib\jbcl.zip;..\lib\jgl.zip;..\java\lib\classes.zip;\notes\notes.jar;\lotus\work\wordpro\book\examples

SourcePath=..\myprojects;..\java\src.zip;..\src\jgl-src.zip;..\src\jbcl-src.zip;\lotus\work\wordpro\book\examples

ClassPath=..\lib\jbcl.zip;..\lib\jgl.zip;..\java\lib\classes.zip;\notes\notes.jar;\lotus\work\wordpro\book\examples
```

Visual Cafe

Visual Cafe, like JBuilder, installs its own Java VM and runtime class library. Also like JBuilder, it has its own .ini file that keeps track of its own set of environment variables. You'll have to edit the file bin\sc.ini (where bin is a subdirectory in the Visual Cafe installation tree), and append your notes.jar path to the CLASSPATH entry. You should also add your Notes directory to the PATH entry. The two modified lines on my system look like this:

```
PATH=%@P%\..\BIN;%@P%\..\Java\Bin;%PATH%;\notes

CLASSPATH=.;%@P%\COMPONENTS\SYMBEANS.JAR;%@P%\..\JAVA\LIB;%@P%\..\JAVA\LIB\SYMCLASS.ZIP;%@P%\..\JAVA\LIB\CLASSES.ZIP;\notes\notes.jar;\lotus\work\wordpro\book\examples
```

Developing Domino Agents and Servlets

Although Notes does not (yet) include a Java development environment, it does (at runtime) use its own Java VM and, like most development tools, it will ignore a CLASSPATH set up in your system's environment in favor of its own. Notes/Domino, of course, will already have included the notes.jar file on its internal CLASSPATH. If you want to make sure Domino's VM will also find your Servlet or other Java class files, you need to append the appropriate directories to the *JavaUserClasses* variable in your notes.ini file.

You can also set the size of the Java VM's internal heap and stack using the *JavaMaxHeapSize* and *JavaStackSize* variables (see Chapter 8 for details).

SUPPORTED JAVA VERSIONS

The Domino Notes Object Interface in release 4.6 was developed using the 1.1.1 release of the Java Development Kit. By the time 4.6 shipped (September 1997), JavaSoft had posted a couple of additional maintenance (bug-fixing) releases, named 1.1.2, 1.1.3, and 1.1.4. Programs you build with any of these releases should work just fine with Domino. If you use version 1.0.2 of the JDK to compile a program it may or may not work for NOI programs. Version 1.0.2 is probably safe for developing Applets that you want Domino to serve up to browsers.

You should keep in mind that JavaSoft will typically post versions of Java only for Win32 and Solaris. Other platform versions of the VM are supplied by individual vendors. IBM, for instance, licenses Java source code from JavaSoft and supplies Lotus with most of the VM implementations that ship with Domino. Thus implementation of a particular release of Java for a particular platform might lag a bit, depending on how quickly the vendor can build, test, and release it after receiving the code from JavaSoft.

D

NOTES OBJECT INTERFACE EXCEPTIONS

As described in Chapter 2, the NotesException class contains a series of *public static final int* declarations for the NOI error codes. The full set of defined codes and their corresponding messages is reproduced in Table D.1.

Readers should be aware of the following caveats, however:

1. The messages are from the English version of the product. They are translated for versions of Domino that are built for other languages.
2. These messages are only the ones that are generated by the NOI piece of Notes. Any error codes reported by NOI that actually belong to core Notes will appear as ERR_NOTES_ERR (value 4000), with the text of the Notes error appended.

3. Messages with replaceable parameters are encoded with placeholders for the replaceable parts. For example in the message, "Directory file %1 not found on path," the "%1" would be replaced with the name of the file.

4. Some of the error messages listed in Table D.1 are obsolete. For example, the message about full text indexing not being available on remote servers was true in release 4.0, but in 4.5 support for remote servers was added. The messages were left in, but they will never appear.

EXCEPTION CODES AND MESSAGES

Exception and Code	Message
ERR_NOTES_ERROR = 4000	Notes error: %1
ERR_SYS_OUT_OF_MEMORY = 4001	Out of memory
ERR_SYS_LOAD_OUT_OF_MEM = 4002	Out of memory or could not load required .dll(s)
ERR_SYS_FILE_NOT_FOUND = 4003	File does not exist
ERR_SYS_DICT_NOT_ON_PATH = 4004	Dictionary file %1 not found on PATH
ERR_NOTES_ERROR2 = 4005	Notes error: %1 (%2)
ERR_SYS_RESOURCE_NOT_FOUND = 4008	Could not find resource
ERR_SYS_LOADING_RESOURCE = 4009	Could not load resource
ERR_SYS_LOCKING_RESOURCE = 4010	Could not lock resource
ERR_SYS_FREEING_RESOURCE = 4011	Could not free resource
ERR_SYS_NOSUCH_RESOURCE = 4012	No such resource
ERR_SYS_WARNING_TITLE = 4016	WARNING
ERR_MAIL_COPEN_FAILED = 4026	Open of message container failed
ERR_MAIL_PAOPEN_FAILED = 4027	Open of public address book failed
ERR_MAIL_LAOPEN_FAILED = 4028	Open of private address book failed
ERR_MAIL_VIM_MESSAGE = 4029	%1
ERR_MAIL_CANT_CREATE = 4030	This object cannot be created with the NEW operator

Notes Object Interface Exceptions

Exception and Code	Message
ERR_MAIL_UNKNOWN_PROP = 4031	Unknown property
ERR_MAIL_INVALID_MSG = 4032	Invalid mail message object
ERR_MAIL_NOPUBLIC_GRP = 4033	Public address book not available
ERR_MAIL_NOPRIVATE_GRP = 4034	Private address book not available
ERR_MAIL_GRPCREATE_FAILED = 4035	Could not create group list
ERR_MAIL_GROUP_DELETED = 4036	The group %1 has been removed from the address book
ERR_MAIL_NAME_REQUIRED = 4037	A file pathname is required
ERR_NOTES_FAILURE = 4038	The requested operation could not be completed
ERR_NOTES_NOSUCH_VIEW = 4039	View %1 not found
ERR_NOTES_NOFTINDEX = 4040	Database %1 has no full text index
ERR_NOTES_DBCREATE_FAILED = 4041	Database creation failed (%1)
ERR_NOTES_DBDELETE_FAILED = 4042	Database %1 could not be deleted
ERR_NOTES_DBOPEN_FAILED = 4043	Database open failed (%1)
ERR_NOTES_INVALID_FORMULA = 4044	Invalid formula (%1)
ERR_NOTES_INVALID_DATE = 4045	Invalid date (%1)
ERR_NOTES_COPY_FAILED = 4046	Note copy from %1 to %2 failed
ERR_NOTES_VIEWOPEN_FAILED = 4047	Open of View %1 failed
ERR_NOTES_NOTEDEL_FAILED = 4048	Note delete failed
ERR_NOTES_NEXTITEM_FAILED = 4049	Item retrieval failed
ERR_NOTES_FINDITEM_FAILED = 4050	Could not find item %1 in note
ERR_NOTES_MODLOAD_FAILED = 4051	Failed to load module %1
ERR_NOTES_PROCFIND_FAILED = 4052	Failed to find proc %1 in module %2
ERR_NOTES_RTWRITE_FAILED = 4053	Write of rich text failed
ERR_NOTES_RTCONVERT_FAILED = 4054	Conversion of rich text failed
ERR_NOTES_FTSRCH_FAILED = 4055	Could not execute full-text search
ERR_NOTES_QUERY_FAILED = 4056	Full-text query (%1) failed
ERR_NOTES_DOCSEARCH_FAILED = 4057	Database search failed
ERR_NOTES_ITEMCOPY_FAILED = 4058	Failed to copy item %1
ERR_NOTES_CREATENOTE_FAILED = 4059	Failed to create new Note
ERR_NOTES_DBNOACCESS = 4060	User %2 cannot open database %1
ERR_NOTES_UNAME_LOOKUP = 4061	Couldn't look up user's group names
ERR_NOTES_SESOPEN_FAILED = 4062	Could not open Notes session

Appendix D

Exception and Code	Message
ERR_NOTES_DATABASE_NOTOPEN = 4063	Database %1 has not been opened yet
ERR_NOTES_SESSION_DATECONV = 4064	Cannot convert date value to string
ERR_NOTES_SESSION_VALNOTSUPP = 4065	Environment variables must be strings, dates or integers
ERR_NOTES_CANT_GETNTH = 4066	Can't get positional note from named View
ERR_NOTES_ATTACH_FAILED = 4067	Couldn't attach file %1
ERR_NOTES_DETACH_FAILED = 4068	Couldn't delete attached file
ERR_NOTES_EXTRACT_FAILED = 4069	Couldn't extract file to %1
ERR_NOTES_DIRSEARCH_FAILED = 4070	Couldn't execute directory search
ERR_NOTES_BAD_INDEX = 4071	Index is out of range
ERR_NOTES_NOSUCH_DIRECTORY = 4072	Directory %1 does not exist
ERR_CDTEXTCREATE_FAILED = 4073	Could not create rich text context
ERR_CDASSIM_FAILED = 4074	Rich text append into item %1 failed
ERR_NOT_RT_ITEM = 4075	Item %1 is not a rich text item
ERR_NOTES_FORMCOMP_FAILED = 4076	Formula could not compile: %1
ERR_NOTES_FORMEVAL_FAILED = 4077	Could not evaluate formula: %1
ERR_NOTES_ITEMCREATE_FAILED = 4078	Could not create field %1
ERR_NOTES_DECRYPT_FAILED = 4079	Could not decrypt note
ERR_NOTES_NOTLOCAL_IDX = 4080	Could not FT index database %1, must be local machine
ERR_NOTES_FTIDX_FAILED = 4081	Could not FT index database %1
ERR_NOTES_NOTEOPEN_FAILED = 4082	Could not open note
ERR_NOTES_RENDER_FAILED = 4083	Could not render OLE image
ERR_NOTES_FILENOTFOUND = 4084	Could not find file %1
ERR_NOTES_UNKNOWN_TYPE = 4085	File %1 is of unknown type
ERR_NOTES_FILEOPEN_FAILED = 4086	Could not open file %1
ERR_NOTES_FILEWRITE_FAILED = 4087	Could not write to file
ERR_NOTES_DATE_NOTSET = 4088	Date value not initialized
ERR_NOTES_NODBNAME = 4089	A database name must be provided
ERR_NOTES_TEMPLCOPY_FAILED = 4090	Update of database %1 from template %2 failed
ERR_NOTES_BAD_UNID = 4091	Invalid universal id
ERR_NOTES_UNAME_REQ = 4092	A user or group name is required
ERR_NOTES_GETACL_FAILED = 4093	Could not read ACL for %1

Notes Object Interface Exceptions

Exception and Code	Message
ERR_NOTES_ACLENTRY_FAILED = 4094	Could not add entry %1 to ACL
ERR_NOTES_ACL_INVALID = 4095	Invalid ACL level
ERR_NOTES_QUERYACL_FAILED = 4096	Could not look up ACL for %1
ERR_NOTES_REFRESH_FAILED = 4097	Could not refresh View %1
ERR_NOTES_OLEPKG_FAILED = 4098	Could not create OLE file from %1
ERR_NOTES_TMPFILE_FAILED = 4099	Could not create temp file
ERR_NOTES_READFILE_FAILED = 4100	Could not read from file %1
ERR_NOTES_RTRENDER_FAILED = 4101	Could not render document
ERR_NOTES_WRONG_CLASS = 4102	Argument is not the correct class
ERR_NOTES_INVALID_ID = 4103	No mail id provided
ERR_NOTES_INVALID_AGENT = 4104	Invalid agent note
ERR_NOTES_VIEWCLONE_FAILED = 4105	Failed to create view
ERR_NOTES_NOVIEWNAME = 4106	You must supply a view name
ERR_NOTES_NEWSGROUPDB_FAILED = 4107	Failed to create newsgroup database
ERR_NOTES_NONEWSGROUPNAME = 4108	You must supply a newsgroup name
ERR_LOG_DBOPEN_FAILED = 4135	Could not open log file %1
ERR_LOG_FOPEN_FAILED = 4136	Could not open log file %1
ERR_LOG_CDCREATE_FAILED = 4137	Could not create text field
ERR_LOG_MAILLOG_FAILED = 4138	Could not open mail log (%1)
ERR_MEM_HVPOOLFULL = 4139	Insufficient memory - LSXBE pool is full
ERR_NOTES_COPYACL_FAILED = 4150	Could not copy ACLs to %1
ERR_NOTES_DOC_NOTINVIEW = 4151	The Document is not in View %1
ERR_NOTES_NOFTQUERY = 4152	You must provide a full text query
ERR_NOTES_NOITEMNAME = 4153	You must provide an item name
ERR_NOTES_NOTEUPDATE_FAILED = 4154	Could not update the Document
ERR_NOTES_NOTELOCATE_FAILED = 4155	Could not locate document in View %1
ERR_NOTES_VIEWDEL_FAILED = 4156	Could not delete View %1
ERR_LOG_CONSTRUCT_FAILED = 4157	Could not form pathname for %1, %2
ERR_SEM_ALLOC_FAILED = 4158	Could not allocate memory for Session
ERR_NOTES_LOOKUP_FAILED = 4159	Could not find name %1 in address book
ERR_NOTES_SEND_FAILED = 4160	Could not send document
ERR_NOTES_NCREATE_FAILED = 4161	Could not create note
ERR_MACRO_IDTBL_FAILED = 4162	Could not create id table for macro

Appendix D

Exception and Code	Message
ERR_MACRO_RUN_FAILED = 4163	Could not execute macro
ERR_NOTES_DBOPEN_NOTLOCAL = 4164	Cannot open databases on machines other than the server running your program (%1)
ERR_NOTES_SIGN_NOPERM = 4165	You must have permission to sign documents for server based agents
ERR_NOTES_ENCRYPT_NOPERM = 4166	You must have permission to encrypt documents for server based agents
ERR_NOTES_ENCRYPT_FAILED = 4167	Document encryption failed
ERR_NOTES_NOSENDTO = 4168	No recipient list for Send operation
ERR_LOG_EVENTPUT_FAILED = 4169	Could not write event: %1
ERR_LOG_INVALID_EVTYPE = 4170	Invalid event type
ERR_LOG_INVALID_SEVERITY = 4171	Invalid severity code
ERR_NOTES_NO_NEWSLETTERDOCS = 4172	No documents to put in Newsletter
ERR_NOTES_MAILDBOPEN_FAILED = 4173	Could not open default mail database
ERR_NOTES_NEWSLETTER_FAILED = 4174	Could not create newsletter
ERR_NOTES_DFLT_VID_FAILED = 4175	Couldn't get default View id for database (%1)
ERR_NOTES_KEYFIND_FAILED = 4176	Get by key failed
ERR_NOTES_RTTEXT_FAILED = 4177	Could not add rich text to item %1
ERR_NOTES_RTDOCLINK_FAILED = 4178	Could not add doclink to item %1
ERR_NOTES_NOPERM_DISKIO = 4179	Disk i/o is a restricted operation
ERR_NOTES_NOPERM_SIGN = 4180	Cannot sign notes when running on a server
ERR_NOTES_NOPERM_ENCRYPT = 4181	Cannot encrypt notes when running on a server
ERR_NOTES_NOPERM_ENVIRON = 4182	Cannot set environment variables when running on a server, or get system variables
ERR_NOTES_NOPERM_ANY = 4183	Restricted operation on a server
ERR_NOTES_NOSERV_DB = 4184	Cannot access foreign servers when running on a server
ERR_NOTES_INVALID_DB = 4185	This database object is invalid (%1)
ERR_NOTES_INVALID_CREDEL = 4186	Cannot create or delete databases when running on a server
ERR_NOTES_INVALID_DOC = 4187	Parent Document is required to make a response Document

Notes Object Interface Exceptions

Exception and Code	Message
ERR_NOTES_DBS_MUST_MATCH = 4188	Parent and Response Documents must be in the same database
ERR_NOTES_RESPONSE_FAILED = 4189	Could not make a response document
ERR_NOTES_NOLISTS = 4190	List types are not valid for this method
ERR_NOTES_CONTAINS_FAILED = 4191	Could not process Contains request
ERR_NOTES_MUSTBE_STRING = 4192	GetDocumentByKey requires a string or string array argument
ERR_NOTES_DESVIEW_FAILED = 4193	Could not access View info in database %1
ERR_NOTES_ITEMARR_FAILED = 4194	Could not create NotesItem array
ERR_NOTES_SRVSEARCH_FAILED = 4195	Could not perform server search on %1
ERR_NOTES_UNKNOWN_SRCHTYPE = 4196	Unknown file type for search
ERR_NOTES_MUSTCALL_FIRSTDB = 4197	Must call GetFirstDbFile before GetNextDbFile
ERR_NOTES_ALLDOCS_FAILED = 4198	Could not retrieve table of all documents
ERR_NOTES_ITYPENOT_TEXT = 4199	Item %1 is not of type Text, special type not set
ERR_NOTES_INVALID_ITYPE = 4200	Unknown special item type for item %1
ERR_NOTES_NOSUCH_FOLDER = 4201	View %1 does not exist
ERR_NOTES_ADDRBOOK_FAILED = 4202	Could not create array of NotesDatabase
ERR_NOTES_NOTCONTEXT_DB = 4203	Can't get left-to-do list, Database %1 is not the agent's database
ERR_NOTES_LTDACCESS_FAILED = 4204	Couldn't access left-to-do-list for agent %1
ERR_NOTES_LTDUPDATE_FAILED = 4205	Couldn't update left-to-do-list for agent %1
ERR_NOTES_BADVIEW_VERSION = 4206	View format is incompatible (%1)
ERR_NOTES_NEED_ADT = 4207	Function requires a valid ADT argument
ERR_NOTES_ACLWRITE_FAILED = 4208	Could not write ACL into database (%1)
ERR_NOTES_RENAME_FAILED = 4209	Function requires 2 role names
ERR_NOTES_NOSUCH_ROLENAME = 4210	Role name %1 not found
ERR_NOTES_PRIVNAME_FAILED = 4211	Could not rename role %1 to %2
ERR_NOTES_READPRIV_FAILED = 4212	Could not get role names
ERR_NOTES_DELPRIV_FAILED = 4213	Could not delete role name %1
ERR_NOTES_DELENTRY_FAILED = 4214	ACL entry name (%1) could not be deleted
ERR_NOTES_NOSERV_EVENTS = 4215	Events can only be logged when running on a server
ERR_NOTES_INVALID_ACLENTRYNAME = 4216	ACL entry name (%1) is invalid

Appendix D

Exception and Code	Message
ERR_NOTES_ENTRYNAME_FAILED = 4217	Could not rename ACL entry %1
ERR_NOTES_NOTLOCAL_REPL = 4218	Source database must be on the local machine to do replication (%1)
ERR_NOTES_REPL_FAILED = 4219	Replication failed (%1)
ERR_NOTES_NOTLOCAL_COMPACT = 4220	Only local databases can be compacted (%1)
ERR_NOTES_COMPACT_FAILED = 4221	Database compaction failed (%1)
ERR_NOTES_TIMEADJUST_FAILED = 4222	Could not adjust date/time
ERR_NOTES_NOSUCH_EMBED = 4223	Invalid embedding type
ERR_NOTES_NOSUCH_EOFILE = 4224	You must provide a file path
ERR_NOTES_NOSUCH_PATH = 4225	File %1 not found
ERR_NOTES_EMBEDARR_FAILED = 4226	Could not create NotesEmbeddedObject array
ERR_NOTES_NOADDRS_FOUND = 4227	No address books were found
ERR_NOTES_DUP_ROLENAME = 4228	The role name %1 already exists
ERR_NOTES_CANTCREATE_FOLDER = 4229	Could not create folder %1
ERR_NOTERENDER_FAILED = 4230	Could not render note to rich text item
ERR_NOFROMFIELD = 4231	Document has no From field
ERR_TEXTLIST_FAILED = 4232	Could not create recipient text list
ERR_NOTES_NOTA_DOCUMENT = 4233	Object passed to EVALUATE is not a NotesDocument
ERR_NOTES_VALIDATE_FAILED = 4234	Unknown error from Document validate
ERR_NOTES_ABSTRACT_BUFFER = 4235	Invalid buffer size for abstract
ERR_NOTES_ABSTRACTING_TEXT = 4236	Item text could not be abstracted
ERR_NOTES_DESAGENT_FAILED = 4237	Could not access agent info in database %1
ERR_NOTES_MIXED_ARRAY = 4238	NotesItem cannot be set to an array of mixed data types
ERR_NOTES_INVALID_DOCLINK = 4239	AppendDocLink requires a NotesDocument, NotesView or NotesDatabase argument
ERR_TEXTLIST_BAD_INPUT = 4240	Problem with input variant
ERR_NOTES_CANTREMOVE = 4241	Cannot remove NotesDocument when instantiated by NotesUIDocument
ERR_NOTES_CANTENCRYPT = 4242	Cannot encrypt NotesDocument when instantiated by NotesUIDocument

Notes Object Interface Exceptions

Exception and Code	Message
ERR_NOTES_CANTCLOSEDB = 4243	Cannot compact a database when instantiated by Notes UI
ERR_NOTES_CANTRUN_OLEOBJ = 4244	Could not activate embedded object %1
ERR_NOTES_CANTSHOW_OLEOBJ = 4245	Could not show embedded object %1
ERR_NOTES_NOEMBEDDED_OBJ = 4246	No embedded object is present, cannot perform this action.
ERR_NOTES_NOSUCH_EMBEDCLASS = 4247	Embedded object class not found in registry
ERR_NOTES_CANTGET_DBSUMMARY = 4248	Can't access database summary info
ERR_NOTES_CANTCOPY_ITEMTYPE = 4249	Can't copy items of type ATTACHMENT or OTHEROBJECT
ERR_NOTES_NEED_DB = 4250	You must specify a parent database
ERR_NOTES_NEED_NOTE = 4251	You must specify a parent document
ERR_NOTES_CANT_LINK_OLE1 = 4252	Can't embed a link on a non-OLE platform
ERR_NOTES_ROLENAME_TOOBIG = 4253	Role name (%1) exceeds maximum length of 15
ERR_NOTES_EOARRAY_FAILED = 4254	Could not create array of NotesEmbeddedObject
ERR_NOTES_ATTACHINFO_FAILED = 4255	Couldn't access attachment information
ERR_NOTES_QUOTAINFO_FAILED = 4256	Couldn't access database size information for %1
ERR_NOTES_DOCNOTSAVED = 4257	The Document has not been saved to disk yet.
ERR_NOTES_ACLNEXT_INVALID = 4258	Could not read ACL for database %1
ERR_NOTES_NOTAFILE = 4259	Object is not a file attachment
ERR_NOTES_CANTFIND_ATTACHMENT = 4260	Could not locate attached file %1
ERR_NOTES_NOSUCH_VERB = 4261	Unknown verb %1
ERR_NOTES_DOVERB_FAILED = 4262	Verb execution failed (%1)
ERR_NOTES_INVALID_ADTTYPE = 4263	Item value cannot be set to object of this type
ERR_NOTES_FTQUERY_FAILED = 4264	Could not perform full text search on the view
ERR_NOTES_NOSUCH_DBID = 4265	Invalid replica id (%1)
ERR_NOTES_OPENBYRID_FAILED = 4266	OpenByReplicaID failed
ERR_NOTES_BAD_UNPROCFT = 4267	UnprocessedFTSearch and UnprocessedSearch are limited to the current database

Appendix D

Exception and Code	Message
ERR_AGENT_NO_RECURSION = 4268	Agents cannot run recursively
ERR_NOTES_CANTGET_MAILSERVER = 4269	Can't open foreign mail server %1 from this server (%2)
ERR_NOTES_BAD_NOTEID = 4270	Invalid note id
ERR_NOTES_DBSECURITY = 4271	Password or other security violation for database %1
ERR_NOTES_DELETE_AGENT = 4272	Can't remove agent belonging to another user
ERR_NOTES_RUN_AGENT = 4273	Can't run a private agent belonging to someone else
ERR_NOTES_NOSUCH_DOCINDEX = 4274	Document index out of range
ERR_NOTES_BAD_SOURCE_CLASS = 4275	Must provide either class or source, but not both
ERR_NOTES_CANT_CHANGE_DEFACL = 4276	Not allowed to change the -Default- entry name
ERR_NOTES_LINKNOCLASS = 4277	Do not provide a class name for embedded links
ERR_NOTES_CANTDO_ARRAYOFARRAY = 4278	Arrays of arrays are not supported
ERR_NOTES_SESSION_CLOSED = 4279	The session has been closed
ERR_NOTES_CANTOPEN_URLDB = 4280	Could not open URL database
ERR_NOTES_NEED_URL = 4281	You must supply a valid URL
ERR_NOTES_INVALID_URL = 4282	Could not locate or open URL (%1)
ERR_NOTES_INVALID_URLHEADER = 4283	You must supply a valid URL header name
ERR_NOTES_NOSUCH_URLHEADER = 4284	Could not locate header (%2) for URL (%1)
ERR_NOTES_NOUNPROC_DOCS = 4285	There are no unprocessed documents in this database
ERR_NOTES_EMBED_FAILED = 4286	Could not embed object
ERR_NOTES_NODEL_CURRENTDB = 4287	Can't remove current database.
ERR_NOTES_INVALID_TIMEEXPR = 4288	Property must be of type Date
ERR_NOTES_RECURSIVE_RENDER = 4289	Can't render a document into an item on that same document
ERR_NOTES_INVALID_ITEM = 4290	Item %1 is invalid
ERR_NOTES_NOMOVETO_PRIVISTUSE = 4291	Can't move document to shared Private On First Use folder (%1)
ERR_NOTES_SAMESRV_REPLICA = 4292	Can't create a replica on the same machine as the source database

Notes Object Interface Exceptions

Exception and Code	Message
ERR_NOTES_CANT_SIGN = 4293	Couldn't sign document
ERR_NOTES_NO_MATCH = 4294	Unable to send mail, no match found in Name & Address Book(s)
ERR_NOTES_AMBIGUOUS_MATCH = 4295	Unable to send mail, multiple matches found in Name & Address Book(s)
ERR_NOTES_DBALREADY_OPEN = 4296	This database object is already open as %1
ERR_NOTES_OLE_NOTAVAIL = 4297	OLE is not available on this platform
ERR_NOTES_ARRAY_NOGOOD = 4298	Array not valid on property set
ERR_NOTES_REGARG_NOTGIVEN = 4299	Required registration argument not provided
ERR_NOTES_MISSING_CERTID = 4300	Certifier id path not supplied
ERR_NOTES_NOCERT_CTX = 4301	Failed to create certifier context
ERR_NOTES_REGFAILED = 4302	Could not register user %1
ERR_NOTES_SRVREGFAILED = 4303	Could not register server %1
ERR_NOTES_CERTREGFAILED = 4304	Could not register certifier %1
ERR_NOTES_XCERTFAILED = 4305	Could not cross certify user %1
ERR_NOTES_RECERTFAILED = 4306	Could not re-certify user %1
ERR_NOTES_NOSUCH_BOOL = 4307	Use True or False for Enabled value
ERR_NOTES_CANTSWITCH_ID = 4308	Failed to switch to id %1
ERR_NOTES_NOSUCH_MAILPATH = 4309	Can't create user mail database, no path provided
ERR_NOTES_BAD_IDFILE = 4310	Error accessing id file %1
ERR_NOTES_CANTADD_USER = 4311	Couldn't add user %1 to address book
ERR_NOTES_CANTADD_SERV = 4312	Couldn't add server %1 to address book
ERR_NOTES_CANTADD_CERT = 4313	Couldn't add certifier %1 to address book
ERR_NOTES_NOCURRENT_AGENT = 4314	There is no current agent, can't open log
ERR_NOTES_AGENTLOG_FAILED = 4315	Logging to agent log failed
ERR_NOTES_NOSUCH_CERTIDTYPE = 4316	Unknown id certification type
ERR_NOTES_NOCURRENT_FTRESULT = 4317	There is no current search result to refine.
ERR_NOTES_IDTBL_FAILED = 4318	Could not create id table
ERR_NOTES_PROF_ARG_MISSING = 4319	Profile name and user name both required
ERR_NOTES_NOSUCH_PROFILE = 4320	Profile document not found
ERR_NOTES_PROFUPDATE_FAILED = 4321	Profile update failed
ERR_NOTES_PROFDELETE_FAILED = 4322	Profile delete failed

Appendix D

Exception and Code	Message
ERR_NOTES_NOSUCH_ARG = 4323	A required argument has not been provided
ERR_NOTES_WRONG_UNID_LEN = 4324	UniversalID must be 32 characters
ERR_NOTES_DESFORM_FAILED = 4325	Could not access form info in database %l
ERR_NOTES_FORMDEL_FAILED = 4326	Could not delete Form %l
ERR_NOTES_NOCLOSE_CURRDB = 4327	Cannot close the context database
ERR_NOTES_FREETIME_FAILED = 4328	Free time search failed
ERR_NOTES_UNIFORM_FAILED = 4329	Could not set Uniform Access on ACL
ERR_NOTES_GETOPTION_FAILED = 4330	Could not access database options for %l
ERR_NOTES_MARKREAD_FAILED = 4331	Could not mark document read
ERR_NOTES_MARKUNREAD_FAILED = 4332	Could not mark document unread
ERR_NOTES_MULTIDB_FAILED = 4333	This operation cannot be performed on multi-database search results
ERR_NOTES_ADDPROF_FAILED = 4334	Could not add user profile to address book
ERR_NOTES_ULOOKUP_FAILED = 4335	Could not access user information on server
ERR_NOTES_INVALID_OBJECT = 4336	Invalid object type for method argument
ERR_NOTES_STAMP_FAILED = 4337	Stamping of document collection failed
ERR_NOTES_BAD_ORGUNIT = 4338	The Organization name must be at least 3 characters
ERR_NOTES_BAD_FTSORT = 4339	Unknown FT option
ERR_NOTES_NOTCONTEXT_COLLEC = 4340	Document collection must come from the agent's database
ERR_NOTES_ECLACCESS_FAILED = 4341	Access not allowed
ERR_NOTES_W32DOM_FAILED = 4342	Could not enumerate users on %l
ERR_NOTES_W32DOM_NOFIRSTUSER = 4343	Must call GetFirstUser before GetNextUser
ERR_NOTES_W32DOM_BADPLATFORM = 4344	The NotesWin32Domain class is not supported on this platform
ERR_NOTES_W32DOM_BADNETAPI32 = 4345	A function could not be loaded from NETAPI32.DLL
ERR_NOTES_W32DOM_DOMAIN_CONTROLLER = 4346	The domain controller could not be found.
ERR_NOTES_TOOMANY_SORT_KEYS = 4347	Too many keys in GetDocumentByKey
ERR_NOTES_BAD_KEYTYPE = 4348	Invalid key value type

Notes Object Interface Exceptions

Exception and Code	Message
ERR_NOTES_CANT_SELF_ASSIMILATE = 4349	Can't append an item to itself
ERR_NOTES_CANT_SELF_COPY = 4350	Can't copy a document's items to itself
ERR_NOTES_POP3_FAILED = 4351	Couldn't get POP3 mail from server %1
ERR_NOTES_ARRCREATE_FAILED = 4352	Error creating LotusScript array
ERR_NOTES_AGSAVE_FAILED = 4353	Agent save failed
ERR_NOTES_CANTREMOVE_AGC = 4354	Cannot remove NotesDocument when it is the Document Context
ERR_NOTES_CANTENCRYPT_AGC = 4355	Cannot encrypt NotesDocument when it is the Document Context
ERR_NOTES_RTSTYLE_CREATEFAILED = 4356	Could not create rich text style
ERR_NOTES_RTSTYLE_APPENDFAILED = 4357	Could not append text style to item %1
ERR_NOTES_RTSTYLE_BADFONT = 4358	Font value must be FONT_ROMAN, FONT_HELV, or FONT_COURIER
ERR_NOTES_NO_CONTEXTDB = 4359	No current database to open mail log in
ERR_NOTES_NULL_APPENDLIST = 4360	Can't append list to a null item
ERR_NOTES_NOSUCH_JAVA_TYPE = 4361	Unknown or unsupported object type in Vector
ERR_NOTES_INVALID_JARRAY = 4362	Vector must contain objects all of the same class
ERR_NOTES_RTSTYLE_BADBOOL = 4363	Style value must be True, False, or STYLE_NO_CHANGE (YES,NO,or MAYBE for Java)
ERR_NOTES_RTSTYLE_BADFONTSIZE = 4364	Font size must be between 1 and 250, or STYLE_NO_CHANGE
ERR_NOTES_RTSTYLE_BADCOLOR = 4365	Color value must be between 0 and 240, or STYLE_NO_CHANGE
ERR_NOTES_RTSTYLE_BADEFFECT = 4366	Effect value must be EFFECTS_SUPERSCRIPT,EFFECTS_SUBSCRIPT,EFFECTS_SHADOW,EFFECTS_EMBOSS,EFFECTS_EXTRUDE,EFFECTS_NONE,or STYLE_NO_CHANGE
ERR_NOTES_NOTREMOTE_DB = 4367	RunOnServer must be used with a remote database
ERR_NOTES_RTITEM_EXISTS = 4368	Rich text item %1 already exists
ERR_NOTES_NOFORM = 4369	No form associated with document.
ERR_NOTES_NOTA_VECTOR = 4370	Input must be an instance of java.util.Vector

Appendix D

Exception and Code	Message
ERR_NOTES_SERVER_SWITCH = 4371	Can't switch IDs on a server
ERR_NOTES_DBDIR_THREAD = 4372	Can't use DbDirectory object on more than one thread

E

CREATING LSXS

The Notes Object Interface in Notes release 4.0 was implemented using an architecture originally called LotusScript Extension, or LSX. This architecture is a specification that tells you how to implement a dynamically loaded code library ("DLL" in Windows, "shared library" in UNIX, "NLM" for Netware, and so on for all the supported Notes server platforms), using C++, which implements a set of LotusScript classes. The LSX library can be loaded and used from any of the Lotus products thatwhich support LotusScript (Notes, but also 1-2-3, Freelance, WordPro and Approach).

A while after release 4.0 shipped, Lotus released a toolkit to assist developers in creating LSXs. Release 2.0 of the LSX Toolkit now supports an enhancement to the LSX architecture to support Java. The new version of the toolkit adds a layer of C-callable code that is compatible with JNI, the Java Native Interface spec from JavaSoft. You can now implement your classes so that they can be called from LotusScript or Java (in fact, the LSX architecture supports method and property invocation from OLE Automation as well).

With the addition of this new Java support, the name "*LotusScript Extension*" is somewhat misleading, but it will probably stick around for a while. Within Lotus there has been support for to begin referring to this technology as "*plug-ins*" instead, but the new name doesn't seem to have taken off yet.

The LSX Toolkit is available for free on the Lotus Web site (the URL is complex, see the entry in the References.nsf links database on the CD-ROM, or go to http://www.lotus.com and wend your way there yourself). It includes template source code and header files, plus some documentation on how to build your own LSX. Code developed using the toolkit can be portable (if you follow the directions) across almost all the supported Notes platforms, client and server (NLM has not been certified as yet).

There's also an LSX generation wizard, implemented as a Notes application, of course. The wizard lets you fill out a form describing your classes, methods, and properties, and then it generates a skeleton C++ implementation for you. All you have to do then is fill in the logic for all the calls. If you're writing a Java interface, then you also need to write a thin layer of Java code that defines your classes and methods. Each Java method calls into one of the predefined JNI entry points generated by the wizard. This is a huge time saver, believe me.

The great thing about the LSX Toolkit, and about the LSX architecture in general, is that you can wrapper existing classes (or C APIs that you would like to expose in an object-oriented way) pretty easily and create modules that are callable from inside any of the Lotus products, or directly from any executable via Java. Yes, you have to be a C++ programmer to take advantage of this feature, but if you want to hook legacy code into the Domino environment via LotusScript or Java

(Agents, buttons, Web server interface, the whole nine yards), it's a huge win.

One new development (not yet released as of this writing, but check the Lotus Web site for updates) is that an upcoming version of the toolkit will support C++ invocation of Notes objects via the LSX interface. Previously, this interface was available only to the LotusScript run time environment. The next toolkit release will document how to pass a Notes NOI object to one of your own class's methods as an argument, and from C++, invoke any of the publicly available methods or properties on that object. Way cool.

F

What's on the CD-ROM

This book (as you've no doubt already noticed) comes with a CD-ROM. This appendix describes what's on the disc, but you should check the **readme.txt file** there for last-minute changes.

This CD can be read by both PC and Macintosh systems. When you insert the CD on a Mac, you might get a "Do you want to rebuild your desktop?" prompt. This is an artifact of the way the CD was manufactured. This is almost always a harmless operation, but it is recommended that you close any open files before responding "Yes". The path names in Table F.1 are in PC format for (my) convenience. Following the table of files are some instructions for installing the sample Notes databases.

The code samples are arranged by chapter in the samples directory. Both **.java** and **.class** files are included, but only the **.java** file names are listed here.

Appendix F

Table F.1 CD-ROM Contents

Directory	Files	Description
\	readme.txt	Description of the contents of the CD-ROM and installation instructions.
	copyright.txt	Copyright notice.
\samples		All the NSF and Java sample files
	References.nsf	A database containing useful Web links and other bibliographic information.
\samples\data	*.nsf	All the NSF files that go with the sample Java programs.
\samples\chap2	Ex21AddrBooks Ex22SetEnv Ex23Eval	Samples from Chapter 2: address books, set/get environment variables, evaluate.
\samples\chap3	Ex31ColValues Ex32Parent Ex33Responses Ex34Attachment Ex35AutoUpdate Ex36lookup	Samples from Chapter 3: column values, finding top parent, getting responses, file attachments, view lookups and auto-update.
\samples\chap4	Ex41RTStyle noteabbr.txt	Sample from Chapter 4: rich text style, Item.abstract dictionary
\samples\chap6	Ex61Reg Ex62News1 Ex63News2	Samples from Chapter 6: id registration and newsletter.
\samples\chap7	Ex74Multi Ex75Crawl	Samples from Chapter 7: multithreaded Application, Web crawler.
\samples\chap8	Ex81Agent Ex82Browser Ex83Multi Ex84CGI	Samples from Chapter 8: multithreaded Agent, return text to browser, enumerate CGI variables.
\samples\chap9	Ex90Agent DbgAgentContext DbgSession	Samples from Chapter 9: debuggable Agent
\samples\chap10	Ex101Conflict	Sample from Chapter 10: creating conflicts
\samples\chap11	HelloNOIServlet HelloNOIServlet2 HelloWorldServlet RunServlet AgentCGIEnumerator AgentOutputStream AgentRequest AgentResponse AgentServletConfig AgentServletContext servlet.cnf	Samples from Chapter 11: sample Servlets, classes for the Agent that runs Servlets. Config file for the Servlet Manager.

Directory	Files	Description
\samples\chap13	Ex13Select table1.txt	Sample from Chapter 13: JDBC example Sample database file
\servlets		This tree contains the JavaSoft Servlet Development Kit.
\NOIDoc		This tree contains HTML files documenting the NOI syntax. You can use a browser to view them.
\LSX		Contains the LSX Toolkit from Lotus.
\LSX\pc		The PC version of the toolkit
\LSX\Unix		The Unix version of the toolkit.

INSTALLATION INSTRUCTIONS

The References.nsf database can be used directly from the CD-ROM in the Notes Client. The databases that go with the sample Java programs should be installed in a subdirectory named "**book** in your Notes data directory. You can copy the files there. The sample Java programs expect the databases to be in the **book** subdirectory, but you can put them somewhere else if you recode the sample programs. They can't be used directly from the CD-ROM, except for browsing, because the sample programs usually modify them.

To install the Servlet Development Kit or the LSX Toolkit, see the instructions for those kits.

The HTML files in the **NOIDoc** directory on the CD-ROM can be browsed directly from the disc using any Web browser. Type the path of the **index.html** file in the **\NOIDoc** directory into the URL line of your browser to start viewing the documentation.

INDEX

$AssistMail Item, 97
$Authors Item, 136
$Fields Item, 178
$FILE Item, 86, 77, 78, 103, 106, 134, 157
$Fonts Item, 141
$Readers Item, 179
$REF Item, 82, 87, 90, 94, 240
$Signature Item, 85, 88, 135
$UpdatedBy Item, 71
?OpenAgent directive, 327
@function formulas, 35, 53, 72, 122
<B> HTML tag, 253

A

abbreviated names, 180
Abstract Windowing Toolkit (AWT), 22, 343
access control list (ACL), 60-63
  entries, *see* lotus.notes.ACLEntry
access, database, 59
ACL (Access Control List)
  class, *See also* lotus.notes.ACL
  methods
    addRole(), 62
    createACLEntry(), 62
    deleteRole(), 62
    getEntry(), 63
    getFirstEntry(), 63
    getNextEntry(), 63
    getParent(), 61
    getRoles(), 61
    isUniformAccess(), 62
    renameRole(), 62
    save(), 63
    setUniformAccess(), 62
  properties, 61-62
ACLEntry
  class, *See also* lotus.notes.ACLEntry
  methods
    disableRole(), 67
    enableRole(), 67
    getLevel(), 63
    getName(), 63
    getNameObject(), 63
    getParent(), 65
    getRoles(), 65
    isCanCreateDocuments(), 65
    isCanCreatePersonalAgent(), 65
    isCanCreatePersonalFolder(), 65
    isCanDeleteDocuments(), 66
    isPublicReader(), 66
    isPublicWriter(), 66
    isRoleEnabled(), 65, 67
    remove(), 67
    setCanCreateDocuments(), 65
    setCanCreatePersonalAgent(), 65
    setCanCreatePersonalFolder(), 65
    setCanDeleteDOcuments(), 66
    setName(), 63
    setPublicReader(), 66
    setPublicWriter(), 66
    toString(), 67
actions, logging, 209, 210, 211
Address Books, 24
  adding users to, 195
  adding ids to, 194, 195
  private, 48
  public, 48, 193

Index

storing ids in, 193, 194
updating, 193
ADMD (Administration Management Domain name), 181
administration activities, 186
administration, Agent, 256-260
administration, database, 57-60
Agent
  administration, 256-260
  Builder, in Notes Client, 168
  cache, refreshing, 258
  class *See* lotus.notes.Agent
  configuration, 173
  context, and debugging, 278
  database access, 255
  environment, 171
  execution, 170
  execution time, maximum, 259
  identity, 250-254
  identity, for Web users, 250
  latency, 260-263
  location, 171
  log, 212
  mail, 87
  methods
    getComment(), 168
    getCommonOwner(), 168
    getLastRun(), 168
    getName(), 168
    getOwner(), 168
    getParent(), 168
    getQuery(), 168
    getServerName(), 169
    isEnabled(), 169
    isPublic(), 170
    remove(), 170
    run(), 170
    save(), 169, 170
    setEnabled(), 169
    setServerName(), 169
    toString(), 171
  new or modified, 128
  output options, 271
  owner, 168
  privileges, 170, 250
  privileges, and HTTP, 172
  saved query, 135
  search query, 168
  security, 40, 254-260
  security, and JDBC, 377
  server name, 169
  signer, 168
  triggering, 8, 381
Agent Manager, 29
  daytime/nighttime parameters, 258
  debug output, 262
  Domino, 381
  end time, 258

environment variables, 260
main loop, delays in, 263
maximum Agents, 259
maximum percentage busy, 259
processes, 259
scheduling cycle, 261
start time, 258
throughput, 260
Agent/Servlet Adapter, 275, 313
AgentBase class, 5
AgentBase.getSession(), 280, 282
AgentBase.NotesMain(), 245
AgentCGIEnumerator class, 326
AgentContext, *See also* lotus.notes.AgentContext class, 27, 212, 246
methods
  getCurrentAgent(), 171
  getCurrentDatabase(), 171, 288
  getDocumentContext(), 171, 271, 325
  getEffectiveUserName(), 172, 283
  getLastExitStatus(), 172
  getLastRun(), 172
  getSavedData(), 173
  getUnprocessedDocuments(), 128, 173-174, 248, 288
  toString(), 175
  unprocessedFTSearch(), 174
  unprocessedSearch(), 174
  updateProcessedDoc(), 129, 175
AgentManagerSchedulingInterval environment variable, 261
AgentOutputStream class, 327, 334
AgentRequest class, 326, 331
AgentResponse class, 326, 331
agents, 5-6, 17
  and replication conflicts, 169
  and search queries, 174
  and selected documents, 173
  background, 255-256
  background, and Newsletters, 203
  creating, 247
  database, 46
  debugging, Chapter 9
  finding, 167
  foreground, 255
  Java, 380, 381-382
  loading servlet programs, 325-330
  private, 65
  server, 250, 256
  special functionality for, Web, 271-276
  unrestricted, 213

writing Chapter, 8
AgentServletConfig class, 326, 332
AgentServletContext class, 326
algorithms, thread unsafe, 302-307
aliases
  form, 178
  view, 108-109
alog4.ntf, log template, 214
AM string ,175
AMGR_DocUpdateAgentMinInterval environment variable, 261
AMGR_DocUpdateEventDelay environment variable, 261
AMGR_NewMailAgentMinInterval environment variable, 261
AMGR_NewMailEventDelay environment variable, 262
AMGR_UntriggeredMailInterval environment variable, 261
Anonymous user, 254, 335
API Program, 136
appending to a text list, 139
Applets, 3-4
  and NOI, 384
  triggering, 8
Application triggering, 8
applications, 2-3, 17
  multithreaded, 220-242
  single-threaded, 217-219
arguments, servlet, 336
atomic operations, 299-300
attached file size, 157
attached forms, document mailing, 96
Auth_Type CGI variable, 272
authentication, user, 254
Author Items, 134-138
Authors flag, 137
AWT (Abstract Windowing Toolkit), 343

B

background Agents, 255-256
background Agents, and Newsletters, 203
backslash character, 75
BASE HTML tag, 242
BeanMachine, Lotus, 352
Binary Large Objects (BLOBs), and NOI, 378
bit bucket, 136
BlindCopyTo Item, 95
Borland JBuilder tool, 352-355
browser, 3

Index

bugs
 in Agent Manager, percentage busy, 259
 in appendDOcLink(), 145
 in Item.contains(), 141
 in registration log, 192
 in Registration.getUserInfo(), 197
 in RichTextStyle effects, 154

C

C API, running Agents from, 172
C/CGI programming language, 7
Calendar Profile, 66
calendar view, 113
canonical names, 181
canonical path name, 191
categorized view, 119
categorized view column, 123
CD Records *See* Composite Document records
certifier id, 185, 186, 194
 file, 191
 hierarchical and flat, 198
 registering, 197-198
certifier password, 190
CGI (Common Gateway Interface)
 programs, 382
 triggering, 8
 variables
  and Agents, 271-276
  and servlets, 325, 326
  in Notes Document, 330
  Auth_Type, 272
  Content_Length, 272
  Content_Type, 272
  Gateway_Interface, 272
  HTTP_Accept, 272
  HTTP_Accept_Language, 272
  HTTP_CONNECTION, 273
  HTTP_HOST, 273
  HTTP_Referer, 272
  HTTP_UA_COLOR, 273
  HTTP_UA_CPU, 273
  HTTP_UA_OS, 273
  HTTP_UA_PIXELS, 273
  HTTP_User_Agent, 272
  HTTPS, 272
  HTTPS_KEYSIZE, 273
  Path_Info, 272
  Path_Translated, 273
  Query_String, 273, 331, 336
  Remote_Addr, 273
  Remote_Host, 273
  Remote_Ident, 273
  Remote_User, 273
  Request_Method, 273
  Script_Name, 273
  Server_Name, 273
  Server_Port, 273
  Server_Protocol, 273
  Server_Software, 273
  Server_URL_Gateway_Interface, 273
child threads
 and Agents, 265-270
 waiting for, 309-310
Class inheritance, 15
Class.forName(), 376, 377
 and dynamic class loading, 292
 and loading servlets, 332
Class.newInstance(), 376
classes, boring, 183
CLASSPATH
 environment variable, 26, 264
 and servlets, 316
cognitive dissonance, and Java Beans, 344
collection class, 123
column
 title, 122
 values, 132
 values, document, 71-76
columns
 categorized, 123
 hidden, 123
 response, 123
 sorted, 123
 view, 72, 122-123
COM and DCOM, 395
comma delimited database, 365
comments, in Agents, 168
common names, 180, 181
compacting databases, 57-58
component model, and Java Beans, 340-341
Component Object Model (COM), 395
Composite Document (CD) records, 135
compressing whitespace in Item text, 139
concurrency, and semaphores, 300-301
concurrent Agents, maximum number, 259
configuration file, for servlets, 315
conflicts, document save, 94
console, Java, 353
constructor
 default, and serialization, 350, 351
 nondefault, for Agent, 282
containment, 16

containment hierarchy, NOI, 351
Content_Length CGI variable, 272
Content_Type CGI variable, 272
context document, for Agent, 171
conversions
 Item values to text, 142
 rich text to text, 148
converting Item values to text, 142
converting rich text to text, 148
converting servlets to Agents, Chapter 11
copying Items, 141-142
copying RichTextItems, 141
CopyTo item, 95
CORBA
 and applets, 388, 390-391
 and Domino, 385, 386-391
 and Java Beans, 391
 and network performance, 389
 skeletons, 387
 vs. RMI, 393-394
country name, in hierarchical names, 181
creating
 databases, privilege, 39
 documents, 178
 forms, 177
 Java Agents, 247
 Log objects, 209
 LSXs, Appendix E
 mail databases, 191, 199
 Name objects, 180
 new Items, 98
 Newsletter objects, 200
 Notes ids, 185-200
 Registration objects, 185
 servlet request/response objects, 331
cross-certifying ids, 185, 196
currency formatting, 176, 177
current Agent, 171
current database, for Agent, 171, 246

D

data reliability, and thrad safety, 297
data sources, for ODBC, 365, 367
data structures, protecting for thread safety, 299-300
data translation formulas, 99
data types
 Item, 98-99

of view keys, 116
data values, and Items, 131
database
  access, 59
  access, and Agents, 255
  administration, 57-60
  Agents, 46
  and Domino web server, 28
  class, *See also*
    lotus.notes.Database
  client API, 361, 363
  constants, 42, 51
    ACLLEVEL_AUTHOR, 42
    ACLLEVEL_DEPOSITOR, 42
    ACLLEVEL_DESIGNER, 42
    ACLLEVEL_EDITOR, 42
    ACLLEVEL_MANAGER, 42
    ACLLEVEL_NOACCESS, 42
    ACLLEVEL_READER, 42
    FT_DATE_ASC, 51
    FT_DATE_DES, 51
    FT_SCORES, 51
    FT_STEMS, 51
  delete, 59
  design elements, 48-50
  drivers, JDBC, 358
  failover, 39
  folders, 46
  forms, 46
  full text index, 52
  index, 53
  manager access, 41
  methods
    compact(), 57-58
    createCopy(), 58
    createDocument(), 57, 232
    createFromTemplate(), 58
    createReplica() 58,
    FTSearch(), 50, 53, 174, 204, 288, 299,
    getACL(), 41, 60
    getAgent(), 48, 167
    getAgents(), 41, 167
    getAllDOcuments(), 41
    getCategories(), 42
    getCreated(), 42
    getCurrentAccessLevel, 42
    getDesignTemplateName(), 43
    getDocumentByID(), 54
    getDocumentByUNID(), 54
    getDocumentByURL(), 54-57
    getFileName(), 43
    getFilePath(), 43
    getForm(), 48, 177

getForms(), 44, 177
getLastFTIndexed(), 44
getLastModified(), 44
getManagers(), 44
getParent(), 44
getPercentUsed(), 44
getProfileDOcument(), 48
getReplicaID(), 45
getServer(), 39, 45, 48
getSize(), 45
getSizeQuota(), 45
getTemplateName(), 43
getTitle(), 45
getURLHeaderInfo(), 57
getView(), 49, 50
getViews(), 46
grantAccess(), 59
isDelayUpdates(), 46
isFTIndexed(), 46
isMultiDbSearch(), 46-47
isOpen(), 39, 48
isPrivateAddressBook(), 48
isPublicAddressBook(), 48
open(), 24, 59
queryAccess(), 59
remove(), 59
replicate(), 60
revokeAccess(), 59
search(), 53, 174
setDelayUpdates(), 46
setSizeQuota(), 45
setTitle(), 45
toString(), 60
updateFTIndex(), 53
navigation, 37
path name, 43
properties, 41-48
queries, 50
relational, 107
replica, 58
replica id, 60
search, 123
searching, 50-57
templates, 43
updates, delaying, 46
URL syntax, 362
views, 46, 49, 50
date-only DateTime object, 163
date adjustments, 162-163
date format
  Java, 159-160
  LotusScript, 160
date formatting, 177
date values, 159
date/time conversion, 159
DateRange
  class *See also*
    lotus.notes.DateRange
  creating, 164
  end time, 164

methods
  getEndDateTime(), 165
  getStartDateTime(), 165
  getText(), 165
  setEndDateTime(), 165
  setStartDateTime(), 165
  setText(), 165
  toString(), 166
modifying, 165
start time, 164
DateTime class *See also*
  lotus.notes.DateTime
methods
  adjustDay(), 162
  adjustHour(), 162
  adjustMinute(), 162
  adjustMonth(), 162
  adjustSecond(), 162
  adjustYear(), 162
  convertToZone(), 163
  getDateOnly(), 160
  getGMTTime(), 161
  getLocalTime(), 161, 164
  getTimeOnly(), 160
  getTimeZone(), 161
  getZoneTime(), 161
  isDST(), 161
  setAnyDate(), 53, 163
  setAnyTime(), 53, 163
  setLocalDate(), 164
  setLocalTime(), 161, 164
  setNow(), 164, 190
  timeDifference(), 164
  toString(), 164
daylight savings time, 161, 162, 163, 177
daytime parameters, Agent Manager, 258
DbDirectory
  class *See also*
    lotus.notes.DbDirectory
  constants
    DATABASE, 38
    TEMPLATE, 38
    TEMPLATE_CANDIDATE, 38
  methods
    createDatabase(), 39
    getFirstDatabase, 38, 59, 301
    getName(), 38
    getNextDatabase(), 38, 59, 301
    openByReplicaID(), 45
    openDatabase(), 39
    openDatabaseByReplicaID(), 40
    openDatabaseIfModified(), 39
    openMailDatabase(), 40
    toString(), 40
DbgAgentContext class, 286-288, 293

Index

DbgSession class, 283-285, 293
DBMS connectivity, 13
DCOM, Microsoft, 386, 395-396
debug output, Agent Manager, 262
DEBUG_AMGR environment variable, 262
debuggable Agent example, 279-283
debugging Agents, Chapter 9
default constructor
  and NOI, 355
  and serialization, 350, 351
  for Java Beans, 340
default mail database, and Newsletters, 203
default value formulas, 99
default view, 113
delays, Agent Manager scheduling, 263
deleting
  Agents, 170
  databases, 59
  forms, 180
  ids on server, 196
  Items, 105-106, 142
denial of service attack, and Agents, 265
Department of Defense, U.S., 194
deserialization
  and Java Beans, 349
  and serialization, 347
Design Refresh, 110
  of forms, 179
design time state, and Java Beans, 348
dessert topping, and floor wax, 278
development environment Java, 247
  for Java Beans, 352-353
development tools, third party, 277-278
dictionary file, 139
digital signatures, 85-86, 97
  and Agents, 256
directory services, Java, 399
disabling Agents, 169
dissonance, cognitive, and Java Beans, 344
distinguished names, 27, 180
DLL, 4, 11
doclinks, 145
  adding to rich text, 145
  in Newsletter class, 201, 204-209
Document
  class, *See also*
    lotus.notes.Document

collections
  nonsorted, 126
  sorted, 126
  See also DocumentCollection, lotus.notes.DocumentCollection
context, for Agent, 171
counter, in view, 120
digest, 138
encryption, 86, 89-90, 136
ID, 54, 80-81
level access control, 136
lookup, by key, 115-119
mailing, 95-97
management methods, 88-98
methods
  appendItemValue(), 95, 98-99, 101, 106
  computeWIthFOrm(), 99-100
  copyAllItems(), 100-101
  copyItem(), 101
  copyToDatabase(), 88
  createReplyMessage(), 89
  createRichTextItem(), 101, 307
  encrypt(), 79, 89-90, 98, 138
  getAttachment(), 78, 101-103
  getAuthors(), 71
  getColumnValues(), 71-76
  getCreated(), 76
  getEmbeddedOBject(), 156
  getEmbeddedObjects(), 77-78, 101
  getEncryptionKeys(), 78
  getFirstItem(), 98, 103
  getFTSearchScore(), 79
  getItems(), 78, 80, 100
  getItemValue(), 104-105
  getItemValueDouble(), 104-105
  getItemValueInteger(), 104-105
  getItemValueString(), 104-105
  getKey(), 80
  getLastAccessed(), 76
  getLastModified(), 76
  getNameOfProfile(), 80
  getNextDocument(), 112,113
  getNextItem(), 104
  getNoteID(), 80-81
  getParentDatabase(), 82
  getParentDocumentUNID(), 82, 87
  getParentView(), 82, 173, 246
  getResponses(), 83-84, 87
  getSigner(), 85-86, 97
  getSize(), 86
  getUniversalID(), 80-81

getVerifier(), 85-86, 97
hasEmbedded(), 86
hasItem(), 105
isEncryptOnSend(), 86
isNewNote(), 87
isProfile(), 80
isProfileDocument(), 49
isResponse(), 87
isSaveMessageOnSend(), 87
isSentByAgent(), 87, 97
isSigned(), 88
isSignedOnSend(), 88
makeResponse(), 90, 240
putInFolder(), 90-91, 114
remove(), 92, 298
removeFromFolder(), 90-91, 114
removeItem(), 105-106
renderToRTItem(), 92, 203
replaceItemValue(), 95, 106-107, 128, 190
save(), 87, 88, 90, 93-94, 95-97, 105, 128, 137, 159, 203, 212, 240, 241
setEncryptionKeys(), 78
setEncryptOnSend(), 86
setSaveMessageOnSend(), 87
setSignedOnSend(), 88
setUniversalID(), 80-81
sign(), 97
toSTring(), 107
profile, 80
properties, 71-88
read access, 137, 178
relevance score, 50
rendering, 92
  in Newsletter class, 201
responses, 83-84, 87, 90, 93
save conflicts, 94
search, by key, 115-119
size, 86
DocumentCollection
  class, *See also*
    lotus.notes.DocumentCollection
data structures, 125
navigation methods, 125-126
for Newsletter objects, 200
methods
  FTSearch(), 126-127
  getCount(), 124
  getFirstDocument(), 125-126
  getLastDocument(), 125-126
  getNextDocument(), 125-126
  getNthDOcument(), 125-126
  getParent(), 124
  getPrevDOcument(), 125-126
  getQuery(), 124
  isSorted(), 124
  putAllInFolder(), 127

Index

removeAll(), 127
removeAllFromFolder(), 127
stampAll(), 128
updateAll(), 128-129, 175
domain, server, 198
Domino
  and servlets, 314-317
  programmability, summary, 380-382
  Release 4.6, 9
  Release 5.0, forecast, Chapter 14
  server ORB, 388-390
  setup for writing Java, Appendix C
DOMINO_SERVLET parameter
  in URLs, 325
  See also servlets
DominoAsynchronizeAgents environment variable, 262, 364
DominoEnableJavaServlets environment variable, 315
driver manager
  JDBC, 358
  ODBC, 365
dynamic class loading, and Class.forName(), 292

E

effective user
  id, 97
  name, 246
  name, for Agents, 172, 250
embedded objects, 77, 86, 135, 143, 146-148
  copying, 142
EmbeddedObject
  class, *See also* lotus.notes.EmbeddedObject
  constants
    EMBED_ATTACHMENT, 158
    EMBED_OBJECT, 158
    EMBED_OBJECTLINK, 158
  methods
    activate(), 158
    doVerb(), 159
    extractFile(), 159
    getClassName(), 157
    getFileSize(), 157
    getName(), 157
    getObject(), 157
    getParent(), 157
    getSource(), 158
    getType(), 158
    getVerbs(), 158

remove(), 106, 159
toString(), 159
embedding
  Java Beans, 348
  OLE links, 147
  OLE objects, 147
enabling Agents, 169
encryption, 78-79
  document, 86, 89-90, 136
  item, 136
  keys, 78-79, 90, 194
end time
  Agent Manager, 258
  in DateRange, 164
Enumeration interface, 27
environment variables, 31-34
  Agent Manager, 260
  AgentManagerScheduling-Interval, 261
  AMGR_DocUpdate-AgentMinInterval, 261
  AMGR_DocUpdateEvent-Delay, 261
  AMGR_NewMailAgent-MinInterval, 261
  AMGR_NewMailEventDelay, 262
  AMGR_Untriggered-MailInterval, 261
  CLASSPATH, 26, 264
  DEBUG_AMGR, 262
  DominoAsynchronizeAgents, 262, 364
  DominoEnableJavaServlets, 315
  Java related, 264
  JavaMaxHeapSize, 264
  JavaStackSize, 264
  JavaUserClasses, 264, 315
error codes 23, Appendix D
errors, logging, 209, 210, 211
event
  codes, in Log class, 211
  handling, and Java Beans, 353
  logging, 211
  model, and Java Beans, 343-345
  queues, 211
  reporting, 211
events in NOI, 344
exact matches, on view searches, 116-118
Exception class *See also* java.lang.Exception
exceptions, 22-23
  NOI, list, Appendix D
execution
  context, servlet, 318
  path, 26
  time, Agent, 259
expanded class syntax, 18

expiration date, for ids, 190, 191
extreme prejudice, terminated with, 244
extrospection, and Java Beans, 345

F

failover, Database, 39
field level replication, 134
field names, in forms, 178
file attachment
  icons, 147
  id, 196
file attachments, 77, 134, 143, 146-148, 155, 159
files, logging to, 210, 213
finally block, 376
  and threads, 218
finding form objects, 177
firewalls, 56
  and remote protocols, 397
flat
  ids, 191
  names, 191
  views, 119
floor wax, and dessert topping, 278
folders, 49, 90-91, 114, 127
  database, 46
  private, 46, 65
  private on first use, 50, 91
  shared, 65
fonts in rich text Items, 141
food fight, and Microsoft, 396
foreground Agents, 255
form aliases, 178
Form
  class, *See also* lotus.notes.Form
  database, 46
  field names, 178
  Item, 100
  name, 178
  finding, 177
  methods
    getAliases(), 178
    getFields(), 178
    getFormUsers(), 178-179
    getName(), 179
    getReaders(), 178-179
    isProtectReaders(), 179
    isProtectUsers(), 179
    isSubForm(), 179
    remove(), 180
    setFormUsers(), 178-179
    setProtectReaders(), 179
    setProtectUsers(), 179
    setReaders(), 178-179
    toString(), 180
formula query, 124

Index

full text
  index, 46, 124
  index, database, 52, 53
  query, 124
  search, 79, 174
    and Newsletters, 201
    and views, 114-115
    limits, 125
    document collections, 126-127

G

garbage collection thread, 229, 240
Gateway_Interface CGI variable, 272
gc, *See* garbage collector
generation, in hierarchical names, 181
GET requests, and servlets, 332
getCommonUserName(), 27
getting ids from server, 196
granularity of DateTime object, 231

H

hidden columns, 123
hierarchical
  ids, 191
  names, 180, 183, 191
home server, 200
HREF HTML tag, 241
HTML, 3
  links, 241
  pages, 240
  tags, 241, 242. 253
  text in Items, 135
HTTP
  Agents, 171
    and output, 244
  server, 29
    and Agents, 250
    and multithreading, 262
    and servlets, 315
    and CGI, 7
HTTP_Accept CGI variable, 272
HTTP_Accept_Language CGI variable, 272
HTTP_CONNECTION CGI variable, 273
HTTP_HOST CGI variable, 273
HTTP_Referer CGI variable, 272
HTTP_UA_COLOR CGI variable, 273
HTTP_UA_CPU CGI variable, 273

HTTP_UA_OS CGI variable, 273
HTTP_UA_PIXELS CGI variable, 273
HTTP_User_Agent CGI variable, 272
HTTPS CGI variable, 272
HTTPS_KEYSIZE CGI variable, 273
HttpServletResponse.getOutput Stream(), 318

I

id file, 71
  storing in address book, 193
id types, 191
id
  cross-certifying, 196
  document, 54
  deleting on server, 196
  getting from server, 196
  intenational, 194
  North American, 194
  recertifying, 197
  registering new certifiers, 197-198
  registering new server, 198
  registering user, 199-200
  switch, 200
  universal, 54
IDE (Integrated Development Environment), 277, 383-384
identity
  Agent, 250-254
  for Web users, 250
IDispatch interface, 156
IDL (Interface Definition Language), 386-387
IDTable, 125
IIOP protocol, 386, 387
IMAP (Internet Mail Access Protocol), 398-400
import statement, 26, 218
InfoBus technology, 344
inheritance in NOI, 15, 143
initials, in hierarchical names, 182
input arguments, servlet, 336
input validation formulas, 99
installing JDBC and ODBC, 364-366
instanceof operator, 32, 33, 76, 105
  and servlets, 332
Integrated Development Environment (IDE), 277
integrated Java development environment, 247

Interface Definition Language (IDL), 386-387
Interface Repository, CORBA, 387
International
  class, *See also* lotus.notes.International
  methods
    getAMString(), 175
    getCurrencyDigits(), 176
    getCurrencySymbol(), 176
    getDateSep(), 176
    getDecimalSep(), 176
    getPMString(), 175
    getThousandsSep(), 176
    getTimeSep(), 176
    getTimeZone(), 176
    getToday(), 176, 190
    getTomorrow(), 176
    getYesterday(), 176
    isCurrencySpace(), 176
    isCurrencySuffix(), 177
    isCurrencyZero(), 177
    isDateDMY(), 177
    isDateMDY(), 177
    isDateYMD(), 177
    isDST(), 177
    isTime24Hour(), 177
  settings, 175
Internet Explorer, 12
Internet Mail Access Protocol (IMAP), 398-400
Internet programmability, 13
interrupting Agents, 248
Intersolv JDBC and ODBC, 365, 368
introspection, 21
  and Java Beans, 341, 345-346, 353
invisible Java Beans, 347
invoking servlets, 314
Item
  and fields, 70-71
  accessor methods, 98-107
  class, *See also* lotus.notes.Item
  constants, 134-136
    ACTIONCD, 134
    ASSISTANTINFO, 134
    ATTACHMENT, 134
    AUTHORS, 134
    COLLATION, 134
    DATETIMES, 134
    EMBEDDEDOBJECT, 135
    ERRORITEM, 135
    FORMULA, 135
    HTML, 135
    ICON, 135
    LSOBJECT, 135
    NAMES, 135
    NOTELINKS, 135

Index

NOTEREFS, 135
NUMBERS, 135
OTHEROBJECT, 135
QUERYCD, 135
READERS, 135
RICHTEXT, 135
SIGNATURE, 135
TEXT, 135
UNAVAILABLE, 135
UNKNOWN, 135
USERDATA, 136
USERID, 136
VIEWMAPDATA, 136
VIEWMAPLAYOUT, 136
data types, 98-99
document, 70-71
encryption, 136
flags, 141
methods
  abstractText(), 138-139
  appendToTextList(), 139
  containsValue(), 140-141, 241
  copyItemToDocument, 141-142
  copyToDocument(), 145
  getDateTimeValue(), 133
  getLastModified(), 133
  getName(), 134
  getParent(), 134
  getText(), 142
  getType(), 134
  getValueDouble(), 132
  getValueInteger(), 133
  getValueLength(), 136
  getValues(), 132
  getValueString(), 132, 142
  isAUthors(), 136
  isEncrypted(), 79, 136
  isNames(), 137
  isProtected(), 137
  isReaders(), 137
  isSaveToDIsk(), 137
  isSigned(), 138
  isSummary(), 138
  remove(), 142
  replaceItemValue(), 306
  setDateTimeValue(), 133
  setEncrypted(), 79, 136
  setNames(), 137
  setProtected(), 137
  setReaders(), 137
  setSaveToDisk(), 137
  setSummary(), 138
  setValueDouble(), 132
  setValueInteger(), 133
  setValues(), 132
  setValueString(), 132
  toString(), 142
name, 134
parent Document, 134

protection, 137
summary flag, 99
types, 134-136
validation, 100
value length, 136
value properties, 132-133
values, 104-105

J

jar file, saving applets in, 349
Java
  Agents, 380, 381-382
    creating, 247
  and JavaScript, differences, 12
  and NOI, 380
  Bean builder tools, 20
    and NOI, 352-355
  Console, 353
    and Agents, 244
  date formats, 159-160
  development environment, and Domino, 383-384
  garbage collection thread, 308
Java Beans, 19
  and Active/X, 340
  and COM Bridge, 156
  and introspection, 345-346
  and serialization, 355
  and servers, 356
  and Domino 5.0, 396-397
  and NOI, Chapter 12
  definition, 339-340
  embedding in applets, 348
  NOI vs. other APIs, 380-381
  platforms, for Domino,
    Appendix C
  properties, 20
Java Database Connectivity
  (JDBC), Chapter 13
Java Development Kit (JDK),
  247, 339
Java Naming and Directory
  Interface (JNDI), 398-400
Java Native Interface (JNI), 352
Java Servlet Development Kit,
  311, 314, 315, 316
Java Virtual Machine, 7
java.beans package
  BeanInfo interface, 340, 345-346
  Beans class, 339
  Introspector class, 345, 346
  Visibility interface, 340, 346-347
  Visibility.dontUseGui(), 347
  Visibility.needsGui(), 347
  Visibility.okToUseGui(), 347
java.io package
  BufferedReader class, 241

Externalizable interface, 350, 352
ObjectInputStream class, 350
ObjectOutputStream class, 350
ObjectStream class, 327, 351
  getSerialVersionUID(), 351
PrintWriter class
  and Agents, 244
  class, 320
  for Agents, 327
  stream, in Agents, 252
Serializable interface, 347, 352
java.lang package, 377
  Class class, 332
  Exception class, 23
  Integer class, 32
  InterruptedException class, 270
  Number class, 32
  Runnable interface, 22
    and Notes threads, 225
  Thread, 21-22, 221
  ThreadGroup
    and Agents, 265
    and AgentBase, 244
java.naming package, 399
  Context interface, 399
  directory package, 399
java.net.URL class, 238-239
java.rmi package, 392
  remote inteface, 392
  RemoteServer class, 392
java.sql package, 358, 361, 364
  Connection class, 367
  DriverManager class, 366
  DriverManager.
    getConnection(), 367, 377
  DriverManager.
    registerDriver(), 377
  ResultSet class, 367
  Statement class, 367
java.util package
  Enumeration interface, 326
  Vector class, 35
Java and LotusScript, differences, 17
javadoc utility, 346
JavaMaxHeapSize environment variable, 264
JavaScript, 10, 12, 13
JavaStackSize environment variable, 264
JavaUserClasses environment variable, 264, 315
  and servlets, 325
javax package, 311 See also javax servlet package
javax.servlet package, 318, 377
  GenericServlet class, 314, 318

Index

javax.servlet.http package
  HttpRequest interface, 326
  HttpResponse interface, 326
  HttpServlet class, 318
  HTTPServletRequest interface, 318, 319
  HTTPServletResponse interface, 318, 319
  Servlet class, 332
  Servlet interface, 318
  service(), 332
  ServletConfig interface, 319, 326
  ServletContext interface, 319, 326
  ServletOutputStream class, 318
JDBC (Java Database Connectivity), Chapter 13
  and SQL, 358
  and testing, 363-364
  and thread safety, 363
  and URLs, 358
  architecture, 360-363
  drivers, 361
    installing, 364
  example, 368-375
  installing, 364-366
  remote naming service, 367
  URL syntax, 366
JDBC/ODBC Bridge, 358, 360, 361
  installing, 364
  registration, 376
JDK (Java Development Kit), 247
JNDI (Java Naming and Directory Interface), 398-400
JNI (Java Native Interface), 352
JScript, 13

K

key
  components, 116
  encryption, 78-79
  lookup in Views, 115-119, 123
keyword
  in hierarchical names, 182
  tags, in distinguished names, 180

L

latency, Agent, 260-263
LDAP (Lightweight Directory Access Protocol), 398-400
left to do list, and Agents, 175
legacy data, and Notes, 359

Lightweight Directory Access Protocol (LDAP), 398-400
LMBCS, 56, 99
loading classes dynamically, and Class.forName(), 292
LocalHost, special TCP name, 252
locks, read and write, 300
Log
  class, *See also* lotus.notes.Log
  constants
    EV_ALARM, 211
    EV_COMM, 211
    EV_MAIL, 211
    EV_MISC, 211
    EV_REPLICA, 212
    EV_RESOURCE, 212
    EV_SECURITY, 212
    EV_SERVER, 212
    EV_UNKNOWN, 212
    EV_UPDATE, 212
    SEV_FAILURE, 212
    SEV_FATAL, 212
    SEV_NORMAL, 212
    SEV_UNKNOWN, 212
    SEV_WARNING1, 212
    SEV_WARNING2, 212
  methods
    close(), 211, 213
    getNumActions(), 209
    getNumErrors(), 209
    getProgramName(), 210
    isLogActions(), 210
    isLogErrors(), 210
    isOverwriteFile(), 210
    logAction(), 209, 211, 271
    logError(), 211
    logEvent(), 209, 211
    openAgentLog(), 212
    openFileLog(), 209, 213
    openMailLog(), 209, 213-214
    openNotesLog(), 209, 214
    setLogActions(), 210
    setLogErrors(), 210
    setOverwriteFile(), 210
    setProgramName(), 210
    toString(), 215
log
  Agent, 212
  object, creating, 209
  mail, in Log class, 213-214
  registration, 192
  template (alog4.ntf), 214
  to file, 213
logging
  events, 211
  to files, 210
  to Notes database, 214
Lotus
  BeanMachine, 352

eSuite, and NOI, 391
Go, and servlets, 313
InfoBus, 344
lotus.notes package, 26
  ACL class, 60-63
  ACLEntry class, 60, 62, 64-67
  Agent class, 167-171
  AgentBase class, 244-250
  AgentContext class, 171-175
  Database class, 24, 41-60
  DateRange class, 29, 34, 99, 116, 164-166
  DateTime class, 29, 32, 33, 99, 116, 159-164
    granularity, 231
    value, on Item, 133
  DbDirectory class, 31, 37
    multithreaded restrictions on, 301-302
  Document class, 69-107
  DocumentCollection class, 41, 123-129
  EmbeddedObject class, 77, 155-159
  Form class, 177-180
  International class, 28, 175-177
  Item class, 131-142
  Log class, 30, 209-215
  Name class, 28, 30, 180-183
  Newsletter class, 30, 200-209, 245
  NotesException class, 23, 211
  NotesThread class, 21-22, 221
  Registration class, 30, 185-200
  RichTextItem class, 92, 143-148
  RichTextStyle class, 30, 146, 148-155
  Session class, 15, 23-37
    and memory management, 307-310
  View class, 107-122
  ViewColumn class, 109, 122-123
LotusScript, 2, 10-11
  Agent, 11
  date format, 160
  global functions, 35
  NotesDocument class, 18
  Variant type, 17
LotusScript Extension (LSX), 10-11, 380
low level reflection, 346
LS:DO (LotusScript Data Object), 358
  and multithreading, 262
LSX
  architecture, and CORBA, 388
  Toolkit, Appendix E
  creating, Appendix E

Index

M

mail
  databases
    creating, 199
    default, and Newsletters, 203
  forward command, 89
  log, 213-214
mailing documents, 86, 87, 95-97
main() method, in applications, 218
marking documents as processed, 129
matching data values, 140-141
maximum Agent execution time, 259
maximum percentage busy, Agent, 259
memory management, and lotus.notes.Session, 307-310
merging rich text items, 145
methods
  and properties, in NOI, 342
  naming conventions, 20
  naming, for Java Beans, 340, 342-343
  overloading in NOI, 17
  See also methods entry under each class name
MFC (Microsoft Foundation Classes), 395
Microsoft 12
  and food fights, 396
  DCOM, 386, 395-396
  Visual J++
    and JDBC/ODBC Bridge, 366
    tool, 352
migrating servlets to Domino, 324-325
MIME encoding, 56, 240
minimum password length, 192
Mozilla, and Agents, 272
muli-valued Items, 132
Multi-database index, 46-47, 52
  and Newsletters, 201
multi-database search, 52
  and Newsletters, 204
multi-user conflicts, 302-303
multi-valued keys, 116
multiple Items of the same name, 141
multithreaded
  Agents, 264-271
  applications, 220-242
  object access, 296
multithreading do's and don'ts, 311

N

name
  common, 180, 181
Name class *See also* lotus.notes.Name
  methods
    getAbbreviated(), 180
    getADMD(), 181
    getCanonical(), 181
    getCommon(), 181
    getCountry(), 181
    getGeneration(), 181
    getGiven(), 181-182
    getInitials(), 182
    getKeyword(), 182
    getOrganization(), 182
    getOrgUnit1(), 182
    getOrgUnit2(), 182
    getOrgUnit3(), 182
    getOrgUnit4(), 182
    getPRMD(), 183
    getSurname(), 183
    isHierarchical(), 183
    toString(), 183
flag, 137, 138, 140
form, 178
given, 181-182
Item, 134
native methods, 16
navigation, view, 108
Netscape Corp., 12
new mail Agent delays, 263
new/modified Agents, 174, 175
newlines, adding to rich text, 144
Newsletter *See also* lotus.notes.Newsletter
  class, 52
  creating, 200
  methods
    formatDocument(), 203
    formatMsgWithDoclinks(), 204-209
    getSubjectItemName(), 201-202
    isDoScore(), 202
    isDoSubject(), 202
    setDoScore(), 202
    setDoSubject(), 202
nighttime parameters, Agent Manager, 258
NOI 9
  and BLOBs (Binary Large Objects), 378
  and default constructors, 355
  and Java, 380
  and Java Bean builder tools, 352-355
  and JDBC (Java Database Connectivity), Chapter 13
  and OLE Automation, 380
  and remote access technologies, 384-398
  and serialization, 351, 355
  and servlets, 380
  applications, writing, Chapter 7
  class diagram, Appendix B
  containment hierarchy, 15, 18-19, Appendix B
  exceptions, list, Appendix D
  applets and CORBA, 390-391
  Java and LotusScript bindings, 380-381
  See also Notes Object Interface
non-document View entries, 120-121
nondefault constructor, for Agent, 282
nonsorted document collections, 126
note id, obtaining, 305-306
Notes
  @function formulas, 5
  and legacy data, 359
  Client scripting, and Java, 383
  date formatk 160
  id typesk 191
  log, and Agentsk 244
  LSX (LotusScript Extension)k 15-16, 380
  macros, 5
Notes Object Interface, 2
  See also NOI
NOTES.INI file, 31, 261
  and environment variables, 364
  and HTTP server, 315
  and servlets, 315
NotesBase.CheckObject(), 306
NotesException class, 23, 211
NotesSQL driver for ODBC, 358
NotesThread *See also* lotus.notes.NotesThread
  and servlets, 323
  class, 238
  methods
    runNotes(), 229
    sinitThread(), 22, 217, 223, 228, 376
    stermThread(), 22, 217, 223, 228, 239, 376
NTF files, 43, 110
number formatting, 176

O

object
  database, and serialization, 350
  inheritance, 19

Index

methods, 19-20
names, user defined, 147, 148
properties, 19-20
reference counting, in LotusScript, 307-308
references, and serialization, 350
sharing, multiple threads, Chapter 10
Object Management Group (OMG), 385
Object Request Broker (ORB), 385, 386
Object.notify(), 270
Object.toString(), 34
Object.wait(), 270
ODBC (Open Database Connectivity), 358
  data sources, 365
  Driver Manager, 365
  drivers, 361
  subprotocol, for JDBC, 377
  installing, 364-366
OLE
  Automation, 9, 156
  Automation handle, 157
  and NOI, 380
  objects, 77, 101, 106, 135, 143, 146-148, 155
    activation not supported, 155
    links, 146
    programming, 395
    verbs, 158
OMG (Object Management Group), 385
Open Database Connectivity (ODBC), 358
operator new, 15, 22, 23
ORB (Object Request Broker), 385, 386
ordering of search results, 118
organization name, 180
  in certifier id, 198
  in hierarchical names, 182
organizational unit, 189, 192
  names, 182
Out of Office Agent, 88
output options, Agent, 271
overwriting file logs, 213
Ozzie, Ray, 35

P

paragraph
  break, in rich text, 144
  size limits, 144
parameterized queries, and JDBC, 367
parameters, servlet, 319
parent Database, 124
parent documents, 82

password length, minimum, 192
password prompt, 27
Path_Info CGI variable, 272
Path_Translated CGI variable, 273
percentage busy, Agent, 259
performance
  and CORBA, 389
  of DocumentCollection navigation, 125
  of View navigation, 120
Perl/CGI Programming language, 7
persistent data
  and Agents, 173
  and serialization, 351
personal Agents, running, 257
PM string, 175
Portability/JavaScript, 12
POST requests, and servlets, 330
prejudice, extreme, 244
private
  Agents, 65, 170
  folders, 46, 65
Private Management Domain name (PRMD), 183
private on first use folder, 50, 91
privileges, Agent, 170, 250
PRMD (Private Management Domain name), 183
processes, Agent Manager, 259
profile documents, 48, 80, 173, 195
profiles, user, 195
property naming conventions, 20
protecting
  data structures, and thread safety, 299-300
  reader lists on forms, 179
  user lists on forms, 179
protocol specifier, for JDBC, 366
public
  address book, 186, 193, 196
  Agents, 170
  readers, 66
  writers, 66
pure Java JDBC, 360
queries
  database, 50
  parameterized, and JDBC, 367
  Agent, 168
  formula, 124
  full text, 124
  saved, 135

Q

Query_String CGI variable, 273, 331, 336

R

read
  access, documents, 178-179
  locks, 300
reader
  Items, 135, 138
  list, view, 110
readers flag, 137
readers, form, 178
readObject(), and serialization, 350
recertifying ids, 185, 197
recipient lists, 96
  in mail log, 213
reflection, low level, 346
refreshing Agent cache, 258
registering
  ids, 185-200
  new certifier ids, 197-198
  new server ids, 198
  new users, 199-200
Registration
  class, *See also* lotus.notes.Registration
  constants
    ID_CERTIFIER, 192
    ID_FLAT, 191
    ID_HIERARCHICAL, 191
    TYPE_CERTIFIER, 199, 200
  methods
    addCertifierToAddressBook(), 194
    addServerToAddressBook(), 194
    addUserProfile(), 195
    addUserToAddressBook(), 195
    crossCertify(), 196
    deleteIDOnServer(), 196
    getCertifierIDFile(), 191
    getCreateMailDb(), 191
    getExpiration(), 191
    getIDFromServer(), 196
    getIDType(), 191
    getminPasswordLength(), 192
    getOrgUnit(), 192
    getRegistrationLog(), 192
    getRegistrationServer(), 193
    getStoreIDInAddressBook(), 193
    getUpdateAddressBook(), 193
    getUserInfo(), 197
    isNorthAmerican(), 194
    recertify(), 197
    registerNewCertifier(), 197-198
    registerNewServer(), 198

registerNewUser(), 199-200
setCertifierIDFile(), 191
setCreateMailDb(), 191
setExpiration(), 191
setIDType(), 191
setNorthAmerican(), 194
setOrgUnit(), 192
setRegistrationLog(), 192
setRegistrationServer(), 193
setStoreIDInAddressBook(), 193
setUPdateAddressBook(), 193
switchToID(), 200
registration
  log, 192
  of JDBC/ODBC Bridge, 376
  server, 186, 193, 194, 196, 198
relational database, 107
  access, and NOI, 357
  connectivity, and Notes, 378
  systems, and servlets, 314
relevance score, 50, 79, 125
  in Newsletters, 202, 204
remote access technologies
  and firewalls, 397
  and NOI, 384-398
Remote Method Invocation (RMI), 392-394
remote naming service, for JDBC, 367
Remote Procedure Call (RPC), 385
Remote_Addr CGI variable, 273
Remote_Host CGI variable, 273
Remote_Ident CGI variable, 273
Remote_User CGI variable, 273
removing
  Items, 142
  Documents, 92
  file attachments, 106
rendering, document, 92
replacing Item values, 106
replica id, database, 45, 60
replica, database, 58
REPLICA_CANDIDATE constant, DbDirectory, 38
replication conflicts, 63
  and Agents, 169
  field level, 134
  of forms, 179
reply messages, 89
Request_Method CGI variable, 273
response
  columns, 123
  documents, 240
responses
  document, 83-84, 87, 90, 93
restricted Agents, 377
  running, 258

restrictions, multithreaded, on DbDirectory, 301-302
result set, database query, 358
rich text
  adding a style to, 146
  adding doclinks to, 145
  adding newlines to, 144
  adding tabs to, 145
  adding text to, 146
  bold style, 151
  color, 151
  effects, 151
  font size, 152
  fonts, 152
  italics, 152
  items, 103, 104
  strike-through, 152
  styles, specifying 148-155
  underlines, 153
RichTextItem
  class See also lotus.notes.RichTextItem
  constants, 158
    EMBED_ATTACHMENT, 146
    EMBED_OBJECT, 146
    EMBED_OBJECTLINK, 146
  methods
    addNewLine(), 144, 146
    addTab(), 145, 146
    appendDocLink(), 145
    appendRichTextItem(), 149
    appendRTItem(), 145
    appendStyle(), 146
    appendText(), 146
    embedObject(), 146-148, 156
    getEmbeddedObject(), 77, 143, 156,
    getFormattedText(), 148
RichTextStyle
  class, See also lotus.notes.RichTextStyle
  constants, 149-151
    COLOR_BLACK, 149
    COLOR_BLUE, 149
    COLOR_CYAN, 149
    COLOR_DARK_BLUE, 150
    COLOR_DARK_CYAN, 150
    COLOR_DARK_GREEN, 150
    COLOR_DARK_MAGENTA, 150
    COLOR_DARK_RED, 150
    COLOR_DARK_YELLOW, 150
    COLOR_GRAY, 150
    COLOR_GREEN, 150
    COLOR_LIGHT_GRAY, 150

COLOR_MAGENTA, 150
COLOR_RED, 150
COLOR_WHITE, 150
COLOR_YELLOW, 150
EFFECTS_EMBOSS, 150
EFFECTS_EXTRUDE, 150
EFFECTS_NONE, 150
EFFECTS_SHADOW, 150
EFFECTS_SUBSCRIPT, 150
EFFECTS_SUPERSCRIPT, 150
FONT_COURIER, 150
FONT_HELV, 150
FONT_ROMAN, 150
MAYBF., 151
NO, 151
STYLE_NO_CHANGE, 151
YES, 151
methods
  getBold(), 151
  getColor(), 151
  getEffects(), 151
  getFont(), 152
  getFontSize(), 152
  getItalic(), 152
  getStrikeThrough(), 152
  getUnderline(), 153
  setBold(), 151
  setColor(), 151
  setEffects(), 151
  setFOnt(), 152
  setFontSize(), 152
  setItalic(), 152
  setStrikeThrough(), 152
  setUnderline(), 153
RMI (Remote Method Invocation), 392-394
  and Domino, 385
  vs. CORBA, 393-394
rmic utility, 392
roles, access control list, 61, 62, 65, 67
root canal, and server administrators, 323-324
RPC (Remote Procedure Call), 385
Runnable interface See also java.lang.Runnable
run(), 225
running Agents, 170
runNotes() method, 21-22, 26

S

saved data document, for Agents, 173
saved query, 135
saving Agent changes, 169, 170

Index

saving applets in jar files, 349
Script_Name CGI variable, 273
Scripting, back-end, front-end, 11
search
  and Agents, 174
  query, 124
  refinement, 127
  results, in Newsletter, 203
Search Scope Configuration document, 47
search site index, 208
searching
  databases, 50-57
  DocumentCollections, 126-127
  Views, 114-119
security
  Agent, 6, 254-260
  and JDBC, 377
  applets, 3
  servlet, 323
selected documents, and Agents, 173, 246
selective privileges, and Agents, 256
semaphore objects, 270
semaphores
  and concurrency, 300-301
  and thread safety, 298
  in Java, 231-232
  read-write, 300-301
sending attached forms, 96
SendTo Item, 95
  in Log class, 213
separators, date, time, number, 176
serializable classes, 340
serialization
  and NOI, 351, 355
  and object references, 350
  and persistent storage, 351
  and version control, 351
  and Java Beans, 347-352
  and Java Beans, 355
  default behavior, 350
serializing Agent execution, 262
server
  administrators, and root canal, 323-324
  Agents, 250, 256
  and Java Beans, 356
  domain names, 198
  id, and servlets, 323
  ids, registering, 198
  name, for Agents, 169
  home, 200
  registration, 186, 193
Server_Name CGI variable, 273
Server_Port CGI variable, 273

Server_Protocol CGI variable, 273
Server_Software CGI variable, 273
Server_URL_Gateway_Interface CGI variable, 273
servlet, 4-5
  and Agents, 323
  and NOI, 380, 382
  and relational database systems, 314
  and server id, 323
  and unrestricted Agents, 332
  and user interfaces, 314
  applets, and CGI, 313
  configuration file, 315
  converting to Agents, Chapter 11
  environment variables, 315
  execution context, 318
  extensions, 314
  in Domino, 314-317
  input arguments, 336
  parameters, 319
  security, 323
  support classes, 326-327
  triggering, 8
  writing, 318-323
ServletOutputStream class, 327
Servlet/Agent Adapter, 323-325
servlet.cnf file, 316, 320
Servlet Manager, 315
  cache, 321
Session, 15
  class *See also* lotus.notes.Session
  in NOI containment hierarchy, 23
  methods
    createDateRange(), 29, 164
    createDateTime(), 29
    createInternational(), 190
    createLog(), 30, 209, 210
    createName(), 30, 180
    createNewsletter(), 30, 200, 288
    createRegistration(), 30, 185
    createRichTextStyle(), 30, 149
    evaluate(), 35
    freeTimeSearch(), 34
    getAddressBooks(), 24, 26, 48, 59
    getAgentContext(), 27, 283, 284
    getDatabase(), 24, 31, 307
    getDbDirectory(), 31
    getEnvironmentString(), 31
    getEnvironmentValue(), 31
    getInternational(), 28
    getNotesVersion(), 28

    getPlatform(), 28
    getURLDatabase(), 28
    getUserName(), 27, 334
    getUserNameObject(), 27
    isOnServer(), 28
    newInstance(), 23, 285, 287, 334
    setEnvironmentVar(), 31
    toString(), 37
setup
  for Java Development tools, Appendix C
  Domino, for writing Java, Appendix C
severity codes, in Log class, 212
shared Agents, 170
shared folders, 65
shrinking text Items, 138-139
signature
  digital, 85-86, 97
  Item, 135
  verification, 85
signed sections, 85
signing Agents, 168, 171
single-threaded applications, 217-219
sinitThread() method, *see* NotesThread.sinitThread()
site searching, 47
skeletons, CORBA, 387
sort options, database queries, 51
sorted columns, 123
sorted document collection, 124, 126
specifying rich text styles, 148-155
SQL queries, and JDBC, 358
SSL and CORBA, 388
stability, and thread safety, 296-297
start time
  Agent Manager, 258
  in DateRange, 164
stermThread() method *see* NotesThread.stermThread()
storing ids in address book, 193
strict containment hierarchy, 351
  and threads, 307
stubs, CORBA, 387
styles, rich text, 148-155
sub-forms, 179
Subject Item
  in Log class, 214
  in Newsletters, 201-202
subprotocol, URL, for JDBC, 366
summary
  data, 71, 72, 138
  flag, 99
    and large Items, 138

Index

sun.jdbc.odbc.JdbcOdbcDriver class, 376, 377
sun.servlet.http package, 311
  HttpRequest class, 331
  HttpResponse class, 318, 331
sun.servlet.ServletLoader class, 331
support for OLE in Java NOI, 143
supported Java versions, Appendix C
surname, in hierarchical names, 183
switching to new id, 200
Symantec Visual Cafe tool, 352-355
synchronization requirements, hidden, 232
synchronize directive, in Java, 231-232
synchronized methods, in NOI, 297
system administrators, and Agents, 255
System variables, 31
System.err redirection, for Agents, 244
System.exit(), 285, 352
System.gc(), 230, 309, 311
  See also garbage collection
System.in stream, in applications, 219
System.out
  redirection, for Agents, 244, 246
  stream, in Agents, 252
  stream, in applications, 219
  synchronization, 232
  println(), and debugging, 278
template, 110
  See also NTF

T

temporary data, 137
terminated with extreme prejudice, 244
testing JDBC, 363-364
text
  adding to rich text, 146
  converting Item values to, 142
  converting rich text to, 148
The View, 16
Thread
  and containment hierarchy, 307
  class *See also* java.lang.Thread
  garbage collection, 229

initialization, 217
methods
  join(), 229
  join(), and Agents, 265
  run(), 221
  sleep(), 229-230
  start(), 21-22, 221, 229
priority 229
  and garbage collection, 308
safety, 38, 231-232, 296-301
  and JDBC, 363
termination, 217
  and Agents, 265
  and garbage collection, 309
  unsafe algorithms, 302-307
throttles, Agent execution, 257
time-only DateTime, 163
time
  adjustments, 162-163
  formatting, 175
  limits, Agent, 244
  zone, 159, 162, 176
  conversion, 161
timer thread, for Agents, 244
today string, 176, 190
tomorrow string, 176
Toolkit, LSX, Appendix E
transient variables, 352
  and serialization, 350
Transportability, Agent, 6
triggering Agents, 381
Triggering server programs, 9

U

U.S. Department of Defense, 194
Unicode in text Items, 139
UNID (Universal ID), 54, 80-81, 94, 107, 111, 135, 240
  and saved data documents, 173
Universal Resource Locator, 3
unopened databases, 37
unprocessed documents, 173, 174, 175
unread marks, 94
unrestricted Agents, 213, 377
  and servlets, 332
  running, 258
updating address book, 193
upgrading servlets to Agents, Chapter 11
URL (Universal Resource Locator), 55
  and input arguments, 336
  and JDBC, 358
  Database, 54
  syntax for JDBC, 362, 366

user authentication, 254
user ids, registering, 199-200
user profiles, 195

V

value
  accessor methods, 98-107
  coercion, 132, 133
  length, Item, 136
  properties, Item, 132-133
variables
  CGI, and Agents, 271-276
  transient, 352
  and serialization, 350
Variants, 17
VBScript, 10, 13
version control, and serialization, 351
View Action
  Agents, 173
  example, 245
View
  auto-update, 120
  class, *See also* lotus.notes.View
  methods
    clear(), 114
    FTSearch(), 114
    getAliases(), 108-109
    getAllDocumentsByKey(), 115-119, 123
    getChild(), 119
    getColumns(), 109
    getCreated(), 109
    getDocumentByKey(), 115-119, 197, 389
    getFirstDocument(), 119
    getLastDocument(), 119
    getName(), 108-109
    getNextDocument(), 119
    getNextSibling(), 119
    getNthDocument(), 119
    getParent(), 109
    getParentDocument(), 119
    getPrevDocument(), 119
    getPrevSibling(), 119
    getReaders(), 110
    getUniversalID(), 111
    getViewColumns(), 122
    isAutoUpdate(), 111-113
    isCalendar(), 113
    isDefaultView, 113
    isFolder(), 114
    isHierarchical(), 119
    isProtectReaders(), 110-111
    refresh(), 121
    remove(), 121
    setAutoUpdate(), 111-113

Index

setProtectReaders(), 110-111
setReaders(), 110
toString(), 122
view columns, 72, 122-123
view indices, 112, 107,108, 120, 121
view keys, 115-116, 132
view navigation, 111-113
  methods, 119-121
view parent, 109
view selection formula, 114
ViewColumn
  class, *See also*
    lotus.notes.ViewColumn
  methods
    getFormula(), 122
    getItemName(), 122
    getPosition(), 122
    getTitle(), 122
    isCategory(), 123
    isHidded(), 123
    isResponse(), 123
    isSorted(), 123
    toString(), 123

Viewmap design information 136
views, 90
  categorized, 107
  database, 46, 49
  flag, 107
  flat, 114
  hierarchical, 107, 114
  searching, 114-119
virtual methods, 223
virus, and Agents, 254
visibility, and Java Beans, 346-347
Visual Basic, 10
visual development tools, and Java Beans, 341

W

W3.org, 57
wait/notify, and Agents, 270
waiting for child threads, 309-310
Web Agents, special functionality, 271-276
  crawler example, 233-242
  retrieval database, 54
  user identity, for Agents, 250
whitespace, compressing in Items, 139
wildcard date/time, 163
World Wide Web Consortium, 57
write locks, 300
writeObject(), and serialization, 350
writing Agents, Chapter 8
writing servlets, 318-323

Y

YAWP (Yet Another Wire Protocol), 395
yesterday string, 176
yielding, in multithreaded programs, 229
Yip, Wai-ki, 182

my2cents.idgbooks.com

Register This Book — And Win!

Visit **http://my2cents.idgbooks.com** to register this book and we'll automatically enter you in our monthly prize giveaway. It's also your opportunity to give us feedback: let us know what you thought of this book and how you would like to see other topics covered.

Discover IDG Books Online!

The IDG Books Online Web site is your online resource for tackling technology — at home and at the office.

Ten Productive and Career-Enhancing Things You Can Do at www.idgbooks.com

1. Nab source code for your own programming projects.
2. Download software.
3. Read Web exclusives: special articles and book excerpts by IDG Books Worldwide authors.
4. Take advantage of resources to help you advance your career as a Novell or Microsoft professional.
5. Buy IDG Books Worldwide titles or find a convenient bookstore that carries them.
6. Register your book and win a prize.
7. Chat live online with authors.
8. Sign up for regular e-mail updates about our latest books.
9. Suggest a book you'd like to read or write.
10. Give us your 2¢ about our books and about our Web site.

Not on the Web yet? It's easy to get started with *Discover the Internet,* at local retailers everywhere.